TamaReel

WOMEN AND EUROPEAN EMPLOYMENT

European employment levels are considered too low and unemployment rates too high. Yet analysis of employment trends requires an understanding of the major changes taking place in the gender composition of the European labour market. The authors of *Women and European Employment* argue that in fact it is women's employment growth which has stopped employment falling even further, and the integration of women into the economy which is associated with the growth of service sector and atypical employment, particularly part-time jobs. By contrast, male employment has been falling and increasing numbers of men have been moving out of the labour force altogether, into inactivity.

This is the first comprehensive and up-to-date study of the contribution of women and men to changing European economic activity patterns covering all fifteen member states. Based on the work of the European Commission's Network of Experts on Women's Employment, it draws on both national and European data sources. The book links trends in the structures of employment with new comparative data on the role of systems of welfare provision in order to explore economic activity patterns by gender. Participation patterns of women still vary widely within Europe, so much attention is paid to the institutions – both in the labour market and welfare – which help to explain these varitations.

The apparently contradictory tendency for women's employment and unemployment to rise is analysed, taking into account changes in industrial/occupational structure and trends at the European, national and regional levels. Many countries continue to pursue inconsistent and discriminatory labour market policies; many still base welfare policies on the notion of a single male breadwinner family. Such policies do affect women as workers, by influencing – for example – the share of women in atypical, informal employment and in inactivity. Nevertheless, women's employment has been increasing in all member states. The authors make the strong argument that policymakers need to recognise the role of changes in gender relations, within the labour market and within the household economy, in the evolution of the European employment system. *Women and European*

Employment is written specifically for policymakers and researchers in labour economics and gender studies.

Jill Rubery is Professor of Comparative Employment Systems at the Manchester School of Management (MSM), UMIST. From 1991 to 1996 she was co-ordinator of the European Commission's network of experts on the situation of women in the labour market. She is the author of *Employer Strategy and the Labour Market* (with Frank Wilkinson, 1994) and *The Economics of Equal Opportunities* (with Jane Humphries, 1995).

Mark Smith is a Research Associate at MSM, UMIST with research interests and publications in patterns of work and labour market transitions.

Colette Fagan is a Lecturer in Sociology at the University of Liverpool. She has published widely on issues of sex segregation, wage systems and working time, including a co-edited volume with Jackie O'Reilly, *Part-Time Prospects: An International Comparison* (forthcoming, Routledge).

Damian Grimshaw is a Research Associate at MSM, UMIST with research interests and publications covering public sector pay and internal labour markets.

ROUTLEDGE FRONTIERS OF POLITICAL ECONOMY

WOMEN AND EUROPEAN EMPLOYMENT

Jill Rubery, Mark Smith, Colette Fagan and Damian Grimshaw

London and New York

First published 1998
by Routledge
11 New Fetter Lane, London EC4P 4EE

Simultaneously published in the USA and Canada
by Routledge
29 West 35th Street, New York, NY 10001

Typeset in Times by Pure Tech India Ltd, Pondicherry, India
Printed and bound in Great Britain by Redwood Books, Trowbridge, Wiltshire

British Library Cataloguing in Publication Data
A catalogue record for this book is available
from the British Library

Library of Congress Cataloging in Publication Data

Women and European employment / Jill Rubery ... [et al].
p. cm. – (Routledge frontiers of political economy)
Includes bibliographical references.
1. Women–Employment–Europe. I. Rubery, Jill. II. Series.
HD6134.W652 1997
331.4'094–dc21
97–6093 CIP

ISBN 0–415–16985–2

CONTENTS

CONTENTS

FIGURES, BOXES AND TABLES

Figures

Boxes

Tables

ACKNOWLEDGEMENTS

This book is based upon research carried out when the authors acted as the co-ordinating team for the European Commission's Network of Experts on the Situation of Women in the Labour Market. Most of the information in this report is derived either from the European Labour Force Surveys for 1983, 1987 and 1992 or from the national reports provided by the network experts. These national reports in turn have been based on national data sources and national studies. Most of the references in this text refer to the national reports for the network; details of the national sources are provided only in the national reports. The authors of the national reports are as follows:

Belgium	D. Meulders, in collaboration with C. Hecq and R. Ruz Torres
Denmark	T. Boje
Germany	F. Maier and Z. Rapp, in collaboration with C. Johnson
Spain	M-L. Moltó
France	R. Silvera, A. Eydoux, A. Gauvin and C. Granie
Ireland	U. Barry, in collaboration with A. O'Connor
Italy	F. Bettio and F. Mazzotta
Luxembourg	R. Plasman
Netherlands	J. Plantenga and M. Sloep
Portugal	M. Chagas Lopes and H. Perista
United Kingdom	J. Rubery and M. Smith
Austria	U. Pastner
Finland	S. Ilmakunnas
Sweden	A. Lofström

We are grateful to the following people for assistance in the preparation of this book: Laurent Freysson from Eurostat who provided the special tabulations upon which much of the analysis presented here is based; Eloise Turner for the detailed work on the preparation of the EC report and for her efficient administration of the project in general; Claire Faichnie for her assistance in the final stages of the preparation of the book; and Maria Stratigaki, Els van Winckel and Agnes Hubert of the Equal Opportunities Unit at the European Commission for their help and support throughout the study. We would also like to acknowledge the help and support provided by UMIST in the administration of the network. Damian Grimshaw is first author of Chapter 5 and Colette Fagan is first author of Chapter 6.

The views expressed in this book are those of the authors and do not necessarily represent those of the European Commission.

1

INTRODUCTION

The most frequently cited criticism of the performance of European economies is their apparent inability to create employment and raise the share of the population in employment. This growing concern with the employment performance of European economies has coincided with the continuing growth of female employment, even in periods of low or negative overall employment expansion. Yet the expansion of female employment, although widely recognised as a feature of modern societies, is still often treated as an independent social phenomenon by labour market analysts, particularly those commenting on trends at the aggregate European level. Differences in employment rates between European countries are not identified as the consequence of differences in female employment patterns and of associated differences in the organisation of the household and family economy (Rubery 1995; Rubery and Maier 1995). Even most analyses of unemployment fail to address, let alone explain, the apparently paradoxical rise in both female employment and unemployment rates. Instead debate over European employment issues remains focused around such issues as the level of labour market regulation (CEC (Commission of the European Communities) 1993a; OECD (Organisation for Economic Co-operation and Development) 1994a, 1994b), with little reference to other social and economic institutions which underpin variations in employment and unemployment rates.

Without a clear understanding of the gender dimensions to the labour market, European employment policy analyses and recommendations can prove to be fatally flawed. For example, not only have policymakers failed to identify the overall low employment rate within Europe as related to low female employment rates in certain countries but also they have regarded the tendency for most new jobs to go to the inactive rather than the unemployed as a puzzle, possibly related to the unemployability of the unemployed, rather than as a consequence of the gendered segmentation of employment demand or the existence of a large hidden reserve of female labour outside the conventionally measured labour force. Flexible and part-time jobs are presented as a possible solution to problems of worklessness,

1

but without analysis of the relationship between sex segregation of employment and atypical work (Maruani 1995).

There is thus a fundamental lack of understanding of gender issues at the heart of European employment policymaking. In part this arises out of the academic tradition in economics of treating the labour market as composed of atomistic individuals, whose role in household, family and welfare systems is often ignored, except in analyses of labour supply functions where household and family systems tend to be treated as an exogenous constraint or as the outcome of an individualised welfare maximisation process (Humphries and Rubery 1984). In particular little attempt is made to link together an institutional analysis of the operation of the labour market with a complementary analysis of the historical and dynamic development of the welfare system and household economy. Yet without this wider institutional perspective on labour markets it may be difficult to explain both variations in labour markets between countries and the role of gender in particular within both the supply and demand structures of labour market systems.

The European Commission has itself explicitly recognised the need for a gender perspective to be introduced within all aspects of decision making if there is to be progress made towards gender equality. In a Communication on mainstreaming, the Commission has committed itself to mainstreaming gender into all its policies and practices (CEC 1996), following the decision at the UN Beijing World Conference on Women in September 1995 that governments should 'use gender impact analysis in the development, monitoring and evaluation of all micro and macro economic and social policies' (section 167 Platform for Action, UN Beijing Conference quoted in EOC (Equal Opportunities Commission) 1996). The reasoning behind the current adoption of mainstreaming as the most effective means of moving the equality agenda forward is the recognition by groups and policymakers concerned with equality that it is the trends in general policies and in the whole array of social and economic institutions which have most impact on future equality prospects. Specific equality-orientated projects have important but possibly marginal effects when they are pitted against a tide of change threatening to reverse even any gains that women have made in the past.

While there is this renewed interest in mainstreaming for policymakers in the equality area, it is not yet clear that the need for mainstreaming gender has been sold to labour market or welfare analysts and policymakers as anything more than special pleading on the part of the women's lobby. The case for mainstreaming needs to be made through a two-pronged approach: first to demonstrate that without a gender perspective, analyses of policies in the field of employment and welfare are likely to be inaccurate and indeed flawed; and second to demonstrate the need for mainstreaming if progress is to be made towards equality. These are in fact two different but interlinked agendas for equality and the case for the first needs to be made through explicit studies of the gender dimensions to social and economic systems which aim to demonstrate to all how a gender perspective can throw new lights on policy issues and on the future of work and employment.

This book aims to contribute to this endeavour through a systematic investigation of the gender dimension to employment in the European Union. The study explores both current differences in gender employment patterns between countries and the role of gender in the changing pattern of employment. Thus the gender dimension is recognised as having both a static and a dynamic aspect. This analysis follows the spirit of previous comparative research undertaken on women and recession in the 1980s (Rubery 1988) which addressed both the question of changes in female employment over time, in particular with respect to changes over business cycles, and the question of how continuing differences between advanced countries in women's employment position could be accounted for.

This latter comparative dimension requires an explanation of the major differences which still exist between European member states in the integration of women into waged work. These variations arise not only out of differences in labour market structure and labour market policies but also from differences in the organisation of the social and household systems and in welfare regimes and state policies. Differences in employment and societal systems provide the backdrop to the analysis of the gender pattern of employment within Europe. Both the societal systems approach to comparative labour market analysis (Lane 1993; Maurice *et al.* 1986; Pfau-Effinger 1993: Rubery 1988) and comparative research on welfare state regimes and social policy have provided a framework within which the persistence of divergence in women's employment patterns can be explained (S. Duncan 1995; Lewis 1992; Sainsbury 1994). Both approaches reject the notion that the variety of gender roles found within advanced economies can be solely or mainly attributed to differences in stage of development or in industrial structure. Instead the importance of path-specific development patterns and of political action is emphasised.

Under the societal systems approach it is not possible to look at one dimension of an economy, for example its labour market system, independently from the role of other social and institutional forces, including, among others, the education system, the industrial system, the legal system, the social and household systems from the prevailing gender ideology. It is these interlocking institutions which explain the particular configuration of both labour market arrangements and gender relations, or the 'gender order' (Connell 1987). Gender relations can be considered the outcome of prevailing social and institutional arrangements but these relations also help to shape the evolution of the social and institutional framework. Identifying single factor causes of differences is ruled out in this approach; instead the evolution of women's employment position must be located within a broad perspective encompassing their role in the economy, the social and household systems and the parallel evolution of social norms and values.

Within the comparative welfare research perspective there is again the rejection of welfare regimes as stages in capitalist development. Instead countries are argued to have adopted and developed particular welfare regimes which close off other likely development paths and which have wide-ranging impacts on both labour market and industrial structure developments. For example Esping-Andersen (1990) proposed a three fold classification of regimes: the American neo-liberal regime where the welfare state acted as a residual safety net; the German corporatist regime where the welfare state provides income maintenance through transfers but is not heavily involved in service provision, much of which is still provided within the domestic economy; and the Swedish social-democratic regime which is based on the principle of most people being in work, and on the direct provision of state services to substitute for domestic provision. This classification of different regimes aimed to describe different degrees of decommodification of labour, that is the protection afforded to workers against the need to sell their labour time, irrespective of the price of labour, in old age, sickness, unemployment, etc. This approach has been criticised widely in feminist literature for failing to address differences between men and women in their position in the process of the commodification of labour; for women the problem is as much their exclusion from the labour market as their requirement to sell their labour without state protection of minimum standards of income (S. Duncan 1995; Lewis 1992; Orloff 1993; Sainsbury 1994). A more salient classification system for women has been argued to be between strong, modified and weak male breadwinner welfare states (see Lewis 1992; Mósesdóttir 1996; Schunter-Kleemann 1996).

However, whatever the problems of developing a classification which takes fully into account women's position in the welfare system and labour market, this type of research has served to demonstrate the importance of welfare regimes in structuring women's role in the wage and the non-wage economy, and the role played by public sector and private sector services in shaping women's employment opportunities. For example the neo-liberal regime has been associated with the growth of private service sector employment for women, the social-democratic regime with public service sector employment, while the corporatist regime has maintained a higher share of domestic services provided within the family economy by non-wage labour. These differences depend upon historical choices concerning the form of the welfare state, choices which are not readily reversed. Thus welfare state and policy research reinforces the societal systems approach in explaining variations between countries, namely that gender differences are rooted in different social and economic institutions and are not subject to a smooth convergence path:

> ...welfare states cannot be seen merely as the byproduct of the industrialisation process; political priorities and decision-making processes lie at the foundation of these welfare states. Once institutionalised, welfare states make a considerable contribution to maintaining the norms and values associated with the role women (and men) are expected to play, with the division of paid and unpaid work, and with the boundaries between the public and private spheres.
>
> (Plantenga and Sloep 1995: 1)

While any cross-sectional analysis of European employment trends will reveal major differences in employment levels, employment forms and indeed social norms and values between European countries, there is nevertheless a danger that excessive focus on these static comparisons will obscure not only the changes taking place within societal and employment systems but also the major tensions and contradictions which exist within member states. Gender relations are playing a very important part in the restructuring of the economy and society, through changes in activity patterns, in employment forms and working time, and through changes in the sectoral and occupational distribution of employment. Many of these changes are occurring despite, not because of, decisions to change the welfare and household regimes. While welfare state regimes are still often premised on the strong male breadwinner household, this approach may be becoming increasingly outmoded and inconsistent with actual changing gender roles in the household and labour market. Governments may create or perpetuate contradictions or inconsistencies, and choose to ignore for political expediency the breakdown of the male breadwinner family as the single or even the most important family form. Nevertheless it is becoming increasingly difficult for governments to cling to a simple model of household and family organisation in framing welfare policy or to maintain the notion that the labour market consists primarily of male full-time continuous participants. There is an increasing blurring of divisions between economic activity statuses on the one hand, and an increasing complexity of social and household arrangements on the other. The dynamic development of gender relations within the labour market system and welfare and family system thus demands an equal level of attention alongside the comparative and largely static analysis of employment and societal systems.

These methodological considerations have informed the structure and presentation of the analysis in the following chapters. The comparative static and the dynamic perspectives have been developed in tandem, with each chapter addressing both issues of difference between countries and issues of change. The concluding chapter brings together the two perspectives through consideration of the likely patterns of convergence or continued divergence in gendered employment patterns in Europe.

Sources of information

This book is based on research undertaken for the European Commission by the Network of Experts on the Situation of Women in the Labour Market. This network consists of an appointed academic expert in every European member state who is charged with drawing up a national report on a specific research topic, to a plan devised by the co-ordinating team, the authors of this book. Much of the information on the institutional and social structures and on the specific characteristics of European labour markets is thus derived from these national reports (see acknowledgements for details). In addition the book draws upon international harmonised data, for example OECD data and studies but particularly upon data from the European Labour Force Survey (LFS), including previously unpublished tabulations (see Box 1.1). Much of the statistical analysis focuses on the period 1983 to 1992. The earliest European Labour Force Survey data available on a harmonised basis are for 1983 and data were also collected for 1987 as this was the first year for which data for Spain and Portugal became available, allowing an analysis of change across twelve European member states (E12) between 1987 and 1992. The period spans a recession to the end of a relative boom in the European economy, with the severest part of the 1990s' recession occurring after 1992 in most countries. This leads to an overestimate of employment growth over recent years.

The research on which this project is based was conceived and begun before the entry of three new member states into the European Union, that is Austria, Sweden and Finland. The first five chapters of the book thus analyse European employment with respect to the twelve states that were in membership in 1994 (referred to as E12). However, once the new member states joined, a parallel research project was set up to cover the same information for the three new member states, as far as was possible with consideration to data limitations. This information on the new member states is summarised in Chapter 6.

It was felt appropriate to discuss these three new member states in a separate chapter for three main reasons. First, for the same reasons as Spain and Portugal appear in the data and analysis only after 1987, there is effectively no or very little harmonised data for the new member states for the period with which we are concerned. The information in Chapter 6 is thus based almost entirely on national sources and as such cannot be readily

Box 1.1 Information on the data used in the book

Most of the data referring to the twelve member states used in this book are from special tabulations of the European Labour Force Survey provided by Eurostat, Luxembourg. Additional European Labour Force Survey data have been taken from Eurostat publications or provided by Alphametrics (UK) Ltd. The European Labour Force Survey uses internationally recognised definitions for the variables used and full details of these can be found in *Labour Force Survey: Methods and Definitions* (Eurostat 1988, 1992) published by Eurostat, Luxembourg (see also Figure 2.1).

Part-time employment

In the 1992 survey a spontaneous answer given by the respondent was used in all twelve member states to determine full, and part-time status (Eurostat 1992: 45). However, in some countries (Greece, Italy and the Netherlands) the number of hours an individual worked was used prior to 1992 (Eurostat 1988: 57).

The Netherlands

In 1987 a change in the survey design of the Dutch Labour Force Survey led to the inclusion of many more short part-time jobs, which has distorted the time series (see Plantenga and Sloep 1995).

The new member states

The data used for the new member states in this book have been taken from a range of sources including *Employment in Europe* (CEC 1994, 1995a), the OECD and the national reports from the experts of the new member states. Until 1995 there was no Labour Force Survey in Austria and this has limited the availability of quantitative information.

Data for Germany

Prior to 1991 data are not available for the former East Germany so in this book we have provided information for the former West Germany and for the Unified Germany for 1992 whenever possible. The convention used in this report for the former West Germany is 'D' or 'Germany (W)' and the Unified Germany is referred to as 'UD'. Please refer to notes of tables and figures for details.

Occupational data

The occupational data used in Chapter 3 for the twelve member states uses previously unreleased data based upon the ISCO 68 occupational classification. Further details on the occupational data and the methodological issues involved using these harmonised data can be found in Rubery and Fagan (1993). There are no data available for Italy. For full details of the occupational classification please refer to Eurostat (1988).

integrated with the discussion of the other twelve countries. Second, the entry in particular of Sweden and Finland into the European Union has changed the balance of European countries and welfare states. Now there are three Scandinavian countries – including Denmark, which has the highest female employment rate among the other twelve states – where there is a strong tradition of high female employment rates based on a large welfare state. The diagnosis of Europe's low employment rate in the early 1990s was in part based on comparisons of the E12 employment rate with that found not only in the US and Japan but also in EFTA (European Free Trade Association) to which Sweden, Finland and Austria belonged. Thus in discussing the European employment rate problem as perceived in the early 1990s it is more appropriate to exclude Sweden and Finland from the analysis.

Finally, although Sweden and Finland continue to have high female employment rates by EU and international standards, these two countries have also suffered the most severe employment collapse in the 1990s of all EU member states. This highlights the problems and complexities of undertaking comparative research, for while these two countries add notably to the average European employment level even in 1992, their inclusion would also add notably to the estimates of employment loss since 1989 or 1990. As their impact upon the European employment story is both specific and significant, it seems worthy of separate consideration.

While there are less strong reasons for excluding Austria from the twelve-country analysis based on employment levels and rates of change, there are even stronger pragmatic reasons, for although Sweden and Finland have only national data for the years in question, their labour force surveys were already quite well harmonised with the rest of the EU while Austria did not have a labour force survey prior to joining the EU.

The plan of the book

The starting-point for the analysis in Chapter 2 is a detailed and largely quantitative analysis of the role of female employment in determining the comparative level of European employment rates and their recent evolution. To identify the role of female employment it is necessary to take into account other influences on employment rates, including changes in population structure and changes in male employment rates, and to establish whether rising rates of part-time work are leading to exaggerations of women's contribution to employment. To clarify the changing employment patterns by gender we also need to explore the interrelationships between age and gender on activity rates. This analysis is undertaken for three main population groups – the young (16–24), prime-age workers (25–49) and older workers (50–64) – and for three activity statuses – employed, unemployed and inactive. This first part of Chapter 2 thus sets out the main trends in economic activity patterns, and the main differences between countries based on conventional definitions of economic activity. In the second part of the chapter the issue of the appropriateness of the definitions of activity, particularly from a gender perspective, is addressed and alternative measures both of employment levels and of available labour supply to measured levels of unemployment are developed. This latter calculation reveals the greater potential for female employment growth in most countries, while also highlighting major differences between countries in the size and composition of the potential labour reserve.

In the third chapter we consider the regional and demand side factors which may explain the economic activity patterns and trends revealed in Chapter 2. The chapter explores both the dispersion of activity patterns within countries by region and the trends in economic activity by region, for those countries where longitudinal data are available. This analysis enables us to examine whether, for example, the coincidental rise in employment and unemployment for women results from divergent regional patterns or from upward movements in both variables within regions. In the second part of the chapter we explore the link between changes in the structure of employment by industry, occupation and working-time and changing gender employment shares. Changes in women's overall share of employment can be the result of the perpetuation of patterns of segregation, that is as a consequence of the expansion of female-dominated sectors, or may result from a change in patterns of segregation. The latter set of changes may involve a move towards a less segregated labour market, with women increasing their share of non-traditional occupations, or towards a more intensely segregated labour market with rising female shares of already female-dominated segments. Both tendencies may even be present in the same labour market. Thus the changing gender composition of employment can be seen to be linked to the structure and evolution of employment sex segregation.

The fourth chapter provides a more in-depth analysis of unemployment by gender and the system of labour market organisation which gives rise to particular patterns of unemployment. To facilitate this analysis the chapter makes extensive use of data on labour market flows between activity statuses. The study of transitions between economic activity statuses provides an opportunity to combine the static and dynamic dimensions to the study. The patterns of entry to and exit from employment, unemployment and inactivity vary by gender, age and stage in the lifecycle, as well as between countries. The pattern of flows is central to understanding changes in employment patterns and activity statuses, but these variations also enrich the understanding of variations in women's position within different labour market systems. Whether the source of the stock of the unemployed comes from first time jobseekers or from job losers will have significant implications for policies to combat unemployment and to reduce gender inequality in unemployment. Similarly, examination of flows from inactivity into employment can cast light on the simultaneous rise in both female employment and unemployment, and the involvement of women in the process of employment restructuring and generation of new employment opportunities. The chapter also explores the influence of other factors, such as educational level and responsibility for children on the risk of unemployment for different groups of women. These analyses highlight the importance of both gender relations and labour market systems for understanding the potential risks of unemployment, and for the types of polices that should be adopted to reduce the disproportionate involvement of women in unemployment.

The fifth chapter takes up this theme of state policies by exploring government policies towards the labour market and how these shape women's position in employment and unemployment. The chapter provides a detailed examination of unemployment benefit systems, non-wage labour costs, active labour market policies, the promotion of flexible employment and policies towards wages and wage moderation. All these state policies are found to have a gender dimension, influencing, for example, women's perceptions of their economic activity status, their access to unemployment benefits and active labour market schemes, the share of atypical work in the economy and women's involvement in these employment forms and the level and trends in wages within female-dominated employment sectors such as low paid jobs or the public sector. From this exploration of the gender implications of the current trends in European employment policies we can identify the need for 'mainstreaming' gender into employment policy design and implementation.

Chapters 2 to 5 focus primarily on the labour market, with the differences in men's and women's role within households appearing as an important but largely implicit explanation of differences in gender roles within the labour market. Chapter 6 switches focus and explores the relationship between household organisation and women's employment rates. The chapter opens by exploring women's waged and unpaid contributions to the household economy and their involvement in the informal economy. It then focuses on state policies towards the household and the individual and the influence of these policies on both women's activity patterns and women's access to benefits over the lifecycle. Three areas of state policy are explored: the tax system and its impact on the incentives for women to work; state policies towards parenting, including maternity and paternity leave and childcare; and the relationship between women's employment patterns and their access to social protection, including unemployment benefit and pensions. This discussion explores not only the constraints of current welfare and tax systems on women's participation in

wage work but also the dangers of moving too rapidly towards an individualised system of benefits if this were to exclude women from access to the
higher benefits that men derive from their more privileged position in the
labour market.

In Chapter 7 the role of women's employment in the new member
states is discussed, with information from national data sources covering
all the main themes addressed in the first five chapters. The discussion
of the new member states helps to clarify and reinforce some of the major
findings from the earlier chapters. For example, the inclusion of these
countries tends to increase further the divergence within Europe of employment and societal systems and the patterns of gender relations: Finland and
Sweden stand at one end of the spectrum with weak male breadwinner
welfare states and a high participation of women in employment, while
Austria has retained a strong male breadwinner welfare system and high
levels of gender inequality. However, the changes taking place within all
three member states reinforce the need for a dynamic perspective: in Austria
women are demanding more access to employment despite the sluggishness
of the welfare and social system's response to changing gender roles,
while in Finland and Sweden many of the gains won by women over recent
decades have been placed in jeopardy by the severity of the recession
and the crisis in public expenditure and the welfare state regimes. Even if
women face major problems within these countries it is also clear that a
return to a strong male breadwinner society is not a policy option on the
agenda, reinforcing the argument that once the labour market and
family and household organisation have developed along a particular
path, some policy options and systems of organisation are effectively
closed off. The integration of women into the wage economy in all
European economies, albeit at different rates and in different forms,
is likely to be an irreversible process of social and economic transformation.

Finally, in Chapter 8 we draw the threads of the argument together in a
concluding analysis which focuses on two main issues: first, the evidence for
or against convergence in the role of women within European employment
systems; second, the need to 'mainstream' gender issues within European
policymaking in the employment and welfare fields. These conclusions
reaffirm the significance of different social and employment systems while
at the same time recognising the forces towards change within these systems, arising both out of state policies and out of the behaviour and
aspirations of women themselves. These dynamic developments in women's
social and economic roles mean that 'mainstreaming' gender requires a
sophisticated approach which eschews simplistic or universalist notions
of women's behaviour and aspirations, and instead recognises the increasing
complexity and diversity of women's employment and social roles.
This means that policies will need to take into account the different

interests of groups of women, divided perhaps by education and generation, country and even region, as well as differences in interests between women and men.

2

THE FEMALE CONTRIBUTION
TO THE EVOLUTION OF THE
EUROPEAN EMPLOYMENT RATE

Concern over the long-term trend in the European employment rate emerged in the early 1990s as a central issue for European policy as a consequence of three interrelated developments. The first area to arouse concern was the evidence of apparent failure within European economies to create jobs in contrast to the job creation record of Europe's competitors, particularly that of the US (CEC 1994, 1995a; OECD 1994a, 1994b). Europe was identified as moving into a period of jobless growth and this failure on the job creation front was likely to lead to a worsening of the two other related problems: the high and rising level of unemployment in Europe and the increasing burden of the non-working population on European welfare state regimes. The latter problem relates to the share of the population not in employment and not solely to the share in unemployment, and an increasing share of new jobs are taken by those outside the labour force instead of those inside. In recognition of these relationships the employment problem in Europe is increasingly considered to be best addressed by focusing not on the unemployment rate but on the employment rate: that is the share of the population in work, with various definitions of the appropriate population according to whether the focus is on the ability to create jobs for the working-age population or on the problems of a high dependency ratio.

This switch in focus from the unemployment rate to the employment rate in practice implies a major shift in traditional concerns over the adequacy of employment opportunities. Conventionally full employment has been defined by reference to the current measured labour force and not with respect to the actual share of the population in work. This measure was used on the basis that those outside the labour force should not be regarded as a hidden labour reserve but instead as fully involved in non-wage activities, primarily domestic work. This division of the population into participants and non-participants has been increasingly found to be non-viable for several reasons. First and most importantly, there has been the persistent rise in female participation, largely undeterred even by downturns in the economic cycle, which necessarily casts doubts on the assumption of a stable inactive part of the population which is happy to be without wage work. Second, there have been rises in inactivity, as well as in unemployment, among other groups, giving rise to the concern that much of Europe's unemployment problem is taking the form of disguised unemployment, manifest in early retirement, prolonged education and discouraged workers. Inactivity levels could be expected to rise because of an increasing demand for highly skilled labour, but the extent to which the reductions in activity among younger or older workers should be considered the result of improved standards of living which allow for longer periods of education or more extensive periods of retirement, has been queried, particularly as both practices increase the burden on the welfare states and the working population.

These trends call into question the traditional divisions of economic activity statuses into the employed, the unemployed and the inactive (Figure 2.1). A focus on the share of the population in employment appears to give a better basis on which to compare comparative employment performance as it is not dependent on the social and institutional influences which determine whether the non-employed are regarded as unemployed or as inactive. While this decision, by European policymakers, has generally been regarded as sensible, given the trends described above, there is a case for arguing that the full implications of this switch in policy focus have yet to be fully recognised and incorporated into policy thinking. By focusing on the share of the population in employment, the rights of women to be in employment are in principle given equal weight with those of men. The discussion of employment policy and performance in, for example, European Commission documents has not been conducted in terms of whether the outcome has been to maintain job opportunities for male breadwinners, rather than to create jobs for second income earners such as students or women in male breadwinner households. This implicit according of equal weight to women's employment alongside men's could perhaps be regarded as a major sea change in employment policy as it implicitly accepts the principles which have underpinned, for example, the Scandinavian labour market models, where it is anticipated, that all other things being equal, most fit adults will be in waged employment, irrespective of gender. Of course a policy objective to raise the European employment rate does not mean that governments are committed to achieving full economic activity status for all the working-age population. Nevertheless the absence of any explicit differentiation by gender in expectations of 'acceptable' employment rates could be seen as a remarkable change of policy for those European governments which have not traditionally given priority to female employment.

These developments are important and could mark a radical break with the past, where even Beveridge's (1944) famous definition of full employment limited expectations to sufficient jobs being available for all the men who were looking for work. However, there are good grounds for more

Figure 2.1 Definitions of labour market status (from the European Labour Force Survey)

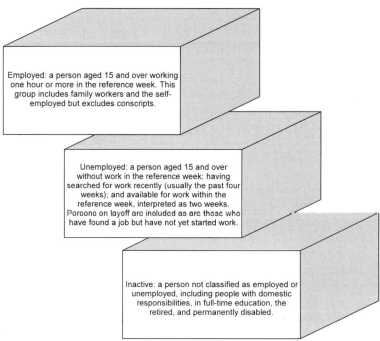

Employed: a person aged 15 and over working one hour or more in the reference week. This group includes family workers and the self-employed but excludes conscripts.

Unemployed: a person aged 15 and over without work in the reference week; having searched for work recently (usually the past four weeks); and available for work within the reference week, interpreted as two weeks. Persons on layoff are included as are those who have found a job but have not yet started work.

Inactive: a person not classified as employed or unemployed, including people with domestic responsibilities, in full-time education, the retired, and permanently disabled.

Source: Eurostat (1992)

than a sneaking suspicion that the full impact of this change of approach has not been recognised by the governments and policymakers concerned. To the extent that the gender issue does emerge in labour market policy analysis, discussion of it is often suppressed as the fact that high employment growth countries may have achieved this through increased integration of women into the economy rather than through a reduction in the numbers of unemployed remains a politically difficult issue to deal with.

Indeed while policy documents refer in gender-neutral terms to employment rate changes, there is a definite implicit and often indeed almost explicit emphasis on the problems of men when the issue of unemployment is discussed. For example, in the Delors White Paper on *Growth, Competitiveness, Employment* (CEC 1993a), there is much discussion of the possibilities of growth of new jobs in the care sector, but it is stated that attention would have to be paid to making these jobs more acceptable to the unemployed or even less degrading, with no acknowledgement that these jobs are currently undertaken in either the waged or the non-waged areas of work by women (CEC 1993a: 20). The discussion clearly had in mind making these jobs more acceptable to and less degrading for unemployed men.

Similarly Commission analyses of the unemployment problem, and indeed some academic analyses of wage and employment trends (Wood 1994) have focused on the problems of unemployment for low-skilled workers, relating these trends to a decline in demand coupled with a rise in the cost of employing low-skilled labour. The concern with low-skilled men in traditional manufacturing or construction manual jobs is either implicit, as in Commission documents, or forms an explicit part of the analysis (Wood 1994). However, even the latter have been criticised for gender-blindness as many of the sectors affected by changing patterns of world trade are female-dominated sectors, and the trends in demand for low-skilled labour do not hold up once the growth of the service sectors and the growth of female employment are taken into account (Freeman 1995). While the genuine policy concern about unemployment continues to focus on the plight of men, and increasingly that of young men, many governments and policymakers find the switch to the use of the employment rate as the method of assessing employment performance to be convenient. Europe's employment performance appears in a better light than if the focus was on the ability of European economies to create jobs capable of sustaining individual adults. Much of the job creation over recent years has been in part-time jobs, often involving very short hours, and taken by those who have access to family income, that is students or young people, women in couple households or those in receipt of state subsidies as either unemployed or retired. While focusing on the employment rate reinforces women's right to work, it also disguises the fact that one male job destroyed is not being replaced, in terms of income generation or working hours, by the creation of one part-time job designed for women or for students. Thus the development of a gender-blind approach to employment rates may be premature if it serves to disguise the changing composition, in quality and quantity of jobs, which underpins the relative stability of overall employment rates. Thus a more disaggregated analysis is required where we identify the role of gender, age and working-time trends in shaping the trends in European employment and unemployment performance.

2.1 Trends in the European employment rate

Contributions to trends in the European employment rate: gender, country and population effects

The long-term trend in the employment rate in the European Union, for the twelve states which were members in 1994, has been downwards; the rate has declined steadily from around 63 per cent in 1971 to around 57 per cent in 1984/5, before recovering somewhat in the period 1986–91 to reach a peak of around 60 per cent, only to fall again to 58 per cent in 1993 (CEC

1994).[1] Inclusion of the new member states within the EU average would undoubtedly increase the overall measured level of the employment rate, but would also underline the problems of falling employment rates in the 1990s; EFTA had already achieved an employment rate of over 70 per cent in 1971 and maintained an upward trend until 1990, when there was a sharp fall to 68 per cent in 1993, caused primarily by sharp falls in employment in two of the new member states, Sweden but particularly Finland. Thus EFTA countries appeared to have escaped the European employment rate problem in the 1970s and 1980s, only to be subject to the same problems and pressures in the 1990s.

In many respects, therefore, the comparisons that are effectively being made between the EU and other competitor countries are those between the EU and Japan and the US. Japan maintained a high and stable employment rate until the late 1980s when it rose yet higher to around 74 per cent. The US started in 1971 with a low employment rate, below that of the EU, but has achieved a rising employment rate, exceeding 70 per cent since 1987 and dipping slightly only in the early 1990s (Figure 2.2). The main difference between the E12 employment rate and those of the USA and EFTA is found in the employment rates of women (although differences in unemployment rates are also significant). Japan has a similar female employment rate to that in the E12, so that the main reason for a higher employment rate in Japan is the high share of older workers in employment, including many above the conventional working-age cut-off of 65. However, the increase in Japanese employment rates in the 1980s and early 1990s has been boosted by rising female employment rates.

This overview of the long-run trends in employment rates has highlighted the significance of the level and rates of change in female employment in international comparisons of employment rates, but has also indicated that the period that we will concentrate on for this study – 1983–92 – may be regarded as relatively unrepresentative of EU experience over the past two to three decades. Employment rates in 1983 had sunk almost to their lowest level over the period, and there was then an unrepresentative rise in employment rates up until 1991 which has since been reversed. Ending the period in 1992 means that we are measuring a net increase over the period 1983–1992, although in practice the employment rate had regained 1980 levels only by 1991 and has since fallen again (Figure 2.2). However, data before 1983 are extremely limited on a harmonised basis, 1987 – the intervening year chosen for this analysis – is the first year for which harmonised data for all twelve countries are available and 1992 was the latest year for which we could obtain LFS data.

Thus, although this book will be looking into the contributions made by men and women to a rising average employment rate, it is important to set this discussion in context and recognise that the rise in the latter half of the 1980s only partially offset previous falls from 1970s' levels, and that

Figure 2.2 Evolution of the EU employment rate

(a) Working age employment rates in EU, US and Japan

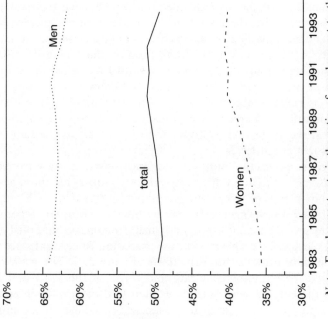

Note: Employment rate is the ratio of employment to the working age population

Sources: CEC (1994, 1995a); OECD (1993b)

(b) Crude EU employment rates for total, men and women

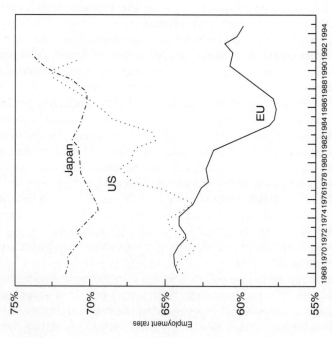

Note: Employment rate is the ratio of employment to the population aged 14+ for 1992 onwards, employment rates are based on the population aged 15+

Source: Special tabulations provided by Eurostat

the experience since 1992 has again been negative. Nevertheless, it is almost certain that whatever the period taken, the relative contributions of men and women to changing employment rates would be found to be similar – negative for men and positive for women – with the main difference whether we were explaining a net fall or rise in the average employment rate.

In this section we are able to include data only for the former West Germany as it is not possible or appropriate to have data for Unified Germany prior to 1990. The exclusion of the former East Germany not only reduces the average female employment rate but also overstates the positive recent contribution of women to employment rate change as in East Germany employment for women has fallen faster than that for men.

There are several different ways of measuring employment rates. So far we have been discussing employment rates measured as the ratio of all persons in employment to the working-age population 15–64 (see first section of Table 2.1). This measure includes in the numerator persons in employment over age 65 but excludes the same persons from the denom-inator and gives an indication neither of the ratio of adult dependants in the economy nor of the success of the economy in providing employment opportunities for the working-age population. In Table 2.1 we have calcu-lated employment rates in the EU using four further measures: all persons in employment as a share of the population aged over 14; persons in employment aged 15–64 as a ratio of the population aged 15–64; persons in employment aged 20–59 as a ratio of the 20–59 population; and persons in employment aged 25–49 as a ratio of the population aged 25–49. The first alternative measure provides an indication of the relative size of the adult population dependent upon those in work, while the other three measures provide an indication of the share of the working-age population – using different measures of working age – who are able to find work. The problem with the narrower definitions of working age (columns 3 and 4) is that they may not provide a good indication of employment performance, if the consequences of poor employment performance are concentrated upon the young or the old, who are not included in these measures. Yet for international comparison the wider definition is also problematical as countries vary in their normal or customary length of education and retire-ment ages, so that variations in employment rates among the younger and older ages are not necessarily directly attributable to lack of employment opportunities.

The trends in the various measures of employment rates in fact follow a similar pattern at EU level, and indeed within most countries. Overall the trend is, as already discussed, slightly upwards, but with the strongest increases found for the narrowest definition – working-age population aged 25–49 – where there is a positive increase in the employment rate for eleven out of twelve countries, and stability in the twelfth, France. Even

Table 2.1 European employment rates by gender and age group (E12), 1992

	14+ crude employment rate (employment/ 14+ population) (%)	Employment rate/15-64 (employment/15-64 population) (%)	Working-age employment rate (employment 15-64/ 15-64 population) (%)	Core-age employment rate (employment 20-59/20-59 population) (%)	Prime-age-employment rate (employment 25-49/25-49 population) (%)
	(1)	(2)	(3)	(4)	(5)
Belgium	46.31	56.83	56.53	66.86	76.49
Denmark	61.96	76.06	74.48	79.77	83.60
Germany[b]	55.26/55.01	67.75/67.16	67.06/66.57	74.50/74.12	78.43/78.96
Greece	44.80	55.42	53.63	62.29	69.31
Spain	39.61	48.78	48.24	55.95	61.69
France	49.84	60.52	60.13	71.12	78.40
Ireland	44.68	52.42	50.82	58.74	61.47
Italy	44.23	53.63	52.75	61.11	69.29
Luxembourg	52.48	61.96	61.52	70.00	76.36
Netherlands	54.80	64.25	63.67	70.33	75.22
Portugal	57.05	68.41	65.91	74.17	81.05
UK	56.12	69.38	68.09	73.90	77.19
E10	51.34	62.62	61.78	69.95	75.68
E12[b]	50.12/50.30	61.18/61.34	60.32/60.51	68.50/68.69	74.32/74.64

Table 2.1 (Contd...)

	Women[a] (%)			Men[a] (%)			All[a] (%)		
	1983	1987	1992	1983	1987	1992	1983	1987	1992
	(6)	(7)	(8)	(9)	(10)	(11)	(12)	(13)	(14)
Belgium	36.4	37.5	44.6	69.9	67.1	68.4	53.1	52.3	56.5
Denmark	64.3	71.0	70.4	76.2	81.0	78.5	70.3	76.1	74.5
Germany[b]	46.3	48.5	55.6/56.0	77.1	76.3	78.3/77.0	61.3	62.4	67.1/66.6
Greece	34.4	36.3	36.2	77.2	74.4	72.3	54.9	54.7	53.6
Spain		26.6	31.3		64.5	65.7		45.3	48.2
France	50.5	49.8	51.3	75.8	71.3	69.3	63.0	60.4	60.1
Ireland	33.4	33.1	36.8	71.5	66.2	64.7	52.8	49.9	50.8
Italy	34.0	34.7	36.7	75.0	72.0	69.2	54.0	53.0	52.7
Luxembourg	38.6	41.8	46.1	78.7	78.4	76.4	58.7	60.1	61.5
Netherlands	34.5	42.4	50.9	68.5	73.7	76.1	51.6	58.2	63.7
Portugal		49.5	55.7		77.2	77.2		62.8	65.9
UK	51.4	56.3	60.8	74.6	76.1	75.3	62.9	66.2	68.1
E10	44.3	46.5	50.4	75.1	73.8	73.2	59.4	60.0	61.8
E12[b]		44.3	48.3/48.8		72.9	72.5/72.4		58.4	60.3/60.5

Source: Special tabulations provided by Eurostat
Notes: a Employment rates measured as working-age employment as a share of working-age population
b Data for Germany and E12 exclude/include the new Länder

when the total population aged 14 and above is used as the basis for the employment rate the trend is upward, particularly for the period 1987–92. Four countries do record a slight fall in the employment rate for the population aged 14+ but these are also the same four countries to record a negative change in the employment rate for the 15–64 working-age population. Thus all countries with a good employment performance for the working-age population record positive increases in the employment rate for the 14+ population.

When we look at the patterns by gender we find female employment rates in 1992 consistently higher than in 1983, except in Greece for the 14+ population, where a rising female population aged 65+ results in a negative employment rate growth (Eurostat 1993b). For most countries there was a consistent increase in both of the two sub-periods, 1983 to 1987 and 1987 to 1992. In Denmark the female employment rate declined slightly between 1987 and 1992, while in France and Ireland it declined between 1983 and 1987 but recovered again by 1992 (Table 2.1). For men the patterns are much more variable, with an overall slight decrease at the E10 level hiding highly variable patterns within member states. The dominant trend is negative: six member states record a decrease in employment rates between 1983 and 1992 and four an increase. While the overall trend is downwards in both periods for E10, five member states record negative changes in both sub-periods – France, Ireland, Italy, Luxembourg and Greece – while Belgium records an overall decline between 1983 and 1992, despite a rise in employment rates in the first period. Of the four countries with an overall increase, only one – the Netherlands – experienced a positive increase in both sub-periods (but even this upward trend may be a consequence of changes in data collection). In the UK and Denmark employment rises in the first period and falls in the second while the opposite pattern is found for West Germany (see Box 2.1 for impact of unification on employment rates for men and women in Germany).

Differences between EU member states are found not only in employment rate trends but also in the actual levels of employment rates. Most of these differences are again explained by divergence in female employment rates. This particularly applies to differences in employment rates for the narrower definitions of working age, such as the 20–59 population, as the wider definitions are influenced by differences in patterns of education and retirement. Figure 2.3 illustrates this finding for the 20–59 population. The male employment rates are shown to diverge only marginally from the EU average while there is much wider variation between the EU average and individual member states' female employment rates. If we rank the countries by overall employment rates for the 20–59 population we find a close matching with the ranking of the countries by female employment rates for the 20–59 population. The two countries where the matching is less close are Germany and Greece, whose positions in the overall employment rate ranking are higher than their position in the overall female employment rate rankings.

Box 2.1 Women in former East Germany have borne the brunt of economic restructuring but still maintain a higher employment rate than women in former West Germany

Including the former **East Germany** in the calculations of the **German** employment rate raises the employment rate for women while decreasing it for men. However, while East German women still have higher employment rates than West German women, the gap has been narrowing rapidly as increasing numbers of East German women end up in unemployment. The East German female unemployment rate rose rapidly from an already high level of 12 per cent in 1993 to 21 per cent in 1992, while the male unemployment rate rose from 8.5 to 14 per cent over the same period. The only exception to this trend was in East Berlin. The experience of East Germany suggests that it is not possible to be confident that the positive employment trends for women in the EU will always be maintained. In the face of high and rising male unemployment, men have begun entering in large numbers jobs which were traditionally done by women. However, the experience of East Germany also underlines the resistance of women to pressures to move into inactivity. Women's employment in East Germany may have fallen from 79 per cent to 65 per cent of the working-age population between 1990 and 1993, but their participation rate fell by a smaller margin, from 84 per cent to 75 per cent, while the potential labour force measure records hardly any change, falling from 89.5 per cent in 1990 to 87.5 per cent in 1993. It is this potential labour force which perhaps provides the best measure of underlying participation rates and is still maintained at a much higher level than for West German women (Maier and Rapp 1995: 32–35).

The 20–59 age group measure could be said to overstate the significance of gender in the determination of the overall European employment rate by underestimating the importance of changes in employment rates by age. Thus for the following analysis we shall concentrate on the employment rate for the 15–64 age population, unless otherwise stated. This measure still differs from the *Employment in Europe* (CEC 1994) definition by excluding those 65+ in employment. However, by this method we will be able to obtain a better understanding of the economic activity statuses of the working-age population.

Table 2.2 shows that the overall employment rate rose between 1983 and 1992 by only 2.3 percentage points from 59.5 to 61.8 (E10, excluding Spain and Portugal) but without the impact of women's rising participation rates the change instead of being weakly positive would have been negative.

Figure 2.3 Employment rates for the 20–59 age group, 1992

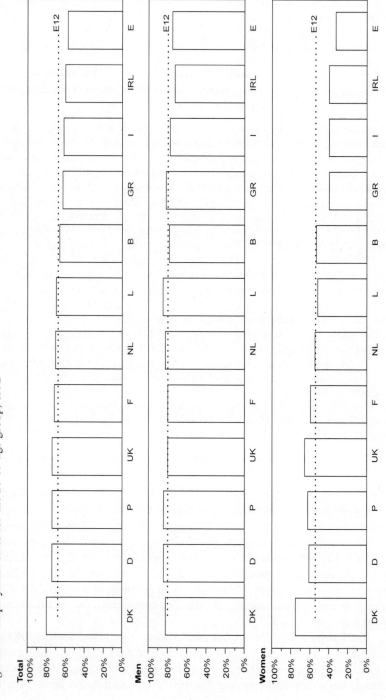

Source: European Labour force Survey (1992),

Table 2.2 quantifies the positive contribution of rising female employment to the overall change in the European employment rate and the negative effect of falling male employment. This exercise required first standardising the measured change in the overall E10 employment rate to eliminate any effects from differential rates of population growth for the ten member states over the time period. This had the effect of raising the measured change in the employment rate from 2.34 to 2.39 percentage points, indicating that changes in population mix by country had somewhat lowered employment rates over the time period. Differential changes in male and female population growth can also impact upon the average employment rate so we also took account of changes in the male and female population shares within each country. Male population growth on average outstripped female population growth in the 15–64 age bracket, accounting overall for a 0.14 percentage point increase in the employment rate, leaving in total 2.25 percentage points to be explained by changing employment rates of men and women. Overall the contribution of the male employment rate to the average E10 employment rate was negative, implying a decrease in the average total employment rate of 0.92 percentage points, while the increase in the average total employment rate contributed by rising female employment rates was greater than the actual overall total employment rate change, at 3.17 percentage points.

Disaggregation of these effects by member state reveals a fairly consistent pattern, with all countries recording a positive contribution from female employment rates, while six out of ten recorded negative contributions from declining male employment rates (see Table 2.2). The actual contribution by member state to the changing European employment rate depends first of all on the relative size of the country and second on the extent of change. These two factors together show a particularly significant role for Germany and the UK in leading to a higher EU employment rate for women, and a significant role for both France and Italy in reducing the EU male employment rate. In the case of France and Italy the negative impact of men on the employment rate was greater than the positive impact of the rise in female employment, so that these two countries together were responsible for a net decrease of over half a percentage point in the European employment rate. Ireland and Greece also made a net negative contribution to the employment rate but all other countries' contributions were positive. Much the same picture emerges when we look at changes over two sub-periods – 1983–87 and 1987–92. The overall increase in the E10 employment rates was stronger in the second than the first period, and this was due to both a stronger increase in women's employment rates and a smaller fall in male employment rates. All the countries identified as making a major contribution to changes at the EU level are in fact large countries, and some of the smaller contributions to the EU employment rate could still be consistent with major changes at the member state level in small countries. Thus

Table 2.2 Percentage point contribution by gender to changes in the E10 employment rate, 1983–92

	1983–7			1987–92			1983–92		
	Changing male to female populations	Changing male employment rates	Changing female employment rates	Changing male to female populations	Changing male employment rates	Changing female employment rates	Changing male to female populations	Changing male employment rates	Changing female employment rates
Belgium	0.00	−0.05	0.02	0.00	0.02	0.13	0.00	−0.03	0.15
Denmark	0.00	0.05	0.06	−0.00	−0.02	−0.01	0.00	0.02	0.06
Germany[a]	0.06	−0.09	0.27	0.04	0.23	0.82	0.09	0.14	1.12
Greece	0.00	−0.05	0.03	0.00	−0.03	−0.00	0.00	−0.08	0.03
France	−0.01	−0.42	−0.06	0.00	−0.19	0.14	−0.00	−0.61	0.08
Ireland	−0.00	−0.03	−0.00	−0.00	−0.01	0.02	−0.00	−0.04	0.02
Italy	0.02	−0.31	0.08	0.03	−0.29	0.21	0.04	−0.60	0.30
Luxembourg	−0.00	−0.00	0.00	0.00	−0.00	0.00	0.00	−0.00	0.01
Netherlands	0.00	0.14	0.21	0.00	0.07	0.23	0.00	0.21	0.44
UK	0.00	0.16	0.51	0.00	−0.08	0.46	0.01	0.08	0.98
E10[a]	0.09	−0.60	1.13	0.07	−0.32	2.01	0.14	−0.92	3.17
Change in the European employment rate	0.09 + −0.60 + 1.13 = 0.61			0.07 + −0.32 + 2.01 = 1.77			0.14 + −0.92 + 3.17 = 2.39		
	59.4 to 60.0%			60.0 to 61.8%			59.4 to 61.8%		

Source: Special tabulations provided by Eurostat
Note: a Data for Germany and E10 exclude the new Länder

Table 2.3 looks at these changes in employment rates within each member state. The four countries where the net change in employment rates were negative in practice tended to experience relatively smaller rates of change than in countries where the employment rate rose. Thus the decreases ranged from 1.4 to 2.8 percentage points (Greece to France), while the increases ranged from 2.6 to 12.0 percentage points (Luxembourg to the Netherlands). The strongly positive increases in six member states provides further evidence of the divergent employment trends over this period. Moreover, the direction of change in employment rates was on average away from and not towards convergence, as three out of the four countries with negative changes had employment rates well below the EU average in 1983 (France excepted).

The only significant contribution to employment rates from men were in the Netherlands (up 3 percentage points – although this change is probably in part the result of a change in the statistical series: Plantenga and Sloep 1995) and in Denmark (up 1 percentage point associated with an increase in the number of young people in work). In three further countries the impact was broadly neutral, varying by less than 1 percentage point. In five countries the decline in the male employment rate made a negative contribution to employment rates of over 1 percentage point, with three making negative contributions of close to or greater than 3 percentage points. In contrast the female contribution to overall employment rates is strongly positive, at over 3 percentage points at the E10 level and exceeding 3 percentage points in six countries. Where female contributions to rising employment rates are modest, the male change in employment rates has tended to be negative, suggesting that although the overall employment performance varies by country, the gender gap remains similar. Indeed the differences in contributions between men and women to the standardised employment rates is remarkably similar across member states, at between 3 and 5 percentage points, whether or not the overall employment rate growth was strong or weak. When we look at the male and female contributions across the two sub-periods we again find fairly similar patterns. However, the consistent positive contribution of women to overall employment rates does not hold, with two countries in each sub-period recording small negative contributions. In each sub-period seven out of the E10 countries recorded negative male contributions, one country more than the number with a negative male contribution for the 1983–92 period as a whole.

Differences in employment rates over the lifecycle mean that overall employment rates are sensitive to changes in the relative size of population age cohorts. The impact of changes in the structure of population can be estimated by calculating the implied employment rate in 1992 with the 1992 population structure but 1983 employment rates (on the assumption that changes in population structure do not change underlying employment

Table 2.3 Percentage point contribution by men and women to changing employment rates within the EU, 1983–92

	1983–7			1987–92			1983–92		
	Male contribution	Female contribution	Employment rate change	Male contribution	Femal contribution	Employment rate change	Male contribution	Female contribution	Employment rate change
Belgium	-1.36	0.55	-0.82	0.62	3.58	4.21	-0.74	4.14	3.40
Denmark	2.43	3.33	5.76	-1.28	-0.29	-1.58	1.16	3.03	4.20
Germany[a]	-0.40	1.15	0.75	1.00	3.53	4.52	0.58	4.74	5.32
Greece	-1.32	0.97	-0.35	-1.00	-0.05	-1.05	-2.31	0.92	-1.39
Spain	—	—	—	0.55	2.36	2.92	—	—	—
France	-2.22	-0.33	-2.55	-1.00	0.74	-0.26	-3.22	0.40	-2.82
Ireland	-2.70	-0.12	-2.82	-0.76	1.78	1.02	-3.46	1.65	-1.81
Italy	-1.46	0.39	-1.07	-1.39	1.00	-0.40	-2.85	1.40	-1.45
Luxembourg	-0.15	1.62	1.47	-1.02	2.17	1.15	-1.17	3.78	2.62
Netherlands	2.64	3.90	6.54	1.21	4.23	5.44	3.85	8.14	11.99
Portugal	—	—	—	0.01	3.22	3.23	—	—	—
UK	0.77	2.49	3.26	-0.40	2.26	1.86	0.37	4.75	5.12

Source: Special tabulations provided by Eurostat
Note: a Data for Germany exclude the new Länder

rate patterns over the lifecycle). For men changes in the age structure of the population (population effect) have had fairly positive impacts on the employment rate over this period, contributing positively to employment rates in nine out of ten cases, and accounting for around 0.7 or more of a percentage point in five countries (the Netherlands and the UK recording increases of over 1 percentage point) (see Appendix Table 2.1). In contrast changing age structure of the female population made a positive impact in only seven out of ten cases, and with the contribution falling below 0.7 of a percentage point in all cases.

To isolate the effect of changing propensities to be employed from changes in age structure, the implied employment rates were calculated for 1992, with 1992 employment rates but 1983 population structure. These results (see Appendix Table 2.1) show that changes in male age-specific employment rates made a negative contribution to the overall employment rate in eight out of ten countries – and a negative contribution of more than 1.5 percentage points in six cases. Only the Netherlands revealed a strongly positive contribution related to upward changes in male age-specific employment rates.

For women the increases were all positive, except for France, which recorded a small negative change of 0.05 of a percentage point. In six countries rising female employment rates by age group accounted for increases in the overall employment rate of 2.5 percentage points and above. In all countries the change in female employment rates standardised for population changes was the main positive contribution to the employment rate while the main negative contribution came from declining male age-specific employment rates. Increases in female age-specific employment rates accounted for 60 per cent to 70 per cent of all the net positive changes in six countries, and in the remaining four provided the main offsetting impact to the net decreases in employment rates derived primarily from decreasing male age-specific employment rates. We also carried out decompositions for the two sub-periods, 1983–87 and 1987–92. The overall patterns are found to be quite similar, except that the population effect exerts a more positive impact on employment rates for both men and women in the second sub-period.

The contribution of part-time employment to changing employment rates

To what extent is the contribution of women to the overall European employment rate exaggerated by the recent expansion of part-time employment? Figure 2.4 and Table 2.4 compare the employment rate changes based on numbers in employment to employment rates calculated on a full-time equivalent basis (counting two part-time jobs as equal to one

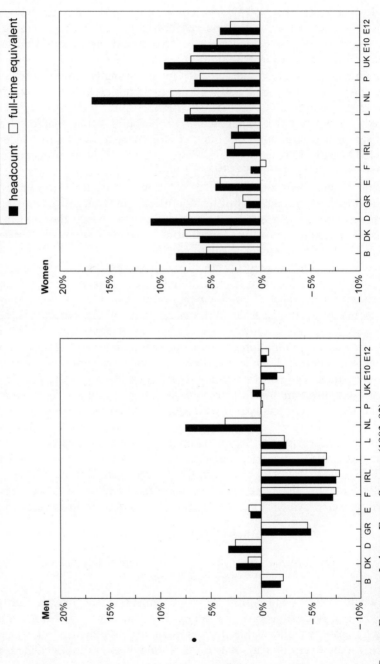

Figure 2.4 Employment rate growth on a headcount and full-time equivalent basis, 1983–92

Source: European Labour Force Surveys (1983–92)
Note: Change in employment rates 1987–92 for Spain, Portugal and E12

Table 2.4 Changes in employment rates by gender: persons in employment and full-time equivalent basis, 1983–92[a]

	Persons in employment			Full-time equivalent		
	Men	Women	Total	Men	Women	Total
Belgium	-1.48	8.27	3.44	-1.53	5.54	2.06
Denmark	2.32	6.09	4.22	1.09	7.69	4.41
Germany[b]	3.04	10.33	7.15	2.46	7.41	5.51
Greece	-4.83	1.77	-1.28	-4.55	2.28	-0.88
France	-6.55	0.79	-2.83	-6.89	-0.46	-3.64
Ireland	-6.81	3.36	-1.95	-7.08	2.50	-2.53
Italy	-5.84	2.73	-1.26	-6.03	2.18	-1.62
Luxembourg	-2.33	7.57	2.85	-2.30	7.24	2.71
Netherlands	7.64	16.41	12.03	4.22	8.85	6.57
UK[b]	0.75	9.48	5.15	-0.30	6.67	3.18
E10[b]	-1.44	6.40	2.67	-2.10	4.36	1.34

Source: Special tabulations provided by Eurostat
Notes: a Employment rates as a ratio of persons in employment aged 15–64 to the population aged 15–64 years
       b Data for Germany and E10 exclude the new Länder.

full-time job). These data reveal that there is still a positive contribution from female employment to employment rates in all countries between 1983 and 1992, except for France, where there is a 0.5 percentage point drop in the full-time equivalent rate for women, but more importantly the female contribution is still systematically greater than that of men. Using the full-time equivalent basis reduces the employment rate increase for women in all countries (except Denmark and Greece where part-time shares have been falling), and does so by considerable margins in Germany (−3 percentage points), the UK (−2.8 percentage points) and the Netherlands (−8.6 percentage points). However, in each of these three countries the female employment rate change, even on a full-time equivalent basis, remains strongly positive, at between 6 and 7 percentage points. The impact of this calculation on measured changes in male employment rates is less significant, but amounts to a decrease of around 1 percentage point in the UK and Denmark and of 3.5 percentage points in the Netherlands. Overall the full-time equivalent calculation reduces the increase in the E10 employment rate from 2.7 to 1.3 percentage points. The impact of this change varies by country, with Belgium, Germany, the UK and particularly the Netherlands experiencing reductions equal to or above the average, while for Greece and Denmark there is even a somewhat greater increase in the full-time equivalent employment rate. If we use the full-time equivalent employment rates to reconsider the ranking of countries by relative employment levels in 1992, we find that two countries move down the hierarchy, the UK and the Netherlands (from second to fourth and from fifth to eighth respectively), while Portugal moves up from fourth to second place (see Figure 2.5). The ranking of countries by female full-time equivalent employment rates follows very closely the ranking for the all (male plus female) full-time equivalent employment rates, with at most one place difference in the ranking for every country. This demonstrates that even after adjusting for differences in part-time rates, female employment patterns are the most significant factor in employment rate variations.

Full-time equivalent calculations help in comparative analysis of employment performance. However, it is important that such standardisation techniques do not obscure the differences between full-time and part-time work, both in terms of types of jobs and in terms of recent employment growth rates. Indeed over the period 1983–92 it is not only in women's employment that part-time job growth has outstripped full-time job growth but also in the case of men's employment. Part-time jobs accounted for 56 per cent of all jobs created among the E10 between 1983 and 1992, and for 54 per cent of new male jobs and 56 per cent of new female jobs (see Figure 2.6 and Table 2.5). Over 75 per cent of all new part-time jobs were taken by women but this also applied to full-time jobs.

Figure 2.5 Full-time equivalent employment rates, 1992

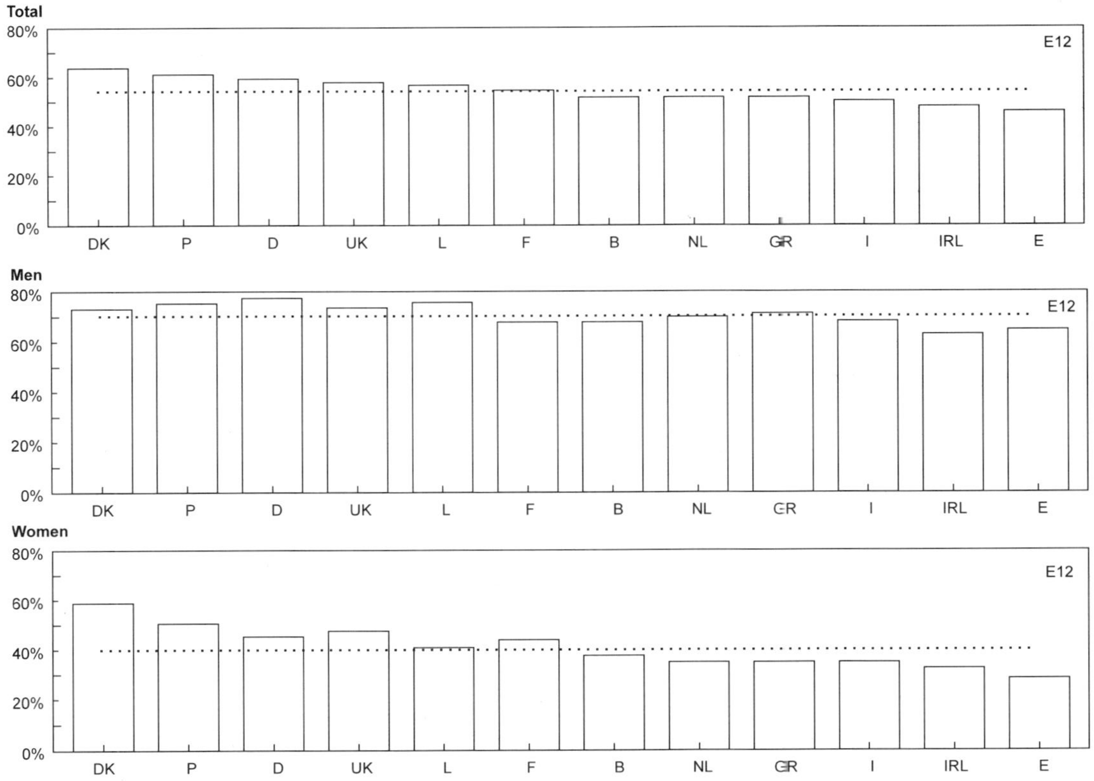

Source: European Labour Force Survey (1992)
Note: Employment rates as a ratio of persons in employment aged 15–64 to the population aged 15–64

Figure 2.6 Composition of employment growth, 1983–92

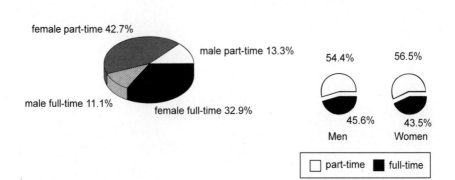

Source: European Labour Force Surveys (1983–92)

Looking at the employment trends by individual country reveals a more diverse pattern. Part-time job growth was by no means a universal pattern, with over 75 per cent of all new part-time jobs for men and for women found in only three countries (Germany, UK and the Netherlands: see Figure 2.7). The actual number of new part-time jobs in the Netherlands is also debatable because of the change in the survey design. There is a more even spread of full-time job growth for women; it is positive in all countries and while Germany and the UK again contributed over 60 per cent of total full-time job growth, Italy also made a significant contribution at over 15 per cent of total job growth. For men the picture is more varied: four countries, but particularly Italy and France, record strong negative falls in full-time employment for men, while Germany dominates the growth in full-time employment, accounting for well over 100 per cent of the total net change in male full-time employment, with the Netherlands the only other country to make a significant contribution to male full-time job growth in the EU (see Figure 2.7). The strongest growth in part-time employment occurred in the first part of the period for men but in the second part for women, although full-time jobs for women also grew more strongly, thus reducing the contribution of part-time jobs to total female employment growth from 60 per cent to 54 per cent between the first and the second period. Nevertheless, the share of part-time jobs in total employment rose for men and for women across both sub-periods. These figures suggest that future employment prospects are closely tied to part-time work in several large EU countries, and that while this growth concerns largely women it is involving an increasing share of men. However, these trends cannot be generalised across all member states given the declining part-time rates in Denmark and Greece over the period. Thus the prospects of part-time work as a form of employment sharing cannot be considered equivalent in all member states.

Table 2.5 Share of new jobs that were part-time, 1983–92

	All (%)			Men (%)			Women (%)		
	1983–7	1987–92	1983–92	1983–7	1987–92	1983–92	1983–7	1987–92	1983–92
Belgium	102.6	42.0	53.5	0.9	9.5	10.3	96.2	49.0	59.9
Denmark	25.9	−2,797.3	6.3	31.6	28.0	43.0	20.2	−248.8	−20.0
Germany[a]	21.3	43.7	39.7	26.9	14.2	16.5	17.0	65.9	57.3
Greece	−19.6	−17.8	−18.8	−155.1	12.1	−22.5	−4.2	−41.2	−17.5
Spain	—	7.0	—	—	−3.5	—	—	13.1	—
France	659.3	40.5	93.4	54.2	13.0	163.7	108.6	47.2	67.9
Ireland	14.1	40.7	80.1	2.9	62.0	26.4	26.9	36.8	35.3
Italy	296.1	27.8	68.8	64.9	−30.5	30.7	36.0	28.4	31.0
Luxembourg	13.6	1.9	7.9	14.1	−15.2	1.0	13.3	9.5	11.4
Netherlands	73.9	70.9	72.5	64.6	36.0	53.5	82.5	89.2	86.0
Portugal	—	22.2	—	—	31.1	—	—	16.1	—
UK	61.5	90.9	68.1	53.8	40.1	146.8	64.9	46.0	57.6
E10[a]	69.1	47.6	56.0	98.9	26.9	54.4	59.7	54.4	56.5
E12[a]		40.6			20.9			47.3	

Source: Special tabulations provided by Eurostat
Note: a Data for Germany and E10/12 exclude the new Länder

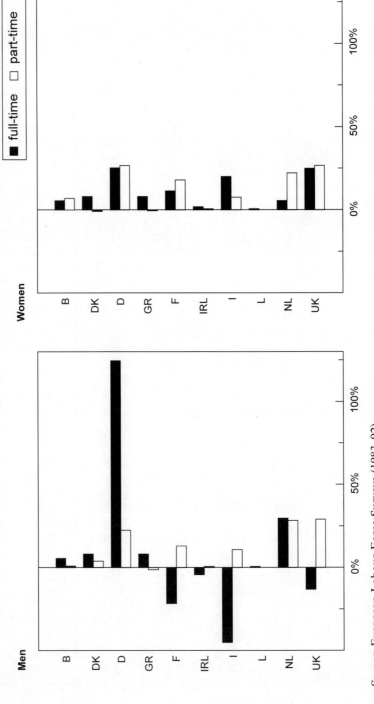

Figure 2.7 Contribution to EU (E10) full-time and part-time job growth by member state and gender, 1983–92

Source: European Labour Force Surveys (1983–92)
Notes: Contribution to full-time job growth sum to 100% for each gender. Contribution to part-time job growth sum to 100% for each gender

To what extent is the growth in part-time jobs associated with the rise in participation of women in the core working-age population – that is over the age range where women have responsibility for children – or to what extent is the growth associated with changes in the incidence of part-time employment for particular age cohorts? These questions have been invest-igated from two perspectives.

First, in Appendix Table 2.2 we calculate that only 44 per cent of the increase in the number of part-time jobs for women over the period 1983 to 1992 is accounted for by rising part-time shares of total employment within each age group (changing age-specific part-time rates) while over half of the part-time job growth (54 per cent) was necessary simply to maintain the same rates of part-time working by age group (population effect). The impact of the changing size and structure of the workforce can be further decomposed into scale and compositional effects, and here we find that the compositional effects, that is the change in the structure of the labour force towards age groups where part-time work is more frequent, explains in fact 77 per cent of the net change in part-time jobs, offset by a 17 per cent decrease in part-time jobs associated with scale effects (that is, the increase in part-time jobs associated with a constant age structure of the population, but changing population size). When we look at these patterns within the two sub-periods we find that the increasing incidence of part-time work within age groups accounted for a higher proportion of part-time job growth in the first than in the second period (55 per cent compared to 37 per cent). For men the pattern is quite different: changes in the incidence of part-time work by age group account for more than 100 per cent of the net growth in part-time jobs, with changes in the size and age structure of the employed workforce acting as a negative influence. These results in part reflect the low part-time employment rates for men at the beginning of the period, reinforcing the evidence that part-time work is a marginal but nevertheless rising form of economic activity for men in the EU.

Disaggregation by member state reveals that in three countries changes in women's part-time employment rates by age group in fact exerted an overall negative impact on part-time job growth (Denmark, Greece and Luxem-bourg) but had a positive impact in the remaining seven, ranging from 23 per cent in the Netherlands to 70 per cent in France of part-time job growth. Similar patterns are found within each of the two sub-periods (see Appendix Table 2.2), except that in the UK the impact of part-time employment rates is negative in the 1987 to 1992 period. When we look at Spain and Portugal over this period we find that changes in the part-time employment rate by age group have a negligible effect in Spain, with all growth accounted for by changes in the structure and size of the labour force, while in Portugal 45 per cent of the net growth is due to rising part-time employment rates within age groups. For men there is a very consistent pattern between the findings at the member state level and those at the E10 level. Changes in the size and structure of the labour force either make a negative contribution or a very small positive contribution to net part-time job growth, with rising age-specific part-time rates accounting for the majority of net part-time job growth in all member states.

The increase in part-time jobs has resulted in an overall increase in the part-time employment rate – from 27.2 per cent to 31.9 per cent for women and from 2.2 per cent to 4.1 per cent for men – over the period 1983 to 1992 at the E10 level. Appendix Table 2.3 decomposes this increase into the share that can be accounted for by a changing age structure of the employed population and the share that can be attributed to changing part-time employment rates by age group. The results show for both men and women that it is the rising part-time employment rates within age groups that are of overwhelming importance, accounting for 4.61 percentage points out of a total change of 4.65 percentage points for women, and for 2.23 percentage points compared to a net change of only 1.86 percentage points for men (see Figure 2.8). Similar patterns also hold within the sub-periods,

Figure 2.8 Decomposition of the growth of the part-time employment rate in the EU, 1983–92

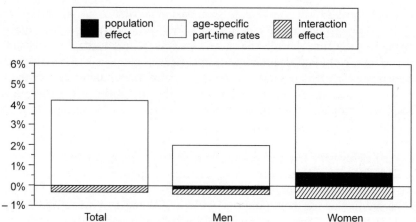

Source: European Labour Force Survey (1983–92)
Note: Population effect + change in age-specific part-time rates + interaction effect
    = net change in part-time employment rate

and in all member states for men. For women we again find a diversity of experience by member states, with Denmark, Greece and Luxembourg all recording negative changes in part-time employment rates, accounted for by declining part-time rates within age categories and not by changes in the age structure of the employed workforce. Spain also records a negative change in the overall part-time employment rate for the second sub-period, but in this case this is due to changes in the age structure of the employed work-force, and not to changes in part-time employment rates within age groups. In most cases the rising age specific part-time rates accounted for mainly by rising part-time rates among women under 40, although countries differ in the extent to which rising rates are concentrated on the very young groups, that is in the period mainly before women become mothers, or whether the rise is found more among the age groups which include mothers. In the UK, the Netherlands, Ireland and France more than 40 per cent of the net change in standardised part-time rates is accounted for by rises in the rates in the under 25s (and Denmark also records a strong rise in part-time rates among this group even though the overall change is negative). In Germany, Italy, and Belgium the rises are more concentrated among older age groups, although the modal group varies from 25–39 for Belgium and Italy to 50–59 in Germany. These findings suggest that the growth of part-time work is by no means solely associated with rising part-time employment rates among mothers in the EU.

Trends in non-employment in Europe

Considering employment rates as a measure of labour market performance means that the residual part of the working-age population constitutes the non-employed which in turn can be sub-divided into the unemployed and the inactive. There are wide variations in the level and composition of non-employment between member states and this section considers these differences within three broad age groups; young persons aged 15–24, prime-age persons aged 25–49 years and older working-age persons aged 50–64 years.

Youth non-employment

At the E12 level (excluding former East Germany) the majority of the youth population, that is those aged 15 to 24, is not in employment: 55.3 per cent of the male youth population and 62.2 per cent of the female youth population were not in employment in 1992 and most were included within the inactive sector of the population (46.2 per cent of the male population and 53.4 per cent of the female population compared to 9.1 per cent and 8.9 per cent respectively in unemployment). This age group encompasses the main population groups attending full-time education but there are wide variations between European countries in non-employment rates, resulting from different participation rates in education, different participation rates of students in paid work, and from differences in unemployment rates.

Figure 2.9 shows that there are six countries with high levels of non-employment in this age group involving 60 per cent or more of the male and female populations. Of these six countries, five – Belgium, France and the

Figure 2.9 Non-employment of men and women aged 15–24 years, 1992

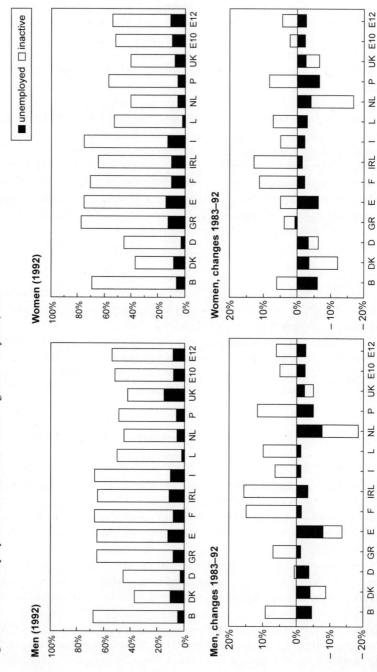

■ unemployed □ inactive

Men (1992)

Women (1992)

Men, changes 1983–92

Women, changes 1983–92

Source: European Labour Force Surveys (1983–92)
Note: Changes 1987–92 for Spain, Portugal and E12

three Southern countries of Spain, Italy and Greece – have both high rates of participation in education and low rates of student participation in paid work (Figure 2.10). The European Labour Force Survey counts individuals working at least one hour a week as in employment even if they are also students. Ireland is the only one of the six countries to have a low share of young people in education (only higher than the UK). In this case the main cause of high non-employment is the high level of youth unemployment, particularly for men. The non-employment situation in the Southern European countries is also in part the result of high levels of inactivity and unemployment even among young persons who are not in education as a consequence of the difficulties of initial labour market entry that young persons face (see Chapter 4).

Luxembourg and Portugal occupy middle positions, with non-employment rates of around 50 per cent (although closer to 60 per cent for Portuguese women) but at the other extreme Denmark, the Netherlands, the UK and Germany all have relatively low levels of non-employment among the youngest age group, with two-fifths or less of men and women not in employment, except for young men in the Netherlands where the share rises to nearly 50 per cent. The UK has less than 30 per cent of women and men aged 15–24 in education compared to around 40 per cent for the remaining countries in this group. One explanation for these low rates of non-employment could be high participation rates of students in paid work but in practice the participation of students aged 15–24 in paid work ranges from less than 10 per cent in Germany, around 20 per cent in the Netherlands and the UK, reaching a high in Denmark of 47.7 per cent and 42.4 per cent for female and male students aged 15–24 respectively (see Figure 2.10). Working students in Denmark are concentrated at the lower end of this age distribution with more than four-fifths of all students in employment aged between 15 and 18 years. Other factors which contribute to the low level of non-employment in these four countries include the dual training system in Germany, which allows young people to combine education and apprenticeship training, thereby resulting in a relatively low share in full-time education, the generally higher levels of part-time employment which provide employment opportunities for students and the generally easier access to the formal labour market than in, for example, the Southern European countries.

Youth non-employment increased in eight member states for men and seven member states for women between 1983 and 1992 (1987–92 for Spain and Portugal). This net increase reflects a fall in unemployment and a larger rise in inactivity. In all member states and for both men and women (except women in Spain and Greece), youth unemployment has declined, measured as a share of the population, by between 6.7 to 1.6 percentage points for women (Belgium to Ireland) and between 6.6 to 1.9 percentage points for men (Netherlands to the UK) (Figure 2.9). The pattern of change in

41

Figure 2.10 Share of men and women aged 15–24 in education by employment status, 1992

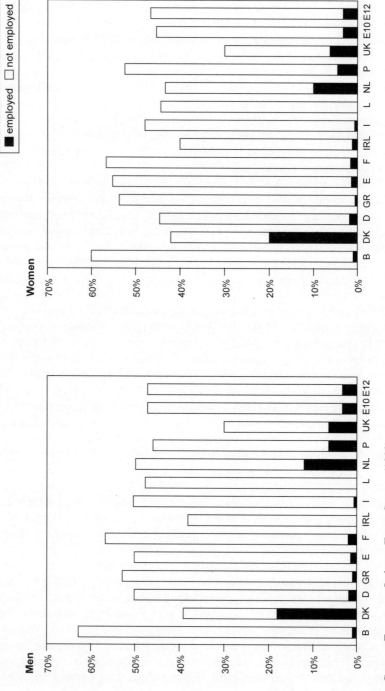

Source: European Labour Force Survey (1992)

inactivity is more mixed: in the Netherlands and Denmark inactivity for young women and men declined considerably, by 12.6 and 11.7 percentage points respectively in the Netherlands and by 8.8 and 4.7 percentage points in Denmark. The large decline in non-employment among the young in the Netherlands must be partly the result of the apparent rise of short part-time employment. This is not necessarily a new development as the changes in the Dutch labour force survey in 1987 are recognised to have increased measured employment, particularly short-time employment. Inactivity also fell for women in the UK and Germany, and for men in the UK but to a lesser extent than in the Netherlands and Denmark. In the remaining countries inactivity has risen among the 15–24 age group, by 0.6 to 15.9 percentage points (Germany to Ireland) for men and by 3.0 to 12.9 percentage points (Greece to Ireland) for women.

Part of the explanation for these changes in rates of non-employment may be found in the significant expansion of the share of teenagers in school between 1985 and 1991 (OECD 1994e: 29). Whether these changes in education are revealed in the non-employment rates depends on the trends in employment activity among students. The share of students who work has remained stable in the case of Italy, France and Belgium, or grown slightly in Portugal and decreased in Ireland. However, in some countries participation in education by teenagers has grown alongside rising shares of students in work. The share of 16–19 year olds in education in Denmark rose from 49.7 per cent to 59.6 per cent and in the UK from 35.4 per cent to 44.2 per cent respectively but at the same time the share of working teenage students also rose. Germany alone experienced a falling share of the teenage population in education. Among the 20–24 age group there has also been a large rise in participation in education, particularly in France, Ireland and Belgium where inactivity rates have also risen, and in Denmark where the high share of working students has modified the rise. Looking at the shares of young people in education demonstrates the wide variation between member states. In six countries – Denmark, Belgium, Greece, Portugal, Spain and France – in 1991 more than a quarter of those aged 20–24 years were in education compared to less than one in ten in the UK. For 16–19 year olds the share of the population varied from a high of 85.1 per cent in Belgium to a low of just 44.4 per cent in the UK.

Young people who are inactive but in education may be of less concern than those who are inactive because of other reasons. Raising the overall standard of education in the economy can increase competitiveness, provide individuals with greater labour market opportunities as well as improving the cultural 'well-being' of a country. *Employment in Europe* (CEC 1995a) suggests that the number of young people in 'full inactivity', that is inactive and not in education, should be of great concern. In 1992 nearly 7 per cent of the 15–24 age group in the EU (including Unified Germany) were inactive in this full sense, and nearly one in ten (9.8 per cent) young women in this age group were 'fully' inactive compared to just 3.4 per cent of men of the same age. The highest levels of 'full inactivity' are found in two Southern countries – Greece and Italy – and the UK and Ireland, with more than 8.5 per cent of the youth population in 'full inactivity' in all four countries in 1992. More startling are the very high rates of 'full inactivity' for the women in these countries; 'full inactivity' for young women exceeded 13 per cent in all four countries rising to nearly 18 per cent in Ireland in 1992. For young men, only Ireland has more than 6 per cent in 'full inactivity' with 13 per cent of the male youth population in neither education nor the labour force. In all member states the share of the female population in 'full inactivity' is greater than that for men with female rates at least twice the male rate in nine countries and more than three times those for men in six countries. Youth unemployment is a problem because large numbers of young people can become disillusioned with the labour market early in their lifecycle but 'full inactivity', particularly for women, must also be considered a serious problem.

Youth unemployment: labour force and population measures compared.

The gender pattern of youth unemployment tends to follow that for the population as a whole, with female unemployment rates on the conventional labour force measure exceeding male rates in all countries except the UK, together with Ireland and Luxembourg for this younger age group. However, in the UK the female rate is 7 percentage points lower while in Ireland and Luxembourg the rates are much closer. Among the remaining countries, in four – Denmark, the former West Germany, Portugal and the Netherlands – the male rate is higher than the female rate but the difference is small. In three Southern European member states – Spain, Italy and Greece – together with France and Belgium, the male rate is considerably lower than the female rate, with the difference ranging from 5 percentage points in Belgium to 17 percentage points in Greece.

The high rates of unemployment often cited for young people may be deceptive because of the lower activity rates compared to older age groups. Conventionally unemployment rates are measured as a share of the labour force but the activity rate for the 15–24 age group for E12 in 1992 on the ILO (International Labour Organisation) definition (see Figure 2.1) was only 50.4 per cent compared to 81.2 per cent for the 25–49 year old age group. This means that a similar share of the population who are unemployed for these two age groups would give rise to a much higher unemployment rate in the younger group. If unemployment is in fact measured as a share of the population, youth unemployment rates fall significantly in all countries compared to the conventional labour force measure (see Table 2.6). Unemployment rates for young people under 25 measured as a share

Table 2.6 Unemployment rates by age group as a share of the population and as a share of the labour force, 1992

Share of the population	Men (%)				Women (%)			
	15–24	25–49	50–64	Total	15–24	25–49	50–64	Total
Belgium	4.2	4.1	1.3	3.5	5.4	6.2	0.9	4.7
Denmark	8.9	7.4	5.6	7.3	8.9	8.4	5.3	7.8
Germany[a]	2.5/3.3	3.1/4.2	3.4/4.2	3.1/4.0	2.4/3.7	3.0/6.0	2.6/4.2	2.8/5.1
Greece	7.4	3.7	1.6	3.8	11.3	5.8	1.0	5.5
Spain	13.8	10.7	6.2	10.4	15.5	12.5	2.3	10.6
France	7.9	6.5	3.8	6.2	9.3	8.8	3.4	7.6
Ireland	12.0	13.4	6.8	11.7	8.8	7.2	2.4	6.7
Italy	11.3	4.5	1.4	5.2	12.5	5.8	0.8	5.9
Luxembourg	2.2	1.3	0.4	1.2	1.6	1.7	0.3	1.3
Netherlands	4.7	3.4	1.5	3.2	5.2	5.1	1.4	4.3
Portugal	4.9	2.3	1.8	2.8	4.9	3.1	0.5	2.9
UK	13.7	9.5	7.7	10.0	7.3	5.0	2.3	4.8
E12[a]	9.1/9.0	6.1/6.2	3.9/4.1	6.2/5.3	8.9/8.9	6.3/6.9	2.1/2.6	5.8/6.2

Table 2.6 (Contd...)

Share of the labour force	Men (%)				Women (%)			
	15–24	25–49	50–64	Total	15–24	25–49	50–64	Total
Belgium	11.3	4.4	2.7	4.8	15.2	9.0	5.1	9.5
Denmark	12.1	7.8	7.3	8.5	12.6	9.5	8.9	10.0
Germany[a]	4.2/5.5	3.3/4.4	4.7/6.0	3.8/4.9	4.3/6.5	4.4/8.1	6.4/10.2	4.8/8.3
Greece	17.2	3.9	2.4	5.0	34.2	10.6	3.7	13.2
Spain	28.0	11.4	9.1	13.7	39.8	23.6	9.6	25.3
France	18.6	6.8	6.9	8.2	25.0	11.5	8.9	12.9
Ireland	24.3	14.5	9.4	15.3	20.8	14.0	10.2	15.4
Italy	24.4	4.9	2.3	7.0	32.9	10.4	3.9	13.9
Luxembourg	4.2	1.3	0.8	1.6	3.2	2.9	1.5	2.8
Netherlands	7.7	3.6	2.6	4.1	8.6	7.9	5.5	7.8
Portugal	8.7	2.4	2.5	3.5	10.8	4.2	1.2	4.9
UK	18.9	10.0	10.4	11.7	11.7	6.7	4.7	7.3
E12[a]	20.0/16.7	6.5/6.6	5.9/6.2	7.9/8.0	19.0/18.9	9.5/10.1	6.2/7.4	10.7/11.2

Source: Special tabulations provided by Eurostat
Note: a Data for Germany and E12 exclude/include the new Länder

of the labour force are around twice that of the prime-age group (25–49 years), at 17.9 per cent compared to 7.7 per cent and just 6 per cent for 50–64 year olds for the E12 in 1992. However, while there are eight countries for men and nine countries for women where the youth unemployment rate exceeds 10 per cent as a share of the labour force, when unemployment is measured as a share of the population there are only four countries for men and three for women where unemployment exceeds 10 per cent. In six countries for men and seven countries for women the unemployment rate more than halves when it is measured as a share of the population rather than the labour force. There are also considerable changes in the ranking of unemployment rates by country, for although Spain still has the highest male youth unemployment rate at 13.8 per cent, it is joined by the UK, also with 13.8 per cent of the male population aged 15–24 in unemployment. For women Spain also has the highest female unemployment as a share of the population at 15.5 per cent and two other Southern countries – Greece and Italy – have unemployment rates of more than 10 per cent. Unemployment rates for men and women aged 15–24 measured as a share of the population are in general closer to those for older age groups and in two countries for men and three countries for women are actually lower than for the prime-age group of 25–49 year olds.

High youth unemployment rates as a share of the labour force may reflect low levels of labour market participation in this age group in some countries and unemployment rates as a share of the population are closer to the rates found for age groups above 25. Nevertheless, the high labour force measures of youth unemployment may be an accurate reflection of the problems faced by the decreasing but still significant share of the population who enter the labour force early, often with low or no qualifications. Moreover, population measures may understate unemployment to the extent that young people continue in education or become discouraged workers as a consequence of poor employment opportunities.

Prime-age non-employment

Among the prime-age population, non-employment is lower than that for those below 25 years of age but there is a more dramatic difference between the sexes. At the E12 level just over one in ten (11.9 per cent) prime-age men are non-employed compared to nearly four out of ten women (38.5 per cent). In 1992 non-employment for men ranged between just over 5 per cent in Luxembourg to over a fifth of the prime-age population in Ireland; at the same time female non-employment rates ranged between nearly three-fifths (59.4 per cent) in Spain to just under a fifth (19.9 per cent) in Denmark (Figure 2.11). In Luxembourg the female non-employment rate is more than eight times that for men and in four more countries – Greece, Portugal, Italy and the Netherlands – the female rate is at least four times the male

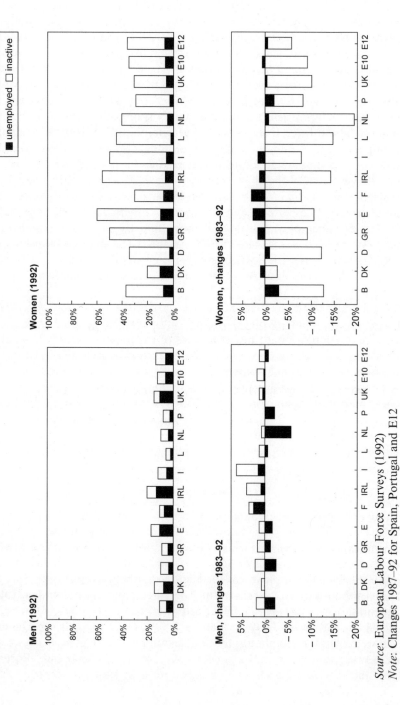

Figure 2.11 Non-employment of men and women aged 25–49 years, 1992

■ unemployed ☐ inactive

Men (1992)

Women (1992)

Men, changes 1983–92

Women, changes 1983–92

Source: European Labour Force Surveys (1992)
Note: Changes 1987–92 for Spain, Portugal and E12

rate. Ireland and Spain have the two highest non-employment rates for both men and women, with male rates at around a fifth and female rates closer to three-fifths. The UK has the third highest non-employment rate for prime-age men yet the third-lowest female non-employment rate. In Germany inclusion of the new Länder reduces the male non-employment rate in 1992 by just over half a percentage point but by nearly 2 percentage points for women, from 34.0 per cent to 32.3 per cent. In Denmark the high employment rate for women means that female non-employment among the prime-age group of women is just 6.8 percentage points higher than the male rate (19.9 per cent compared to 13.1 per cent).

This prime-age range covers the peak child-rearing years and the period when most men are expected to be in the labour force. As a consequence the non-employed women are more often inactive, while for men there is a more even split between inactivity and unemployment. For women inactivity rates for the 25–49 age group range from just over one in ten in Denmark to over two-fifths in five countries (Ireland, Spain, Greece, Italy and Luxembourg). Female unemployment rates (as a share of the population) among the prime-age group are all less than one in ten except in Spain with a rate of 12.5 per cent in 1992. In Luxembourg the female unemployment rate, as a share of the population, was just 1.7 per cent, less than one twenty-fourth of the rate of inactivity, and in eight countries female unemployment was less than a fifth of the inactivity rate. Higher ratios of unemployment to inactivity were found in Spain, France and Denmark, but whereas in France and Denmark the high ratios resulted from low inactivity as well as high unemployment, in Spain both inactivity and unemployment rates were high in comparative terms.

For men inactivity rates were below one in ten in all member states in 1992 ranging from just under 4 per cent in Luxembourg and Belgium to just under 8 per cent in Ireland but even for this group, which covers the population category most likely to be part of the active population, unemployment rates (as a share of the population) were lower than inactivity rates in seven out of twelve member states and at the E12 level male inactivity and unemployment rates were almost equal at 6.1 per cent and 5.8 per cent respectively. These data suggest the inadequacy of current measures of unemployment which exclude, for example, discouraged workers. Male unemployment rates as a share of the population in 1992 ranged from a high in Ireland and Spain of more than one in ten prime-age men (13.4 per cent and 10.7 per cent) to less than 3 per cent in Portugal and Luxembourg (2.3 per cent and 1.3 per cent).

Looking at the trends since 1983 we can see that female non-employment has been falling, reflecting rising employment rates, while male non-employment rates have been rising. Between 1983 and 1992 the E10 non-employment rate for men rose by 2 percentage points and female non-employment fell by 10 points; most of these changes in non-employment were accounted for by shifts in inactivity which rose by 1.8 percentage points for men and fell by 10.1 percentage points for women. Figure 2.11 shows how in all member states prime-age female inactivity fell over the period and male inactivity rose (except in Portugal where it fell very slightly by 0.2 of a percentage point). The largest fall in female inactivity, of almost 20 percentage points, was in the Netherlands.[2] Inactivity rates also fell significantly in all remaining countries: by between 7 and 14 percentage points (including Spain and Portugal where the fall is measured only over

---

Box 2.2   Women's labour supply behaviour is subject to both structural and cyclical effects, but the relative importance of these effects varies between countries

Trends in the employment rate have to be interpreted against long-term trends in the organisation of households and employment. In the mid-1950s in **Denmark** the typical family included a housewife outside the labour market and a husband working 48 hours per week for 49 weeks per year. Today the typical family consists of two individuals both working full-time 37 hours per week for 46 weeks per year. The annual labour supply of the average family has consequently risen by 40–50 per cent (Boje 1995: 15).

While **Italy**, like all other European countries, has been experiencing a long-term increase in female labour supply, there is beginning to be evidence of discouraged worker effects; particularly in the South for women. This is shown in part by the recent fall in first-time jobseekers among women in the South, a trend which does not seem consistent with demographic patterns. However, even though volatility of women's labour supply is still higher than men's, it is perhaps the persistence of women's job search that is most worthy of comment, given the mean average job search of first-time jobseekers of twenty-six months. The more educated the woman, the more persistent she is in her participation in the labour market although, except for graduates, education does not seem to improve significantly her chances of employment; it only reduces the likelihood of her becoming a discouraged worker (Bettio and Mazzotta 1995: 80, 107).

In **France** women's activity rates have risen faster than their employment rates, suggesting that the trend increase in participation has become relatively independent of employment opportunities, with a reduction in the importance of cyclical variations in activity rates. However, the stability of the trend probably hides two countervailing tendencies; a rise in discouraged workers entering the labour force when demand is high and an added worker effect when employment demand is low, both serving to maintain a high female unemployment rate. The result of the trend increase has been an increase in the share of economically active women aged 25–49 from one in two to eight in ten (Silvera *et al.* 1995: 3, 5, 89–92).

---

the 1987–92 period) except in Denmark where the fall was only 2 percentage points, in part because of the low inactivity level for women even in 1983. In six countries some of the decline in inactivity was accompanied by a rise in female prime-age unemployment (as a share of the population) ranging from less than 1 percentage point in Denmark to a 3.6 percentage point rise in France. In the other six member states unemployment rates have remained stable (in Luxembourg) or fallen, contributing to the general fall in female non-employment.

Decreases in the rate of inactivity for women can be considered part of a long-term structural trend towards higher employment rates for women. Women's labour supply increase has come to be seen as increasingly independent of actual employment opportunities, and representing an irreversible social development (see Box 2.2). However, Italy is perhaps providing a salutary reminder that women's long-term emancipation and integration into waged work is not independent of the supply of employment opportunities. Long-term unemployment in Italy is beginning to result in discouraged worker effects and falls in female participation in the South (see Bettio and Mazzotta 1995).

The rises in male prime-age inactivity between 1983 and 1992 have been most dramatic in Ireland and Italy (3.7 and 4.0 percentage points), both countries where unemployment has also risen (0.7 and 1.9 percentage points). France and the UK are the only other countries where both inactivity and unemployment have risen for men, but in the case of France the rises in non-employment have been dominated by unemployment. In half of the member states, rises in male prime-age inactivity have resulted in falling shares of the male prime-age population in unemployment, suggesting a rise in the share of men leaving the labour market rather than remaining in unemployment and searching for work.

Prime-age unemployment: labour force and population measures compared

When unemployment rates are measured as a share of the population rather than the labour force, prime-age female rates tend to converge with male rates but they continue to exceed male rates (Table 2.6). This underscores the problem of unemployment for prime-age women, for despite a higher share of the population being involved in non-wage work activities a higher share of the female prime-age population is counted among the measured unemployed.

In four countries – Greece, France, Italy and Spain – female prime-age unemployment as a share of the labour force was greater than 10 per cent in 1992, reaching nearly a quarter in Spain (23.6 per cent) compared to only two countries (Spain and Ireland) where the male rates reached double figures. It is in three Southern countries – Spain, Italy and Greece – that the female to male unemployment rate differential was highest in 1992. For example, in Spain female prime-age unemployment exceeded male prime-age unemployment by 12 points compared to a gap of under 2 percentage points in former West Germany, Luxembourg and Portugal. The UK and Ireland stand out as the only countries where male unemployment rates are higher than those for women in 1992, but in Ireland the difference is less than a percentage point while in the UK male unemployment rates exceeded the female rate by more than 3 percentage points. These higher measured unemployment rates for women are at best an underestimate of the relative problems faced by women in gaining access to employment as it is in this age group that the hidden unemployed and discouraged workers are most likely to be concentrated.

Older-age non-employment

Non-employment rates for the 50–64 age group are higher for both men and women compared to the prime-age groups; around two-fifths of men (37.5 per cent) and two-thirds (67.7 per cent) of women in this age group were non-employed in 1992. For women non-employment rates ranged from over 80 per cent in Belgium to less than half the female population aged 50–64 years (45.3 per cent) in Denmark (Figure 2.12). For men, the share of the population who were non-employed in 1992 was lower but still high, ranging from less than a third in Denmark to over half in Belgium. This age group will generally exclude women caring for young children but will incorporate many, both men and women, who have left the labour market as part of early retirement programmes or because of lower retirement ages for women in some member states. The rise in unemployment during recessionary periods has meant that older workers have often become less competitive in the labour market and if made redundant they have fewer training opportunities to re-enter employment and this has contributed to the high levels of inactivity, among both men and women. Older workers have been offered a range of exit routes from the labour market and in most EU countries have been able to leave the labour market via conversion of unemployment benefits into early retirement programmes, long term sickness benefits and invalidity schemes (OECD 1992).

Following a similar pattern to the prime-age group, female non-employment rates fell during the 1980s while for men they rose. The E10 male non-employment rate rose by 5.7 percentage points between 1983 and 1992, mostly occurring before 1987, while for women the non-employment rate fell by 2.5 percentage points. Within member states the pattern of change in non-employment has been more varied. In the majority of countries women's non-employment has fallen mainly as the result of declining

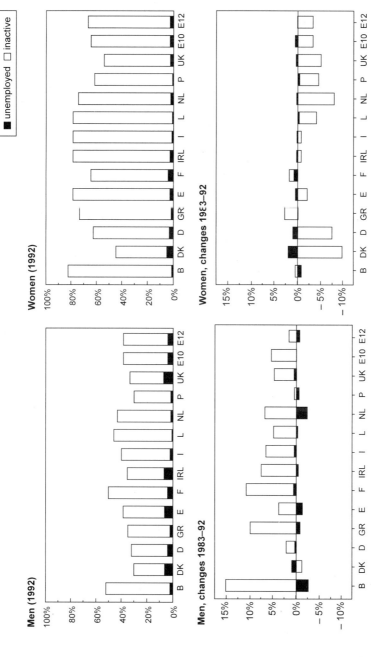

Figure 2.12 Non-employment of men and women aged 50–64 years, 1992

Source: European Labour Force Surveys (1983–92)
Note: Changes 1987–92 for Spain, Portugal and E12

levels of inactivity particularly in Denmark, the former West Germany and the Netherlands where inactivity rates fell by 7 percentage points or more between 1983 and 1992. In a further three countries – the UK, Portugal (1987–92) and Luxembourg – inactivity rates for women fell by more than 3 percentage points. In Greece, France and Belgium female inactivity rates rose but in the case of Belgium this coincided with a fall in unemployment while in the other two countries unemployment rose along with inactivity. Luxembourg and Portugal, along with Belgium, are the only countries where female older age unemployment fell between 1983 and 1992, while in all other member states unemployment rose very slightly, exceeding a 1 percentage point rise only in Denmark and the former West Germany.

Obviously retirement ages within the EU member states affect the recorded levels of inactivity and unemployment of the 50–64 age group. In five out of twelve member states – Germany, Greece, Italy, Portugal and the UK – men and women have different retirement ages with women able to retire at 60 compared to 65 for men in Germany, the UK and Greece; 55 compared to 60 in Italy and 62 compared to 65 in Portugal. Four out of five of these member states (Greece excluded) have plans to equalise retirement ages in the future (Whitting *et al.* 1995). In the remaining member states retirement ages range from 60 in France to 67 in Denmark. Despite the different retirement ages of women between member states we can see that there is considerable convergence between member states in inactivity rates for women aged 60–64, certainly as compared to 50–59 age ranges. Inactivity rates for women in 1992 aged 50–9 range from 25 per cent in Denmark to between 70 per cent and 75 per cent in Ireland, Spain, Italy, Belgium and Luxembourg. For the 60–64 age group, inactivity rates range from a low of just over 70 per cent in Denmark and Portugal to 95 per cent in Belgium with nine member states having female inactivity rates between 80 per cent and 95 per cent in 1992. For men, inactivity in the age group above 60 is generally much higher than in the 50–59 age group in all member states; only three countries have inactivity rates below 50 per cent in the latter age group compared to rates below a third for the 60–64 group in all member states except Belgium.

The changes in male non-employment between 1983 and 1992 have been quite different from the patterns found for women, with inactivity rates rising by 5 percentage points or more in eight out of twelve countries, with rises in Belgium, France and Greece of 15.2, 9.8 and 9.6 percentage points respectively. In France unemployment among the 50–64 age group also rose adding to the increase in inactivity for the age group, whereas in Greece and Belgium and five more member states (including Spain and Portugal between 1987 and 1992) unemployment fell. For men, as we saw for women, the changes in unemployment were small and only in Belgium and the Netherlands did male unemployment for the 50–64 age group change by more than 1 percentage point, with falls of just over 2.5 percent-age points in both cases. The sharp rises in male inactivity among this older age group demonstrate the trend of older men leaving the labour market, sometimes taking early retirement but also becoming discouraged workers and long term sick as they find fewer labour market opportunities. In the three countries – Belgium, Greece and France – with the largest rises in male inactivity, most of the increases occurred between 1983 and 1987 but in the other member states the increases were either more modest and more even over the time period or, as in the cases of Luxembourg and Ireland, concentrated between 1987 and 1992.

Older age unemployment: labour force and population measures compared

Unemployment rates for the 50–64 year olds measured as a share of the labour force are generally lower for both men and women than in younger age groups, except in the former West Germany where they are higher for both men and women and the UK and France where the male unemploy-ment rate for this age group is higher than for the prime-age group. Once again female unemployment rates as a share of the labour force are higher than male rates in all countries except the UK, together this time with Portugal (Table 2.6).

With the low levels of participation in this older age group, particularly among women, the unemployment rates fall significantly when measured as a share of the population rather than the labour force; in fact the female unemployment rate for 50–64 year olds as a share of the population is lower than the male rate in all EU member states.

Distribution of unemployment and inactivity within the working-age population

The continued high rates of youth unemployment have tended to disguise the decline in the proportion of unemployment concentrated in this age group. Between 1983 and 1992 the share of the E10 unemployed aged 15–24 fell from over two-fifths (42.8 per cent) to less than a third (30.8 per cent). When we examine the patterns across member states we find that the changing size of the youth cohort and increased participation in full-time education has reduced the concentration of unemployment among young people. Nevertheless, the 15–24 age group still accounted for a large share of the total unemployed particularly in the Southern member states where initial access to employment can be hard (Appendix Table 2.4). In Italy, Greece and Portugal the young in 1992 still accounted for around two-fifths or more of total female unemployment and of total male unemployment. These high concentrations in the Southern member states are a significant reduction on the shares of the early 1980s. In 1983 more than two-thirds of Italian unemployment was concentrated in this age group; in 1987 for women in Spain and men and women in Portugal the figure was more than half. Greece stands out as the only country where young men have actually increased their share of unemployment over the period, from 34.7 per cent to 39.9 per cent between 1983 and 1992.

The declining concentration of unemployment on the youngest age groups has had different effects in different member states; in the majority of member states the change in the distribution of unemployment has shifted towards the prime-age 25–49 year olds with the share of unemployment for the over 50s remaining stable, so that in 1992 prime-age women accounted for more than two-thirds of unemployment in five countries and prime-age men more than two-thirds in four countries. In the former West Germany the 50–64 age group has increased its share of the unemployed for both men and women, while the share of unemployed in the prime-age group has remained stable; in Denmark for men and the UK for women both age groups have increased their share of total unemployment as the youth share has declined.

The distribution of working-age inactivity between the age groups has a strong gender pattern with more than a third of all inactive women being of prime-age (25–49 years) in all member states except Denmark (Appendix Table 2.4). In four countries – the UK, Ireland, Luxembourg and the Netherlands – more than two-fifths of inactive women are aged 25–49 years. For men the prime-age groups account for only between a tenth and a fifth of male working-age inactivity, except in Denmark, and the greatest concentrations of inactivity are in the age groups below 25 and above 50. For men the 15–24 age group accounts for more than two-fifths of all working-age inactivity in five countries and more than a half in a further three countries, whereas for women the youngest age group accounts for a much lower share of inactivity because of the higher concentrations in the prime-age group.

Over the 1980s the changing patterns of employment have produced quite different changes in the distribution of male and female working-age inactivity. Rising female employment rates have meant that the prime-age groups now account for a falling share of female inactivity in all member states, except Denmark where the prime-age share of inactivity has risen from 25 per cent in 1983 to 29 per cent in 1992 owing, in part, to rising employment rates among students. The shift in the concentration of inactivity away from the prime-age groups has led to greater concentrations of female working-age inactivity in the older age groups in some countries but not to the same extent as the concentration of male inactivity among the 50–64 year olds. In eight countries the share of female working-age inactivity in the 50–64 age group has risen but in all cases, except Greece, the rise was less than 5 percentage points. There has also been a rise in the concentration of female working-age inactivity in the age group below 25 in six countries.

For men in nine countries there have been rising concentrations of inactivity in the prime-age group with the E10 average rising from 11 per cent to 14.9 per cent between 1983 and 1992. Trends among older men towards early retirement and leaving the labour market have also increased the concentration of inactivity in the over 50 age group where in 1992 more than two-fifths of all working-age inactive men were found in eight member states. In the Netherlands and the former West Germany, the share of male inactivity in the 50–64 age groups rose from less than a third in 1983 to more than two-fifths in 1992. In Spain, Portugal, Italy, France and Ireland, there have actually been falling concentrations of inactivity in the 50–64 age group in spite of rising absolute values (except Portugal) as a consequence of greater rises in inactivity in the younger age groups.

The changing patterns of participation of the labour market throughout the lifecycle has meant that there is a falling concentration of inactive women in the prime-age group as female employment and participation in the labour market increases, whereas for men declining employment rates in many member states have led to a rise in the concentration of inactive men in the prime working-age group, despite simultaneous rises in inactivity in younger and older sections of the population.

Summary

Behind the fairly stable trends in overall employment rates lie significant changes in the gender and age patterns of participation and in the shares of full- and part-time jobs. The trends among women towards increasing employment rates and decreasing inactivity and the opposite trends among men have tended to reduce gender differences in activity patterns. These findings still hold, although less strongly, when account is taken of the change towards higher levels of part-time working. Even on a full-time equivalent basis, female employment rates have made a positive contribution to average employment rates while the male contribution has by and large been negative. However, there are still problems in interpretation of recent trends arising from ambiguities over appropriate measures of economic activity status. To what extent does the growth of marginal part-time work, among young people, students, as well as prime-age women, overstate the employment rate in some countries? And to what extent are those classified as inactive in practice part of a hidden labour reserve? So far we have accepted Eurostat definitions of economic activity status as relatively unproblematic, but we now need to explore the implications of adopting different definitions of employment, unemployment and inactivity.

2.2 Reconsidering current definitions of economic activity

The changing nature and composition of European labour markets means that the current definitions of employment and unemployment are becoming increasingly inappropriate and even obsolete. The persistence of job shortage and long-duration unemployment, the rise in atypical modes of employment, the increasing entry into employment direct from inactivity, and the increasing tendency to combine education and employment all create problems for conventional definitions of economic activity, giving rise to marginal employees, discouraged workers and hidden unemployed. The ILO definition of unemployment is used by Eurostat to generate harmonised unemployment statistics for the EU, but its requirement that the unemployed should currently not be in employment, have searched for work over the past four weeks and be available to start work in the next two weeks may be regarded as too stringent a test (see Figure 2.1).

Box 2.3a Definitions of activity status may overstate women's involvement in formal employment but understate unemployment, underemployment and women's role in the informal economy

The problems of defining unemployment are illustrated by three different measures currently in use in **Belgium**. In 1992 the ILO unemployment rate gave a female unemployment rate of 10.8 per cent for women while the rate based upon respondents' self-definition of unemployment was much higher at 15.6 per cent. The male unemployment rate by self-definition was also higher than the ILO rate at 7.6 per cent compared to 5.7 per cent. However, in 1987 and 1983 the two measures gave similar results. The most common measure of unemployment in Belgium is that collected by the administrative authorities, which gives a total of 700,000 looking for a job compared to 567,000 under the self-definition and 405,000 under the ILO definition. This category is further sub-divided into the unemployed job searchers (508,000) and others looking for a job, which includes many of the involuntary part-time workers. Here the problem of defining unemployment becomes caught up with the problem of defining employment and employment rates. Labour market policy in Belgium has encouraged a high share of the unemployed to take up part-time work, by allowing people even unemployed for half a day to claim unemployment benefit. As a consequence, approximately 50 per cent of female part-timers and 90 per cent of male part-timers fall into this involuntary part-time category, and have faced major disincentives in moving into full-time work because of high marginal tax rates as benefit entitlement is lost. Budgetary constraints are leading to the phasing out of this system, but the scheme raises the question whether these people should be considered employed or unemployed (Meulders 1995 60–61).

In **Ireland** the social welfare system discourages women from signing on independently as unemployed (see Chapters 5 and 6). It is estimated that

---

only 50 per cent of female unemployed are registered as unemployed compared to 85 per cent of male unemployed. Moreover, as the male breadwinner
model remains dominant, it is probable that even the high levels of female
long-term unemployment are an underestimate of the underlying long-term
unemployment rate as more women than men are likely to reclassify themselves as inactive if they fail to find work (Barry 1995: 21).

The high correlation found in **Portugal** and elsewhere between increasing
female participation rates and increasing employment suggests that it may
be more appropriate to talk of 'labour slack' which can include those not
formally included as unemployed, rather than unemployment. Many women
in Portugal for example fail to register at a Job Centre, for a range of factors
including the social stigma of registration and the involvement of women
outside the labour market in clandestine work (Lopes and Perista 1995: 14).

In **Germany** statistics include two definitions of the labour force – the conventional definition including the employed and the unemployed and a second
definition known as the potential labour force, which includes not only the
employed and the unemployed but also a definition of the labour reserve. This
labour reserve includes all persons who are not registered as unemployed but
who would take up employment immediately under positive labour market
conditions. It includes those people who remain in training due to labour
market constraints (extended periods spent in education) as well as older
people in early retirement schemes (Maier and Rapp 1995: 3). German statis-
ticians have still faced difficulties in defining economic activity status. Since
1990 those in marginal part-time jobs, i.e. outside social security, have been
included as in employment in the microcensus whereas previously they were
excluded. Moreover, survey research shows that in 1989 2.5 million women
wanted to enter employment but only 17 per cent had actually been registered
as seeking work, with a further 24 per cent unemployed without being registered and 58 per cent categorised as inactive after an interruption for family
reasons, etc. Younger and more educated women were particularly unlikely to
be included on the unemployment register (Maier and Rapp 1995: 38–39).

Similarly the classification by Eurostat of persons who had done any paid
work in the reference week as employed may be regarded as too generous a
measure of employment status. These problems among others led to
changes in definitions and in survey methods in a number of countries,
and to the adoption of multiple measures (see Box 2.3). Not all these
changes necessarily help to provide more appropriate measures of economic
activity status.

A useful model with which to analyse the blurred boundaries of employment, unemployment and inactivity has been developed by Freyssinet
(1984, cited in Silvera *et al.* 1995: 36). Figure 2.13 shows the four intersec-
tions between the three parts of the population. At the intersection between
employment and inactivity we find those persons who have voluntarily

> ### Box 2.3b   Definitions of activity status may overstate women's involvement in formal employment but understate unemployment, underemployment and women's role in the informal economy
>
> The current Labour Force Survey definitions used in **Spain** are criticised as inappropriate for categorising economic activity statuses of Spanish women. The assignment of anyone working one hour a week to employment over-estimates employment and fails to provide an adequate analysis of precarity and underemployment. On the other hand, the requirement to be actively seeking work and to be available for work is biased against women whose domestic responsibilities make it more difficult for them to fulfil these expectations, even when they would like to enter employment. Women's role in the rural economy is also often underrecorded, sometimes recorded as part-time when actual hours of work suggest it is full-time work (Moltó 1995: 25).
>
> **Italy** has recently changed its definitions of economic activity status to bring it more into line with international definitions. One change has involved raising the minimum working age to 15 from 14. More importantly two new definitions of unemployment have been introduced to measure unemployment; under the first, to conform to international standards, persons are treated as unemployed only if they have looked for work over the past 30 days; under the second, broader definition they are counted as unemployed if they have looked at some time over the past 6 months or have taken a competitive examination for entry into employment during the past 2 years. This latter definition (although broad by international standards) has considerably tightened up on previous definitions where anyone who had looked for work over the previous 24 months was included. The effect of the tightening definition is to reduce measured unemployment for women relative to men and for Southern women in particular (Bettio and Mazzotta 1995: appendix 1).
>
> In the **Netherlands** in 1987 a change to the wording of the questionnaire led to the discovery of a large number of previously hidden workers on short hours. In order to make the Netherlands data more comparable with other countries, there has been a further change to the data introduced in 1992. Now only those people who work at least 12 hours a week or are actively seeking a job for a minimum of 12 hours are included in the labour force. Previously those working for less than 12 hours but at least 1 hour were included as in employment, but in order to be classified as unemployed, persons needed to be looking for at least 20 hours of work. The new definitions should decrease the measured employment rate but increase the measured unemployment rate. These changes will affect men as well as women: as young men are often employed on short hours work, although it will reduce the share of prime-age women in employment and increase the share in unemployment (Plantenga and Sloep 1995: 2, 3, 34).
>
> In **France** there are three definitions of unemployment in use: the ILO definition, the Ministry of Labour Statistics based on the number of jobseekers registered, and the census definition which includes all who declare themselves

to be unemployed and do not state that they are not seeking work, together with mothers with children, pensioners and housewives who explicitly state that they are seeking work. There is no requirement either to be available for work or to be actively seeking work; thus the census definition is both extensive and subjective (Silvera *et al.* 1995: 33).

opted to have shorter working time than the norm. Although these people are in an ambiguous position between two labour markets states, they are perhaps of less concern to policymakers than those individuals who are involuntarily in intermediate statuses. Between employment and unemployment we find those persons who are involuntarily working shorter hours than the norm. These, mainly the involuntary part-time workers, can be considered part employed, part unemployed or possibly underemployed. Between the two forms of non-employment, inactivity and unemployment, are unemployed people who are being retrained or have been phased into retirement as well as discouraged workers and persons already in early retirement. At the intersection of all three sections of the population we find the informal or black economy and homeworking. This section of the economy can draw upon labour from the inactive, unemployed and employed populations; indeed much informal sector work is carried out by those in full-time formal employment. These blurred boundaries between employment and non-employment represent 'the range of intermediate statuses found in a society faced with the problem of organising mass unemployment and sharing out of available work' (Silvera *et al.* 1995: 36).

In 1982 the ILO formally defined underemployment as 'when a person's employment is inadequate'; two main components of underemployment can be distinguished from this, that is visible and invisible underemployment (OECD 1992). The visible component of underemployment can be

Figure 2.13 Interrelationship between employment, unemployment and inactivity

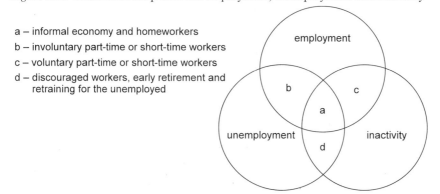

a – informal economy and homeworkers
b – involuntary part-time or short-time workers
c – voluntary part-time or short-time workers
d – discouraged workers, early retirement and
    retraining for the unemployed

Source: Freyssinet (1984, cited in Silvera *et al.* 1995: 36) considered as those persons involuntarily working shorter hours, the involuntary part-time, who can be identified using labour force survey data. The invisible component of underemployment, as the name suggests, is harder to define and measure and includes persons who are not fully utilising their skills and education. The next section considers the effect of the inclusion of involuntary part-time workers in a measure of underutilisation of potential labour supply using data from the European labour force surveys. The invisible element of underemployment tends to affect women more and this is most clearly demonstrated by the way the large gains in educational attainment of women have not translated into a correspondingly large increase in female representation in relatively well paid non-manual occupations (OECD 1992). Similarly the occupational downgrading of women in the returner countries after a spell out of the labour market also demonstrates how female skills and education are not fully used in the labour market (Rubery and Fagan 1993).

Alternative definitions of the employment rate

The first problem in defining the employment rate is determining the relevant population. Some of these problems – whether to include only the working-age population or even a sub-section – have been discussed in section 2.1. However, a further problem arises with respect to the actual definition of the population – that is, whether to include or exclude migrant labour, and how to treat an increase or decrease in population due to migration flows which themselves may be at least in part a product of changing employment opportunities? Thus, if the employment rate is used as a measure of economic performance, it may be misleading if better economic performance leads to an increased migration rate thereby reducing the employment rate. In these circumstances net measures of job creation may be a more useful measure. In actual practice over recent years this issue has been relatively unimportant in most EU countries – and indeed the EU performance relative to the US looks worse on a job creation measure because of the much faster growth of population, in part through migration in the US. Overall the trends within the EU have been towards a low emigration, controlled migration model (CEC 1995b), with net flows accounting for a much lower share of the population than was the case in the 1950s and 1960s when there were significant flows between EU member states, from Southern to Northern countries. Two countries, Luxembourg and Germany, can be singled out as having significant migration and/or transborder flows.

Luxembourg has always had a high level of migrant and/or transborder workers. Until the mid-1970s the Luxembourg labour shortage was filled mainly by the Portuguese but since that date it has mainly been filled by transborder workers. If the number of all workers in Luxembourg including transborder workers is divided by the resident working-age population in Luxembourg then the employment rate is 75 per cent, while the employment rate of the working-age residential population is only 56 per cent (Plasman 1995: 3). In this case transborder flows have compensated for a low female participation force in Luxembourg.

Germany is the other country where migration has had a significant impact on employment rates over recent years (Figure 2.14). The ending of the impact of the baby boom on domestic labour supplies was compensated by a rise in migration, both between the former East and the former West (thereby depressing employment rates in the West) and from Eastern Europe. Between 1983 and 1993 there was an increase in German nationals living in West Germany of 2.5 million, including migrants from East Germany and from central and Eastern Europe. In addition there was a net flow of 1.9 million from the rest of the European Union and elsewhere of non-German nationals. These two sources of migrants accounted for 8.4 per cent of the population in the former West Germany in 1993 and for 7.8 per cent of all in employment (Maier and Rapp 1995: 17). Projections of the labour supply in Germany expect a further decrease in the male national labour supply, and that this decrease will be offset by both an increase in female labour supply and continued net migration.

The Southern countries of Europe are also beginning to see increases in their immigrant labour forces. In Greece, for example, there are estimated to be around half a million illegal foreign workers, most of whom have arrived since 1992 (Cavouriaris *et al.* 1995: 11). One issue is where the migrants are working, and whether they compete with mainly male or mainly female labour for jobs, and indeed whether their employment shows up in measured statistics of employment. There is some evidence in Italy and Spain that immigrant labour, although mainly male, is employed in sectors where there are high shares of female labour – such as services, including tourism. In Germany the industries in which non-EU labour is employed include traditional male industries such as mining, construction and car manufacture, often involving night work and shift work, as well as some female-dominated sectors such as hotels and catering, health care and private households. Thus the impact of immigration on gender differences in employment rates is uncertain. In Italy foreign labour is estimated to account for 18 per cent of the irregular labour force and only 3 per cent of the formal labour force (Bettio and Mazzotta 1995: 32), suggesting that much of the economic activity of migrants may go unrecorded, thereby perhaps contravening the expected boost to measured employment rates from short-term migration. No such expectation can be held with respect to longer-term migration flows; ethnic minorities are often the groups with the lowest employment rates due to discrimination. Research in the UK has shown that the employment rates of ethnic minority men tend to fall below even those of white women (Rubery and Smith 1995: 85) and in the Nether-

Figure 2.14 Trends in net migration per 1,000 population in the EU, 1960–92

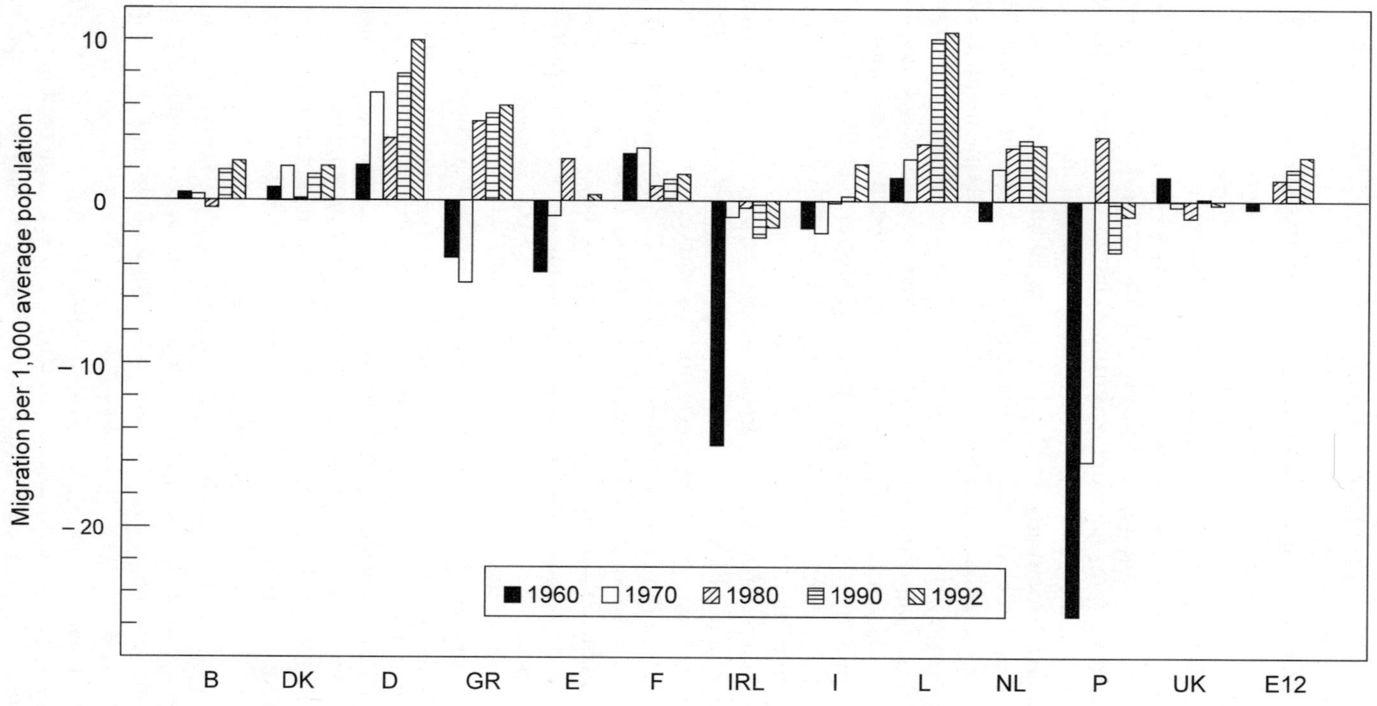

Source: Eurostat (1994a)

lands the population without Dutch nationality has a participation rate of only 44 per cent compared to a Dutch national rate of 58 per cent, a gap which has widened over recent years (Plantenga and Sloep 1995: 17). One important dimension to the problems of social exclusion, and to the associated problems of defining unemployment or potential labour supply, is that of racial and ethnic discrimination. The concentration of high unemployment among such groups may lead to high rates of discouraged workers, thereby reducing both employment and unemployment rates.

Once the question of appropriate population measures has been addressed there is the further problem of defining employment. Much of the increase in employment in many member states can be largely attributed to an increase in part-time working, usually by women. Section 2.1 illustrated how employment rates and employment growth were reduced when considered on a full-time equivalent basis – with one part-time job equal to half of a full-time job. This section explores further the impact on employment rates of adjustments for different working hours in the European Union. Over half of part-timers in the EU usually worked less than 20 hours a week in 1992 and in the three countries with the highest part-time rates – Denmark, the Netherlands and the UK – more than a quarter of part-timers usually work less than 10 hours a week. In Denmark more than half of all part-timers usually work less than 10 hours a week, many of these probably young persons in education as we have already seen. In 1991 Denmark had the highest shares of teenagers working part-time for both men and women than any other member state (Rubery et al. 1995). To consider those workers on very short hours as equivalent to the standard full-time workers may be highly misleading, particularly when making cross-country comparisons, and these workers may be considered more akin to the workers in the informal sector in the Southern European countries. To work such short hours implies a level of dependence on another source of income. For students this may mean their parents, a loan or a state grant but for many women these short hours imply dependence on another source of wage income usually from a male breadwinner.

Table 2.7 shows the employment rates excluding these marginal workers to give an indication of their impact on different member states. In all countries except Denmark, the Netherlands and the UK the 1992 employment rate – calculated here as all persons in employment over the working-age population aged 15–64 – falls by less than 1 percentage point when persons working less than 10 hours a week are excluded and only in the Netherlands does the employment rate fall by more than 5 percentage points. When we consider the female 10+ hours employment rate the picture is quite different. In the three countries with the highest part-time rates – Netherlands, Denmark and the UK – the female employment rate is more than 5 percentage points lower and in a further five countries – Portugal, Ireland, France, former West Germany and Luxembourg – the

Table 2.7 Impact on working-age employment rates of excluding persons usually working 10 hours or less and 20 hours or less a week, 1992.

	Male employment rates (%)			Female employment rates (%)			Total employment rates (%)		
	All persons rate	+10 hours rate	+20 hours rate	All persons rate	+10 hours rate	+20 hours rate	All persons rate	+10 hours rate	+20 hours rate
Belgium	68.8	68.7	67.9	44.8	44.0	36.2	56.8	56.4	52.1
Denmark	80.7	76.6	73.9	71.3	65.8	58.6	76.0	71.2	66.3
Germany[a]	79.1/	78.5/	77.6/	56.2/	52.9/	43.4/	67.8/	65.9/	60.7/
	77.6	77.0	76.1	56.2	53.7	45.8	67.2	65.5	61.1
Greece	74.9	74.8	74.2	37.2	36.9	35.6	55.4	55.2	54.2
Spain	66.3	66.2	65.5	31.7	30.9	28.6	48.8	48.3	46.8
France	69.8	69.6	68.4	51.5	50.2	44.8	60.5	59.7	56.4
Ireland	67.3	66.8	65.6	37.3	35.9	32.4	52.4	51.5	49.1
Italy	70.4	70.3	69.9	37.2	36.9	35.1	53.6	53.4	52.3
Luxembourg	77.1	77.1	77.1	46.7	45.5	41.1	62.1	61.5	59.4
Netherlands	77.0	72.1	69.6	51.2	41.3	32.8	64.3	56.9	51.4
Portugal	80.6	80.1	79.1	57.4	56.4	54.1	68.4	67.6	66.0
UK	76.9	75.2	73.6	61.8	54.8	43.0	69.4	65.0	58.3
E12[a]	73.6/	72.7/	71.7/	48.9/	46.1/	39.8/	61.2/	59.3/	55.6/
	73.5	72.6	71.6	49.3	46.6	40.4	61.3	59.5	55.9

Source: Special tabulations provided by Eurostat
Note: a Data for Germany and E12 include/exclude the new Länder.

employment rate is more than 1 percentage point lower. The 10+ hours male employment rate is significantly different from the normal employment rate only in Denmark and the Netherlands (more than 4 percentage points) and in all other countries except the UK the employment rate changes by less than 1 percentage point.

Persons usually employed for 20 hours or less a week work around half or less than half of the average hours in the EU. Working for more than 20 hours might therefore be regarded as a prerequisite for full integration into employment. Excluding persons working 20 hours or less reduces the E12 employment rate by more than 5 percentage points and the UK and the Netherlands employment rates by 11 and 13 percentage points respectively. Excluding women working 20 hours a week or less leads to an 18 percentage point fall in the female employment rate in both the Netherlands and the UK (see Table 2.7), compared to a 9 percentage point fall at the European level. The other two high part-time countries – Denmark and Germany – also experience significant falls, with female employment rates 12 percentage points lower than when all persons in employment are considered. Even in countries where there are medium levels of part-time employment – Belgium, France and Luxembourg – the female 20+ hours employment rate is more than 5 percentage points lower. Only in Greece is the female 20+ hours employment rate similar to the normal employment rate, changing by less than 2 percentage points. Once again for men the change in the employment rate is less dramatic, with the 20+ hours employment rate less than 2 percentage points lower at the EU level and in nine countries. Only in Denmark and the Netherlands is the difference between the 20+ hours and the normal employment rates for men more than 6 percentage points.

These patterns illustrate how the three highest part-time countries – Denmark, the Netherlands and the UK – stand out with the highest shares of workers on marginal hours. Short hours working has a much stronger gender dimension in the UK such that exclusion of those on short hours significantly affects the female employment rate but has a much smaller affect on the male employment rate, while in Denmark and the Netherlands the employment rate for both sexes is significantly reduced. In all other countries the effect of excluding short and very short hours working has a negligible effect on the male employment rate and a variable impact on the female employment rate, with the smallest effects in the Southern European countries where part-time employment is less common.

Between 1983 and 1992 the E10 employment rate – calculated here as all persons in employment divided by the working-age population – rose by 2.2 percentage points but this disguises a 2 percentage point fall for the male rate and a 6 percentage point rise in the female rate. By excluding the workers on very short hours (10 hours or fewer) the overall employment rate rose by just 1.5 percentage points whereas the male employment rate fell further by more than 2.5 percentage points and the female rate rose by

5.1 instead of 6.1 percentage points. Excluding persons usually working 20 hours a week or less reduces the increase in the overall European employment rate to just 0.6 of a percentage point and in the female European employment rate from 6 to 3.6 percentage points while the male employment rate fell by nearly 3 percentage points.

As we have seen above, in some countries some young people in education also have jobs particularly in Denmark, the UK and the Netherlands. Students in employment, in common with all persons on very short hours, are dependent on other sources of income. Although the earnings from part-time work provide vital income, in many cases this will not be their main source of support. By excluding these persons in education who also work from the 1992 employment rate, the overall European employment rate (E12) falls by just over half of 1 percentage point from 61.3 to 60.7 per cent. In eight countries excluding young people in education who are also working causes the male and female employment rates to fall by less than 1 percentage point. In the UK and Portugal, exclusion of working students reduces male and female employment rates by just over 1 percentage point, slightly more for women in the UK and slightly less in Portugal. It is in Denmark and the Netherlands, that working students have a significant impact on employment rates; excluding students reduces the employment rates by 5 and 3 percentage points respectively. Female employment rates are more affected by the exclusion of students than male rates in Denmark and the Netherlands with employment rates falling by 5.9 and 3.8 percentage points for women compared to 4.3 and 2.9 percentage points for men. The high labour market involvement of students in Denmark goes some way to explaining the high Danish employment rate but, as we have already seen, the Danish employment rate remains high even when considering the age groups above 25.

A further problem of classification relates to those on leave from employment, whether on maternity, parental, long-term sickness or sabbatical/education leaves. This type of arrangement is increasing in all countries, especially for maternity leave where the number increased from 229,000 to 667,000 in the E12 between 1983 and 1992 (OECD 1995a: 184). Moreover, in Denmark, for example, there has been a recent set of policies to increase leave from work for a wide range of reasons as part of a policy to help work sharing. It is probably double counting to include those on leave as in employment as well as those acting as substitutes, but where a person is not replaced, excluding those on leave underestimates the share of those with an employment attachment. However, it is also not necessarily appropriate to classify those on leave as either inactive or unemployed.

Unpaid family workers are an example of a labour market group who are not 'in employment' in the conventional sense. Persons undertaking unpaid work for the family may be regarded as operating between the formal and informal labour market. Family workers accounted for just under 2.5 per cent of the European workforce (including Unified Germany) in 1992, but the majority of family workers are women and they accounted for over 4 per cent of female employment compared to just over 1 percent of male employment. There is a strong country dimension to the distribution of family work with three Southern European member states having the highest rates of family work, ranging from 3.4 per cent of employment in Italy to 12 per cent in Greece, compared to the UK where the question relating to family workers was introduced for the first time only in the 1992 Labour Force Survey, revealing just 0.7 per cent of those employed as unpaid family workers. Excluding family workers from the employment rate measure reduces the 1992 E12 employment rate by just under 1.5 percentage points but the female rate falls by over 2 percentage points compared to just 0.8 of a percentage point fall for men. In Greece, where over a quarter of women are unpaid family workers, exclusion of family workers reduces the female employment rate by nearly 10 percentage points (9.7) and in five more countries – Spain, Italy, France, Belgium and Denmark – by more than 2.5 percentage points. For men, only in the three Southern countries with the highest levels of family work – Greece, Spain and Italy – does the employment rate fall by more than 1 percentage point with the exclusion of male family workers.

The Southern countries tend to have a high share of informal sector work, and it may be in part for this reason that there is a low share of recorded part-time work as much informal sector may be part-time (Cavouriaris *et al.* 1995: 8). However, as we have already seen, in Figure 2.13, the informal economy cannot be considered synonymous with particular economic activity statuses, and even unpaid family labour is by no means necessarily informal in the sense of illegal, but instead is part of the normal system of the operation of family firms in many countries. To the extent that informal work involves persons employed in the formal economy as well, its measurement would not affect employment rates – although its formalisation might create new jobs for the unemployed or inactive. Some persons who are categorised as unemployed or inactive may be working long hours or earning high sums in the informal sector, and to that extent current measures underestimate economic activity (see Box 2.4). However, many non-employed persons in the informal sector are likely to be undertaking work which may be regarded as marginal to economic activity – not necessarily because it involves either short hours, irregular work or low skill but because it generates low levels of income. Women may be particularly likely to be engaged in the informal sector because social security systems and family systems based on a male breadwinner model make it more possible for women to work without social security cover. This work may conform to formal sector wage work in many respects: it may be regular, involve long hours of work and even be integrated into the formal economy, to the extent that informal work is used to produce goods

Box 2.4 Informal sector activities are both complements to and substitutes for formal sector work, but prime-age women may be more likely to be solely engaged in informal work outside the social security system

In **Portugal** there is a high level of economic activity outside the formal sector – including non-wage family work and clandestine work often carried out as complementary to participation in the formal economy, as is suggested by the high formal sector employment rates for both men and women. Resistance to flexible working schedules has been attributed to the demands of such activities including tending agricultural smallholdings (Varegao and Ruivo 1994). Indications of the extent of informal sector work include a high level of activity among children under 14. However, not all informal sector work is outside the formal sector; there is also a high level of illegal work in the form of illegal filling of permanent positions by temporary workers (Lopes and Perista 1995: 34, 13).

In **Spain** the development of the informal sector 'contributes to blur the frontier between employed and unemployed, between the active and the inactive' (Moltó 1995: 24). Moreover within the informal sector there are strong gender divisions, with the men mainly involved in subcontracting and the women mainly in homeworking, and the men primarily engaged at the beginning and end of their careers while women act as homeworkers during their core working ages as well. One critical reason for women's greater involvement in the informal sector is that they are more willing or perhaps more able to work outside of social security coverage. Women have been estimated to account for 60 per cent of irregular employment outside of social security protection (Moltó 1995: 24, 63).

In **Italy** much of the impetus behind the redefinition of unemployment (see Box 2.3b) was to try to resolve the issue as to whether high unemployment in Italy was in fact disguising rising participation in the informal sector. However, while unemployment has continued to rise in the 1980s, especially in the South, there has been no corresponding rise in the estimates of the number of labour units involved in the irregular economy. The irregular economy (disguised employment plus second jobs) remains an important source of activity in Italy for both women and men, accounting for more than 20 per cent of all employment, measured in standard labour units (Bettio and Mazzotta 1995: Tables A13–A16).

There are no direct data on the informal sector in **Germany**, but some indirect evidence that it may be increasing in importance for women comes from an increase in the number of women with second jobs between 1987 to 1992, most of these being jobs under 15 hours a week and therefore likely to be outside the social security system (Maier and Rapp 1995: 16)

In **France**, 'while more female than male non-wage workers are still involved in informal, less well-remunerated activities, the number of those engaged in such activities is declining while the number of those in formal employment is rising (increasing numbers of women are now wage workers and employers, while fewer are family workers)'.

70

This changing pattern of female participation in non-wage work is not in itself indicative of the evolution of informal activities, such as voluntary work, second jobs, homeworking, work in the black economy and peripheral activities'. These activities serve to blur the definitions of employment, unemployment and inactivity but it must be remembered that involvement in the informal sector is not necessarily indicative of underemployment: earnings in the informal sector can exceed those in the formal sector in some cases, and persons involved in the informal sector may do so out of choice and/or in addition to operating within the formal sector (Silvera *et al.* 1995: 31).

The definition of the informal sector in the **UK** is particularly problematic because of the legal exclusion of many non-standard workers from the tax and social security system. Thus employment forms which may be submerged or hidden in other countries, as they avoid or evade taxation and regulation, may be entirely legal in the UK and thus potentially more likely to be included in the measured formal sector (Rubery and Smith 1995: 196).

and services sold in the formal economy, but its main distinguishing characteristic is likely to be its low pay. If the informal sector were to be measured and included along with the formal economy, one important issue to be discussed is whether the value of the informal economy should be measured more by hours of work or value of the product. Here we come up against similar problems confronted in trying to measure the value of work in all spheres – by input or by output – and thus the invisibility of the informal sector is but one of the problems in deciding how to take it into account in employment rate measures.

Alternative measures of unemployment and underemployment

The changing nature of European labour markets means that the definition of unemployment is also inadequate, missing many potential workers who would like to work or would like to work more. The most commonly used definition of unemployment is that of the ILO which requires that individuals are not currently in employment, have searched for work in the past four weeks and are available to start in the next two weeks. Discouraged workers are those who would like to work but who believe that none is available so they do not search and are therefore excluded from the ILO count of unemployment and regarded as inactive. There are also other categories of persons who do not meet the requirements of the ILO definition and are therefore recorded as inactive rather than unemployed even though they would like to work and may even have been seeking work. This section measures unemployment and labour supply as a proportion of the working-age population rather than the labour force. Using the working-age population as the denominator makes the rate less susceptible to definitional changes of unemployment and different levels of labour market participation and therefore gives a clearer picture of the scale of the problem. The unemployment rate calculated as a share of the working-age population reduces female rates more than male rates because of the lower female activity rates, particularly in Ireland, Spain, Italy and Greece. Nevertheless, female unemployment rates remain higher than male rates in ten out of twelve countries, and lower in the UK, with the female rate in Ireland falling below the male rate for 1992 but not in 1983 or 1987.

Data presented by the OECD (1995a) show how discouraged workers are concentrated in the core age group of 25–54 years in all EU countries for which there are data, except for the UK where there are greater concentrations in the age groups over 55, particularly for men. The OECD data also show how the UK is the only nation where men make up a greater proportion of discouraged workers than women, with women accounting for around two-thirds or more in most OECD nations. Using information on the previous work experience of discouraged workers, the data show how in the majority of countries most discouraged workers have 'remote' work experience, not having worked within the past three years (see Figure 2.15). The long period of time since many discouraged workers last worked suggests that they 'would most likely face problems similar or worse than the long term unemployed' in finding work (OECD 1995a: 45). Additionally, some discouraged workers have never worked, particularly in Italy and Greece where more than two-thirds and three-quarters of male and female discouraged workers respectively had no work experience. The other two Southern member states also had higher than average shares of discouraged workers with no work experience, particularly women, with 33 per cent and 51 per cent of Spanish and Portuguese female discouraged workers having never worked (see Figure 2.15). In all other EU member states in 1993 more than 80 per cent of discouraged men and women had had some work experience. The higher shares of discouraged workers in the Southern member states with no work experience reflects the problems that individuals face in gaining entry to the formal labour market.

The strict ILO definition of the unemployed is useful for comparative research in providing a harmonised definition of unemployment but it can also be restrictive by excluding individuals who may meet some but not all the criteria of the definition and for whom the categorisation of inactive is inappropriate. By comparing jobseekers with the ILO unemployed we can measure the share of individuals who are not in employment and are seeking work but are not included within the harmonised unemployment count. Comparing the 'jobseeker rate' with the ILO unemployment rate, calculated as a share of the population, we find that the EU jobseeker rate for men is just over 1 percentage point higher and for women it is nearly 2 percentage points higher (1.8 percentage points) (Table 2.8). For women in

Figure 2.15 Share of discouraged workers with little or no work experience, 1994

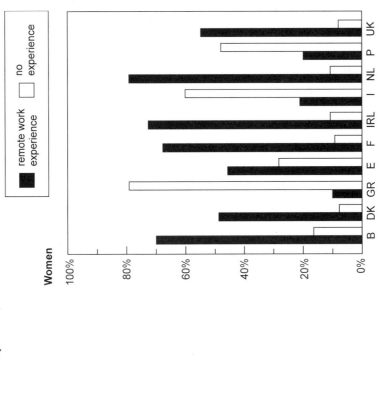

Men

Women

Source: OECD (1995a)

Note: Remote work experience is 3 years or more since last job

Table 2.8 Alternative measures of unemployment and underutilisation as a share of the working-age population (15–64 years)

	ILO unemployed[b] as a share of the labour force		ILO unemployed		Jobseekers[c]	
	Men (%)	Women (%)	Men (%)	Women (%)	Men (%)	Women (%)
Belgium	4.79	9.51	3.46	4.71	4.42	6.08
Denmark	8.30	9.88	7.31	7.82	8.45	9.08
Germany[a]	4.91	8.23	4.01	5.07	5.08	6.55
Greece	4.91	12.87	3.87	5.50	4.44	6.66
Spain	13.57	25.07	10.42	10.60	10.90	11.47
France	8.13	12.88	6.18	7.62	6.67	8.88
Ireland	14.89	15.24	11.78	6.71	14.20	9.16
Italy	6.92	13.76	5.24	5.93	7.96	10.42
Luxembourg	1.89	3.17	1.48	1.53	1.40	1.75
Netherlands	4.05	7.78	3.25	4.32	4.57	6.76
Portugal	3.37	4.75	2.81	2.86	3.14	3.48
UK	11.54	7.30	10.04	4.87	10.79	5.71
E12[a]	7.88	11.12	6.29	6.17	7.42	7.98

Table 2.8 (Contd...)

	Jobseekers and discouraged workers[d]		Jobseekers and inactive wishing to work[e]		Underutilisation rate: jobseekers, inactive wishing to work and involuntary part-time workers[f]	
	Men (%)	Women (%)	Men (%)	Women (%)	Men (%)	Women (%)
Belgium	5.56	7.41	7.25	9.53	7.73	13.27
Denmark	9.19	10.31	11.71	13.34	12.62	17.89
Germany[e]	5.08	6.55	5.82	7.95	5.98	8.85
Greece	4.54	7.24	5.23	9.16	6.16	10.06
Spain	10.93	11.59	13.32	17.15	13.50	17.85
France	6.70	9.03	7.12	9.99	8.04	13.70
Ireland	14.47	9.53	18.09	15.78	19.45	17.34
Italy	8.12	11.69	9.45	14.25	10.28	15.51
Luxembourg	1.40	1.75	2.14	4.04	2.14	4.81
Netherlands	4.93	7.92	9.03	16.03	9.81	17.35
Portugal	3.14	3.65	4.42	6.28	4.86	7.70
UK	11.02	6.02	13.33	12.28	14.41	14.70
E12[e]	7.56	8.42	9.04	11.63	9.67	13.45

Source: Special tabulations provided by Eurostat
Notes: a Data for Germany and E12 include the new Länder
b ILO unemployed are all those persons who sought work in the past four weeks, are available for work within one week and do not currently have a job
c Jobseekers are persons who sought work in the past four weeks, not all of whom are included in the ILO unemployment count
d Discouraged workers are inactive persons not seeking work because they believe no work is available
e Inactive wishing to work refers to those wishing to work but not searching for work
f Involuntary part-time workers refers to persons in part-time employment who would like to work full-time but were unable to find full-time employment.

Italy, the Netherlands and Ireland there are significant increases in labour supply with the 'jobseeker rate' compared to the unemployment rate, with the former exceeding the latter by 4.5 percentage points in Italy and by 2.5 percentage points in the Netherlands and Ireland. In five further countries the female jobseeker rate is more than 1 percentage point higher, whereas for men the jobseeker rate exceeds the ILO unemployment rate by 2 percentage points only in Ireland and Italy and by 1 percentage point in only three other member states.

If we add the discouraged workers, that is those who are not looking for work as they believe there are no jobs available, to the jobseekers the share of the male E12 population (including Unified Germany) included rises by just over a tenth of a percentage point and the female share by just under half of 1 percentage point. Women accounted for three-quarters of all discouraged workers in the EU in 1992 and in four member states – France, Greece, Italy and Portugal – women made up over four-fifths of discouraged workers. Only in Belgium, the UK and Luxembourg did women account for less than 60 per cent of discouraged workers. The inclusion of discouraged workers has least impact on the measurement of a labour reserve for men and women in Germany and Luxembourg and men in Portugal, Spain and France. Belgium is the only country where the male population share rises by more than 1 percentage point with the inclusion of discouraged workers but a rise of over 1 percentage point is recorded in four countries for women, namely Belgium, Denmark, the Netherlands, Italy and Belgium.

The European Labour Force Survey asks inactive individuals who are not actively seeking work if they would like to work. The individuals who wish to work are effectively unemployed even though they are not seeking work. Some from this group will be discouraged workers but there will be a much larger group who are not seeking work for a whole host of reasons, including the continuing tendency for women to define themselves as housewives rather than as unemployed or jobseekers. Economic activity status is still influenced strongly by social norms, even if social norms are changing, and the status of housewife is decreasing in importance in most countries, albeit at different rates (see Box 2.5). If we include persons wishing to work who are not actually seeking work along with jobseekers, there is a further rise in the share of the male population at E12 level of almost 1.5 percentage points, and in the female population share of over 3 percentage points. The increase in the male population share was over 2 percentage points in five countries, namely Denmark, Spain, Ireland, the Netherlands and the UK, but for women nine countries recorded a rise of 2 percentage points or more, reaffirming that a higher share of women than men who are currently inactive would like to work and do not give the reason that there are no jobs available as their reason for not looking for work

---

Box 2.5: 'Housewife'...a declining but ambiguous category.

Changes in female roles have been slow to take hold in **Ireland** as is evidenced by the failure of the share of older women – i.e. those aged 45–64 – engaged in housework to fall during the 1980s: 71 per cent saw themselves as housewives in 1983 and 70 per cent in 1992. However, the pace of change among the younger generation is much faster with the share of housewives among the 25–44 age group falling from 63 per cent to 49 per cent over the same period (Barry 1995: 10).

Belgium is another country where the older generation has maintained a high level of inactivity, but here too the share of housewives fell from 62 per cent to 51 per cent of the 20–59 year old population over the very short period 1987 to 1992 (Meulders 1995: 11).

In the **Netherlands**, out of the 2.1 million women who are regarded as part of the working population by the Labour Force Survey, fewer than 1.9 million actually define themselves as in the labour force, the rest defining themselves as housewives, students or other. Among those categorised as unemployed by the survey, the discrepancy is even worse with only 18.2 per cent of the unemployed defining themselves as such (Plantenga and Sloep 1995: 10–11). These findings appear to run in the opposite direction to the situation in Belgium where more women define themselves as unemployed than comply with the ILO definition of unemployment. However, the extensive short hours working in the Netherlands appears to pose particular problems of definition.

In **Denmark** there is evidence of a polarisation taking place in the female population with an increase not only in the number of women in permanent employment but also in the number of women who are receiving social benefits, alongside a decline in the share of women declaring themselves to have other sources of support, which includes housewives. Thus the category of housewife and the concept of economic dependence on the spouse is becoming less and less relevant in Denmark (Boje 1995: 29).

In the **UK** over three-quarters of inactive women were looking after the home in 1979, but by 1991 the share had fallen to two-thirds. The decline in inactivity has not been as fast as the decline in the share of housewives as at the same time there has been a sharp increase in the share of long-term sick, from under 5 per cent to 13.2 per cent of persons counted as inactive from 1979 to 1991 (Rubery and Smith 1995: 73).

If we now compare this broad definition of those who are currently not in employment but would like to work with the ILO unemployment definition we find a rise of 2.75 percentage points in the male population share but a much larger rise of 5.46 percentage points in the female population share for the E12 (including Unified Germany) (Table 2.8). This provides support for the argument that there is a higher level of hidden female unemployment. The substantial rise in measured available female labour supply is a possible indicator of the barriers women face when considering entering the labour market including, for example, domestic and childcare responsibilities or fiscal systems which make working uneconomical. In all member states, including those who wish to work boosts the measure of available female labour supply relative to the ILO unemployment definition more than the measured available male supply. The largest rises for women occur in the Netherlands, Ireland, Italy, the UK and Spain (11.7, 9.9, 9.8, 7.4 and 6.6 percentage points above ILO unemployment population rates respectively). The sharp rise in the Dutch and the UK unemployment rates indicates that a high level of part-time employment does not prevent the situation where many women want to work but do not search for jobs. Ireland and Spain have two of the lowest female employment rates in Europe; so too does Greece but here the rise in the female labour supply was only a relatively modest 3.7 percentage points. Rises of more than 4 percentage points are found in Denmark and Belgium. The lowest rise for women was in France, a country with comprehensive childcare facilities which may reduce hidden unemployment, but there was also only a small rise in Germany where childcare is less available. The largest increase in measured labour supply for men resulting from including those who would like to work but are not actively seeking work above the ILO unemployment population rate was found in Ireland with a 6.3 percentage point rise, followed by the Netherlands (5.8), Belgium (4.8), Denmark (4.4), Italy (4.2) and the UK (3.3). In all other member states measured male labour supply rose by less than 3 percentage points.

While this last definition has provided the broadest definition of those who may be considered available for work but who are not in employment, there is another category of the potential labour reserve, and that includes those currently in employment but who are underemployed. The rise of atypical forms of employment has resulted in underemployment of persons in part-time employment who would like to work full-time but were unable to find full-time employment.

We can add these involuntary part-timers to the population who are either jobseekers or the inactive wishing to work but not seeking work, to provide a global measure of the underutilisation rate of the working-age population. This rate of underutilisation of the working-age population shows that the equivalent of 9.7 per cent and 13.5 per cent of the male and female working-age population are either not working enough or would like to work, compared to ILO unemployment rates of 6.3 per cent and 6.2 per cent for men and women respectively (Figure 2.16). This represents an increase of 0.6 percentage points for men and 1.8 percentage points for women over the broad definition of jobseekers and inactive wishing to work. For men the increase is less than 1 percentage point in all cases except the UK and Ireland (where the increases are still below 1.5 percentage points), suggesting that although a higher share of male part-timers are involuntary part-timers this does not significantly affect the potential male

Figure 2.16 Share of the population who are unemployed and underutilised, 1992

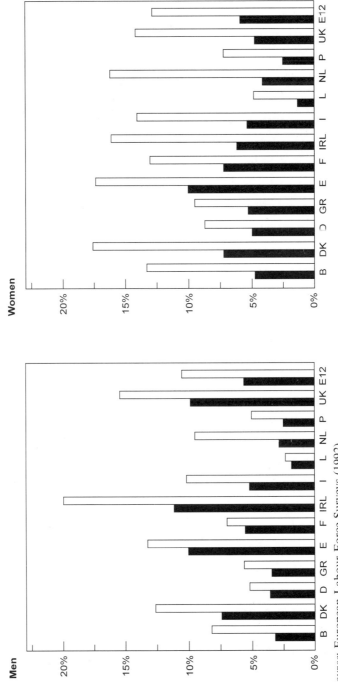

Source: European Labour Force Surveys (1992)
Note: Data include the new German Länder

labour reserve. However, for women in Belgium, Denmark and France, including the involuntary part-timers raises the potential female labour reserve by over 3 percentage points, and eight out of twelve countries recorded increases of at least 1 percentage point.

When we look at the underutilisation rates by country we find that four countries, Denmark, Spain, Ireland and the Netherlands, have female underutilisation rates of more than 17 per cent and a further four have rates between 13 per cent and 16 per cent. The factors which give rise to high underutilisation rates are, however, quite different. For example, while Denmark tops the list followed by Spain when we look at the underutilisation rate, this reflects to a large extent the high share of involuntary part-timers in Denmark, which itself may be in part a function of the benefit system, whereby those who work part-time but who do so involuntarily may continue to be eligible for full-time social protection benefits. Spain by contrast has very few involuntary part-timers, but also has a large share of the female population not included in employment, in the ILO unemployment measure or even in this measure of the potential labour reserve, while in Denmark most women are either in employment or form part of a potential labour reserve. Thus the factors which may lead to a high level of hidden unemployment are on the one hand an actual high level of inactivity coupled with high unemployment rates, as in the case of Spain, or alternatively, a social norm whereby most women expect to be in employment, as in the case of Denmark. The countries with a relatively low female potential labour reserve include only one high employment country, Portugal, while the low potential reserves in Greece, Germany and Luxembourg may reflect social norms where it is more common for women to define themselves as outside the labour market.

If we compare the ranking of countries by unemployment population rates and by underutilisation rates we find a number of countries where their position in the ranking changes significantly. Most dramatic is the situation for the Netherlands, which has the third highest underutilisation rate, but the third from bottom unemployment rate. France in contrast has the third-highest unemployment rate but only the seventh-highest underutilisation rate. Germany and Greece also have relatively higher unemployment rates compared to their underutilisation rates, while the UK has a high underutilisation rate relative to its unemployment rate. All other countries changed rank by no more than one place.

For men the average potential labour reserve is lower than for women, but the range is actually greater, with nearly one-fifth of Irish men falling into this category, suggesting a much higher level of hidden unemployment among men in this country than in others. Ireland also has the highest measured unemployment rate for men, followed by Spain and the UK, and these three countries top the list of countries with a high male potential reserve or underutilisation rate. Thus although the extent of hidden unemployment varies by country, those with high measured unemployment rates also tend to have high levels of hidden unemployment. This pattern is confirmed if we rank the countries by ILO measured unemployment population rates and by the male underutilisation rate, as we find only two countries where their position in the ranking changes by more than one place. Germany has a relatively higher male unemployment rate than male underutilisation rate, while the Netherlands has a relatively higher male underutilisation rate, sixth in the overall ranking, compared to the measured unemployment rate, tenth in the overall ranking.

Summary

Economic activity statuses should not necessarily be considered as mutually exclusive. Definitions of activity status which focus on actual activities – for example, whether someone undertook waged work or sought waged work in the reference week – fail to explore individuals' perceptions of their economic activity status or their economic activity aspirations. Moreover, definitions of employment status may be argued to be too wide, encompassing all forms of employment including short hours and unpaid family work, while unemployment definitions may be too restrictive, omitting many people who would like to work and would be available for work if employment opportunities were expanded. These ambiguities of status affect both sexes, but are particularly evident in the case of women. Women may be less likely than men to see themselves primarily as wage workers, and thus may move more readily into domestic or informal work as an alternative to unemployment. Moreover, they may be less able to look actively for work as they are often engaged in domestic duties, and/or may use mainly informal areas for seeking work. Employment definitions for women are also more problematic because of the higher involvement of women in short part-time work, in unpaid family work and in leave from employment for maternity or childcare.

3

WOMEN'S EMPLOYMENT RATES AND STRUCTURAL AND REGIONAL CHANGE

The factors which shape the gender pattern of economic activity include not only societal factors and influences but also the pattern of employment demand. Gender segregation is a feature of all advanced societies and thus the pattern of demand, defined by region, industry, occupation and working-time contract, will have major implications for the overall economic activity statuses of men and women. It would not be correct to regard the gendered pattern of demand as independent of societal effects, as the pattern and form of gender segregation still varies despite being strong and pervasive in all societies (Rubery and Fagan 1995). Nor, however, is it the case that regional or indeed industrial or occupational effects can be regarded as simply subservient to the impact of societal norms and values. It may, for example, be the lack of development of service sector employment which constrains women to social roles as housewives or as unpaid family helpers, and not strong social norms. Moreover, social norms may vary between regions, independently of the structure of demand for labour within regions.

Investigation of the regional and compositional demand effects helps to clarify the extent to which trends in employment by gender represent the outcome of compositional changes in employment opportunities, with women's employment expanding and men's contracting due to the growth and decline of traditional female-oriented industries and occupations on the one hand and male-dominated sectors on the other. This analysis also reveals whether the growth of female employment is associated with changing patterns of segregation, including the entry of women into non-traditional areas, and/or an increase in the intensification of segregation, with the growth of, for example, part-time jobs perhaps serving to increase the concentration of women in certain areas and to intensify the exclusion of men.

3.1 Regional patterns of change in economic activity by gender

Regional variations in employment rates within member states

Explorations of regional variations in employment rates are limited by available data. European Labour Force Survey data disaggregated by regions are available for all countries in 1992 but for previous years the regional data are less complete and are available in a comparable useful form for only seven countries for 1987 and only four countries for 1983. The data used in this section are based on the NUTS (Nomenclatures of Territorial Units) classification at level I in most cases (see Eurostat 1988 and 1992). On this basis, Denmark and Luxembourg are treated as each constituting one region only.

The extent of regional variation revealed by these data are first of all a function of the regional classifications used; in some cases this classification level may be too broad to reveal the main geographical variations in economic activity patterns. In some countries the classifications may be influenced more by political than by economic or geographical divisions; in Germany some regions are in fact mainly metropolitan areas, separated out in the data because of their independent political status as separate Länder. Thus when we compare the extent of regional variations using this classification we are not necessarily giving a true comparative picture of regional or geographical variations between countries.

With these provisos in mind, Figure 3.1 compares the size of the gap between highest and the lowest employment rates within member states, revealing major national differences in the extent of regional variations in employment rates. Italy, France and Germany have the widest variations in total employment rates (15 percentage points or more), and perhaps surprisingly the highest and lowest employment rates in Germany are found among the old and not the new German Länder. Spain, the UK and Greece also have significant variations (over 10 but below 12 percentage points), while the range of employment rates revealed in the Netherlands, Portugal, Belgium and Ireland are more modest at under 8 percentage points. When we look at variation by gender by region we find a similar ordering of countries for both genders by size of variations, but we find one group of countries (Belgium, Greece, Spain and the UK) where there is considerably more variation in employment rates for men, and another where the regional variations for women are greater (Germany, France, Italy, Portugal, Ireland and the Netherlands) (Figure 3.1). Within these groups of countries the size of the gender gap varies; in the Netherlands for example the range for women exceeds that for men by less than 1 percentage point, while in Italy it is 14 percentage points greater at over 27 percentage points, compared to 13 for men. Germany and France also record high variations in employment rates for women at 18 percentage points, but the next-highest gap is in Spain at 10.6 percentage points. For men the largest gap between highest and lowest is 13 percentage points in Italy, Spain and the UK, but more countries reveal a gap of over 10 percentage points for men (six) than is the case for women (four).

When we look at the pattern of change in variations in employment rates over time, for those countries for which we have data, we find that

83

Figure 3.1 Regional variations in employment rates, 1992

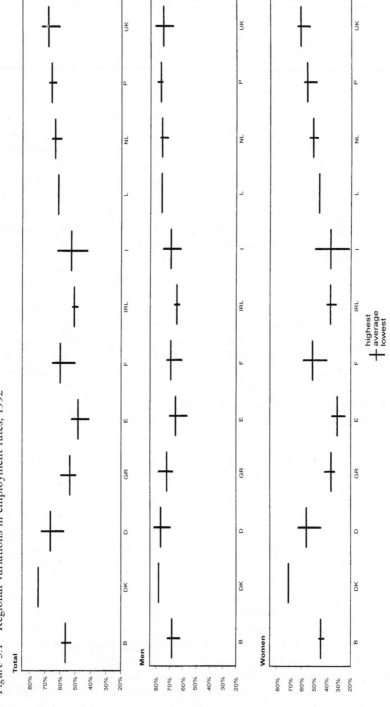

Source: European Labour Force Survey (1992)

employment rates have tended to diverge for men in six out of seven countries while there is a somewhat more mixed and opposite pattern for women, five with converging rates but two, Italy and France, with diverging rates (see Appendix Table 3.1). Female employment rates converged most in Spain, down from over 17 percentage points in 1987 to 11 percentage points in 1992. Male employment rates showed the strongest tendencies towards divergence in Italy and France, with increases of 4 to 5 percentage points in the range between 1983 and 1992. The UK is the only country where employment rates for both men and women converged taking the period 1983 to 1992 as a whole and the later 1987–92 period, but this convergence followed a widening of employment rate variations by region during the 1983–7 period for both sexes. The recession of the late 1980s and early 1990s hit the UK earlier than other EU member states and affected for the first time Southern as much as Northern regions, perhaps accounting for the trend to convergence in the later period (see Box 3.1).

We have already identified in section 2.1 that while the direction of change in male employment over this time period was quite varied by country, female employment rates rose in all member states. For both men and women the net overall trends at national level are also largely maintained at the regional level. The main exception to the universal tendency for female employment rates to rise is France where only four out of eight regions recorded a positive increase in female employment over the 1983–92 period, although the 1987–92 period shows a more consistent upward trend. In France the decline in employment was found in some regions with already low employment rates, such that the lowest regional employment rate actually fell from around 41 per cent to under 40 per cent. Similarly in Italy the two out of the eleven regions where employment rates actually fell for women were located in the South, that is, with below average employment rates even at the beginning of the period (see Box 3.1).

In Belgium, Italy and France employment rates for men fell in every region over the period 1983–92, in line with national trends. In the period 1987–92 downward trends were also recorded in every region in France and all but one region in Italy, while Belgium experienced an increasing male employment rate in every region. Again in line with national trends in the Netherlands and in the old German Länder employment rates rose in every region except for one of the Länder over the 1987–92 period. In the UK the majority of regions also showed increases in employment rates for 1983–92, with only two out of eleven showing decreases. However, between 1987 and 1992 the UK pattern was more mixed with six out of eleven regions recording falls and five increases, resulting in a small national decrease in male employment rates over this period. Spain also showed a mixed pattern by region with three regions recording falls and four increases in male employment rates. Overall, however, there appears to be more evidence of

---

Box 3.1 National aggregate patterns of employment and gender relations are called into question by continuing North–South divisions in Italy and East–West divisions in Germany

Divisions in **Italy** between North and South have widened since the mid-1980s. Most employment growth has been in the North and most unemployment growth in the South. Male employment rates fell by 8 percentage points in the South and by 4.6 in the North. Female employment rates in the South also declined but by only 0.5 percentage points, while rising by 4.7 percentage points in the North. Employment fell in the South partly as a result of the curtailing of subsidies, reducing economic activity especially in construction and thereby reducing male employment in particular. However, the small decline in female employment rates in the South must be considered against the background of already very low employment rates combined with very high unemployment rates even at the start of the period. Some of the widening gap between the North and the South and the continuing strong gender divides within each region may be disguised by new definitions of unemployment that have reduced in particular measured female unemployment in the South. Moreover there is evidence of an increase in discouraged female workers in the South as the number of female first-time jobseekers in measured unemployment has fallen.

However, variations are found within the South and the North; in the North the region of Lazio, in and around Rome, experienced higher than average female employment growth while most of the falls in employment for women and men were concentrated in Campania and Sicily reflecting the phasing out of subsidies to the Mezzogiorno and the weakness of the South's industrial base which was unable to withstand recent recessionary pressures. In contrast Emilia-Romagna in the North with a strong female industrial employment base is leading the way out of recession as export growth expands in the export-oriented consumer goods industries of the 'Third Italy' (Bettio and Mazzotta 1995: 39–40 and Appendix 1).

The differences between East and West regions of **Germany** in patterns of female economic activity are found more in the form of non-employment and in the shares of part-time work than in employment rates. In fact the falls in employment in East Germany have tended to reduce the gap in employment rates between East and West. However, a much lower share of non-employed women in the East are found in inactivity, and among employed women part-time rates in the East vary from 10 to 15 per cent, but in the West from 30 to 37 per cent. For men there is also an overlap in employment rates between East and West with Saarland in the West and Saxony in the East having relatively low employment rates, both characterised as having a high proportion of traditional industries such as coal and steel (Maier and Rapp 1995: 29).

---

divergence in trends for male employment between countries than by region within countries, while for women the positive upward trend is found fairly universally at the national and the regional level.

Despite the variations between regions in employment rates, there are still systematic differences in employment rates by gender, such that the highest regional employment rate for women is still below the lowest regional employment rate for men in every member state. France comes closest to having overlapping employment rates by gender with the lowest employment rate for men by region exceeding the highest employment rate for women by only 2.5 percentage points. The gap between the lowest male and the highest female employment rates is also relatively low in the UK (5 percentage points) and Germany (8 percentage points), but in the remaining countries for which we have data the gap is sizeable, ranging from 12 to 26 percentage points.

Variations in employment rates by region for women might be expected to be associated on the one hand with higher service sector employment, and on the other with high rates of part-time work, especially in countries where part-time is a significant employment form. However, a simple examination of the ranking of regions by either share of services in total employment or the share of part-time work in female employment reveals no systematic relationships. Out of ten countries, only three recorded the highest female employment rate in the region with the highest share of employment in services. Moreover, even for these countries there is no evidence of any systematic tendency for a high services share to coincide with high female employment rates across all the regions. Italy in particular shows a poor relationship between services sector shares and female employment as it is in the South where services take on relatively greater importance. As female employment rates will be affected by the level as well as the composition of employment, we also looked at the relationship between the share of services and the share of women in all employment, but again found no evidence of simple correlations in Germany, Italy, France, Spain, Portugal or the UK. However, Belgium, the Netherlands and Greece do reveal the same rank order for regions by share of services and share of women in total employment.

High shares of part-time work in total employment might be expected to increase not only the female share of employment but also the female employment rate, as work is shared over a larger number of persons. Again, however, there is no systematic pattern. There is no country where the region with the highest female part-time rate has also the highest female employment rate, and there was only one case where the highest female part-time rate coincided with the highest female share of employment. No countries reveal systematic relationships between high part-time and high female employment rates but this absence of a relationship is not because of a lack of variation in part-time rates between regions. Four countries had variations in female part-time shares by region of 10 percentage points or more, although the high range in Germany of 24 percentage points is due to the different traditions of part-time work between the old and the new

Box 3.2 Regional variations in female employment patterns reflect differences in geographical features, in urbanisation, in demography, industrial structure and in social norms

Not all but most of the island regions of the member states tend to have lower employment rates and higher unemployment rates than the mainland. This applies for example to the Azores and Madeira, to Northern Ireland, to Sicily and to some extent to the Canaries for men. The main exception is the **Greek Islands**, which have the highest female employment rate, although we do not know what share of women are here employed as unpaid family workers, which may distort the employment comparisons.

In **Ireland** the highest female participation rate is found in the East but when the East is sub-divided between Dublin and the rest, Dublin is found to have a female participation rate 8 percentage points higher than the latter. Lower female employment in the West is likely to be associated with two factors: unrecorded work of farmers' wives (Braithwaite, 1994: 62) and demographic factors, specifically the high emigration rates of the middle age groups (Barry 1995: 11).

Not all urban areas result in higher employment rates. The Attica region in **Greece** (which includes Athens) has the lowest employment rate for both men and women, and increases in unemployment around Athens have accounted for no less than 28 per cent and 39 per cent of the increase in total female and male unemployment since 1988 (Cavouriaris *et al.* 1995: Table 3).

In **Germany** the Länder with the highest female employment rates include the metropolitan areas such as Berlin on the one hand, and, on the other hand, the less industrial areas such as Bavaria, where services predominate. Women have lower employment rates in the old industrial regions such as Saarland and North Rhine Westphalia, indicating, perhaps, either the continuation of the male breadwinner model in these heavy industrialised areas where male manual worker earnings are relatively high, or perhaps the slow down in employment opportunities in these areas (Maier and Rapp 1995: 29–32).

In the **UK**, industrial structure is important in explaining the traditionally higher unemployment rates and lower employment rates in **Wales**, the **North of England**, **Northern Ireland** and to some extent **Scotland**. The impact of the recent recession on service industries which are concentrated in the South has done much to reduce regional divergence. However, convergence has also come about through rises in employment within low employment areas; Wales experienced a 13 percentage point rise in female employment over the 1983–92 period compared to 10 percentage points elsewhere (Rubery and Smith 1995: 105).

Changes in female employment shares are not only a consequence of, but also a part of the process of employment restructuring and growth. Regions in **France** with the highest rates of change in feminisation of the labour force are also those with the highest rates of job creation (the West, South West and the Mediterranean), but where job growth has been slow female employment has fallen and the increase in feminisation has been less marked (Silvera *et al.* 1995: 42).

German Länder (see Box 3.1). France has both wide variations in female employment rates by region and wide variations in female part-time shares, but taking account of these differences by calculating full-time equivalent employment rates does not make a significant difference to the size of regional variations. If we compare the range of female employment rates by region on a headcount and a full-time equivalent basis (see Appendix Table 3.1) we find that although in seven cases the range is reduced on the full-time equivalent basis, in three cases it is actually greater. Moreover, even within those seven countries where part-time work does tend to widen the regional dispersion of female employment rates, the decrease in variation on the full-time equivalent basis is modest; less than 1 percentage point in four cases and accounting for a decrease of over 2 percentage points only in the case of the UK. Of the three countries recording increases, two, Belgium and Spain, recorded very slight differences, but Portugal recorded a widening of over 2 percentage points as part-time work is more common in areas with low overall female employment rates. Thus little of the regional variation within countries can be explained by differential rates of part-time working. Overall regional differences in employment rates require explanations along a number of dimensions, including geographical characteristics, level of urbanisation, industrial and demographic structures as well as social norms and values (see Box 3.2).

Regional variations in non-employment rates within member states

Regional variations in non-employment rates are the obverse of regional variations in employment rates. Non-employment takes the form of either unemployment or inactivity and Figures 3.2 and 3.3 track the extent to which variations in employment rates by region are reflected in unemployment or inactivity rates (measured as shares of the population) by member state and by gender. Regions are ranked by employment rates and thus the employment rate curve falls from left to right. The extent to which the unemployment and/or the inactivity curve rises smoothly from left to right or shows a more varied or ragged pattern will indicate whether or not there is a systematic relationship between low employment rates and high unemployment or high inactivity rates. For men the expectation might be that unemployment rates would rise primarily to offset low employment rates at a regional level. Figure 3.2 supports this expectation to some extent. Certainly in almost all countries unemployment rates rise in regions with low employment rates. There is no clear trend in Portugal or the Netherlands in part because employment rates show little variation, but in Greece the unemployment rate tends to remain flat despite variations in employment rates. In Greece most of the variation in employment rates is compensated for by rising inactivity rates, but there is also some evidence of rising inactivity rates in countries where unemployment also rises with declining

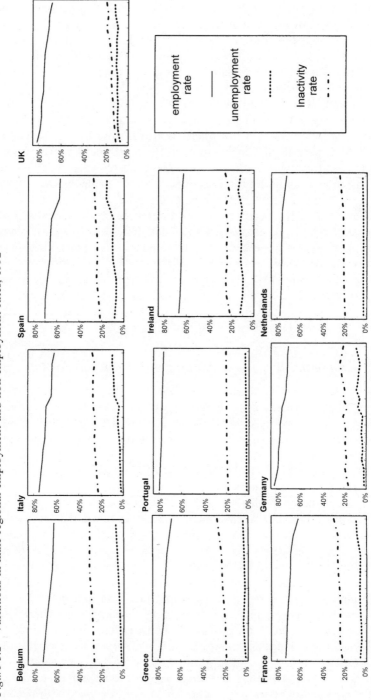

Figure 3.2 Variations in male regional employment and non–employment rates, 1992

Source: European Labour Force Surveys (1992)
Note: Data are based on NUTS I regional classification except for Ireland, where data are based on NUTS III

Figure 3.3 Variations in female regional employment and non-employment rates, 1992

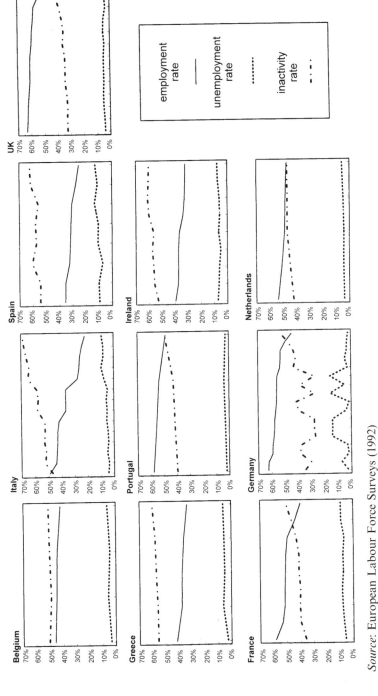

Source: European Labour Force Surveys (1992)
Note: Data are based on NUTS I regional classification except for Ireland, where data are based on NUTS II

employment rates. Variations are relatively small, but again most countries have discernible upward trends except perhaps for Portugal.

For women the pattern is very different (Figure 3.3). In most countries the compensation for low employment rates by region is found primarily in higher inactivity rates. There is a marked upward trend in all countries except for Belgium, and Germany where the differences between former East and West Germany in women's integration into the labour force leads to a complex relationship between employment rate levels and rates of unemployment and inactivity, with higher unemployment rates relative to inactivity in the East and vice versa in the West (see Box 3.1). In contrast there is a strong upward movement in unemployment rates only in Italy, Spain and Belgium.

Figure 3.4 traces the same relationship for pooled data for all NUTS II regions in nine European member states for men and women (data for the UK, Denmark and Luxembourg are at NUTS I level). For both men and women there is a clearer upward trend in inactivity rates as employment rates fall, although unemployment rates are fairly consistently higher in regions with the very lowest employment rates. For unemployment rates in particular, however, the figures reveal more the lack of a relationship with employment rates as there is considerable movement around the slight upward trend. The upward trend in inactivity rates is also far from con- sistent; in particular for women the regions with high employment rates appear to divide between some with high and others with low inactivity rates, and it is these differences which give rise to a series of high peaks in the unemployment rates at the left hand side of the distribution. Thus when employment rates are high there seems to be strong regional and country differences in the extent to which the rest of the female population is unemployed or inactive, but at low employment rates there is a much more consistent tendency for a high and rising share of the female popula- tion to be inactive. The upward trend line is much steeper for women, reflecting the wider variations in employment rate and the relatively gentle upward slope in unemployment rates. There is much less difference in the gradients of the two lines for men, and considerable variation around the slight upward trend in both the inactivity and the unemployment rates. However, for both men and women unemployment rates on a popu- lation basis seem to be a relatively poor predictor of the employment rate in the region and variations in activity rates are overwhelmingly important for women and somewhat more significant than unemployment population rates for men.

If we look in more detail at trends in inactivity rates by region within countries we find that by and large the move at the regional level in the same direction as at the national level. For women there was an extremely consistent pattern at regional level with all reporting decreases except for two regions in Southern Italy, reflecting a possible increase in discouraged

Figure 3.4 Employment, unemployment and inactivity rates at regional (NUTS II) level by gender, 1992

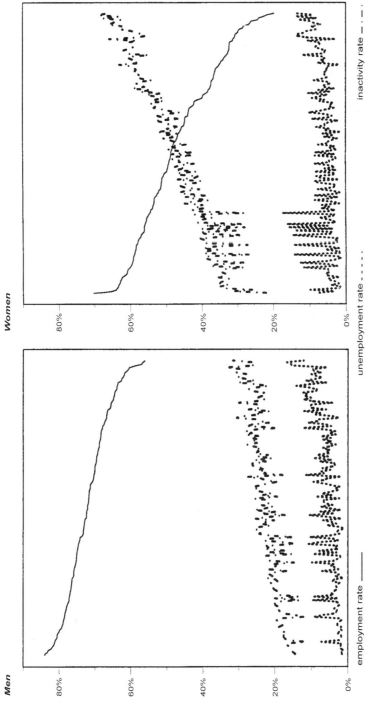

Source: European Labour Force Survey (1992)

Note: Data are based on NUTS II regional classification except for the UK, Denmark and Luxembourg, where data are based on NUTS I workers in this area of very high unemployment. In Belgium, France and Italy male inactivity rates rose in all regions over all time periods considered, while in Spain and the Netherlands there was also an upward trend in all regions except one. Germany and the UK are the only countries for which we have data where male inactivity rates move in different directions by region; for West German regions only (and excluding Berlin), five Länder reported an increase and five a decrease in male inactivity rates between 1987 and 1992, while in the UK five decreased and six increased inactivity rates over this time period, although for the period as a whole the direction of change was more clearly downward, with eight out of eleven reporting falls.

Three countries stand out as having very wide variations of female inactivity rates between regions. Germany has the largest range at nearly 26 percentage points, and although this is boosted by the divergence in behaviour between East and West Länder (see Box 3.1), the range is still nearly 18 percentage points if only the Western Länder are considered. Italy also has a range above 20 percentage points (22.7), reflecting the wide differences in participation rates between North and South (see Box 3.1). France is perhaps the most surprising inclusion in the list as not only is the range wide at over 15 percentage points, but also it has been rising over time. Portugal and the UK also have relatively wide dispersions with a range of over 9 percentage points, but the remaining five countries have variations which are no greater and sometimes smaller than those found in inactivity rates for men by region. Indeed in four out of the five remaining countries men's inactivity rates vary more than those for women (Belgium, Greece, Portugal and the Netherlands – although only by a small margin). Ireland, however, shows more variation for women than for men. Despite the evidence of variations in inactivity rates by region, in all countries a higher share of women were in inactivity in every region than even the highest male regional inactivity rate.

Turning now to unemployment rates by region (Appendix Table 3.2), we find much more divergent patterns in trends over time in unemployment rates because of different national patterns of unemployment trends. These differences reflect differences in the timing of the business cycle as well as long-term trends, so we shall not investigate trends in unemployment rates further. Of more interest here is whether variations in unemployment rates are influenced more by gender or by region; that is to what extent is being a woman or a man a better predictor of the risk of unemployment than living in a particular region. We look first at the unemployment rates by population to retain consistency with the analysis so far presented but we shall look later at these issues by the more conventional labour force unemployment rates. Using the population measures we find first that there are only two countries where the risk of unemployment appears to be systematically higher for one gender irrespective of the region; thus the lowest regional population unemployment rate for men is greater than the highest regional unemployment rate for women in two countries, the UK and Ireland. In all other countries there was at least some overlap in the population unemployment rates by region for men and women, with the Netherlands coming closest to having the opposite pattern to that found in the UK and Ireland, with higher female regional population unemployment rates than the highest male regional unemployment rates, except for one region. Germany has overlapping male and female population unemployment rates for the West German Länder, but for the East German Länder female unemployment rates are consistently much greater, often close to twice the rates for men in the same Länder. Within regions, even on the stricter test of unemployment population rates, women's unemployment is still often higher than men's. The main exceptions to this pattern are obviously the UK and Ireland, but also the West German Länder and a minority of regions in other countries[1].

Where unemployment rates are particularly high for men and there are wide differences in male and female activity rates, it is clearly difficult for women's population based unemployment rates to exceed those for men. Thus when we turn to labour force based unemployment rates (see Appendix Table 3.2) we find even more evidence of a higher risk of unemployment for women within regions, and also more countries where female unemployment rates on the labour force measures are consistently greater than the highest male regional unemployment rate. Using the labour force measure of unemployment considerably reduces the number of regions where male unemployment rates exceed those for women. For example, whereas all the old German Länder and all Irish regions recorded higher male unemployment rates on a population basis, on the labour force basis female unemployment is higher than male unemployment in all but two German Länder, new and old taken together, and also exceeds male unemployment in four out of eight Irish regions. Only in the UK does the female unemployment rate remain persistently below male unemployment rates in all regions. However, although the unemployment rates on a labour force measure tend to be higher in all countries relative to male unemployment rates, countries still differ in the extent to which the risk of unemployment can be said to be primarily related to gender or primarily related to region. The countries where region clearly predominates over gender now include only Ireland and Germany (especially but not exclusively differences between the old and the new German Länder, but even within the old German Länder male and female unemployment rates overlap). However, in Italy there is a strong regional and gender effect, especially when we look at unemployment rates for Southern and Northern regions grouped together. Here male unemployment in the North is in fact somewhat above female unemployment in the South, even though female unemployment rates are more than twice male unemployment rates in both North and South. Moreover, although on average female unemployment rates in the North and male unemployment rates in the South are similar, when we look at the regions within the North and the South we find much higher male unemployment rates in some Southern regions than are found in any Northern region for men or for women. There is also some overlap in unemployment rates for men and women across regions in Spain, with male unemployment rates in two regions exceeding the two lowest female regional labour force unemployment rates.

However, in Spain gender is clearly a more important determinant of unemployment risk than region as unemployment rates for men rise above a fifth in only two out of seven regions but fall below a fifth in only one region for women. Greece and France are also countries where being a woman is in general a more important factor in explaining the risk of unemployment than being in a particular region, although in Greece female unemployment rates in the islands do fall below male unemployment rates on the mainland, and in France unemployment rates for men in two out of eight regions overlap with the higher range of unemployment rates for women. Meanwhile in the Netherlands and Portugal, female unemployment rates in all regions exceed the highest male regional unemployment rates. Belgium is a country where this pattern used to apply, with all female unemployment rates in 1983 exceeding the highest male regional unemployment rate. However, over the 1980s regional differences have taken on greater importance such that the female unemployment rate in the Flemish region now falls below the male unemployment rates in both Walloon and Brussels, even though within each region female unemployment rates exceed the corresponding male unemployment rates by a clear margin.

Cross-country comparisons of regions

We can use the Eurostat data to compare regional patterns of employment across countries and not just within the borders of individual member states. Comparing female employment rates in 1992 we find, not surprisingly, that the highest employment rate is in Denmark at 70.4 per cent but after Denmark the immediate rankings are dominated by the UK and Germany with five of the top decile regions from the UK and two from Germany – Bavaria and the combined labour market of East and West Berlin (see Table 3.1). If we examine the top quartile of regions the group also includes all UK regions except Northern Ireland, four more Germany regions (two from the new Länder), Île de France and Northern Portugal. In the bottom decile the regions are dominated by Spain and Italy, with all the Italian regions from the South of the country along with the Spanish regions of the Canaries, South, Centre and North East. The remainder of the lower quartile includes Attica, the capital city region of Greece, as well as Madrid and five regions from Ireland.

Table 3.1 Upper and lower quartiles of female regional employment rates, 1992[a]

Upper quartile		Lower quartile	
Rank and region	Employment rate (%)	Rank and region	Employment rate (%)
1 Denmark	70.40	59 Mid-West (IRL)	37.37
2 East Anglia (UK)	63.34	60 Lazio (I)	36.68
3 East Midlands		61 Abruzzi and Molise (I)	
(UK)	62.73		36.64
4 Bavaria (D)	62.60	62 East (E)	35.61
5 South East (UK)	62.41	63 North West (E)	35.37
6 Berlin (D)	62.25	64 South West (IRL)	33.84
7 South West (UK)	61.65	65 Attica (GR)	33.46
8 Yorkshire &		66 Midlands (IRL)	32.67
Humberside (UK)	60.82		
9 Scotland (UK)	60.67	67 Madrid (E)	32.31
10 North West (UK)	59.57	68 North East (IRL)	32.24
11 West Midlands		69 South East (IRL)	32.13
(UK)	59.31		
12 Baden-Württemburg		70 North East (E)	31.74
(D)	59.27		
13 Hamburg (D)	59.19	71 Canaries (E)	30.56
14 Île de France (F)	58.51	72 South (I)	27.48
15 North (UK)	58.37	73 Centre (E)	27.34
16 Brandeburg (D)	58.29	74 Sardinia (I)	26.27
17 North (P)	58.13	75 South (E)	24.98
18 Wales (UK)	57.93	76 Campania (I)	24.11
19 Saxony (D)	57.79	77 Sicily (I)	21.72

Note: a Data are based on NUTS I regional data (NUTS II for Ireland) from the European Labour Force Survey. The regions have not been weighted by population so that the top and bottom quartiles will represent different shares of the EU population

If we compare the ranking of regions by male employment rates to that for female employment rates, we find that in the top decile East Anglia and the South West of the UK remain in unchanged rankings while Bavaria climbs from fourth to first place and Denmark only just remains in the top decile with the eighth-highest male employment rate (Table 3.2). Also in the top decile of male employment rates are the Portuguese and Greek Islands, both regions in the lower half of the female rankings. In the lowest decile of male regional employment rates are two regions of Belgium (Brussels and Walloon) and the North of France all in the middle of the female rankings. Also new to the lowest decile is the North West and Donegal region of Ireland joining the Canaries, South Spain, Sicily and Campania, all of which were included in the lowest decile of female employment rates. Overall only twenty-seven regions moved by fewer than 10 rankings and only four remained unchanged, demonstrating the wide variation between relative regional male and female employment rates.

Table 3.2 Upper and lower quartiles of male regional employment rates, 1992[a]

Upper quartile		Lower quartile	
Rank and region	*Employment rates (%)[b]*	*Rank and region*	*Employment rates (%)[b]*
1 Bavaria (D)	82.08 (4)	59 Centre (E)	65.98 (73)
2 East Anglia (UK)	81.19 (2)	60 Mediterranean (F)	65.82 (46)
3 Baden-Württemburg (D)	80.39 (12)	61 South West (IRL)	65.60 (64)
4 Islands (P)	79.70 (39)	62 Mid-West (IRL)	65.23 (59)
5 Hessen (D)	78.81 (22)	63 North West (E)	64.64 (63)
6 Islands (GR)	78.57 (52)	64 Midlands (IRL)	64.63 (66)
7 South West (UK)	78.52 (7)	65 East (IRL)	64.58 (54)
8 Denmark	78.47 (1)	66 South (I)	64.33 (72)
9 Schleswig-Holstein (D)	78.41 (21)	67 Sardinia (I)	63.99 (74)
10 Rhineland-Palatinate (D)	78.38 (26)	68 West (IRL)	63.95 (58)
11 North (P)	77.98 (17)	69 South East (IRL)	63.91 (69)
12 Lower Saxony (D)	77.52 (31)	70 Walloon (B)	63.87 (50)
13 West-Netherlands (NL)	77.49 (25)	71 Sicily (I)	63.69 (77)
14 South East (UK)	77.21 (5)	72 North West & Donegal (IRL)	62.68 (56)
15 East Midlands (UK)	77.18 (3)	73 Brussels (B)	62.35 (44)
16 Hamburg (D)	76.97 (13)	74 Campania (I)	61.85 (76)
17 Luxembourg	76.40 (42)	75 North (F)	61.08 (53)
18 East-Netherlands (NL)	76.08 (38)	76 South (E)	57.77 (75)
19 South (P)	76.01 (28)	77 Canaries (E)	57.07 (71)

Notes: a Data are based on NUTS I regional data (NUTS II for Ireland) from the European Labour Force Survey; regions have not been weighted by population – see Table 3.1
b Numbers in parentheses are the female regional employment rate rankings as shown in Table 3.1

In view of the wide variation in part-time rates between countries and regions, we have also considered the rankings of regional female employment rates on a full-time equivalent basis. This ranking of full-time equivalent employment rates provides a very different pattern compared to that observed previously; Denmark remains at the top of the ranking but the UK does not appear in the top decile at all, which instead is dominated by Germany (five regions) along with North Portugal and Île de France (Table 3.3). The rest of the upper quartile includes more German regions (five) as well as five regions from the UK and the Southern mainland of Portugal. The lowest decile effectively remains unchanged with only North East Spain losing its place to South East Ireland. The remainder of the lower quartile is interesting because it includes the North, East and South Netherlands all falling more than 20 rankings from their position in the female headcount ranking. Overall those regions which have fallen furthest are in the UK (all falling 10 rankings or more) and the Netherlands (20 rankings or more) and the major climbers (more than 10 rankings) are regions in former East

Germany and mainland Portugal, along with Emilia-Romagna in Italy (+14) and the Greek Islands (+10).

Table 3.3 Upper and lower quartiles of female regional full-time equivalent employment rates, 1992[a]

Upper quartile		Lower quartile	
Rank and region	*Employment rates (%)[b]*	*Rank and region*	*Employment rates (%)[b]*
1 Denmark	57.56 (1)	59 North West (E)	33.61 (63)
2 North (P)	55.43 (17)	60 South Netherlands (NL)	33.16 (40)
3 Berlin (D)	54.79 (6)	61 East (E)	32.88 (62)
4 Brandeburg (D)	54.14 (16)	62 East Netherlands (NL)	32.84 (38)
5 Île de France (F)	54.02 (14)	63 Attica (GR)	32.35 (65)
6 Saxony (D)	53.40 (19)	64 Madrid (E)	31.05 (67)
7 Saxony Anhalt (D)	53.38 (20)	65 North Netherlands (NL)	30.92 (41)
8 Thüringia (D)	52.31 (23)	66 South West (IRL)	30.52 (64)
9 Mecklenburg West Pomerania (D)	52.27 (24)	67 Midlands (IRL)	29.73 (66)
10 Bavaria(D)	51.71 (4)	68 North East (IRL)	29.26 (68)
11 South (P)	50.65 (28)	69 North East (E)	29.21 (70)
12 Hamburg (D)	49.43 (13)	70 South East (IRL)	28.99 (69)
13 South East (UK)	49.07 (5)	71 Canaries (E)	28.28 (71)
14 Baden-Württemburg (D)	48.27(12)	72 South (I)	25.73 (72)
15 East Anglia (UK)	47.88 (2)	73 Centre (E)	25.10 (73)
16 East Midlands (UK)	47.46 (3)	74 Sardinia (I)	24.67 (74)
17 Scotland (UK)	47.03 (9)	75 South (E)	23.26 (75)
18 Hessen (D)	46.60 (22)	76 Campania (I)	22.88 (76)
19 South West (UK)	46.41 (7)	77 Sicily (I)	20.51 (77)

Notes: a Data are based on NUTS I regional data (NUTS II) for Ireland) from the European Labour Force Survey; regions have not been weighted by population – see Table 3.1

b numbers in parentheses are the female employment rate rank based on a head count basis, as calculated on Table 3.1

The different rankings of regional employment rates show the wide variations that exist across the European Union, with female employment rates in the top decile around double those in the lowest decile. In contrast for men the ratio of top decile employment rates to lowest decile rates is only about one and a quarter. The full-time equivalent comparisons demonstrate how part-time employment has distorted the Dutch and UK female employment rates in comparison with the rest of Europe but in Denmark, another high part-time country, the female employment rate remains the highest even on a full-time equivalent basis.

3.2   Impact of segregation by industry, occupation and employment contract

Industrial structure versus industrial segregation effects

To what extent has increased female employment been associated with the changing structure of industry or changing demand for women within industries? This issue is investigated through a shift-share analysis of employment change by industry (NACE 1 digit) (Appendix Table 3.3). For the period 1983–92 we find for the E9 (data for Italy not available in addition to Spain and Portugal) that around three-quarters of the increase in female employment is accounted for by the changing structure and scale of industrial employment (industry effect) and only 21 per cent is explained by rising female shares within industry (share effect) – the remaining 4 per cent is accounted for by the interaction term. We can further divide the industrial change element into two components, the changing scale of employment, given a constant structure of industry (the scale effect) and the changing composition of industrial employment (the weight effect). Both have had a positive effect on women's employment but the largest component of the industrial change (56 percentage points out of 75) is accounted for by the scale effect and only 17 percentage points by changing composition of employment.

From these two sets of decompositions it appears that over half of the growth of female employment over this period has been due simply to an expansion of employment opportunities, independent of any specific segregation effect and only 17 per cent has been due to the 'weight effect' – that is changes which favour women because of gender segregation by industry. This may appear as a rather minor role for segregation until we look at the comparative experience for men. There we find a parallel but opposite effect of the weight effect reducing male employment over the period, for while the weight effect increased female employment by 1.1 million it decreased male employment by an equal but opposite amount. Thus, assuming neutral compositional effects, the expanding scale of industrial employment, would have led to an increase in male employment of 5.7 million and of 3.6 million in female employment, but the changing composition of employment in fact resulted in employment growth due to structural scale effects of only 4.4 million for men compared to 4.9 million for women (Figure 3.5).

The picture for men deteriorates further when we look at changes in employment related to changing gender shares within industries. Most changes over recent years in segregation have been towards rising female shares, resulting in desegregation in some male-dominated sectors but further increases in female segregation in industries where they are already concentrated. Thus rises in the share of women within industries does not necessarily imply moves towards greater integration and desegregation

100

Figure 3.5 Decomposition of the change in female and male employment (E9), 1983–92

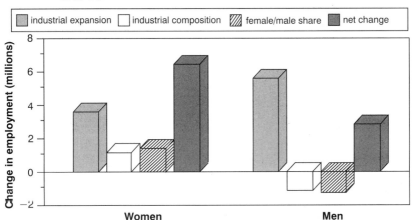

Source: European Labour Force Surveys (1983, 1992)

(Rubery 1988). Indeed many of the changes within industry shares may be due to differential rates of expansion and contraction in male-dominated and female-dominated occupations within industries. Blue collar production work within industries has been in decline, primarily affecting men, while white collar work, particularly clerical and administrative, within industries has been maintained or has expanded mainly increasing opportunities for women. The result has been that although women have increased their share of more male-dominated sectors, segregation by occupation remains strong within the sectors. Given the recent historical process of change, it comes as no surprise to find that changes in gender shares have increased female employment by 21 per cent of the total increase or by 1.4 million while male employment had decreased by the same and opposite amount. Nearly half of the share effect derives from rising female shares within 'other services', evidence again of increasing gender segregation in employment, particularly in areas of fastest growth. Female employment prospects have thus been boosted relative to male employment both by favourable trends in industrial composition, and by continuing increases in female shares in most industries, but with a notable effect in the faster-growing and already female-dominated services.

This pattern at the E9 level is repeated at the member state level. There is a consistent positive weight effect for women's employment, thus showing that in all countries structural change increased women's employment by more than would be the case if there had been an even expansion of industrial demand, and likewise decreased male employment below that predicted assuming even expansion. In all countries there is also a positive share effect for women, and thus an opposite negative share effect for men. In most countries the share effect is sizeable, ranging from 19 per cent to 44 per cent of total female employment growth, with the exception of Denmark where the share effect accounted for only 4 per cent of total female employment growth (see Figure 3.6). However, Denmark already has high female employment shares, suggesting that a plateau in the degree of segregation may be reached with high participation rates.

When we look at the data split into two periods – 1983–7 and 1987–92 – we find some tendency for a stronger share effect in the second period and thus a weaker structural and scale effect. The period after 1987 included the strong period of European growth between 1986 and 1990, which may have attracted more women into employment who had remained outside of the labour market as hidden unemployed during the earlier period of slower growth. Between 1987 and 1992 there was a net increase of over 4 million female jobs compared to 2.4 million in the four years to 1987. The stronger share effect is found at the E9 level and also in six out of nine member states. Again nearly half of this share effect at the E9 level derives from changes within other services, but the share effect is positive in all sectors except agriculture in the second period but in the first period the share effect, while still positive overall, is negative in three out of ten sectors. Relative substitution within sectors of women for men has thus increased in importance as a source of female employment growth over the period, while changes in industrial structure in women's favour, that is a positive weight

Figure 3.6 Decomposition of the change in female employment, 1983–92

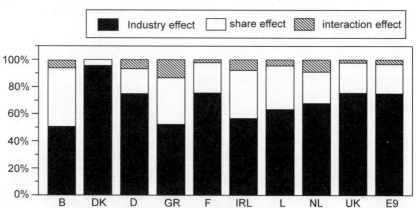

Source: European Labour Force Surveys (1983–92)
Note: Industry effect + share effect + interaction effect = net change

effect, had more impact in the first than the second part of the period at the E9 level.[2]

Women's employment has increased, measured not only by numbers of women employed in line with general employment expansion, but also as a share of total employment. A similar shift-share analysis can be carried out to determine to what extent increasing overall female shares of employment are explained by changes in industrial composition or by changing female shares within industries. As the overall expansion of employment over this period does not enter into this analysis of change in the female employment share we can expect these results to indicate a lower importance to structural effects and a greater importance to share effects than in the previous shift-share analysis. Over the period 1983–92 the female employment share rose nearly 3 percentage points at the E9 level (Appendix Table 3.4), with 1.34 percentage points accounted for by changes in industrial composition and 1.63 percentage points by increasing female shares within sectors. This relatively even distribution at the E9 level hides quite a diverse pattern within member states. In six countries the share effect exceeds the structural change effect: by particularly large margins in Belgium, the Netherlands and Luxembourg; by sizeable margins, but based on an overall lower change in female employment shares in Germany and Greece; and by a very small margin indeed in Ireland (Figure 3.7). Of the remaining three countries, the structural change effect is strongest, by a very small margin in the UK, but significantly stronger in both France and Denmark. The differences between the two sub-periods are even more obvious using this shift-share analysis. In the earlier period – 1983–7 – the structural change effect

Figure 3.7   Decomposition of the change in female share of employment, 1983–92

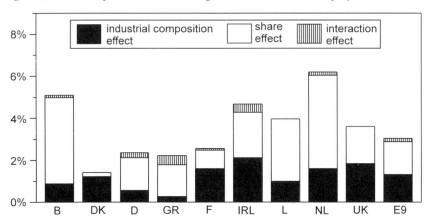

Source: European Labour Force Survey (1983, 1992)
Note: Industrial composition effect + share effect + interaction effect = change in
   female share of employment

103

dominated the share effect not only at the E9 level but also in six out of the nine countries. In contrast in the later period the share effect is dominant in ten out of eleven countries (including Spain and Portugal). Only in Denmark is the structural effect larger but even here the difference is only marginal, compared to an actual negative share effect in the earlier period.

Industrial restructuring and part-time employment

Part-time employment has been one of the major sources of overall employment growth and of female employment growth in particular. But to what extent is this growth due to changing tendencies to use part-time work within industrial sectors, or to the expansion of sectors where part-time work has long been used? To answer this question we have estimated the contributions to total employment growth which derive from structural change but divided into full-time and part-time jobs, and the contributions to total employment growth accounted for by changes in the relative incidence of full- and part-time jobs within industries. At the E9 level changing shares of part-time work within industries accounted for just over a third of total employment growth between 1983 and 1992. In contrast the expansion of sectors that use part-time employment had a relatively small effect (15 per cent) and industrial growth and change actually contributed more to full-time employment (65 per cent). In the latter sub-period, 1987–92, increased shares of part-time working within sectors contributed just less than a third to total net job growth at the E9 level. The inclusion of Spain and Portugal reduces the contribution of part-time shares to 23 per cent for the E11 but the part-time structural or industry effect remains the same (16.3 per cent).

At the member state level there is considerable diversity of experience (Appendix Table 3.5). For example, if we consider the share of all new jobs accounted for by changing shares of part-time work within industries between 1983 and 1992, we find very significant proportions in France, Ireland, the Netherlands, Belgium and the UK, ranging from 82 per cent of total job growth in France to 36 per cent in the UK. These estimates underline the significance of changing labour use strategies in explaining the growth in part-time employment in a range of countries. However, in Germany, Luxembourg, Greece and Denmark the contribution varies from only 4 per cent in Germany to a negative 24 per cent in Denmark (that is, decreasing incidence of part-time work in fact led to job loss equivalent to 24 per cent of total job growth). When we look at the period 1987–92 we find a relatively similar picture except that the part-time share effect is less significant in France and also Ireland. It is also very low in Spain, accounting for less than 1 per cent, but relatively high in Portugal at 28 per cent.

In contrast to the part-time share effect, we find little evidence that part-time job growth resulting from structural change (that is, the expansion of sectors that use part-time labour) made a major contribution to employment growth in many countries. Denmark, with the lowest overall increase in part-time work, except for Greece where it declined, in fact had the highest part-time industry effect accounting for 35 per cent of total job growth (offset by the negative 24 per cent part-time share effect). The UK and the Netherlands had the next highest part-time growth effects, accounting for 24 per cent and 18 per cent of total job growth respectively, but in all other countries the part-time industry effect accounted for 13 per cent or less of total job growth. A similar pattern is found for the later sub-period 1987–92 with part-time job growth due to industrial change accounting for over 30 per cent of total job growth in the UK and Netherlands, but elsewhere making only a relatively small contribution to employment growth. Thus it is the changing incidence of part-time work within sectors rather than a shift to industries using part-time jobs which caused the high share of part-time jobs within all new jobs in the EU. Nevertheless, part-time job growth is concentrated by sector within other services and distributive trades and catering – and accounted for 70 per cent of all part-time job growth during 1983–92 (in the E9) (73 per cent of female and 60 per cent of male part-time jobs). Other services accounted for 46 per cent alone, and for almost half of all new female part-time jobs. The concentration of new part-time jobs in these sectors was high in most countries, in fact rising to 94 per cent in France, 95 per cent in Luxembourg, 97 per cent in Portugal, between 1987 and 1992, and 113 per cent in Ireland (owing to the fall in part-time work in agriculture). Only Denmark and Greece, the countries with low or negative rates of part-time job growth, did not conform to this pattern.

Occupational structure and occupational segregation effects

Gender segregation is more conventionally measured by occupation than by industry. Occupational data at the international level are, however, much less widely used than industrial data and there are considerable question marks over the comparability of such data as are available. So far only data for broad occupational groups are available, and for analysis of trends we still have to rely on data collected under the ISCO (International Standard Classification of Occupations) 68 system which has frequently been criticised for reliability and for inconsistency in its approach to occupational classification. Since 1992 occupational data have been available on the new ISCO 88 basis but this does not provide a basis for analysing changes over time. Using the ISCO 68 data we have information on broad occupational groups for the years 1983, 1987 and 1990, although as we documented in earlier reports data are not available for all countries for all years. Our previous work has revealed that these data can be used to detect trends within countries, as the coding appears to be relatively consistent from year to year and changes in female shares of occupational groups are consistent with more detailed and accurate national data, although we would not wish to place too much emphasis on the differences between countries in distributions of employment by occupational groups (Rubery and Fagan 1993).

Using these data we have attempted to identify the relative importance of change in the scale and structure of occupations versus change in the female shares of occupational groups in explaining female employment growth over the 1983–90 period (see Appendix Table 3.6). We are not able to make a straightforward comparison with the results for industry structure versus share effects at the European level because occupational data are only available for six countries covering the period 1983–90, and for ten countries for the very short period 1987–90. From the data that are available, however, we find a relatively similar pattern to that for the industry shift-share analysis – namely a much higher share of female employment growth accounted for by changes in the scale and structure of occupations than by increasing female shares of occupational groups. For the E6 the growth effect accounted for 82 per cent of total female employment growth over the 1983–90 period and the share effect for only 16 per cent. Moreover, of the 82 per cent growth effect, 55 percentage points were due simply to the increasing scale of employment and only 25 to the changing structure of occupations. When we look at the two sub-periods – 1983–7 and 1987–90 – we find a somewhat higher share effect in the first period and a very low share effect in the second period. However, these results can be shown to be strongly influenced by the composition of member states included in the European level analysis, for when we look at the changes over the 1987–90 sub-period for the E10 we find a higher share effect – 12 per cent compared to 1 per cent for the E6, indicating that there is diversity of experience within member states. Nevertheless the overwhelming tendency is for the growth effect to exceed the share effect. Only in Greece and Ireland during the 1983–1987 period was the share effect more important than the growth effect.

Appendix Table 3.7 shows a shift-share analysis of the changes in female employment shares. This is done both for all persons in employment and on a full-time equivalent basis. The latter set of calculations enables us to control for changes in the full-time/part-time composition of occupations; changes in working-time patterns affect both the structure of occupations, measured on an employment headcount basis, and the female employment shares, as most of the part-timers are women. Because of the restricted number of countries available, it is more interesting to look at individual countries than at European averages. Looking at the female employment shares on a 'headcount' basis first, we find there is in fact quite a wide

106

divergence of experience between countries: structural change effects dominate over growth effects in Belgium, Germany (1987–90), Greece, Spain (1987–90), the Netherlands (1987–90), Portugal (1987–90) and Ireland (1983–90 and 1987–90 but not 1983–7). Structural change effects dominate in France, and Luxembourg (1983–90, 1987–90 but not 1983–7), and also the UK (1983–90 taken as a whole, and 1987–90 but there are strong share effects in 1983–1987). The results for the UK for the period 1987–90 may not be reliable due to problems of missing data, particularly for men in 1990. It is notable that there is less evidence of share effects becoming more important in the second sub-period than was the case for the industry level analysis – but some of the industry share effects may have reflected relative growth of occupations such as administrative and clerical relative to production occupations, so there is not an expectation that the two sets of analyses should point in the same direction.[3]

One problem in fact of interpreting the occupational data is the close interrelations between some of the occupational groups and sectoral divisions; for example, service occupations and agricultural occupations may be regarded as much as industrial as occupational classifications. However, more detailed analysis of the contributions to the overall share and structural change effects reveals strong effects from the professional and the clerical categories, indicating that these results are not solely reflecting industrial structure change but also change in occupational categories. For the majority of countries both the structural change and the share effects are dominated by these two occupational groups. This supports our earlier analyses of segregation changes which showed an increasing importance of professional jobs in women's employment, and indeed of clerical jobs, particularly in the Benelux and Southern countries of the EU where female shares of clerical work were fairly low at the beginning of the 1980s (Rubery and Fagan 1993).

The full-time equivalent calculations tend to reduce the estimated increase in female employment shares, except in Greece and Luxembourg. What is notable is that the share effect still remains positive in almost all countries (Luxembourg and France in 1987–90 are the main exceptions), indicating that women's employment share within occupations is rising independently of rising shares of part-time employment.

Segregation by industry, occupation and employment contract: future employment prospects for men and women

Overall the direction of change over recent years has favoured the employment of women. Industrial and occupational restructuring has had a negative impact on male traditional jobs and has expanded the share of female traditional jobs. This restructuring in favour of women's jobs has occurred both at the sectoral level, and within sectors. Moreover, the increasing use of part-time work has also acted to increase the employment of women, although here most of the change has involved increasing use of part-time work within sectors, perhaps indicating more of a substitution of part-time for full-time jobs within female job sectors. However, even on a full-time equivalent basis, women's employment has tended to expand in both relative and absolute terms.

So far we have been considering the pattern of change primarily from the perspective of the quantity of employment. These patterns of employment change also have implications for the quality of jobs. Summarising the impact on the quality of jobs is more complex as there are clearly divergent experiences both between countries and between groups of women. The increasing share of women employed within sectors and occupations is evidence of the pattern found in previous reports of both decreasing and increasing segregation. Women have been making breakthroughs into tra-ditional male higher level jobs and at the same time expanding their share of already feminised lower skilled or lower paid occupations and sectors. The dominance of 'other services' in female employment growth is particu-larly significant: this sector accounts for most of the job growth stemming both from industrial change and from changes in female employment shares.

Future employment prospects for women will depend strongly both on the pattern of structural change and on the extent of discrimination in recruitment and selection processes. The experience of East Germany pro-vides a salutary reminder that where male unemployment increases, women's access to traditional job sectors may even be restricted (see Box 3.3). Desegregation has occurred in areas of feminised work such as clerical and bank work. However, the French national report for the Beijing Con-ference presents an alternative optimistic scenario where the development of new job areas, not tied to gender stereotypes, should expand and diversify female employment opportunities (see Box 3.3). Whatever the prospects for changes in gender patterns of recruitment and selection, these have to be set against structural changes which now appear to be threatening female job areas, such as clerical work, which up to now have been relatively protected from restructuring. Another important area which up to now has offered a relatively safe haven is the public sector (see Box 3.4). This sector has not only provided relatively stable and often reasonably well-paid employment but also changed the conditions under which care work is undertaken – from private domestic in the household, to the public provi-sion of services based on market wages. Current proposals in many coun-tries to 'reform' the public sector thus pose threats to female employment on two counts – threats to the pay level and job security associated with public sector employment, and threats to the availability of public services. The quality of employment opportunities cannot be fully described by

---

Box 3.3 Occupational change

In **Denmark** there has been a structural change in the female labour force from unskilled and low-level employees to high and middle-level employee occupations. This development in the female occupational structure is argued to be the main reason for the shift in employment from part-time to full-time jobs. Still more women want full-time employment to be able to utilise their educational achievements (Boje 1995: 36).

In the former **East Germany** around 40 per cent of unemployed women come from clerical occupations. This concentration arises for two reasons: the overstaffing in these administrative occupations under the previous regime and the entry of men into what were previously regarded as solely female occupations such as bank clerks. This reverse desegregation has been fuelled by the high unemployment among men and the rising status of some of these occupations under the new regime (Maier and Rapp 1995: 35).

In **France** the national report prepared for the UN World Conference on Women in Beijing identified the factors accounting for the increased rate of female activity to include not solely the growth of traditional female jobs in the service sector but also the development of new jobs which had a less gender-specific image than traditional jobs, and the rapid pace of technological change which had reduced the importance of physical differences in working and employment conditions (Silvera et al. 1995: 61).

---

reference to either occupation or sector; also important are the characteristics of organisations in which women are employed and the nature of the employment contract. Public sector organisations are likely to provide better employment conditions than private sector organisations to which public service work may be subcontracted. These differences in quality of job opportunities do not, however, appear in current employment statistics. Even within the private sector women are often overrepresented in small firms where employment conditions are less likely to be favourable, although the situation varies between member states (see Box 3.5).

Women are also overrepresented in temporary contracts and in part-time jobs. Part-time work tends to increase female employment segregation and is also more associated with unstable employment and insecure contracts than full-time work. Thus employment trends which may favour women's employment – towards more part-time or more temporary jobs – may also be leading to a deterioration in the quality of work for women. Demand side changes probably dominate the overall employment patterns, and much of the recent albeit delayed growth of part-time jobs in Southern countries is attributable primarily to demand side patterns (see Box 3.6). However, women are not necessarily passive actors in the labour market.

Box 3.4 Public sector employment

The growth of the public sector has played a particularly important role in the development of female participation, especially in Scandinavian countries such as **Denmark**. Not only has the socialisation or decommodification of care work released female labour for the labour market, but also it is precisely in the public service industries delivering the care work where most women have found paid work, or have become 'commodified'. Current proposals to roll back the welfare state will hurt women twice, reducing their access to paid work and increasing their obligation to undertake unpaid care work. There is little mobility between public and private sectors in Denmark, and such mobility as does exist tends to be somewhat higher from private to public rather than vice versa. This segregation of the labour markets will reinforce women's dependence on future employment trends in the public sector (Boje 1995: 33).

In **Spain** there has been a particularly rapid rise in the female share of the public sector – up over 12 percentage points from 29 per cent to nearly 42 per cent between 1983 and 1992. Part-time jobs have also expanded rapidly in the public sector, albeit from a much lower starting-point even than in the private sector (Moltó 1995: 48, 51, 102).

Box 3.5 Representation in small and medium-sized enterprises

In **Spain** women appear to be underrepresented in small enterprises (fewer than 50 employees) and to have a higher share of contracts in medium and large firms. However, when only employees on permanent contracts are considered, women's representation by size of firm is fairly similar; the difference arises only because of a high concentration of women on temporary contracts especially in enterprises with more than 250 employees. Here women's share rises to 47 per cent of all on temporary contracts compared to an overall share of those on temporary contracts of 35 per cent (Moltó 1995: 61).

Information from **Germany** in 1987 suggests that women are overrepresented in small firms compared to men: 54 per cent were employed in firms with under 50 employees compared to 48 per cent of all employees. Within sectors there was no particular evident tendency for women to be overrepresented systematically in small enterprises, except in the industrial sectors; for example women accounted for only 20 per cent of employees in enterprises with 1,000 or more employees compared to shares ranging from 26 to 35 per cent in all other size ranges (Maier and Rapp 1995: Table 2.1.5).

In **France** women are overrepresented in small and medium-sized enterprises according to data relating primarily to the private sector; only 9 per cent of women employees are in enterprises with more than 500 employees compared to 13 per cent of men. Most of this overconcentration in small firms can be explained by sector effects, relating to the high share of small enterprises in private services. A different picture might be found if the public sector were included (Silvera *et al.* 1995: 68).

In Denmark, the declining shares of women in part-time work is directly attributed to rising educational levels and job attainment by women, resulting in demands by women to use their skills and attributes more fully in the labour market (see Box 3.1). However, it is not necessarily the case that women in all countries will be able to exert this type of influence on labour market trends, and women's employment growth may remain associated with the growth of more casualised and more part-time employment forms.

Box 3.6 Part-time job growth

Part-time work has recently grown rapidly in **Spain** and **Portugal**, from a very low starting-point. This may suggest some convergence between Southern and Northern countries, although similar patterns are not found in **Italy** and **Greece**, where part-time work has fallen or remained stable. In Spain the evidence suggests that the growth in services, retail and catering has been demand side driven. More information is necessary to identify whether this growth is due to changes in industrial organisation and patterns of work organisation in services (Moltó 1995: 49, 54).

4

UNEMPLOYMENT, GENDER AND LABOUR MARKET ORGANISATION

Unemployment rates for women have grown alongside employment rates. Thus although recent economic conditions have increased women's employment opportunities relative to past trends, these opportunities have not kept pace with the share of women seeking wage work. Moreover, although women appear to be doing better than men in maintaining their employment, they are doing this from a lower overall base. Thus women constitute the largest source of labour reserve in the European Union and there are many more women without work than is the case for men.

The lower overall employment rate for women can in fact provide some of the explanation for the simultaneous rise in employment and unemployment; because of the large hidden reserve, unemployed women have to compete with non-employed women when jobs become available and thus the risk of remaining unemployed may be high despite new job opportunities for women, simply because of the overall size of the available female reserve. Obviously, other factors intervene to explain which groups of women become trapped in unemployment. However, although there is a tendency across most of Europe for women's unemployment to exceed that of men's, the actual characteristics of the female unemployed are quite different between member states. These different characteristics arise both out of the system of gender relations and out of the organisation of the labour market, and the different nature of the unemployment problem may demand different policy solutions. This chapter explores the nature of the unemployment problem in different member states, drawing extensively on information on transitions between economic activity statuses as well as on studies which have identified factors which affect the risk of unemployment by gender, age or country.

4.1 Gender differences in unemployment rates

The unemployment rate of women, as we have documented (see Chapter 2), exceeds that of men in all member states except the UK, and in Ireland for 1992. The gap between male and female unemployment rates has narrowed over recent years – from around 3 percentage points in 1983 to just over 2 percentage points in 1992 at the E10 level (but at the E12 level this gap widens to 2.8 percentage points due to the large gender gap in Spain: see section 2.1). Much of the narrowing of the gap can be attributed to the decreasing importance of youth unemployment over the 1980s in total unemployment. As young people constitute a higher share of the female labour force than the male labour force in many countries, high youth unemployment tends disproportionately to boost the female unemployment rate. The decrease in the gender gap has been much smaller for the 25–49 year old population; here the gender gap was around 2.7 percentage points at E10 level in 1983 but by 1992 this gap had narrowed to only around 2.3 percentage points. Moreover, by 1992 there was a larger gender gap for the 25–49 year old population than was found for the whole working-age population (15–64) at both the E10 and the E12 level (2.3 percentage points compared to 2.1 for E10 and 3 compared to 2.8 for E12), in contrast to the situation in 1983 when the gender gap for the 15–64 population exceeded that for the 25–49 population by 0.3 of a percentage point.

Thus the problem for women's unemployment has become increasingly that of unemployment among the core working-age group and not solely or mainly that of youth unemployment. Unemployment rates for young people have risen again in the recent recession but this has in fact disproportionately affected young men. Moreover, because of the decreasing participation rate of young people, even though actual unemployment rates have returned to the very high levels of the early 1980s, the impact on average unemployment rates for the whole working-age population is much reduced. Thus the issue becomes more that of explaining the continuing high ratios of female unemployment relative to men throughout the age structure.

Although the UK stands out as the exception, with lower unemployment rates for women at all age ranges, there are, as we have already seen, also notable differences in the pattern of unemployment rates between the other member states. Seven countries – eight when we include the rates for Unified Germany – have a significant gender gap in unemployment rates, ranging from 3.4 percentage points in the case of Unified Germany to 11.6 percentage points in the case of Spain. Three of the Southern countries – Spain, Greece, Italy – have the highest gender gaps, followed by Belgium, France, the Netherlands and Unified Germany. Denmark, Portugal, former West Germany and Luxembourg also have higher unemployment rates for women but the gap is only around 1 percentage point, while Ireland in 1992 actually recorded a slight negative gender gap, reversing the positive gaps found in 1983 and 1987.

In all the countries with a large gender gap the female unemployment rates exceed the male rates for all age groups, at least up to age 50 and often beyond. Nevertheless, even within these countries there is some difference

113

by age groups in the relative size of the gender unemployment gap. Thus in Greece it is young women in particular who experience very high rates of unemployment relative to their male counterparts, while in the Netherlands the gender unemployment gap emerges more for the older age groups, with very little difference found for the 15–19 year age group in particular. In the countries with small overall gender unemployment gaps there tends to be more variation between age groups in the size and direction of the gender gap. One feature appears to be common across all five countries (Denmark, Portugal, former West Germany, Luxembourg and Ireland) and it is that young male adults appear to have a similar or worse experience of unemployment than young female adults (aged 20–24) in these countries (except in Portugal but here the gap is less than half of 1 percentage point). However, the UK still stands out as the only country with significantly higher male unemployment rates in every age category.

4.2 Flows into and out of unemployment, employment and inactivity

Some insight into the labour market processes that result in the higher measured female employment rate in most member states, and into the variations between member states, can be obtained by consideration of labour market flows (see Figure 4.1). Table 4.1 shows the rates of flows in and out of unemployment, together with the female share of flows into unemployment and the female share of the long-term unemployed. The first point to note is that the average unemployment rate is not correlated with the rate of inflows into unemployment. In fact for most of the member states the rate of inflow is relatively low, varying only between 0.1 and 0.3 per cent of the source population (see note to Table 4.1) for nine out of eleven member states (no data for Luxembourg). Two countries stand out as having high rates of inflow into unemployment – the UK and Denmark at 0.6 and 0.7 per cent of the source population – but these countries have unemployment rates close to or only slightly above EU averages. The key factor determining average unemployment rates is the outflow rate, and it is this rate that varies most over the cycle. Thus we find the comparison between countries in Table 4.1 cannot be taken as representing a stable ordering of countries by outflow rate as this will depend on the position of the country with respect to the economic cycle. Nevertheless, we find patterns here which help explain variations between countries in unemployment experience. For example, the very high rates of unemployment in Spain seem associated with the very low outflow rates from unemployment, while the low unemployment rates in the former West Germany are associated with a low inflow and a relatively high outflow rate. Denmark, but particularly the UK, both have high outflow rates to compensate for their high inflow rates.

Figure 4.1 The dynamics of unemployment

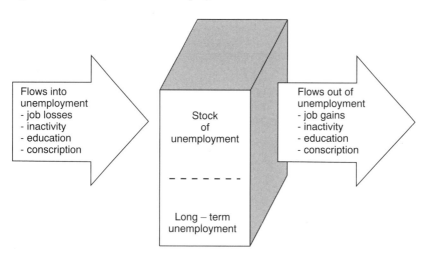

Table 4.1 Flows into and out of unemployment by gender, 1990

	Inflows	Outflows	Women as % of total inflows	Women as % of long-term unemployed	Women as % of labour force
	% Of source population[a]				
Belgium	0.3	5.1	64	64	39.2
Denmark	0.7	8.3	44	56	46.2
Germany	0.2	8.0	52	49	40.9
Greece	0.2	5.6	45	69	37.1
Spain[b]	0.2	2.0	39	60	35.2
France[b]	0.3	5.5	48	60	43.8
Ireland	0.3	4.2	33	30	33.5
Italy	0.2	3.6	53	61	36.7
Netherlands	0.1	5.6	59	50	39.2
Portugal	0.1	3.1	63	65	42.9
UK	0.6	13.4	52	26	43.1

Sources: OECD (1993a: Table 3.3); special tabulations provided by Eurostat
Notes: a Working-age population (15–64) less the unemployed for inflows; total unemployment for outflows
b Data for 1991

The second part of Table 4.1 shows both the female share of inflows into unemployment and the female share of long-term unemployed. In all cases except for Ireland the female share of inflows into unemployment exceeds that of their share of the labour force. This finding provides some clue to the higher female unemployment rate as a disproportionately high share of women enter unemployment on an annual basis; the measured unemployment rate reflects both rate of entry into unemployment and duration of unemployment. This greater tendency for women to enter unemployment undoubtedly in part reflects their higher share of labour market transitions, measured as changes in employment status from employed, unemployed or inactive, and may also reflect their employment in more unstable employment positions, such as temporary jobs, resulting in a higher share of frictional unemployment.

Women are also overrepresented, relative to their share of the labour force, among the long-term unemployed, and for some countries – mainly Belgium, Portugal, former West Germany and the Netherlands – this high share is accounted for, or more than accounted for, by the high female share of entries into unemployment. Thus in Belgium and Portugal women account for just under two-thirds of both the entries into unemployment and the long-term unemployed, while in Germany and the Netherlands the female share of long-term unemployed is around 50 per cent, somewhat lower than the female share of entries into unemployment.

In another set of countries the female share of long-term unemployment is even higher than their share of entries into unemployment – even though the entry share exceeded the female share of the labour force. Here, women's higher unemployment rate is due not only to a higher risk of entering unemployment but also to an even higher risk than men of remaining unemployed. These countries include Denmark, France and Italy, where the female share of long-term unemployed is between 8 and 12 percentage points higher than the female share of entries into unemployment. Greece and Spain are also in this group, where the female share of long-term unemployed is some 21 to 24 percentage points higher. The UK again stands out as an exception, for although women account for a disproportionate share of the inflow into unemployment, they are heavily underrepresented among the long-term unemployed, at only 26 per cent of all long-term unemployed. This share is not that much below the share found in Ireland, but in the latter country women account for only a third of the inflows into unemployment, close to their share of the labour force.

Flows into unemployment

To understand the problem of unemployment we need information not only on the stock of persons who are unemployed but also on the patterns of change in economic activity status which lead people to enter unemployment. Do the unemployed move into unemployment from employment or from inactivity? What share of those who start to look for work were employed or inactive prior to seeking work? And do these patterns vary by country and indeed by gender?

These questions can be investigated using a range of data available from the Labour Force Survey. Figure 4.2 shows the share of the unemployed

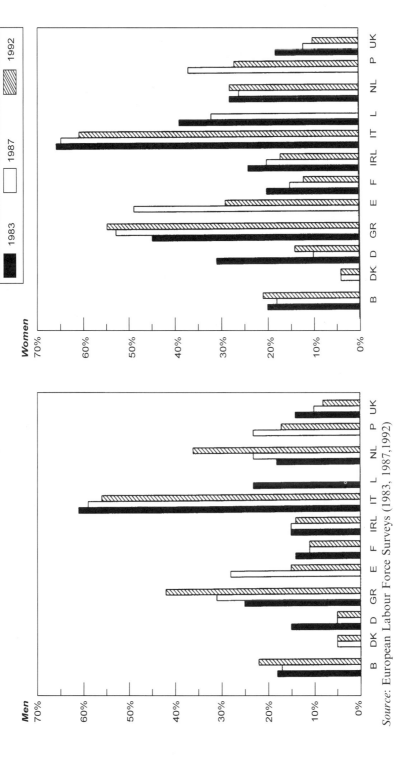

Figure 4.2 Share of the unemployed aged 15–64 who have never worked, 1983–92

Source: European Labour Force Surveys (1983, 1987, 1992)

who have no previous experience of employment. This reveals major differences between countries and indeed changes over time in the share of first jobseekers among the unemployed. First jobseekers are more important within the unemployed in the Southern countries, but even within these countries there are marked differences and trends. For example, first jobseekers account for the majority of the unemployed, both male and female, in Italy but the share is falling gradually. Greece has the next-highest share of first jobseekers among the unemployed at 55 per cent for women and 42 per cent for men, but in contrast to Italy the share is rising. In both Spain and Portugal the share of first jobseekers among the unemployed has fallen rapidly since 1987 for both women and men. There have also been gradual declines in the shares of first jobseekers among the unemployed in most of the Northern countries (four out of seven for men and women), with the Netherlands the only country other than Greece to record a significant rise. For most countries, therefore, the majority of the unemployed have had some work experience at some time in the past, and this applies to women as well as to men. It is only Greek and Italian unemployed women who tend not to have had any work experience, with first jobseekers accounting for 55 per cent and 61 per cent of all unemployed respectively, while in all other countries at least 70 per cent of unemployed women had worked at some time in the past.

The Labour Force Survey also provides information on what respondents who are currently seeking work were doing immediately before they started to seek work. These data include some persons who, although seeking work, do not conform to all the requirements to be classified as unemployed and are thus in the inactive category. These data, however, provide more direct information on whether the unemployed primarily come from employment, education or other forms of inactivity. Table 4.2 shows the employment status of those seeking employment in 1992 immediately before the person started to seek employment. At the E12 level nearly two-thirds of men but only 49 per cent of women (45 per cent excluding the new Länder) had started seeking work from employment, while only around 18 per cent of men and women had started seeking work from full-time education. Major gender differences are found when we look at the shares seeking work from domestic activity; this accounted for 29/27 per cent (excluding/including the new Länder) of women jobseekers, but for less than 2 per cent of male jobseekers. One in twenty male jobseekers had come from conscription, an activity status of no relevance for most women.

There is, however, still no standard European pattern of flows into unemployment or jobseeking; Table 4.2 provides evidence both of the continuing strong differences between member states in both labour market and household organisation and of their implications for gendered patterns of unemployment. First, although entry into unemployment from domestic responsibilities is overwhelmingly a female preserve, when we look at the

Table 4.2a Situation of jobseekers immediately before starting to seek work, 1992

	Men			Women		
	% Working	% Education	% Conscription	% Working	% Education	% Domestic work
Belgium	56	15	4	51	14	22
Denmark	77	20	—	77	20	3
Germany[a]	73/80	9/6	2/1	58/76	7/4	25/14
Greece	47	17	24	25	31	39
Spain	77	13	4	54	20	21
France	80	6	4	72	8	17
Ireland	72	16	—	35	22	39
Italy	24	39	13	14	33	45
Luxembourg	51	—	—	—	—	42
Netherlands	60	30	2	48	25	21
Portugal	64	15	4	49	18	30
UK	73	17	—	39	17	38
E12[a]	64/65	18/18	5/5	45/49	20/18	29/27

Table 4.2b Change in shares of jobseekers by situation immediately before starting to seek work, 1983–92/1987–92[b] (percentage point change)

	Men			Women		
	% Working	% Education	% Conscription	% Working	% Education	% Domestic work
Belgium	−8	−0	−1	−3	−1	−4
Denmark[b]	+5	−4	—	+3	−20	—
Germany[b]	−8	+3	−1	−1	+1	+1
Greece	−16	+1	+9	−4	+3	−2
Spain[b]	+18	−13	−2	+20	−22	+3
France	+15	−7	−1	+22	−10	−4
Ireland	+5	−7	—	+8	−12	+2
Italy	+14	−4	+6	+9	−2	+5
Luxembourg	−14	—	—	−2	—	+8
Netherlands	−11	+9	−2	+17	−8	−13
Portugal[b]	—	—	—	—	—	—
UK[b]	0	+1	—	+1	+1	−2
E10[bc]	+3	0	0	+6	−3	0

Source: Special tabulation provided by Eurostat
Notes: a Data for Germany and E12 exclude/include the new Länder
  b 1987–92
  c Excludes Portugal and Spain

119

data by member state we find that the share of females seeking work who were previously engaged in domestic responsibilities ranges from only 3 per cent in Denmark to 45 per cent in Italy. Five countries have ratios of 38 per cent or above, while four are in the 20 per cent to 30 per cent range and two in the 10 to 20 per cent range (including Unified Germany), with only Denmark recording under 10 per cent. A high share of women seeking work following a spell of domestic responsibilities could be expected to be associated with a number of country-specific factors or characteristics, for example, with high shares of women in inactivity, with labour markets where the risk of unemployment is concentrated at the point of entry into careers, or with labour markets where the women returner pattern of participation prevails. The countries with a high share of jobseekers previously engaged in domestic activities fit these expectations to some extent: four of the five countries have relatively low participation rates among women which increases the likelihood that the unemployed will come from domestic activity, and these include two of the Southern countries (Greece and Italy) where initial integration is difficult. The only country with high participation is the UK, but this has a returner pattern of participation. What is perhaps surprising is the absence of the two other main returner countries (Germany and the Netherlands) from this category; Germany has a relatively low share of women jobseekers coming from a spell of domestic work, even when the former West Germany is looked at compared to Unified Germany (25 per cent compared to 14 per cent) suggesting perhaps that German 'housewives' may move more easily into work once they start to seek work, thus cutting out spells of being a jobseeker, or that German housewives do not identify themselves as jobseekers as readily as, for example, British women who have taken time out for domestic responsibilities. The Netherlands data are difficult to interpret as the share has varied considerably over recent years. In contrast the shares of the unemployed coming from domestic work for most countries remained fairly stable over the period 1983–92 (Table 4.2).

Table 4.3 provides some further information on the share of women who had been involved in domestic tasks before becoming unemployed (note here that the data, drawn from a study using 1989 ELFS, relate to the unemployed and not the broader category of jobseekers as in Table 4.2). This shows the proportion of unemployed women in this category for five age categories for 1989. What is striking is the high shares of unemployed women who were previously undertaking domestic work in the age categories above 25 in both the Southern countries of Greece and Italy and in three returner countries, the UK, the Netherlands and Ireland (here classified as a returner country for, although the number of returners is still relatively low, continuous participation is still relatively uncommon). In Germany, despite also having a women returner participation profile, the share of women aged 25–34 who are unemployed after a domestic spell is only 27 per cent compared to 60 per cent in the UK, 55 per cent in the Netherlands and 52 per cent in Ireland. France and Spain join Germany in having a relatively low share even of core-age women during the child-bearing phase of the lifecycle being in domestic work prior to becoming unemployed; these low ratios probably reflect two very different influences – a high rate of integration of women in France and indeed Belgium among younger age groups, and the high incidence of temporary employment in Spain, leading to a high share of the unemployed with immediate past work experience.

Table 4.3 Percentage of unemployed women 'keeping house' immediately before unemployment, by age group, 1993

	14–24	*25–34*	*35–44*	*45–54*	*55–64*	*Total*
Belgium	9.5	16.5	22.0	(15.4)	—	15.9
Denmark	—	—	—	—	—	(2.8)
Germany	9.6	26.7	28.9	20.9	10.4	23.5
Greece	20.7	56.0	65.3	47.3	—	40.4
Spain	9.5	18.0	35.1	27.9	19.2	16.9
France	6.6	21.1	31.0	14.3	(7.6)	17.6
Ireland	(12.1)	52.0	68.6	(68.5)	—	42.2
Italy	36.1	60.0	70.9	63.6	48.4	49.5
Luxembourg	—	—	—	—	—	(49.2)
Netherlands	12.8	54.9	65.5	66.5	(54.6)	47.3
Portugal	31.9	38.9	44.6	(58.9)	—	37.2
UK	31.4	60.3	56.6	48.9	34.4	47.2
E12	20.5	37.4	45.5	32.7	19.3	31.4

Source: Eurostat (1993a: Table 3.3)

When we look at the data for share of jobseekers previously in work we find further evidence of diversity between member states. For men there is an overall higher share of jobseekers previously in work, but even here there is significant variation: six countries have shares between 70 and 80 per cent, four have shares between 51 and 64 per cent, and Greece and Italy have even lower shares of jobseekers who were in work at 47 per cent and 24 per cent respectively (Table 4.2). These figures are indicative of quite a different situation – the problem of initial entry into the labour market. In Greece the share of jobseekers previously in work has fallen, but in Italy it has risen from a remarkably low level of 9 per cent in 1983. Other countries with strong increases in the share in employment prior to seeking work include Spain (58 per cent to 77 per cent 1987–92), France (68 per cent to 80 per cent) and Portugal (55 per cent to 64 per cent 1987–92).

For women we find even greater country diversity in shares of jobsee-kers previously in work: three countries (France, Denmark and Unified

Germany) have shares above 70 per cent; four between 40 and 60 per cent (Belgium, Spain, the Netherlands and Portugal – plus former West Germany) while five have shares below 40 per cent (three with shares between 30 and 40 per cent – the UK, Ireland and Luxembourg – but Greece and Italy again with the lowest shares at 25 per cent and 14 per cent respectively). Six countries have had rapid rises in the share of jobseekers who were in work: Spain (33 per cent to 54 per cent 1987–92), Germany (60 per cent to 76 per cent 1987–92), France (51 per cent to 72 per cent), Italy (5 per cent to 14 per cent), the Netherlands (31 per cent to 48 per cent) and the UK (24 per cent to 39 per cent). These changes in shares of women jobseekers previously in work are likely to reflect three interrelated factors: higher work experience in general among the female population; more flexible labour markets increasing risk of job loss for those in employment; and declining shares of young people among the unemployed.

The share becoming jobseekers from full-time education also shows variations by country. For men the share reaches or exceeds 30 per cent in two cases – Italy and the Netherlands – while seven countries have shares between 10 and 20 per cent, and Germany (both Unified and former West Germany) and France have shares below 10 per cent. France has witnessed a marked decline in the share of jobseekers coming from full-time education over the 1980s, probably associated with a rise in special employment schemes for young people (Silvera *et al.* 1995: 84). The only other countries where the share has fallen significantly for men are Spain and Ireland, again associated with declines in the share of young people among the unemployed. The pattern for women is relatively similar to that for men, except that Greece joins Italy with a share over 30 per cent and Ireland and the Netherlands have shares over 20 per cent; otherwise the same countries have shares, between 10 and 20 per cent and below 10 per cent. The gender gap in shares of jobseekers coming from full-time education is usually quite small. The main exception is Greece, where 31 per cent of female jobseekers come from this source compared to 17 per cent male jobseekers, but this is due to high shares of men seeking work after conscription. Spain, Ireland and France have all seen decreases in the shares entering unemployment from full-time education over recent years.

Further information on the pattern of flows into jobseeking can be gleaned from Table 4.4 which shows the economic activity status immediately before the jobseeker started to seek work, this time divided into first jobseekers and those with previous work experience (see Figure 4.3 for description of status prior to becoming a jobseeker). The share of first jobseekers differs somewhat from the data given in Figure 4.2, which considered only those who are classified as unemployed, while these data include all those currently seeking work, but the basic pattern of differences between Southern and Northern countries remains.

Table 4.4 Situation of jobseekers immediately before starting to seek work by previous work experience, 1992

Men	Never worked		Worked before			Those who have never worked as share of all jobseekers (%)
	% Education	% Conscription	% Working	% Education	% Conscription	
Belgium	62	11	72	—	—	24
Denmark	81	—	82	16	—	6
Germany[a]	39/40	—	79/85	6/5	1/1	8/5
Greece	35	49	82	—	4	44
Spain	69	13	41	2	2	16
France[b]	41	18	88	1	3	12
Ireland	84	—	87	—	—	17
Italy	62	18	57	6	6	59
Luxembourg	—	—	65	—	—	—
Netherlands[b]	63	6	80	11	—	36
Portugal	70	—	76	4	4	23
UK	84	—	81	10	—	10
E12[a]	62/62	15/15	81/82	6/5	2/2	23/21

Women	Never worked		Worked before			Those who have never worked as share of all jobseekers (%)
	% Education	% Domestic	% Working	% Education	% Domestic	
Belgium	60	23	65	—	21	22
Denmark	88	—	81	16	3	5
Germany[a]	31/34	31/23	64/80	5/3	24/13	10/5
Greece	51	43	58	3	35	57
Spain	58	31	76	4	17	30
France[b]	46	39	82	1	13	14
Ireland	82	12	44	4	47	23
Italy	49	46	38	8	44	62
Luxembourg	—	—	44	—	47	29
Netherlands[b]	63	7	56	10	27	27
Portugal	56	36	65	4	28	18
UK	76	13	44	8	42	13
E12[a]	52/52	38/38	63/67	5/5	26/23	31/28

Source: Special tabulation provided by Eurostat
Notes: a Data for Germany and E12 exclude/include the new Länder
   b High share of those coded as 'never worked' claimed to be working immediately before seeking work (France: 19% male, 12% female; Netherlands: 27% male, 26% female).

The main prior activities of men who are first jobseekers are full-time education or conscription. The latter takes on major importance in Greece, accounting for 49 per cent of first jobseekers who in turn account for 44 per cent of male unemployed. Overall 15 per cent of E12 male first job seekers moved into jobseeking from conscription, but this category was significant (accounting for at least 10 per cent of first jobseekers) in only five countries. In contrast over half of all first time male jobseekers had previously been in full-time education in all countries except Greece (because of the high share

Figure 4.3   Situation of jobseekers immediately before starting to seek work

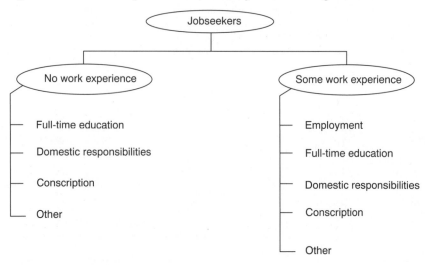

Source: Eurostat (1992)

coming from conscription) and Germany, where the low share may be the result of the dual training system in Germany[1] and the prevalence of part-time education in the school to work transition. Among those male job-seekers who had previously worked, the overwhelming majority become jobseekers direct from employment. In all countries, except Italy and Luxembourg, more than 70 per cent of all those jobseekers with previous work experience had been working immediately prior to seeking work. Denmark, the Netherlands and the UK had a relatively high share of those with previous work experience entering jobseeking from full-time education, perhaps indicating the increasing integration of wage work and education in these three countries.

For women the two main sources of first jobseekers are full-time education and domestic activity. Domestic activity is a more important source of first jobseekers for women than conscription is for men, accounting at the E12 level for 38 per cent of all female first jobseekers. Consequently the share of women entering from full-time education is lower than for men (52 per cent compared to 62 per cent). However, there is considerable variation between countries in the share coming from domestic work, ranging from 7 per cent in the Netherlands to 46 per cent in Italy. Denmark has such a small share of women in this category that no accurate estimate can be given. The division of the sample by previous work experience helps to sort out those countries where women are leaving domestic activity for the first time and attempting to enter wage employment, and those where women tend to enter wage employment and then quit to look after children. About a quarter (26 per cent) of all women (E12 excluding former East Germany) who had previously had work experience entered jobseeking from domestic activities, but again there is evidence of variation by country. Five countries had shares of 35 per cent or more, including two Southern countries (Greece and Italy), and three countries where there is a developed or emergent returner pattern – the UK, Ireland and Luxembourg. In Portugal, Germany and the Netherlands, between 24 per cent and 28 per cent of women entered employment from domestic activity, with the latter two countries again failing to show the high share of women returners that might be expected from their participation patterns, suggesting a higher share go straight into employment from inactivity. The countries with the lowest shares of those with previous work experience entering from domestic activities include three with established or emerging continuous employment patterns for women (Belgium, France and Denmark) together with Spain. In the last case the low share of women entering from domestic activities may in fact be a reflection of the large share forced to enter jobseeking from employment as a consequence of the high share of women on temporary contracts in Spain. Only 13 per cent of unemployed women with previous work experience entered from domestic activity in Unified Germany, compared to 24 per cent when only the former West Germany is considered. This difference reflects both the very high share of East German women among the unemployed and the different career profiles of East and West German women.

While the data we have been examining so far refer to the economic situation of jobseekers immediately before they started their current period of job search – and thus can refer to economic activity statuses at different points in the past – data from the LFS also allow us to look at the economic activity statuses of the unemployed one year prior to the survey. This reveals a similar pattern; a much higher share of women enter unemployment from inactivity than is the case for men at the E12 level and within each country (Figure 4.4 and Table 4.5). For men all shares are below 27 per cent (excluding Greece), while for women six countries have shares of 37 per cent and above and only Denmark has a share below 20 per cent compared to six countries for men. These higher shares entering from inactivity result in lower shares entering from employment in most countries than is the case for men.

These differences in labour market flows between countries reflect different systems of labour market organisation as well as different patterns of female integration into the wage economy. Greece and Italy can be singled out as still having a low share of jobseekers with previous immediate work experience, a high share, particularly among women, coming from full-time education and also a high share of women jobseekers coming from domestic activities. These findings fit a labour market system where there are difficulties in initial integration into employment for both women and men, but

Figure 4.4 Labour market flows: European averages (E12), 1992

A Inflows into unemployment / inactivity / employment

B Outflows from unemployment / inactivity / employment

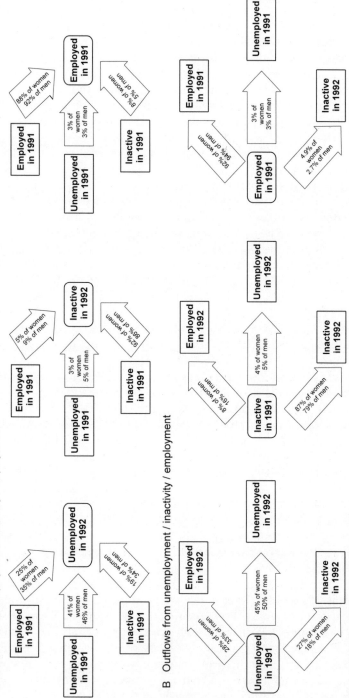

Source: European Labour Force Survey (1992)
Notes: A employed + unemployed + inactive = 100% in 1992
B employed + unemployed + inactive = 100% in 1991

Table 4.5 Share of unemployed who were employed, unemployed or inactive one year previously, 1983–92

	Men									Women								
	Employed (%)			Unemployed (%)			Inactive (%)			Employed (%)			Unemployed (%)			Inactive (%)		
	1983	1987	1992	1983	1987	1992	1983	1987	1992	1983	1987	1992	1983	1987	1992	1983	1987	1992
Belgium	28	18	24	52	69	49	20	14	27	16	13	21	64	72	49	20	15	31
Denmark	44	69	61	38	22	23	18	9	15	38	58	55	35	32	29	27	10	16
Germany[a]	44	38	38/47	42	50	41/37	15	13	22/17	39	28	33/50	39	50	35/32	23	23	32/18
Greece	48	38	33	17	34	33	36	28	34	20	16	15	21	46	35	59	38	50
Spain	—	19	34	—	64	46	—	17	20	—	11	19	—	65	55	—	24	26
France	38	36	39	44	51	42	18	13	19	25	27	30	44	47	40	32	25	31
Ireland	35	24	26	55	70	66	10	7	7	24	17	21	23	31	29	53	52	50
Italy[b]	17	—	16	54	—	62	29	—	22	9	—	11	49	—	44	42	—	46
Luxembourg	43	39	45	36	37	—	20	49	24	31	32	36	20	—	—	49	47	40
Netherlands[b]	38	—	31	42	—	45	—	16	26	21	—	24	21	—	39	59	76	37
Portugal	—	30	44	—	53	30	13	14	14	—	17	33	—	58	39	—	26	27
UK	33	30	43	55	56	42	18	—	19	28	28	36	33	28	27	39	44	36
E10[c]	34	—	35	48	—	46	18	—	—	24	—	26	40	—	37	36	—	37
E12[a]	—	—	35/37	—	—	46/45	—	—	19/18	—	—	25/28	—	—	41/40	—	—	34/31

Source: Special tabulations provided by Eurostat

Notes: a Data for Germany and E12 exclude/include the new Länder
      b 1987 data omitted as show very large movements between statuses compared to 1983 anc 1992
      c Excludes Portugal and Spain

also one where once integrated there is a relatively low risk of job loss for those in formal sector work, for men and for women. The result of this type of labour market system is often an 'opt in/opt out' labour market participation pattern for women, with those who successfully integrate into employment staying in work while other women remain inactive and/or discouraged workers. However, there is also evidence in some Southern countries – namely Spain and Greece – of an increase in the entry of middle-aged women into unemployment from inactivity, suggesting that this model may be breaking down as women's desire to enter wage work spreads into the older age cohorts. Indeed the share of female first jobseekers aged below 25 fell from 81 per cent to 57 per cent between 1983 and 1992 (Moltó, 1995: 82). Spain still has an 'opt in/opt out' pattern of participation but makes greater use of flexible employment, particularly temporary contracts. Thus unlike Greece and Italy the unemployed are not primarily first jobseekers, or entering unemployment from inactivity, but instead include a higher share of those who are long-term participants but unable to secure a permanent job. Problems of initial integration appear much less problematic in countries such as Germany where most of the jobseekers come from those in employment, possibly as a result of the dual training system that reduces the share of persons excluded from employment at the start of their careers (Maier 1995).

While the overall data reveal continuing differences between countries, there is also evidence of some degree of convergence as, for example, more flexible labour markets and higher shares of women in work reduce the share of jobseekers coming from various forms of inactivity into unemployment. In Denmark, for example, the higher share of jobseekers with work experience may in part be attributed to the frequent use of temporary layoff in Denmark. High levels of unemployment benefits allow firms to use temporary layoff as means of labour demand adjustment in Denmark without facing opposition from workers. Moreover, higher benefits allow employees to move between jobs without risk of major income loss (Boje 1995: 41). This is a different kind of flexibility from that found in countries where ending of fixed term contracts is an important source of entry into unemployment, as this is an involuntary ejection into unemployment independent of the existence or adequacy of benefits. Ending of temporary contracts is cited as an important and often increasing source of entry into unemployment particularly for women, for example, in Spain and Belgium (see Box 4.1). In Italy job loss became an increasing source of unemployment for both men and women, and in Greece dismissal and redundancy increased for women but more so for men, while ending of fixed term contracts reduced in importance for both. In Portugal the ending of fixed term contracts is a more important cause of entry into unemployment for women than for men, but the share affected fell in both cases significantly since the late 1980s (from 77 per cent to 35 per cent for women and from 62 per cent to 30 per cent for men from 1987 to 1992: Lopes and Perista 1995: 43), associated probably in part with a change in legislation with respect to employment contracts in 1989 which reduced the distinction between permanent and temporary contracts (González and Castro 1995).

Box 4.1 Employment flexibility increases women's risks of unemployment

In **Belgium** in 1991 ending of a limited term contract was the reason why nearly 36 per cent of the female unemployed who had been employed within the past three years left their job, up from 24 per cent in 1983. The comparable figures for men were 24 per cent and 18 per cent (Meulders 1995: 59).

In **Spain**, although we do not know how many of those entering unemployment came from a temporary contract, we do know that 90 per cent of women on a temporary contract had taken the job because they could not find a permanent contract. As temporary contracts account for over a third of Spanish women in employment, it seems that temporary contracts are often the only options open to the unemployed, and are also likely to lead to further spells of unemployment (Moltó, 1995: 91).

In **Italy** deregulation policies have been introduced with the apparent aim of stimulating employment. However, while the effects of this policy on employment are not yet fully known, there is some evidence that it is fuelling unemployment – albeit mainly short-term unemployment by Italian standards. This deregulation policy has been introduced alongside a policy towards unemployment where it is redundant workers who are protected and most of the burden is passed onto first jobseekers or intermittent workers, most of whom are women (Bettio and Mazzotta 1995: 95)

In **France**, ending of a temporary job is an important cause of entry into unemployment for both men and women, accounting for 35 per cent of the male unemployed and 33 per cent of the female unemployed; but because of the higher share of women among the unemployed, women in fact account for 54 per cent of all those entering unemployment after the ending of a temporary job (Silvera *et al.* 1995: 84–87).

To the extent that more flexible employment contracts result in a higher share of the unemployed coming from employment instead of inactivity, it can be argued that such policies only shift the burden of unemployment and do not tackle the underlying problem. Moreover, women who are disproportionately affected by problems of integration into employment may also be disproportionately affected by flexible employment strategies. Thus, the problems women face in seeking integration into wage work may now by no means over once a position is found if this is a temporary post. However, the balance of the argument may also depend upon the relative chances of someone with at least some recent work experience moving back into work; evidence from Italy certainly suggests that much of the long-term unemployment is still concentrated among first jobseekers, and those who become unemployed as a result of flexible employment policies at least have a better chance of moving back into employment quickly. The mean duration of job search of first jobseekers has risen dramatically in Italy, from 13 to 15 months for men and women respectively in 1983, to 25 and 26 months in 1992. However, the majority of job losers get a job within the first 4 to 12 months and there has been no marked increase in length of job search over the 1980s (Bettio and Mazzotta 1995: 16; see also Box 4.2). It may also be important for women to be able to make entry relatively quickly into employment after education, to reduce the likelihood that marriage and motherhood will precede entry into a career, thereby reducing long-term career chances.

Box 4.2   Do first-time jobseekers find it harder to find employment?

The Southern countries provide mixed evidence on the relation between entry into unemployment and duration of job search. In **Portugal** the duration of job search for first time jobseekers has been found to be much the same as those with previous work experience, for both men and women (Lopes and Perista 1995: 39–41). In **Italy** the job search duration of first time jobseekers is much longer (Bettio and Mazzotta 1995: 16)

Flows out of unemployment and inactivity

Women, as we have already seen, tend to find it more difficult than men to move out of unemployment. Thus in most countries women constitute a disproportionate share of the long-term unemployed, and indeed often account for a higher share of the long-term unemployed than of the flows into unemployment. The influence of differences in labour market characteristics is still evident in the data on duration of unemployment, although interpretation of these data are complicated by the impact of the cycle on the shares of long-term unemployed. However, four countries stand out as having a very high share of long-term unemployment among women over the whole time period, namely three of the Southern countries, Spain, Greece and Italy, together with Belgium (Table 4.6). The share of the long-term unemployed among the female unemployed population now exceeds 50 per cent also in Ireland, but this represents a significant rise over 1983 where the share was only 25 per cent. The pattern for men is less clear cut, but the highest rates of long-term unemployment were recorded in Ireland, Italy and Belgium in 1992 and in Belgium, Italy and the UK in 1983.

Table 4.6 Share of unemployed remaining unemployed for twelve months or more, 1983–92

	1983		1987		1992	
	Men (%)	Women (%)	Men (%)	Women (%)	Men (%)	Women (%)
Belgium	60.0	70.3	72.2	76.1	56.3	61.0
Denmark	27.3	37.4	23.6	34.3	25.3	28.5
Germany	40.7	37.7	47.2	49.2	37.0[b]	30.6[b]
Greece	24.6	44.6	35.4	54.1	38.2	57.2
Spain	—	—	60.8	71.8	34.9	52.7
France	39.4	44.9	47.0	51.4	32.0	36.7
Ireland	42.3	24.8	70.2	58.2	63.1	51.3
Italy	53.6	58.4	63.6	68.4	58.3	58.1
Luxembourg	(36.8)	(31.1)	(39.9)	(29.0)	—	—
Netherlands	49.0	49.9	50.7	41.3	47.0	41.6
Portugal	—	—	50.6	61.6	25.0	36.5
UK	52.3	36.0	52.9	32.1	39.7	26.6
E12	47.2[a]	46.0[a]	54.7	56.3	40.2[b]	42.1[b]

Source: Special tabulations provided by Eurostat
Notes: a Data for E10
b Data include new Länder

The UK is often presented as a relatively flexible labour market but this has not prevented the development of persistent long-term unemployment, especially among men. Some analysts have suggested that women face fewer problems of social exclusion resulting from long-term unemployment, but this perspective has been challenged by a study in France (see Box 4.3).

Box 4.3   Is long-term unemployment less of a problem for women?

One study in **France** has suggested that women may be less affected by the processes of social exclusion associated with long-term unemployment and exclusion from the labour market. Women may suffer less from the loss of occupational identity, are less likely to be living alone and less likely to suffer from isolation and disinvolvement with the family. However, another study has challenged this analysis, arguing that women who live outside a stable relationship are especially vulnerable, facing risks of prostitution, of being victims of violence and of their children being taken into care. The presence of young children provides access to benefits, but as they grow up access to benefits declines and the risks of social and psychological decline increase. Those women left alone in middle age also face high risks of exclusion as they have little training and face difficulties in supporting themselves and their children (Silvera *et al.* 1995: 27).

131

Table 4.7 Share of unemployed changing activity status over the year, 1982–92

Men	% Remaining unemployed			% In employment one year later			% Inactive one year later		
	1982–3	1986–7	1991–2	1982–3	1986–7	1991–2	1982–3	1986–7	1991–2
Belgium	67	71	49	26	21	18	6	8	33
Denmark	50	37	33	36	44	55	13	18	12
Germany	61	67	45/43[a]	30	17	30/33[a]	9	16	25/24[a]
Greece	48	54	45	49	43	44	—	3	11
Spain	—	62	51	—	34	43	—	4	6
France	47	52	52	40	36	35	13	12	13
Ireland	70	72	62	18	17	14	11	12	23
Italy[b]	58	—	45	38	—	27	4	—	27
Luxembourg	50	46	35	44	41	57	—	—	—
Netherlands	68	60	30	22	28	26	11	12	44
Portugal	—	47	32	—	43	50	—	9	17
UK	60	57	58	26	32	29	14	11	13
E10[c]	58	—	50	31	—	30	11	—	21
E12[a]	—	—	50/49	—	—	33/33	—	—	18/18
Women									
Belgium	75	76	43	17	15	21	8	9	36
Denmark	52	36	33	35	45	51	13	19	16
Germany	55	51	31/37[a]	30	13	27/28[a]	15	36	43/35[a]
Greece	64	70	58	26	22	25	10	7	17
Spain	—	72	63	—	21	27	—	7	10
France	48	54	50	31	27	30	21	20	20
Ireland	52	58	50	29	25	22	19	17	27
Italy[b]	66	—	43	27	—	23	8	—	34
Luxembourg	40	—	—	51	61	60	—	—	—
Netherlands	58	56	23	30	33	22	13	11	54
Portugal	—	54	32	—	28	40	—	19	29
UK	49	42	37	32	40	38	19	19	25
E10[c]	56	—	41	29	—	28	15	—	31
E12[a]	—	—	45/45	—	—	28/28	—	—	27/27

Source: Special tabulation provided by Eurostat
Notes: a Old Germany/new Germany
      b 1987 data omitted as show very high rate of change compared to other years
      c Excludes Portugal and Spain.

We have further information relating to the flows out of unemployment from the labour force survey. Figure 4.4 and Table 4.7 show the economic activity status at the time of the survey of those unemployed twelve months earlier. The aggregate E12 data show that women are more likely to enter inactivity from unemployment than men while men are more likely to move into employment or remain unemployed over the period of a year. Table 4.7 also reveals a fairly widespread tendency not only for the share of the unemployed remaining as unemployed to fall between 1983 and 1992 but also for the share moving from unemployment to inactivity to rise, for both men and for women. Changes in the shares moving into employment are much less consistent, dependent upon whether the reductions in shares remaining unemployed are partially, fully or even more than fully compensated by shares moving into inactivity.[2]

In two countries for which we have national data – Spain and Italy – we find that women have a stronger probability of moving from unemployment into inactivity. In Italy women have as much chance of moving from unemployment into inactivity (16 per cent to housewife status, 4 per cent to student status) as into employment (20 per cent), while men have both a stronger likelihood than women of moving into employment (31 per cent) and a lower likelihood of moving into inactivity (0 per cent to being a 'housewife', 5 per cent to being a student) (Bettio and Mazzotta 1995: Table 7). Women also have a higher chance of remaining in unemployment (57 per cent compared to 52 per cent). In Spain flow data which trace changes in activity status reveal that women account for two-thirds of transitions between unemployment and inactivity, somewhat under one in two of the transitions between employment and inactivity but only around one in three of the transitions between unemployment and employment and vice versa. Women also account for more than half of the transitions from inactivity to employment, missing out on the unemployment status (Moltó 1995: 107–110).

The share of the inactive who are still inactive one year later is higher than the corresponding shares for the unemployed, but lower (as we see below in table 4.9) than the shares maintaining employed activity status between the two dates (Table 4.8). These results are unsurprising given that unemployment is a state which most people wish to move out of, employment is a state which most people wish to retain, and inactivity may fit both categories, depending on the reason for inactivity. Men are somewhat more likely to move out of inactivity than are women, suggesting that it is a somewhat less desirable or stable state for prime-age men, and/ or that most inactive men are undergoing education which comes to a finite end (Figure 4.4). However, there are also major differences in transition rates between countries. The UK and Denmark have high transition rates out of inactivity – in all years but particularly for Denmark in 1991/2 – possibly associated with a tendency to combine education and employment. The male transition rates in 1991/2 are 38 per cent and 52 per cent, and the female rates 23 per cent and 42 per cent for the UK and Denmark respectively. The next highest rate for men is 21 per cent (the Netherlands) and for women 14 per cent (France and the Netherlands). Transition rates are less than 10 per cent for men in Belgium and Luxembourg, and for women in Belgium, Luxembourg, Greece, Spain, Italy and Portugal.

Table 4.8 Share of inactive still inactive one year later, 1983–92

	Men (%)				Women (%)		
	1983	1987	1992		1983	1987	1992
Belgium	88	91	90		94	96	93
Denmark	75	73	48		81	78	58
Germany	83	88	82/82[a]		93	94	89/89[a]
Greece	79	87	87		93	95	93
Spain	—	82	75		—	93	90
France	82	85	84		88	89	86
Ireland	83	86	89		90	89	89
Italy[b]	86	—	84		94	—	91
Luxembourg	86	88	91		93	95	94
Netherlands[b]	84	—	79		91	—	86
Portugal	—	88	85		—	94	92
UK	75	71	62		84	79	77
E10[c]	82	—	79		91	—	87
E12[a]	—	—	79/79		—	—	87/87

Source: Special tabulation provided by Eurostat
Notes: a Old Germany/new Germany
   b 1987 data omitted as show very high rate of change compared to other years
   c Excludes Portugal and Spain

Transitions to and from employment

So far we have been looking at flows from unemployment or inactivity into other economic activity statuses. However, in order to understand labour market processes we also need to look at flows into and out of employment. As is to be expected, the majority of those in employment, both male and female, are still in employment one year later, and thus the interest focuses on differences in the shares moving out of employment into unemployment and inactivity between countries and over time. Similar shares of women and men move into unemployment over the period of a year at the E12 level but women are more likely to move into inactivity, thus slightly reducing the probability that women will be in employment a year later (Figure 4.4). Figure 4.5 categorises the countries by the share of the employed entering unemployment and inactivity. We treat 2 per cent or less moving into unemployment as a low rate of transition, 2 per cent to 4 per cent as a medium rate and over 4 per cent as a high rate, and use the same categories for movement from employment into inactivity. If we first compare the pattern for men and women in 1992 by country, we find that all the countries have high and medium rates of transition into inactivity for women compared to only eight of the countries for men. We also find that nine of the countries have medium or high rates of transition

134

Figure 4.5 Flows from employment into unemployment and inactivity, 1983–92

Flows into unemployment

Men

Flows into inactivity	1983 Low	1983 Medium	1983 High	1987 Low	1987 Medium	1987 High	1992 Low	1992 Medium	1992 High
Low	I	B, D, GR	IRL, UK	B, L, NL, P	D	E, IRL, UK	B, GR, P		IRL
Medium	L	F	DK, NL		DK, Gr, F		I, L, NL	D, F	E, UK
High									DK

Flows into unemployment

Women

Flows into inactivity	1983 Low	1983 Medium	1983 High	1987 Low	1987 Medium	1987 High	1992 Low	1992 Medium	1992 High
Low					B				
Medium	I	B, D, GR	DK, IRL	L, P	D, GR	E, IRL	L, P	B, D, GR	IRL
High	L	F, Nl, UK			NL, UK	F, DK	I	NL, UK	DK, E, F, (UD)

Notes: UD = Unified Germany, D = former West Germany Low = 0–2%, Medium = 2–4%, High = > 4%

into unemployment for women compared to only six for men, suggesting that women's attachment to employment status is more precarious than that of men.

When we look at the patterns by member state we find Denmark has the highest rates of transitions for both men and women out of employment into unemployment and inactivity. These high transition rates may be associated with the use of unemployment benefit as a means of funding temporary layoffs in Denmark. For women France and Spain also come into the highest categories on both counts, but Denmark is the only country to have a high rate of transition into inactivity for men. Ireland also has a high transition into unemployment for women and a 3.7 per cent transition into inactivity, so that it is close to being categorised with the high transition countries on both counts. Three more countries have high transitions for men into unemployment but medium (in the case of Spain and the UK) and low transitions into inactivity, in the case of Ireland. The opposite patterns tend to hold for women, with three countries having high rates of transition into inactivity but with medium (in the case of the UK and the Netherlands) and even low (in the case of Italy) rates of transition into unemployment.

Although the patterns are complex, the typologies of labour market systems which are now becoming relatively familiar are evident; the Southern countries (except for Spain) together with Belgium and Luxembourg tend to have relatively low rates of transition into unemployment, while the less regulated labour markets of Ireland, UK, Denmark (not state regulated, with low employment protection but high trade union organisation) and Spain (with high levels of temporary employment to offset stronger regulation of permanent contracts) tend to have higher rates of transition into unemployment. Other countries, such as Germany and France in the case of men, tend to fit into the middle category. The rates of transition into inactivity reflect both labour market systems and patterns of social reproduction. For example the high rates of transition into inactivity among Italian women may be associated with the very high rates of long-term unemployment, and thus with a discouraged worker effect; those leaving employment for whatever reason may not think it worthwhile to seek for work. Certainly these flows into inactivity have increased in Italy along with higher and longer-term unemployment. Similarly in Spain the high rate of movement into inactivity may also reflect the high rate of unemployment. The high rates of transition into inactivity in the UK and the Netherlands may be more associated with the persistence of the returner model of participation. In Denmark and France, the high rates are somewhat at odds with other data indicating relatively continuous careers for women, thereby raising questions – which cannot be answered by available data – as to whether these rates are indicative of high rates of early retirement in these countries.

When we look at these transition matrices for the years 1983 and 1987 we can identify some differences in patterns but also a high degree of similarity. For men fewer countries had high or medium rates of transition to inactivity in the earlier years, but the number of countries with medium to high transition rates to unemployment was actually higher. Ireland, the UK, Denmark and Spain tended to have the highest rates of transition to unemployment, and again the remaining Southern and Benelux countries rather lower rates (except for the Netherlands in 1983), while France and Germany tending to occupy middle positions. For women there were also somewhat fewer countries with high transitions into inactivity in the earlier years, but in all years few if any countries had low transitions to inactivity. The distribution of countries by transition into unemployment remained very stable, with Italy, Portugal and Luxembourg having low rates of transition, Belgium, Greece, Germany, the Netherlands and the UK medium rates, and Spain, Denmark, Ireland and France high transitions (except for France which had a medium transition rate in 1983). The countries which increased their rates of transition into inactivity were Italy, Spain and Denmark, while Luxembourg reduced its transition rate into inactivity from high to medium over the same period.

Looking at the flows into employment – that is the share of those employed who a year earlier had been unemployed or inactive – we find, unsurprisingly, a higher rate of inflow from inactivity for women than men but there are similar shares moving in from unemployment (Figure 4.4 and Table 4.9). The female inflow rate is higher than the male inflow rate in all countries but there are again differences in levels between countries. Spain, the UK and Denmark have the highest inflow rates for both men and women in 1992, although only the UK maintained a high inflow rate of more than 10 per cent for each of the three years and for women only. The rates of movement into employment from unemployment tend to be lower than the rates of inflow from inactivity in all years; the inflow tends to be greater for women but the gender gaps tend to be smaller than when the rates of inflow from inactivity are compared. Thus flows from unemployment for men do not compensate for the higher flows from inactivity for women, with the result that a lower share of employed women were in employment a year previously. Thus in all countries we have the situation that access to employment appears to be somewhat more fluid for women than for men, yet this greater fluidity or flexibility does not prevent women accounting for a disproportionate share of the long-term unemployed. What is important to note of course is the high share of entrants to employment coming from inactivity for women, so that where jobs are available to those outside employment it may be the inactive who are preferred over the unemployed.

Table 4.9 Share of employed who were unemployed or inactive one year earlier, 1983–92

	Men (%)						Women (%)					
	Unemployed			Inactive			Unemployed			Inactive		
	1983	1987	1992	1983	1987	1992	1983	1987	1992	1983	1987	1992
Belgium	1.8	1.6	0.9	2.8	2.7	2.9	3.2	3.0	2.5	4.5	3.1	4.2
Denmark	2.9	1.4	3.6	3.7	4.5	12.2	2.8	3.1	5.0	5.8	6.8	14.2
Germany	1.3	0.8	1.0/1.5[a]	4.2	2.3	3.7/3.5[a]	1.8	1.1	1.5/2.2[a]	5.9	3.6	6.8/6.2[a]
Greece	1.1	1.5	1.7	3.4	2.5	2.8	1.2	1.9	2.3	5.4	3.8	4.1
Spain	—	7.3	6.1	—	3.5	7.8	—	7.3	7.9	—	7.2	11.4
France	2.4	3.4	2.6	3.5	3.5	4.4	3.4	3.7	3.5	6.9	6.1	7.2
Ireland	2.5	3.5	2.8	2.3	2.6	2.6	2.5	3.1	2.4	9.6	9.7	9.1
Italy	2.1	—	2.8	2.3	—	4.2	3.3	—	3.8	5.1	—	7.1
Luxembourg	0.7	0.7	0.8	3.2	2.7	2.3	1.4	1.5	1.1	9.0	5.1	5.6
Netherlands[b]	1.6	—	1.7	3.5	—	4.6	1.7	—	3.2	7.2	—	9.1
Portugal	—	3.1	1.7	—	1.9	3.2	—	3.3	2.6	—	2.9	4.4
UK	3.3	4.1	2.8	3.9	4.4	8.1	2.4	3.1	2.2	10.0	10.9	12.2
E10[c]	2.2	—	2.2	3.5	—	5.0	2.6	—	2.7	7.0	—	8.4
E12[a]	—	—	2.6/2.6	—	—	5.2/5.1	—	—	3.1/3.1	—	—	8.5/8.2

Source: Special tabulation provided by Eurostat
Notes: a Old Germany/new Germany
     b 1987 data omitted as show very large movements between statuses compared to 1983 and 1992
     c Excludes Portugal and Spain

4.3   Risk of unemployment, according to domestic responsibilities and education and training

Domestic responsibilities and unemployment

Unemployment rates are higher for women with current childcare responsibilities than for those without. At the E12 level in 1989 the unemployment rate for women with a child under 18 was 12.3 per cent compared to 7.6 per cent for all women (see Table 4.10). Young women with children are particularly likely to have high unemployment rates: for women aged 14 to 24 the unemployment rate for mothers was a high 32.4 per cent compared to 11.1 per cent for young women without a child. Having a young child is also associated with a higher risk of unemployment; for those with a youngest child aged under 5 the risk rose to 17.5 per cent and for those with a youngest child 5 to 9 the risk was 12.5 per cent, slightly above the average for all mothers. These increased risks of unemployment for mothers are found in almost all member states, the main exception to this pattern being Denmark. However, even here maternity increases the risk of unemployment for women aged under 25 and more detailed national data do find an increased risk of unemployment for mothers after controlling for factors such as household position and occupational status. However, this disadvantage disappears for highly educated women living in couples with a child

138

(Boje 1995: 52). Having a pre-school child has a particularly strong impact on the unemployment rates of women in the UK, a finding consistent with the well-known problems women face in the UK in finding jobs to fit with childcare arrangements in a society with very limited public provision.

Table 4.10 Unemployment rates for women with and without children and by age of youngest child, 1993

	Unemployment rates (%)					
	All ages		14–24		All ages Youngest child:	
	At least one child < 18	No child < 18	At least one child < 18	No child < 18	0–4	5–9
Belgium	13.9	10.2	31.4	16.0	16.9	14.6
Denmark	8.8	9.5	28.7	12.7	9.5	8.0
Germany	10.2	6.2	20.3	5.5	13.9	10.7
Greece	10.4	6.9	26.7	23.3	15.4	11.1
Spain	22.0	16.1	45.4	29.9	26.9	21.7
France	13.0	10.1	34.4	15.2	17.1	12.7
Ireland	22.1	9.7	—	—	22.0	22.2
Italy	13.4	8.1	40.0	28.3	19.2	14.3
Luxembourg	—	—	—	—	—	—
Netherlands	15.9	9.3	36.8	13.4	16.2	20.2
Portugal	7.0	4.5	20.3	—	10.5	7.3
UK	9.4	5.0	32.2	6.0	16.6	7.8
E12	12.3	7.6	32.4	11.1	17.4	12.5

Source: Eurostat (1993a: Tables 4.2 and 4.4)

Domestic responsibilities can also affect the type of work sought by the unemployed. European Labour Force Survey provides information on whether the unemployed are seeking self-employment, full-time paid employment or part-time paid employment. The first point to note is the wide variations between member states in the shares of female unemployed seeking part-time work: from under 10 per cent in Greece, Spain and Portugal, to 47 per cent in the UK and 72 per cent in the Netherlands (see Figure 4.6). As women have roughly similar domestic roles in European Union states these differences are more attributable to differences in labour market organisation, and/or differences in the extent of female participation, than to differences in responsibilities. The share of part-time work within the female labour force is clearly related to the shares of the female unemployed seeking part-time work; whether this is because women are expressing different preferences due to different attitudes to part-time work and/or to women working, or whether these differences simply reflect realistic assessments of opportunities is open to question.

Figure 4.6   Share of unemployed women seeking a part-time job, 1983–92

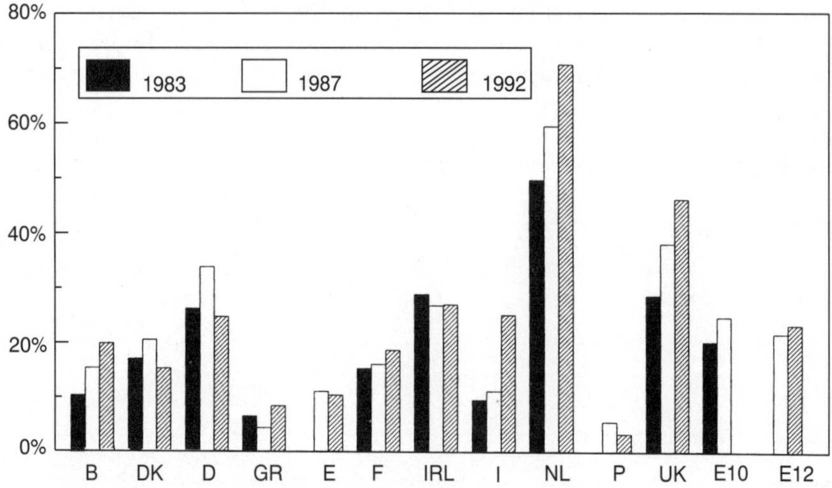

Source: European Labour Force Surveys (1983, 1987, 1992)

However, there is no simple correlation between shares of part-time jobs among women and the share of the unemployed seeking part-time jobs. Denmark stands out in particular as a country with a higher share of part-time working but a low share of the unemployed who are looking for part-time work. This finding fits with the general trend away from part-time work in Denmark and the decreasing influence of women's domestic responsibilities on their labour market participation patterns. Belgium, Germany and France are also countries with medium to high shares of part-time work for women but where the share of the unemployed seeking part-time work is below the average share in the labour force. Ireland, Italy, the UK and Netherlands, however, have higher shares of the unemployed seeking part-time work than the overall share in part-time work, even though the latter two countries have the overall highest part-time rates in the EU. All these countries, except for Ireland, have also registered increasing shares of the unemployed seeking part-time work.

The responses to the question on the type of employment sought are broken down in 1992 by age of respondent, and in 1990 by marital status (see Table 4.11). For all countries except Denmark the share of older women, (25+) wanting part-time work is greater then the average share wanting part-time work. The much higher share of young women seeking part-time work in Denmark reflects the general importance of part-time work among all young people in Denmark, as well as the decline in part-time working among women of core working age. Comparing the data broken down by age in 1992 to the data broken down by marital status in

1990 suggests that marriage is a stronger indicator than age of desire for part-time work, but that the marriage effect is particularly strong in Germany, Ireland and to some extent in Denmark, as 22 per cent of unemployed married women wanted part-time work in 1990 compared to only 13 per cent of women aged over 25 in 1992. However, the 22 per cent figure is still way below the average part-time work share in Denmark.

Table 4.11 Share of unemployed married/all women and unemployed young/prime-age women seeking part-time work, 1990–2

	1990		1992	
	All unemployed women (%)	Unemployed married women (%)	Unemployed 15–24 (%)	Unemployed 25+ (%)
Belgium	19.5	25.6	12.9	22.1
Denmark	18.2	22.0	23.1	12.9
Germany	37.5	47.7	12.8	26.5
Greece	6.7	9.1	6.9	9.4
Spain	9.0	15.1	7.9	11.9
France	17.8	24.9	7.3	22.7
Ireland	32.4	52.0	—	37.2
Italy	12.5	23.0	13.7	35.1
Netherlands	67.3	82.8	55.6	77.3
Portugal	6.1	6.0	—	—
UK	42.9	53.5	28.2	55.7
E12	22.4	33.2	13.4	27.7

Source: Special tabulation provided by Eurostat

Education and training as a protection against unemployment

In all countries women are increasing their involvement in education and training, entering the labour force later and competing with men on the basis of similar if not higher qualifications, albeit maintaining a gender divide in the selection of subjects studied. Table 4.12 shows that in six out of ten countries for which we have data that women are equally or more likely to be in tertiary education men and that in four of these countries the female enrolment rate exceeds that of men by 5 percentage points or more. In contrast only in Germany is the enrolment rate of men more than 5 percentage points higher than for women. Even when the enrolment rates for university education alone are considered, women still have higher or approximately equal rates in five countries and again only in Germany is there a significant gap in favour of men.

141

Table 4.12 Entry to tertiary education, 1992[a]

	Non-university tertiary education			University education			Total		
	All (%)	Men (%)	Women (%)	All (%)	Men (%)	Women (%)	All (%)	Men (%)	Women (%)
Belgium	25.3	19.1	31.8	27.3	29.4	25.1	52.6	48.5	56.9
Denmark	11.2	12.8	9.6	41.5	36.4	47.0	52.8	49.2	56.6
Germany[b]	12.5/	11.4/	13.7/	35.3/	45.4/	24.8/	47.8/	56.8/	38.5/
	16.0	12.6	19.6	33.0	41.4	24.1	49.0	54.0	43.7
Greece	13.4	—	—	15.9	—	—	29.3	—	—
Spain	—	—	—	43.3	40.8	45.9	43.3	40.8	45.9
France	17.3	16.0	18.7	30.6	26.6	34.8	48.0	42.6	53.5
Ireland	17.8	17.7	18.0	22.1	21.9	22.3	39.9	39.5	40.4
Italy	0.4	0.3	0.6	41.3	41.4	41.2	41.7	41.6	41.8
Netherlands	—	—	—	40.1	40.7	39.4	40.1	40.7	39.4
UK	10.3	9.9	10.7	26.6	27.5	25.6	36.9	37.4	36.3

Source: OECD (1995b: 150)
Note: a (new entrants as % of population in the theoretical starting age)
    b Old Germany/new Germany

More qualified workers face a lower risk of unemployment over the lifecycle than less qualified workers. However, this finding does not necessarily hold at the point of entry into the labour market; in some countries it is those with higher-level qualifications which may face particular difficulties in securing an appropriate initial job. Nor do women necessarily benefit to the same extent as men from the protection of education and training against unemployment (see Box 4.4). To investigate the influence of education we use OECD data that give us information on unemployment rates by gender, level of education and age for 1991 for ten member states (excluding Luxembourg and Greece).

We can first of all divide the countries into those where unemployment rates are strongly negatively related to educational level for all ages and genders and those where unemployment rates may be negatively related to educational levels for workers aged over 25 but are positively (or non-linearly related) for those aged 20 to 24 (Table 4.13). The countries that fall into the second category are Italy, Portugal and Spain, with all other countries found in the first. Within these categories there are strong differences in the strength of the relationship between education and unemployment even for male unemployment patterns: for example, in Ireland the male unemployment rates by education vary between a high of 26.3 per cent and a low of 3 per cent, while in the remaining countries in this category thevariation is only from a maximum of 14 per cent to a low of under 2 per cent. In some countries the main dividing line is between those with level 0/1 or level 2 education (primary and compulsory secondary), while others have a more graduated effect, with significant declines in unemployment rates still between level 3 (low level vocational and preparation for further

---

Box 4.4   Education is not sufficient to protect women against unemployment

National data for **Denmark** show that while a short period of higher education provides some protection against unemployment, unemployment rates start to rise again for those with extended higher education, suggesting there may be problems even within the Northern countries for some highly trained people to integrate into the labour market, perhaps particularly in the context of public sector cutbacks. This effect was found to be particularly strong for women (Boje 1995: 54). National data for **Belgium** show that unemployed women are better qualified than unemployed men: 66 per cent of women compared to 56 per cent of men had some qualifications (Meulders 1995: 63). Among first-time jobseekers in **France**, there is a growing polarisation of qualification levels, with the number of first-time jobseekers without qualifications rising at the same time as the share of graduates among first time jobseekers has doubled. Women with low-level technical and vocational qualifications are reducing their representation among first-time jobseekers (Silvera *et al.* 1995: 96).

---

education), level 5 (further education non-degree) and level 6/7 (degree and above).

In the three countries where higher unemployment among under 25 year olds is positively related to university level education we find that even for over 25 year olds there is not a strong negative relationship between educational levels and unemployment rates, although higher education (level 6/7) does provide some protection for women over age 25 in all three countries.[3] These are also the three countries with the highest youth to adult unemployment rates, and thus the unemployment in these countries is that of initial entry into employment, a problem that appears exacerbated for those young people with higher educational qualifications. Only national data are available for Greece, and not split by age category. This shows those with middle level education facing the highest relative unemployment rates.

If we now consider the gender differences in unemployment rates by educational level for those aged over 25 we find a varied pattern. Belgium, Denmark, France and Portugal fall into one group of countries where women with lower education face an increased risk of unemployment relative to men, but where this increase narrows as educational levels increase. Germany and the Netherlands fall into the opposite category where the unemployment rates of low educated men and women are relatively similar but the gap widens against women as educational levels increase. These results are consistent with these countries still having a pattern of women returner participation, so that even more highly educated women may face problems of re-entry into the labour market. The UK and Ireland also show

Table 4.13 Unemployment rates by educational attainment, 1993

Age 20–24			Level				
		All	0/1	2	3	5	6/7
Belgium	Male	11.2	26.0	11.1	7.1	6.1	5.4
	Female	18.3	38.1	26.4	16.7	5.7	4.5
Denmark	Male	14.0	—	23.0	11.7	14.7	9.5
	Female	17.5	—	33.9	14.8	14.6	12.3
Germany	Male	5.7	—	9.5	4.7	4.7	4.3
	Female	7.4	—	11.7	6.4	6.9	5.4
Greece	Male	24.1	29.0	22.5	21.6	—	38.8
	Female	36.9	38.4	38.0	34.4	—	39.0
Spain	Male	15.6	—	23.1	11.1	6.1	6.2
	Female	22.5	—	32.7	19.9	11.0	10.9
France	Male	22.9	51.5	26.2	16.7	16.4	12.2
	Female	17.3	41.5	29.5	12.6	12.0	8.6
Ireland	Male	23.7	27.1	18.4	32.5	—	42.9
	Female	32.5	39.3	27.1	36.8	—	50.0
Italy	Male	8.0	21.4	7.0	6.1	—	—
	Female	8.5	20.8	8.7	7.4	—	—
Netherlands	Male	7.2	6.7	8.3	8.4	9.5	16.1
	Female	13.3	12.8	15.0	16.5	4.6	16.1
Portugal	Male	7.2	6.7	8.3	8.4	9.5	16.1
	Female	13.3	12.8	15.0	16.5	4.6	16.1
UK	Male	15.0	—	28.3	12.0	7.2	13.6
	Female	10.0	—	21.4	9.0	3.5	7.4

Age 25–64			Level				
		All	0/1	2	3	5	6/7
Belgium	Male	4.7	14.4	3.5	2.0	1.6	1.4
	Female	11.1	28.0	12.7	7.5	2.9	2.3
Denmark	Male	8.8	—	13.0	7.9	5.2	4.6
	Female	11.1	—	15.3	10.6	6.1	4.7
Germany	Male	5.0	—	10.0	5.0	3.3	3.4
	Female	8.1	—	10.1	8.1	6.7	6.3
Spain	Male	9.6	10.7	10.5	7.3	—	5.8
	Female	19.4	18.3	26.1	21.5	—	13.6
France	Male	6.0	7.3	8.9	4.9	2.6	2.8
	Female	10.1	11.0	14.6	9.0	4.4	5.0
Ireland	Male	15.9	26.3	16.9	8.5	5.4	3.0
	Female	8.1	15.5	12.0	5.6	4.2	4.2
Italy	Male	3.4	3.0	3.3	4.0	—	3.4
	Female	10.9	9.5	12.4	11.6	—	7.4
Netherlands	Male	3.4	12.4	4.0	2.5	—	—
	Female	8.2	13.5	10.1	8.2	5.2	—
Portugal	Male	2.3	2.4	1.7	2.0	1.2	0.9
	Female	5.8	6.1	6.2	4.6	0.7	2.8
UK	Male	7.8	—	13.4	6.8	4.3	2.5
	Female	6.2	—	7.6	6.1	3.2	4.2

Source: OECD (1993a: Table 7.b.1)
Notes: Level 0/1   Primary education and compulsory education
      Level 2   Compulsory secondary
      Level 3   Low-level vocational and preparation for further education
      Level 5   Further education non-degree
      Level 6/7   Degree and above

similar patterns to Germany and the Netherlands, except that in this case it is the low educated men who face higher unemployment risks more than low educated women; as education increases the gap narrows, and is in fact reversed with women facing higher unemployment risks than men at educational levels 6/7 in both countries. The reasons for the relatively low unemployment rates of women in both countries is thus a result of lower female unemployment rates for less-skilled workers. Spain and Italy form another group of countries where the relative disadvantage faced by women is maximised among women with middle level qualifications. These higher unemployment rates are indicative of general problems in both countries in the effectiveness of vocational and professional training programmes which seem to be failing to provide appropriate skills to help women enter the labour force.

If we look at gender differences in unemployment rates for people aged 20–24 by education we find another set of diverse patterns. In the UK and Ireland young women have lower unemployment rates than young men at almost all educational levels, and in the Netherlands there is relatively little difference between the male and female rates. In all other countries young female unemployment rates are higher on average than young male unemployment rates. In Belgium, Denmark and France there are particularly increased unemployment risks for women with low levels of education relative to those for men; in France and Denmark there is a reduction in the size of the gender gap at higher educational levels but the risk remains higher for women while in Belgium young women with educational levels 5 or higher have a slightly lower unemployment risk than their male counterparts. In Germany there is a higher risk of young women being unemployed at all levels of education but the gap varies only between 1.1 and 2.2 percentage points. In the three countries where unemployment rates are highest for those with level 6/7 education – Italy, Spain, Portugal – this finding applies particularly in Spain and Portugal to young men, but is an equally strong if not stronger effect for young women in Italy. In Spain and Portugal unemployment rates for young women do not vary markedly with educational levels: in Spain the range is from 34 to 39 per cent, while in Portugal it is from 13 to 16 per cent, except for level 5 which has an unemployment rate of less than 5 per cent (but this group may be quite small). In Italy the unemployment rates for young women at level 6/7 are 50 per cent compared to rates of between 27 per cent and 39 per cent for the other educational levels. In all three countries there are significant gender gaps in unemployment rates for low educated young men and women; in Portugal the unemployment rates for women up to education level 3 are around twice those for young men; in Spain they are around 60 per cent higher except for the low educated, where women face only around 30 per cent higher risk. In Portugal highly educated young men and women in fact face the same unemployment rate of 16 per cent, while in Spain and Italy women face an even higher risk than the very high risk already faced by highly educated young men (39 per cent compared to 34 per cent in Spain, 50 per cent compared to 43 per cent in Italy).

Box 4.5   Training programmes need to be well-regarded by employers if they are to help women to work

In **Spain** the high unemployment rates for middle qualified workers can at least in part be attributed to a poor vocational or professional training programme which is not well targeted at industry's needs. Women in the middle range suffer particularly high rates of unemployment (Moltó 1995: 111).

In the **UK** women face a double problem; first, they have less access to on-the-job training than men, so that the chance of a single woman aged 20 receiving training has been estimated to be reduced by one-third compared to her male counterpart, while the chance for a woman of the same age married with children is reduced by four-fifths. Second, even if they do receive training, the tradition of informal and non-credentialised training in UK means that this training is most help if a person continues in employment in the same organisation, but tends not to be recognised if a person switches jobs, or even worse, interrupts employment. Thus British women are vulnerable to occupational downgrading if they leave the labour market, even if they were in receipt of training in their old job (Green 1991; Rubery and Smith 1995: 165–167).

Women perhaps face greater disadvantages in gaining access to useful training than they do in negotiating the education system (see Box 4.5). These problems are particularly acute when training is left up to employers, and when it is not highly regarded by employers or considered non-transferable. Training programmes can be helpful in smoothing the transition from school to work, but where they are closely integrated into the employment system they may smooth this transition through maintaining and even reinforcing, rather than challenging the existing gender division of labour (see Box 4.6). Moreover, just as women seem to have moved into equal and even first place in the education league there is renewed emphasis on further and lifelong training which could act to their disadvantage (see Box 4.7).

Nevertheless, most evidence suggests that women are taking active steps to improve their own position in the labour market through the acquisition of both training and education. In part this higher participation may be a response to poor employment prospects, and thus may be regarded as disguising an increase in discouraged workers, but the impact of these changes is to reduce somewhat the disadvantage faced by women in the labour market (see Box 4.8). One perhaps unintended impact of women's greater involvement in education and training is a greater likelihood that

Box 4.6   Training systems smooth the process of transition from school to work but at the same time reinforce gender segregation

In **Germany** the transition from school to work is eased by the extensive training system. This helps to reduce youth unemployment for both men and women. Education and training are perhaps more important than gender in determining risk of unemployment: calculations of unemployment rates by gender and skill suggest that unskilled men and women both face the highest risks. Nevertheless the pattern of education and training is still highly gendered with young men more involved in apprenticeships and young women in vocational schools, following training programmes which tend to reinforce the pattern of occupational sex segregation of employment (Maier and Rapp 1995: 13).

In the **UK** training programmes for young people have also served to reduce measured unemployment, but again these programmes have tended to reinforce and not reduce sex segregation. This reinforcement comes both from the preferences of trainees and from the set of financial incentives in place for training providers; funding is linked to the success of trainees in obtaining subsequent employment, so training providers have a financial incentive not to risk training men and women for non-traditional jobs where obtaining employment may be more difficult (Rubery and Smith 1995: 179–181).

Box 4.7   Just when women were closing the gap in initial education and training, the new emphasis on further training and lifelong learning may open it again

In **Germany** the labour market is characterised by a clear structuring of 'occupations' or 'professions' as a means of allocating jobs, income and career development. Access to vocational training and further training thus becomes a major issue for women's position in the labour market. Employment interruptions have always penalised women as they lose out on career tracks, but the growing importance of further vocational training may mean that employment interruptions will become an even greater impediment to professional careers than they were in the past when basic vocational training was regarded as an adequate basis for performing skilled tasks (Maier and Rapp 1995: 41).

In **France** a higher share of women pass the Baccalauréat and proceed to higher education, but, as the share of the population passing the Baccalauréat increases, the advantage that this currently gives to women may reduce. Moreover, fewer women opt for the more prestigious scientific Baccalauréat. Men still receive more continuing training than women although the gap is small (44.4 per cent of men have received training since the beginning of their career compared to 41.3 per cent of women, but it is in manual and low level white collar jobs that the largest gender gaps are found) (Silvera *et al.* 1995: 22).

Box 4.8   Should women's increasing participation in education be considered evidence of disguised unemployment or of women taking action to overcome their disadvantages in the labour market?

In **Italy** women under 25 are more likely to extend education in response to increased unemployment than are men. Women have also higher completion rates than men and completing courses on time is increasingly becoming more important in obtaining a position than the qualification itself. This higher participation in education could be regarded as evidence of discouraged workers among women, but also suggests that Italian women are taking action to improve their employability. Women are also more involved in training than men, constituting over 70 per cent of trainees. However, education still provides less protection against unemployment for women than for men (Bettio and Mazzotta 1995: 24–30).

One study in **France** has shown that young men are often facing a greater financial crisis when unemployed, and thus may have less opportunity to seek an appropriate position, and are guided by the Employment Services immediately into precarious work. Women may have less immediate need of work and are able to select a training course which gives them a greater chance of a standard contract at the end of the course (Silvera *et al.* 1995: 87).

---

women will participate in the formal instead of the informal economy (see Box 4.9), and thus in the long-term the effect may be to reduce the share of women who are discouraged workers.

Box 4.9   Education and training as a route into formal employment?

In **Portugal** women's participation in initial vocational training programmes tends to have little effect on measured unemployment; instead it is more likely to lead to women moving from the informal economy or inactivity to the formal wage economy. Women who received vocational training increased their employment rate prior to that before training by 11 per cent, albeit by a lower percentage than for men (13 per cent). Unemployment rates remained roughly the same, while the share of women who were family workers prior to training declined (Lopes and Perista 1995: 53–54)

4.4   Conclusions: the impact of labour market organisation on women's risk of unemployment

Women face a generally higher risk of unemployment than men for a series of reasons. First, women have a lower employment rate than men and thus by definition there is greater potential female labour reserve, which may or may not be mobilised into actively seek work and thus counted as unemployed. Second, women in most countries have higher rates of transition between economic activity statuses than is the case of men; this fluidity of economic status, and the greater insecurity attached to women's employment positions, can and does result in a relatively high female stock of unemployment. In addition women tend to suffer from relatively long-term unemployment, possibly in part because new recruits are as likely or in fact more likely to be drawn from women outside the labour force as from the unemployed. Finally, women continue to face discrimination in the labour force; this manifests itself in a higher share of women being employed in precarious jobs which may increase the flow into unemployment, in women facing higher unemployment rates at every level of education so that even strategies adopted by women to improve their position on the labour market may have only limited effects, and in women who have current domestic responsibilities for young children facing greater difficulties in securing employment than women without domestic responsibilities in almost all countries.

However, within this general model of gender differences in unemployment risk, there is also evidence that the particular system of labour market organisation, and the particular pattern of female labour market participation has an impact on the extent and incidence of female unemployment. There is a significant difference, for example, between those countries where the unemployment is concentrated on the young, almost irrespective of education, and those where women's unemployment is more evenly spread through the age groups. The share of women entering unemployment from inactivity is high in a range of countries, but for different reasons; in some cases they are mainly first jobseekers, but in others women returners with some previous labour market experience. In yet other countries there are more fluid movements between employment, unemployment and inactivity, either because of a high rate of job instability as in Spain, or because of different ways of combining education and work as in Denmark.

These differences in the processes which lead to unemployment for women mean that detailed analysis of the particular causes of women's higher risk of unemployment are required before policy prescriptions can be determined; for example in the Southern countries the problem perhaps lies both with the general problems of young people finding work, and the more specific gender issue of the assistance provided by the family to young men compared to young women (Pugliese 1995). Here policies to improve young women's education to enable them to search for jobs independently of the family may be critical, but in other countries the issues may revolve around how to help women returners or women with low access to vocational qualifications. Under these conditions general policy prescriptions for all European states as to how to reduce the gender gap in unemployment may not be appropriate. Instead policies to reduce the gender unemployment gap need to be integrated with mainstream policies to reduce both the measured and the hidden rates of unemployment taking account of the particular characteristics of the labour market and social and economic environment in the member state.

5

STATE POLICIES AND WOMEN'S EMPLOYMENT AND UNEMPLOYMENT RATES

State policies regulate the financial position of those in unemployment and influence the success of unemployed workers in re-entering employment. Sections 5.1 and 5.2 evaluate the relation between different 'passive' labour market policies and the position of men and women in the labour market. These policies aim to replace a proportion of lost income for a limited period and, in some countries, are supported by universal access to a minimum standard of living regardless of employment experience. Section 5.3 will discuss the gender issues involved in the 'active' labour market policies pursued by the different member states, which aim to improve the 'employability' of unemployed workers. We do not attempt here to describe systems of social security in full as comprehensive descriptions exist in annual CEC publications such as *Employment in Europe* and *Social Protection in Europe*. The following discussion focuses on those aspects of the social security system which impact positively or negatively upon women's relative economic position among the unemployed. In this chapter we concentrate on the differences between member states with regard to the provision of unemployment compensation and social assistance. In Chapter 6 similar attention will be paid to social security policies regarding pensions for old age.

One possible aim of the following analysis might be to rank the different state policies found in member states according to a measure of gender equity. For example, it may be possible to group countries according to how their system of unemployment insurance increases or reduces the relative level of protection women face as employees compared to men. Such a ranking, however, must also account for broader differences between countries with regard to the distinct philosophies of distributive justice which underpin each country's social security system, and which affect the risks faced by all employees. For example, one study proposed the grouping of member states into four general categories of social security systems according to their general method of financing and allocating social security protection (CEC 1993b: 16). In the first category, the system of compensation for the unemployed aims primarily to maintain previous levels of income by linking individual benefits closely to unemployment insurance contributions. Germany, France, Belgium and Luxembourg all have social security systems which follow these general principles of insurance practice. Those in work contribute to insurance funds, and these contributions entitle them to receive a proportion of their earnings when unemployed. General taxation finances a complementary system of unemployment assistance which ensures minimum levels of income to those who have not contributed to the fund, as well as those who are ineligible for or who have exhausted their entitlements to benefit payments.

In the second category, benefits are financed by general taxation and are more closely tied to needs. Denmark, the UK and Ireland are classed within this category (CEC 1993b). In the UK and Ireland, benefits are paid at a flat rate to all unemployed, thus providing a universal entitlement to a subsistence living standard which bears no relation to previous income. In common with the first category, further social assistance is means tested. While Denmark relies on general taxation as a means of financing, it deviates somewhat from the categorisation since it compensates the unemployed according to the level of their previous income. The report does acknowledge Denmark's poor fit and it is unclear why Denmark is categorised along with the UK and Ireland rather than with the first category. Indeed, recent changes in Denmark's unemployment insurance system highlight the difficulties of categorising countries according to needs-based systems financed by general taxation or insurance-based systems financed by individual contributions. On the one hand, the Danish system has moved closer to an insurance-based system as the state contribution to expenditures on unemployment benefits was replaced in 1994 by an additional contribution paid by employers and employees as a percentage of income. On the other hand, replacement of lost income has increasingly become a matter of ensuring basic minimum levels of income since the maximum threshold level below which the replacement rate applies has been significantly reduced over recent years (Boje 1995: 59–60).

The third category occupies an intermediate position and includes Italy's less-developed system of social security and the system found in the Netherlands which relies on a diverse range of financing methods. Finally, in the Southern member states of Spain, Portugal and Greece, systems of social security are still in their infancy and unemployment assistance is not designed to provide a universal level of minimum income (CEC 1994).

While there are problems in classifying member states according to whether the unemployment system rewards individuals according to need or following general insurance principles, further problems arise if we consider the extent to which women face disadvantages in the access to and level of unemployment benefits they receive in each country. Where social security systems are founded on insurance principles, entitlement to benefits may require a long period of continuous employment involving a minimum level of weekly hours. Such regulations act to exclude many women who have interrupted their career paths, or who have worked part-time. Moreover, given the gender pay inequity which exists in all member states, women will be disadvantaged in comparison to men by insurance-based systems, given that the level of unemployment compensation is calculated in proportion to previous individual earnings. It would appear, then, that women may enjoy more equitable treatment under needs-based systems which guarantee a minimum income entitlement or make a flat-rate payment. However, other obstacles to fair treatment arise if these flat-rate systems pay very low rates to single adults, but offer either substantial additions according to the number of dependants in the household, or are supplemented by a large component of means-tested benefits. In both systems, therefore, it is likely that the level of compensation received by women will, in practice, be less than the compensation for men, and may restrict women who are married to unemployed men from seeking work. The following analysis aims to identify in more detail those characteristics of social security systems which impact upon the relative position of women compared to men within each country.

5.1 Unemployment and unemployment benefits

According to the ILO definition of unemployment, we saw in Chapter 4 that women were overrepresented among the unemployed in the majority of member states in 1992. This penalty is compounded by the fact that women are less likely to receive unemployment compensation once unemployed, compared to men. For the European Union (the twelve member states as defined in 1992), the share of women unemployed according to ILO criteria who were receiving unemployment compensation in 1992 was 28 per cent compared to 33 per cent of unemployed men (see Table 5.1). Figures for the different countries reveal a wide variation in these ratios in terms of both the scale of protection provided to those in unemployment and the degree to which unemployment compensation is unevenly distributed between men and women. For countries such as Belgium, Denmark and Germany, a relatively high proportion of both men and women in unemployment are entitled to unemployment compensation. At the bottom end of the scale, in the Mediterranean countries of Greece, Italy, Portugal and to some extent in Spain, unemployment compensation is not available to the vast majority of unemployed men and women. For those member states that lie in between these poles, the probability of receiving unemployment benefit is largely dependent upon the sex of the claimant. Although unemployed women in all member states, with the exception of Luxembourg, are less likely to receive unemployment compensation compared to unemployed men, this is less obvious in countries at the upper and lower ends of the ranking yet very clear in the UK, Spain, Ireland and the Netherlands. In these mid-ranking countries unemployed women are roughly half as likely to receive unemployment compensation relative to unemployed men. This evidence reflects two factors that characterise systems of unemployment compensation: first, the stringency of eligibility conditions which restrict access to unemployment benefits; and second, the degree to which a country's system of unemployment compensation establishes independent as opposed to derived rights.

Table 5.1 Percentage share of unemployed men and unemployed women in receipt of unemployment compensation (benefit or assistance), 1992

	% Share of women	*% Share of men*	*% Share of unemployed women in total unemployment*
High share			
Denmark	84.3	84.4	51.1
Belgium	84.0	85.2	57.6
Germany	73.7	75.7	55.4
Medium share			
Ireland	43.8	83.1	36.0
France	42.5	51.7	56.0
UK[a]	32.0	70.0	32.6
Netherlands	25.9	58.8	56.6
Spain	21.9	38.7	51.1
Luxembourg[b]	30.7	26.6	41.4
Low share			
Portugal	16.2	18.2	52.9
Greece	5.8	11.3	60.4
Italy	5.2	6.0	53.7
E12	27.8	32.6	50.9

Source: Eurostat (1994c)
Notes: a Data are missing for the UK and therefore approximated from 1990 data in CEC (1992b)
  b Data are missing for Luxembourg and therefore figures refer to 1991 data provided by the national expert based on the annual ILO Census

Where figures are available, national measures of unemployment reveal an even greater extent of sex bias in terms of independent access to unemployment compensation. For example, in Spain, national data demonstrate a widening of the gap between women's and men's access to compensation in comparison to European Labour Force Survey data: 19 per cent of women registered as unemployed received unemployment benefits compared to 50 per cent of men in 1992 (Moltó 1995). National data for 1993 in West Germany also show that although women's share among those registered as unemployed is equivalent to their share of the labour force, only 61 per cent of women registered as unemployed received either unemployment benefits or assistance compared to 77 per cent of all men. Thus, discussions at the national level in West Germany are more likely to focus on the sex bias in access to compensation, an issue which is hidden by the LFS data. By contrast, data for East Germany show that women in this case were overrepresented among those registered as unemployed (63.9 per cent share compared to a 48.2 per cent share of the labour force in 1993), yet once unemployed they were equally likely compared to men to receive benefits or assistance (Maier and Rapp 1995: Tables 2.3.3.1.1 and 2.3.3.1.2).

Indeed, the 1994 report of *Employment in Europe* highlights the dangers of discussing European employment issues solely with regard to the harmonised LFS data as the LFS definition captures different groups of people compared to national measures of unemployment (see Chapter 2). For example, in 1992 only 63 per cent of those counted as unemployed across the E12 under national definitions were included in the LFS (CEC 1994). This suggests a high proportion of discouraged workers, as the ILO definition requires that the person has actually looked for work during the past four weeks (see Chapter 2). Disaggregating the data by member state, LFS data underestimate the registered count by at least 20 per cent in every country except Spain. These problems of definition have particular implications for a gender analysis of unemployment. In nine of the twelve countries, women registered as unemployed are less likely than men to be counted in the LFS measure. The weak overlap is most significant in Greece, Portugal, Italy and Ireland, where less than 40 per cent of women registered as unemployed were counted in the LFS. The possible explanation is that women registered as unemployed are less likely to continue looking actively for work, perhaps relying on more informal networks and in the meantime devoting themselves to domestic or informal work.

Conversely, only 78 per cent of those counted as unemployed in the Community by the LFS were registered as unemployed in the member states in 1992 (CEC 1994). This discrepancy in definitions was lowest in Belgium, Spain, Germany and France, where more than 80 per cent of LFS unemployed were registered as unemployed, and highest in Portugal and Greece, where the proportions were 49 per cent and 13 per cent respectively. Again, the differences in definitions have particular implications for women in unemployment. Only 73 per cent of LFS unemployed women for the Community as a whole were registered as unemployed compared to 82 per cent for men (CEC 1994). This suggests that women who are both available and seeking work are more likely than men not to register as unemployed, possibly due to biases in access to unemployment benefits. For example, unemployed women in the UK and Germany are faced with conditions of eligibility to unemployment benefits which may require availability for full-time work. Although some exceptions are made for persons with significant responsibility for children or other dependants, it is likely that this rule acts as a significant disincentive against women's decision to register as unemployed. In the UK, the share of women counted among unemployed persons available and seeking work under the ILO definition is 34 per cent compared to a share of unemployment benefit claimants of 24 per cent (autumn 1994; Rubery and Smith 1995). In Ireland, for a couple living together and both registered as unemployed, the maximum payment is exactly the same as the case where only the primary claimant registers – the only difference being that if claims are made individually then each receives half the combined rate. Again, this discourages women from registering as unemployed and they are ultimately classified as 'engaged in home duties' in labour force statistics (Barry 1995: 31). In other countries, however, the national measure may discriminate positively in counting women as unemployed. For example, in Italy, the national count includes employees working part-time less than 20 hours or on fixed term contracts of four months or less; both groups are excluded from the LFS measure (Bettio and Mazzotta 1995). In Portugal, the share of registered unemployed in receipt of benefits has increased substantially from 22 per cent in 1987 to 50 per cent in 1993 (Lopes and Perista 1995: 62). It is possible that the low initial coverage rate has caused many unemployed not to register, thus increasing the observed ratio of beneficiaries to registered unemployed. However, given that the actual number of people in receipt of benefits increased from 67,000 to 167,000 during the six-year period, it is likely that the increased incidence of benefit recipients will have a positive effect on the incentive for those in unemployment to register at job centres.

The following discussion evaluates the problems that women face in claiming unemployment benefits by a consideration of the differential conditions peculiar to each country's system of unemployment compensation. Eligibility conditions which require a continuous employment history and meeting minimum weekly hours or earnings thresholds exacerbate women's experience of unequal entitlement to benefits. Where unemployed workers are ineligible or have exhausted their rights to unemployment benefits, most member states provide some form of unemployment assistance. However, where this takes household income as the reference, women again lose their right to independent unemployment compensation. Hence, the period during which benefits can be claimed irrespective of household income is also a key factor. Other institutional regulations of importance to women's access to unemployment compensation include the rights of those who have worked or seek to work part-time, the use of availability for work tests and expectations relating to childcare arrangements.

156

Eligibility conditions for unemployment benefits

Workers with discontinuous employment history

Entitlement to unemployment benefits typically depends on satisfying a certain number of contributory payments throughout a specified period preceding termination of employment. Emphasis on a long, continuous employment history excludes many employees who have short or discontinuous employment experience and those who are subject to precarious employment conditions. Women are likely to predominate among such groups, both as a result of maternity or childcare leave, or as a result of a higher incidence of women employed in precarious jobs. Table 5.2 shows that all member states require a minimum period of insured employment. Emphasis on continuous employment is high in Portugal and Ireland, where the claimant must have been in insured employment for around 75 per cent of the stated previous period. This amounts to 540 days of the previous 24 months in Portugal, and 39 weeks in the previous 12 months in Ireland. The most favourable treatment for workers with short or interrupted work histories is found in Spain and Denmark, and to a lesser extent in Greece and Germany. In these four countries claimants are required to have been in insured employment for less than one-third of the stated past period. Unemployment insurance in Spain is accessible to persons who have made contributory payments for 52 weeks in the previous 6 years, and in Germany the requirement is 360 days in the previous 36 months.

In some countries, where claimants are either ineligible for the standard unemployment benefits or have exhausted their entitlement rights, access to an extended period of reduced benefits or unemployment assistance is also contingent upon meeting a certain qualifying period of employment. For example, in France the claimant must have completed five out of the previous ten years in employment in order to claim unemployment assistance. In Germany, entitlement to unemployment assistance requires at least 150 days' contributory employment in the preceding year. Finally, in the Netherlands, entitlement to an extended period of wage-related unemployment benefits is contingent upon 52 daily wage-related payments in three of the preceding five years (although this is set to change, see below).

In recognition of the penalties faced by women with discontinuous employment histories, childcare is counted as qualifying employment in France, Germany and the Netherlands – although the stringent conditions which accompany these measures in Germany largely serve to offset any expected gains. In France, five years' employment in the preceding ten years is normally required for entitlement to unemployment assistance. For persons who have stopped work to raise a child, this period may be reduced by one year for each dependent child up to a maximum of three years (Silvera *et al.* 1995: 101). In Germany, childcare leave counts towards the qualifying period of twelve

months during the preceding three years as long as the claimant was previously employed or in receipt of unemployment benefits. Women who have
experienced longer periods out of the labour force are excluded (the average
employment interruption of mothers is six years) (Maier and Rapp 1995: 56).
Regulations in the Netherlands are slightly more favourable. In determining
the work history requirement for the extended benefits, years in childcare for
children under 6 years old can be counted directly (6–12 year olds count as 50
per cent) (Plantenga and Sloep 1995: 43).

Table 5.2 Grouping of countries by eligibility conditions for unemployment benefits
according to their reliance on continuous work history

		Continuous work history requirements
	Low	
Spain		52 weeks in past 6 years
Denmark		26/17 weeks in past 36 months (full-time/part-time); 12 months' contributions total; 300/150 hours in past 10 weeks
Greece		125 days' contributions in past 14 months
Germany		360 days in past 36 months
	Moderate	
France		6 months in past 12 months
UK		50 weeks in past 2 years
Italy		12 months in past 24 months and 24 months' contributions overall
Luxembourg		26 weeks in past 12 months
Netherlands		26 weeks in past 12 months
Belgium		312–624 days in past 18–36 months (see text for proposed reforms) (varies by age)
	High	
Portugal		540 days in past 2 years
Ireland		39 weeks in past 12 months; 3 days in any period of 6 consecutive days

Sources: National reports
Note: The figures presented for Italy are not entirely comparable due to the multi-level system
of redundancy and unemployment benefits in operation. The figures refer to eligibility to the
system of 'ordinary unemployment benefits' which although comparable to other member
states as a form of compensation is in fact the lowest level of benefits and makes up only 8%
of all fully subsidised yearly equivalent units of benefits paid in 1993. The more common
payments, although highly selective, take the form of redundancy payments (of between 80 and
100% of previous lost income) and involve different eligibility requirements (Bettio and Mazzotta 1995: Tables A–E).

The degree of institutionalised bias inherent in contribution record
requirements has worsened in Spain, France and the Netherlands, where
this particular eligibility condition has been tightened in recent and
proposed legislative changes. Although Spain has relatively favourable
provisions compared to other member states, prior to June 1994 qualifying

conditions required only six months in the previous four years (Moltó, 1995: 116). Following recent reforms in France, the link between the unemployed person's contributions record and the period of entitlement to benefits is much tighter (Gauvin *et al.* 1994: 94). In the Netherlands, eligibility conditions for unemployment benefits have been subject to extensive legislative review aimed at tightening requirements for continuous employment history by merging the extended period of wage-related benefits with the first tier of benefits. According to proposals for forthcoming reforms, wage-related benefits are payable only to those who satisfy both a requirement of 26 weeks of contributory payments in the previous 39 weeks and a labour history requirement of three years of contributory payments in the previous four years. Those unemployed who fail both these conditions receive a 'continuation payment' (unemployment assistance) set at 70 per cent of the minimum wage (or 70 per cent of their previous daily wage – whichever is lower) (Plantenga and Sloep 1995: 45).

Workers in part-time employment

In the majority of member states, entitlement to unemployment benefits is also contingent on meeting minimum weekly working-time conditions while in previous employment and sometimes requires the ability and willingness of the unemployed to accept full-time work. In many countries this results in the outright exclusion of some groups of part-time employees from protection against the risks of unemployment which has a direct impact on women who are concentrated in low-paying and part-time jobs. Different eligibility conditions for unemployment compensation affect the decision to enter part-time employment. This is not to suggest, however, that there is an easy one-to-one relation between the favourable eligibility conditions and the rate of part-time employment. For example, in Germany, the rate is low compared to the UK (15 per cent and 23 per cent of the labour force respectively), yet both impose high risks for part-time workers by relatively stringent requirements for eligibility to unemployment compensation (Maier 1992).

Table 5.3 categorises member states into three groups according to the availability of unemployment benefits for part-time workers. In Ireland, Germany, the UK and to a lesser extent in Belgium, entitlement to benefits is most heavily oriented towards the conception of full-time work specified in terms of either weekly contractual hours or earnings. In the Netherlands, France and Spain, accessibility to unemployment benefits is relatively more favourable.

The UK and Ireland are the only member states to include a minimum earnings threshold below which employees neither make contributions nor receive benefit payments, although in Ireland part-time workers who previously earned between IR£30 and IR£70 per week are entitled to reduced payments. In Germany and the UK, there is the additional requirement of being willing and able to seek full-time employment (introduced in the UK from 1 November 1996) – although exceptions to the full-time jobseeking rule are made in Germany for unemployed workers who must care for children or other dependants; in these circumstances they are required to seek work involving more than 18 hours per week. (The state has only recently acknowledged that entitlement regulations which required women to prove childcare arrangements were discriminatory; in practice, however, it is likely that labour offices still conform with past regulations: Maier and Rapp 1995: 57.)

Table 5.3 Eligibility requirements for unemployment benefits affecting part-time workers in countries with medium to high levels of part-time employees, 1994

	Minimum hours or pay threshold for full entitlement to benefits	Additional entitlement conditions for unemployed part-time employees
Low		
Netherlands	None	—
France	None	Reduced benefits for working-time below a certain threshold
Spain	12 hours per week (or 48 per month)	—
Medium		
Denmark	15 hours per week	Reduced entitlement for work of 15–30 hours per week
Luxembourg	16 hours per week	Working time of less than 20 weekly hours counts as only half a contributory payment
High		
Belgium	More than 18 hours per week (or 3 hours per day)	—
Ireland	18 hours per week; IR£70 per week	Reduced benefits for previous weekly earnings of IR£30–IR£70
Germany	18 hours per week	Must be available for full-time employment
UK	UK£57 per week	Must be available for full-time employment

Sources: Maier (1992); national reports
Note: Greece, Portugal and Italy are excluded from the Table as the share of female employees in part-time jobs is relatively low (less than 10%). Interestingly, however, the Greek social security system does not distinguish between part-time and full-time employment since eligibility is dependent upon meeting a minimum number of daily contributory payments.

In Denmark, those insured as part-time workers receive reduced entitlements (Maier 1992: 47). The situation is similar in France, where employees with a part-time or a fixed term contract receive reduced entitlements to compensation. In France, this is due to the strict relation between the duration of unemployment benefits and the individual's record of contributory payments: this varies from an entitlement to four months at the standard level of benefits for those in employment during six months in the past year (for any age), to nine months of payments for those in employment during fourteen months in the past two years (for ages 25–

49) (Silvera *et al.* 1995: 100). In many countries, the benefits received are not proportional to the contributions paid. Information is not available, however, to calculate the precise relation between individual contributions and benefits received. This requires evaluation of the relation between the reduced level of contributions and the reduced benefits received for part-timers employed below the threshold level and comparison of this ratio with that for full-time employees. A degree of equity is maintained in Denmark, where part-timers employed between 15 and 30 hours per week receive pro rata benefit payments up to a maximum limit restricted to two-thirds of the threshold for full-time insured workers (Boje 1995: 61).

An additional feature in some countries involves adaptations of the unemployment insurance structure to encourage the acceptance of part-time employment or reduced working-time as an alternative to unemployment. In the Netherlands, benefits are available to workers who lose more than 5 hours per week (or 50 per cent of working time if weekly hours are less than 10). In Denmark, individuals with full-time insurance (employed for more than 30 hours per week) can claim supplementary benefits when working part-time for a maximum duration of 12 months provided they are immediately available for a full-time job. The effects of this practice in Denmark are partly reflected in data on the number of insured females in the labour force between 1981 and 1993, which demonstrate a clear trend from part-time to full-time insurance. As this is significantly greater than the shift from part-time to full-time employment among women, it suggests that many women have accepted part-time work along with supplementary benefits while seeking full-time work (Boje 1995: 59). Similar provisions exist in Belgium and France where workers with entitlement to the standard unemployment benefits continue to receive benefits if they take up part-time work (Maier 1992: 48–49). In Germany, full-time workers who become unemployed and then take up part-time employment are entitled to full-time benefits if they experience unemployment within a period of three and a half years after taking up part-time employment. Although such changes in policy recognise the importance of part-time work in job creation, the new condition underlines the disadvantages experienced by those in long-term part-time employment. Also, various schemes exist in Italy designed to compensate for lost earnings due to reductions in hours worked. Where the employee has accepted reductions in hours to avoid redundancies, 80 per cent of lost earnings are replaced through 'Wage Supplementation' schemes. Voluntary employee decisions to move to short-time working are usually covered by a 'Solidarity Contract' which replaces 75 per cent of lost earnings (until the end of 1995). However, access to these schemes is not possible for many employees in small industrial firms and service sectors (Bettio and Mazzotta 1995: 61–62).

In Germany, Ireland and the UK, provisions allowing unemployed persons to work up to a maximum number of hours while continuing to receive benefits are subject to severe restrictions, which ultimately create little, or no, positive incentives for the acceptance of part-time employment. In the UK and Germany, claimants earning more than a negligible amount (UK£10 for an unemployed couple in the UK from 1996; DM30 in Germany) face deductions in compensation on all excess earnings: in Germany, 50 per cent of the excess is deducted from benefit payments; and in the UK the claimant retains only the initial UK£10, as 50 per cent of the excess is deducted and the other 50 per cent is saved by the state to be refunded once the claimant's job involves 24 or more hours, or the claimant's unemployed partner is employed for more than 16 hours (Rubery and Smith 1995: 173). In Ireland, in the case of an unemployed couple receiving benefits, once the woman earns above IR£60 per week, the male claimant loses entitlement to the Adult Dependant Allowance and half of any Child Dependant Allowance. Also, under means-tested unemployment assistance, the male claimant is assessed as having half of any income earned by the female claimant above IR£45 per week (Barry 1995: 31–32, 55–56).[1] In each country, therefore, it is clear that such policies do not provide a major stimulus to participation in part-time work. Hence, in failing to act as a proper system of earnings insurance, the system of unemployment benefits imposes punitive marginal tax rates which restrict opportunities to boost household income while unemployed, and thus reinforces the divide between work-rich and work-poor households (Rubery and Smith 1995: 174). Moreover, even if such thresholds are argued to be necessary, it is not clear why the UK and Germany set them at such a punitive low level compared to Ireland. At current exchange rates, the German and British thresholds are approximately equivalent, and represent a quarter of the earnings disregarded in the Irish system. A broader treatment of these policies and the practice of in-work benefits in the UK is provided in Chapter 6, where we identify in more detail the effects of these policies on participation and the reinforcement of the 'unemployment trap'.

The restrictive policies found in Germany, the UK and Ireland contrast with the more supportive policies found in Belgium, which are far more likely to strengthen the bridge between unemployment benefits and stable employment. In Belgium, unemployment beneficiaries who work part-time have benefits deducted in proportion to weekly hours worked rather than according to an earnings threshold. Following implementation of this policy in 1983, by 1991 part-time employed beneficiaries made up 35 per cent of all beneficiaries and 45 per cent of all part-time workers. The policy of encouraging part-time employment was initially viewed as an anti-unemployment measure, both by providing a bridge out of unemployment and by reducing working-time. However, between 1983 and 1990, further information reveals that the proportion of part-time workers who were not seeking full-time work fell from 37 per cent to 12 per cent suggesting, it is argued, an inefficient reliance on state subsidies provided to those in work (OECD 1994b: 199).

Other excluded groups of workers

The relative economic position of the unemployed in Italy, Greece, Spain and Portugal is determined less by the relation between eligibility conditions and the sex of the claimant, than by the degree to which the social system provides coverage across all sectors of employment. Typically, stronger coverage is found in manufacturing rather than the service sector and in these Southern countries there is a relatively large informal economy in both manufacturing and services. Major holes in coverage mean that the past employment patterns of employees and their contractual status are less important than the actual sector of employment.

In Greece, the social security system offers weak protection due to the wide division between formal and informal work in the economy. This affects thousands of women working informally as homeworkers in traditional sectors of the Greek economy. Legislation in 1985 and 1986 was designed to integrate informal workers into the social security net by defining homeworking as dependent work and therefore obliging employers to pay the appropriate social security costs. However, in practice the effect was negligible, largely because employers were unwilling to increase costs by 20 to 25 per cent. In response, further legislation in 1990 exempted 30 per cent of labour costs paid to employees as a piece rate. Again, however, there has been little change in employer strategy (Cavouriaris *et al.* 1995: 47). In Spain, coverage has been continuously expanded since 1984; the share of registered unemployed in receipt of benefits increased from 38 per cent in 1985 to 75 per cent in 1993. However, particular groups of workers remain excluded, namely domestic workers, temporary workers in agriculture not living in the Southern regions of Spain, self-employed workers, students and civil servants (Moltó 1995: 115–116).

In Italy, the system of social security offers far from complete coverage. In 1993, of the total number of registered jobseekers (2,359,000), the majority (1,774,000) were first-time jobseekers and re-entrants who are excluded from the social security system. Therefore, less than 25 per cent of the total unemployed population was eligible for any form of unemployment compensation (Bettio and Mazzotta 1995: 70). For those in employment, the multi-level system of social security includes more generous forms of protection for the traditional sectors in industry and construction. Redundancy payments (or 'wage supplementation') were originally designed to protect employees in large industrial firms and have only recently been extended to some service sectors, including retail, newspapers and tourism, as well as cleaning subcontractors that work in firms eligible for wage supplementation. Women are therefore generally expected to predominate among those eligible for the lowest level of benefits ('ordinary unemployment benefits'), that is, employees in small firms or in excluded service sectors who are ineligible for the more generous wage supplementation schemes. In addition, apprentices, homeworkers and employees on fixed term contracts are excluded altogether from wage supplementation schemes so that women employed as homeworkers or with fixed term contracts only have access to 'ordinary unemployment benefits'. The limited evidence available demonstrates that in 1993 women were underrepresented among those eligible for either of the two forms of compensation. Women constituted 41 per cent of benefit recipients compared to a share of 53 per cent of total unemployment (Bettio and Mazzotta 1995: 61–70).

Duration of non-means-tested benefits and access to unemployment assistance

Where unemployed workers are ineligible or have exhausted their rights to unemployment benefits, most member states provide some form of unemployment assistance. However, where this takes household income as the reference, women lose their right to independent unemployment compensation. Hence, the period during which benefits can be claimed irrespective of household income is a key factor in assessing the relative economic position of different social groups among the unemployed.

Table 5.4 Grouping of countries according to duration of non-means-tested unemployment benefits

	Duration of standard rate of unemployment benefits
Long	
Belgium	Unlimited: subject to responsibility for dependants and average duration of unemployment in the region
Denmark	Up to 7 years
Netherlands	Up to 5 years: subject to past employment
Medium	
Germany	6–32 months: subject to age and past employment
Portugal	10–30 months: subject to age
France	4–27 months: subject to contributions record and age
Luxembourg	12–24 months: subject to age and difficulty in re-employment
Spain	120–720 days: subject to contributions record
Short	
Ireland	Up to 15 months: subject to age
UK	12 months (6 months from August 1996)
Greece	5–12 months: subject to age and contributory record
Italy	180 days: for 'ordinary unemployment benefits'

Sources: National reports
Note: See Appendix Table 5.1 for details of conditions

For many member states, the duration of unemployment benefits is a function of either the number of contributory days in employment or the age of the claimant or both (see Table 5.4). Therefore, those women with less than a fully continuous employment history who are not excluded at the first stage of entitlement to benefits are likely to experience unequal treatment in the form of a reduced period of non-means-tested benefits. The shorter the duration of unemployment benefits, the sooner unemployed workers have to rely upon forms of unemployment assistance which are paid to those in financial need. As entitlement to unemployment assistance typically depends upon an assessment of household income, and, as women are often in partnership with an employed man, women's claim to unemployment compensation will then take the form of derived rights rather than independent rights. This causes additional problems for women since once they lose individual entitlement to either unemployment insurance or assistance, they may also be exempt from active labour market programmes of training and recruitment (see section 5.3).

The member states can be grouped according to whether the duration of benefits is long, medium or short (Table 5.4). Although Belgium and Denmark are characterised as having a long duration of benefit payments, this requires some qualification. In Denmark the maximum duration of benefit payments has recently been restricted. During the 1980s, claimants nearing the end of their 2.5 years' entitlement to benefits were entitled to a 'Job Offer' of seven to nine months, sufficient to guarantee future entitlement to benefits. Then, in response to evidence showing a large number of persons moving recurrently from claimant status to Job Offers, reforms in 1988 limited the unemployed to two Job Offers. Further reforms in 1994 reorganised these transitions into two periods, potentially increasing the maximum duration of benefits to seven years. During the first three years, 'Period 1', the person is obliged to participate in subsidised work or training for twelve months, and during 'Period 2' the worker may be required to participate continuously. Hence, the seven-year maximum may include only two years of passive receipt of benefits (OECD 1995a: 124–125). The reforms also enable many workers to extend the period of benefits through entitlement to one-year extensions for both parental and educational leave (Boje 1995: 63). In Belgium the benefit system is midway between an insurance and an assistance scheme providing relatively low benefits for an unlimited duration. However, the standard rate is enjoyed for an unlimited period only by recipients who claim responsibility for dependants as the head of the household, although compensation is suspended once the person's duration in unemployment is greater than one and a half times the average regional duration of unemployment, controlling for age and sex. Claimants without dependants are subject to a decreasing scale of payments after the twelfth month (Meulders 1995: 62, 82).

The duration of non-means-tested benefits is particularly short in Ireland, the UK, Greece and Italy. In Ireland and the UK, women who have exhausted their rights to unemployment benefits or are ineligible are then subject to a household means test. Whatever the disadvantages this poses for unemployed female workers, however, the situation is more favourable relative to Greece and Italy, where there is no national scheme of further assistance to the long-term unemployed or to those ineligible for benefits (although there are regional policies in the South of Italy which ensure a limited degree of income support to families in need) (Bettio and Mazzotta 1995: 51).

Given that the evidence in Table 5.4 does not distinguish between receipt of benefits and receipt of unemployment assistance, it is useful to draw on national data in order to assess women's relative access to benefits compared to unemployment assistance. In former West Germany, although a relatively similar share of all registered unemployed women and men receive unemployment benefits (49 per cent and 54 per cent respectively), only 16 per cent of registered unemployed women receive unemployment assistance compared to 29 per cent of men. This means that almost one-third of all registered unemployed women in West Germany receive no financial compensation compared to around one-fifth of men (Maier and Rapp 1995: 59–60), reflecting the characteristics of the means-tested unemployment assistance scheme, which involves a low income threshold for the partner's income. In Spain, however, the evidence gives the contrary result. In 1993, women registered as unemployed made up 32 per cent of benefit recipients compared to 45 per cent of unemployment assistance recipients (Moltó 1995: 119–120). Given the relatively 'female friendly' eligibility conditions for unemployment benefits, it is likely that this evidence reflects the greater difficulty women face in re-entering employment (in 1992, for example, 53 per cent of women remained unemployed for at least twelve months, compared to 35 per cent of men), as well as the less stringent contributions record for entitlement to unemployment assistance.

Recent changes

The continuation of recessionary conditions and high unemployment into the mid-1990s in many member states has maintained strong pressure on unemployment expenditures due to both the large proportion of workers registering as unemployed and the increased period over which benefits need to be paid. In response, many countries have restricted access to benefits and reduced the level of benefits payable.

Recent changes in some countries highlight the contradictions in implementing a set of labour market policies which on the one hand promote so-called flexible employment practices among employers and on the other hand restrict the rights of employees in atypical employment to social security protection. This is true to some extent in the Netherlands and France. In the Netherlands, the proposed merger of the first two tiers of benefits and the tightening of eligibility conditions has been described above. In addition, however, as a means of diminishing the penalty faced by those ineligible to benefits under the new conditions the proposals also include an extension of the 'continuation payment' from one to two years (Plantenga and Sloep 1995: 42–44). An additional restrictive feature involves the proposed merger of the two schemes which provide unemployment assistance. Currently, one scheme is available to former employees and young first time jobseekers and obliges claimants to apply for jobs. The other scheme covers those who have few ties with the labour market and does not require them to make job applications. The largest group of beneficiaries of the latter group are female single parents (57 per cent of all beneficiaries in 1990). The merger of the two schemes will oblige those women protected by the second scheme to make job applications with a general exception made for parents responsible for children under 5 years old. The estimated impact of this legislation will increase the labour supply by 100,000 single mothers and 47,000 single, older women (Plantenga and Sloep 1995: 45–47). Finally, changes proposed for 1996 aim to increase the scope for means testing by removing the guaranteed right to an earnings retention allowance for those in receipt of unemployment benefits. The proposed legislation will decentralise the responsibility for determining whether an unemployed worker is eligible for additional income to the municipal level, thus increasing the opportunity for discretionary bias exercised against the interests of women (Plantenga and Sloep 1995: 47–48).

Since the 1992 reforms in France, eligibility conditions for unemployment benefits and assistance have become more restrictive, which has had particularly adverse implications for women in precarious employment and single unemployed women with insufficient contributions. The only groups who improved their position were unemployed workers with between four and six months' employment in the reference period, who received benefits for one more month after the reforms, and the group of unemployed with relatively high past earnings (Gauvin et al. 1994: 94). Evidence collected to assess the general impact shows that the fraction of unemployed who were ineligible for benefits rose by 16 per cent between June 1993 and June 1994 and the share of unemployed who had exhausted their claim to benefits and were ineligible for unemployment assistance (the 'specific solidarity allowance') rose by 38 per cent (Silvera et al., 1995:98–99).

In Spain and Denmark, where restrictions have occurred these have been partially offset by an expansion in coverage. In Spain, contributory record requirements were tightened in June 1994 from six months in the past four years to twelve months in the past six years, and the exemption of benefits from taxation was removed. Contrary to the expected outcome, however, national unemployment data shows a significant growth in the percentage of registered unemployed in receipt of benefits – from 38 per cent in 1985 to 75 per cent in 1993. Nevertheless, this may be partially the result of a relatively higher proportion of unemployed people who lack the incentive to register due to stricter eligibility conditions (Moltó, 1995: 115). In Denmark, where unemployment insurance is voluntary, there has also been a rise in coverage through increased voluntary membership of insurance funds. Between 1983 and 1993 the share of insured full-time and part-time workers increased from 67.2 per cent to 74.3 per cent among men and from 68 per cent to 81 per cent for women. The higher rate of coverage among women may be for two reasons: first, more men are self-employed or are employed in the private sector where the rate of coverage is lower in general; and second, the risk of unemployment has been slightly higher for women (Boje 1995: 59).

In the UK, changes proposed in the 1996 reforms will decrease women's independent right to unemployment benefits outright, primarily due to the decrease in the period of non-means-tested benefits from twelve months to six. In addition, the reforms will impose stricter availability-for-work tests which refer to a minimum norm of 40 hours per week. Women with caring responsibilities are given only limited attention by a vague and discretionary exception for those with an undefined 'significant' level of responsibilities. (Rubery and Smith 1995: 174–175). Hence, unemployed women in the UK are faced with both tightened rules of access and reduced entitlement to contributory benefits even though the rate of contributory payments have actually increased in recent years.

Replacement rates

Once eligible for unemployment insurance, the relative economic position of different social groups in unemployment is, in part, a function of the different procedures by which the replacement rate is calculated in different member states. This varies between, on the one hand, those member states which primarily aim to replace individual earnings and, on the other hand, those which aim to provide a universal minimum entitlement. Groups with lower average earnings, such as women, will receive lower actual benefits than high-wage groups in countries where the system calculates the level of benefits as a direct proportion of previous earnings, although the effect is modified where a maximum earnings or payment threshold applies. Conversely, women will enjoy more equitable treatment, and in fact a higher replacement rate, where benefits are paid as a fixed amount or where compensation guarantees a minimum income entitlement. This is not to suggest that equitable compensation is an appropriate measure of fair treatment, as the flat-rate benefits paid may be very low, and thus disadvantage all groups. Moreover, flat-rate payments are often paid to single adults and then topped up either by substantial additions for the number of dependants in the household, or by a large component of means-tested benefits. In both cases, women will tend to receive lower payments than men.

Despite these institutional considerations which impact upon different labour market groups, many economic analyses which incorporate a measure of the replacement rate – such as attempts to demonstrate a positive relation between the level and duration of benefits payable and the average duration of unemployment, or analyses that try to account for the impact of 'the cost of job loss' on worker productivity – not only assume full coverage of receipt of unemployment benefits, but also generally treat benefit payments as a homogeneous payment.

Two OECD reports, however, accounted for gender differentials in unemployment compensation. One study attempted to demonstrate the relation between the relative levels of unemployment benefits received by men and women and the ratio of total male to total female unemployment for a number of OECD countries (OECD 1994b: 171–183). Differences in compensation received by men and women are based on a proxy for household position: men's level of benefits are calculated as the average of payments made to a single person and to someone with a dependent spouse; women's benefits represent the average of a single person's benefits and a person with a spouse in work. Given this information, a correlation is found between the ratio of benefit payments received by men and women and the ratio of male and female unemployment. A previous OECD report found a positive correlation between the ratio of the replacement rate paid to long-term unemployed women relative to the average rate for all in long-term unemployment and the share of women registered among the long-term unemployed (OECD 1991: 204–208). The calculation of the replacement rate for women assumes that married women do not receive unemployment assistance when unemployment insurance benefits are exhausted since their spouse is working.

In both cases, therefore, household position is used as a proxy for calculating different replacement rates for men and women. The assumption is that married men are more likely to claim an allowance for a dependent spouse while in unemployment, and that a married woman will be worse off as a result of the greater likelihood that her spouse will be at work. This is an important addition to an understanding of the relation between household organisation and the different levels of benefit payments, and thus the different incentive effects of benefits for men and women. What is surprising, however, is that in neither study does the calculation of replacement rates take into account women's inferior average earnings capacities relative to men, since there is no reference to earnings data disaggregated by sex. Earnings referred to in OECD (1991) use annual pay data for the full-time 'average production worker' in manufacturing. In OECD (1994b), the same source of pay data is combined with pay data derived from dividing the National Account income by the level of full-time equivalent employment (accounting for the incidence of part-time work); the average of the two sources provides the basis of earnings statistics used (OECD 1994b: Annex 8A). Consequently, both approaches fail to incorporate the important influence of labour market organisation and segmentation on the position of the unemployed.

Consideration of the relation between replacement rates and gender wage differentials raises serious methodological problems. First, the relative replacement rates paid to women may tend to increase in countries where benefits are paid at a flat rate and decrease where benefits are earnings related. Second, the attempt to correlate levels of benefits with unemployment levels does not take into account the possibility that women may switch between registered unemployment and inactivity depending upon certain characteristics of the benefits system, as well as between employment and unemployment.[2] The first criticism is addressed in the following discussion of male and female replacement rates in the member states calculated as a function of both differential earnings opportunities and household position. The second criticism is addressed in the discussion of active labour market policy (section 5.3) and the evaluation of the impact of the social security system on labour market participation (section 6.2).

The evidence in Table 5.5 shows the actual replacement rates for men and women in the twelve member states. Calculations refer to male and female workers who are registered as unemployed, eligible for entitlement to the standard rate of benefits and previously earned the respective average wage as a full-time manual worker in manufacturing (see Appendix Table 5.2 for details). The replacement rates shown consider the initial period of unemployment only, and therefore ignore those differences between countries resulting from changes in the replacement rate formulae as the period of unemployment increases.[3] Relatedly, no reference is made to the different durations of entitlement to unemployment benefits experienced by unemployed men and women, which may reduce women's relative replacement rates either as a result of women's greater likelihood of shifting on to means-tested assistance prior to men, or due to women's limited access to extended periods of unemployment benefits. Also, Table 5.5 refers to the gross level of unemployment benefits for all countries, despite the fact that, following recent changes in Ireland and Spain, Greece is now the only country in the EU to exempt unemployment compensation from taxation (National reports; OECD 1991: 201).

The majority of member states calculate the replacement rate as a proportion of previous earnings subject to a maximum threshold. The UK and Ireland are the only cases where a fixed amount is payable to all eligible registered unemployed workers regardless of past income, and Italy is the only case where the percentage rate of compensation for 'ordinary unemployment benefits' is applied to all earnings. The level of replacement rate in Italy is largely dependent on access to the particular scheme of compensation. The lowest level of 20 per cent for 'ordinary unemployment benefits' applies to workers from small industrial firms and most parts of the service sector. Higher rates of 80 per cent and more are available for workers in large industrial firms and the construction sector in the form of 'wage supplementation' or 'turnover benefits', which offer protection to those temporarily laid off or with a reduction in working time.

Table 5.5 Replacement rate for initial period of unemployment benefits based on average gross weekly earnings of men and women working as full-time manual workers in manufacturing, October 1993

	Formula for replacement rate	*Addition for dependent spouse*	*Threshold level*	*Replacement rates for full-time manufacturing manual workers*			
				Ratio of gross benefits to gross earnings for a single person		*Ratio assuming men claim for a dependent spouse*	
				M	*F*	*M*	*F*
Belgium	55%	5%	yes	0.44	0.55	0.48	0.55
Denmark	90%	no	yes	0.63	0.77	0.63	0.77
Germany	60% (of net earnings)	no	yes	0.34	0.32	0.34	0.32
Greece	40%	10% of benefit	yes	0.25	0.32	0.28	0.32
Spain	70%	no	yes	0.66	0.70	0.66	0.70
France	(40.4% + FF 1,645) or 57.4%	no	yes	0.58	0.63	0.58	0.63
Ireland	IR£55.60 p.w.	IR£35.50	n/a	0.21	0.33	0.33	0.33
Italy	20%	no	no	0.20	0.20	0.20	0.20
Luxembourg	80%	no	yes	0.80	0.80	0.80	0.80
Netherlands	70%	no	yes	0.70	0.70	0.70	0.70
Portugal	65%	no	yes	0.65	0.65	0.65	0.65
UK	UK£45.45	UK£28.05	n/a	0.15	0.25	0.25	0.25

Sources: National reports and additional information provided
Note: See Appendix Table 5.2 for details

The degree to which lost earnings are compensated for while in unemployment varies enormously between member states. Six countries stand out as offering relatively high replacement rates: Denmark, Spain, France, Luxembourg, the Netherlands and Portugal, where actual replacement rates for men and women range between 58 and 80 per cent. In contrast, compensation is extremely limited in Ireland and the UK as a result of the low flat rates, and Italy where the results refer to the least generous scheme of compensation.

Separate results for men and women which account for differential average earnings and the effects of maximum threshold levels reveal the extent to which men and women experience unequal levels of compensation within each country and the relative level of benefits between countries. Clearly, women gain from systems which offer high absolute levels of compensation as well as those which ensure gender parity among the eligible unemployed. Of the four countries with the highest replacement rate formulae, women's relative level of compensation compared to men in Luxembourg and the Netherlands mirrors the average gender differential in earnings; high maximum earnings thresholds in both countries mean that men and women receive the same proportion of previous earnings. In contrast, the compensation differential in Denmark and Spain is narrower than the degree of gender pay inequality in employment. In Spain, for example, women previously earning the average wage in manufacturing receive the maximum replacement rate as the maximum earnings threshold lies above women's average earnings yet below men's average earnings. Also, in France, women benefit from the application of a dual replacement rate formula which involves payment of either 40.4 per cent plus a fixed amount of FF 1,645 per month or 57.4 per cent, according to which is the higher (limited to a range between FF 3,983 and 75 per cent of past earnings). Inclusion of the former option benefits low-paid workers, and therefore women.

Among countries where the replacement rate is generally low for all unemployed workers (Germany, Greece, Ireland, Italy and the UK), women experience greater gender parity only in those countries which practise a flat-rate compensation system (UK, Ireland and, in practice, Greece where the threshold is so low that actual payments amount to a flat-rate system). In Ireland, however, where both partners in a household are registered as unemployed, the total receipt of unemployment benefits is always the sum of one single person's rate and an allowance for an adult dependant, whether both claim individually or only one person claims. As men are predominantly the primary claimants, women have little incentive to register as unemployed and are therefore more likely to receive compensation indirectly (Barry 1995: 31). Furthermore, where a claimant is receiving a single parent's allowance or a deserted wives' allowance, only half the personal rate of benefit is payable and no addition is made for child dependants (Barry 1995: 26–27). In Italy, women receive an equivalent proportion of lower earnings compared to men, and Germany is the only case where men receive a higher proportion of earnings than women. This is the result of basing the calculation of replacement rates on net earnings which is disadvantageous to many women who are penalised by the effects of Germany's household-based cumulative tax structure. Women married to men earning higher wages are subject to relatively higher tax rates and therefore receive a relatively smaller replacement rate. Also, as both men and women pay social security contributions according to gross earnings, women in this situation do not receive their rightful compensation, in effect wasting contributions (Maier and Rapp, 1995: 57).

The final column in Table 5.5 takes into account the greater likelihood that unemployed men, rather than women, will receive additional compensation for a dependent spouse. Such a mechanism exists in only four member states (Belgium, Greece, Ireland and the UK), although others do include allowances for dependent children – an issue which is not considered here (see Appendix Table 5.2 for details). In Ireland and the UK, receipt of a dependent spouse allowance by the male claimant equates the man's recalculated replacement rate with that of a female single claimant.

The treatment of part-time workers, in terms of the relative level of benefit payments received, varies between member states. In the Netherlands there are no exceptions to part-timers' entitlements to benefits; eligibility depends upon the loss of 5 working hours or at least 50 per cent of normal hours if the working week is 10 hours or less. In Denmark and Spain, for those unemployed part-time workers who meet the relatively moderate eligibility conditions (previously employed more than 15 and 12 hours per week respectively), calculation of the actual replacement rate is made according to specific part-time threshold levels. In Denmark, the threshold level was DKr 1,695 per week for part-time workers compared to DKr 2,545 for full-time workers. In Spain, thresholds apply to part-time employment on a pro rata basis by accounting for the hourly minimum wage. In the UK and Ireland, the universal flat-rate benefit provides a potentially high replacement rate for part-time workers. For example, an unemployed female part-time worker in the UK with average earnings in manufacturing would have received a replacement rate of 50 per cent in 1994. However, although payments do not distinguish between part-time and full-time workers, the system of eligibility conditions in the UK is designed to exempt many part-time workers from coverage. Consequently, part-timers who lose their jobs are unlikely to enjoy relatively high benefit payments as they must first meet strict availability for work requirements (of 40 hours per week from November 1996) and satisfy the required number of contributory payments (Rubery and Smith 1995: 218–220).

Since the mid-1970s, restrictive practices in many member states have led to a decline in actual replacement rates. According to OECD calculations for the period 1972 to 1990, this trend is particularly evident in Belgium, Denmark, Germany, Ireland, the Netherlands and the UK (see Table 5.6). The massive decline in the UK, bringing it close to the bottom of the ranking in 1990, is partly due to changes in the formula of indexation during the 1980s from upgrading according to average earnings to a link with the retail price index (Rubery and Smith 1995: 218). In Germany, the drop in actual replacement rates between 1980 and 1990 is partly explained by a change in the replacement rate formula in 1986 – from 68 per cent of net earnings to 63 per cent for persons without children. The most widespread changes have occurred in France. Following changes in July 1993, the range of unemployment benefits (basic allowance, exceptional basic allowance and end-of-entitlement allowance) were replaced by a single sliding-scale allowance. Under the new conditions, the rate of payment is reduced by between 15 per cent and 17 per cent every four months. Also, the link between the unemployed person's record of contributions and the period of entitlement to benefits is much tighter (Gauvin *et al.* 1994: 94). The institutionalisation of stronger insurance principles may disadvantage many women by enhancing the significance of discontinuous or short employment history and working-time.

Table 5.6 Replacement rates of unemployment benefits[a]: comparisons across member states (E9), 1972–90

	1972	1980	1990
Belgium	0.83	0.73	—
Denmark	—	0.60	0.47
France	0.34	0.41	—
Germany	0.74	0.64	0.42
Ireland	—	0.43	0.35
Italy	0.11	0.14	0.08
Netherlands	—	0.93	0.75
Spain	—	0.39	0.40
UK	0.43	0.28	0.16

Source: OECD (1993a: 105)
Note: a Calculated as the ratio of actual payments of unemployment insurance benefits per unemployed recipient to the average wage of all production workers

In the Netherlands, the maximum earnings threshold has remained unchanged between 1993 and 1995. Hence, although in 1993 the threshold was greater than average earnings in manufacturing for both men and women (see Appendix Table 5.2), it is likely that actual replacement rates will have fallen below 70 per cent for 1995, particularly for male manual workers in manufacturing. In Germany, the replacement rate formula was reduced again in 1994 – from 63 per cent with an additional 5 per cent child allowance to 60 per cent with an addition of 7 per cent. Child allowances were introduced in 1986, replacing the universal entitlement of all unemployed workers to 68 per cent of previous net earnings (Maier and Rapp 1995: 57). Further examples of restrictive changes include Spain, which has recently established unemployment compensation as a taxable source of income and the UK where legislative change proposed for 1996 will abolish the adult dependant allowance – currently paid independently of requiring the partner to seek work – and integrate payments with the income-related 'Jobseeker's Allowance' (Rubery and Smith 1995). In fact, Greece appears to be the only country where change has occurred in the opposite direction. Maximum earnings thresholds, against which the replacement rate is applied, were 30 per cent higher in 1994 than in 1993. Calculations for 1994 earnings data show that this secured higher actual replacement rates for unemployed men and women (31 per cent and 40 per cent respectively). However, few policies appear to have been implemented in Greece to alter the very low share of registered unemployed in receipt of compensation, which is among the lowest in the European Union (see Table 5.1) .

5.2   Non-wage labour costs

The design of unemployment compensation systems varies enormously between member states. Not only do member states provide very different levels of financial support to those in unemployment, but also they rely on very different means of financing the system of social security. For example, whereas in some countries funding is largely reliant upon employer and employee earnings-related contributions, in others the revenue is primarily drawn from general taxation. These differences inspire much of the current European debate on national competitiveness which maintains that both the level of social security protection and the means of financing have a direct effect on the burden of non-wage costs to the employer, which, other things being equal, affects the competitiveness of employers in each country. Despite the lack of evidence for the negative effects of too high non-wage costs, formulation of policy at the European level stresses the need to reduce employer contributions to social security in order to increase the creation of low-wage, low-skilled labour which is seen as a key element in raising the employment rate (Dreze and Malinvaud 1994 cited in Maier and Rapp 1995: 54). This argument applies in particular to those countries that have regressive systems of contributions which impose disproportionate costs on low-wage labour. In contrast, however, there is also evidence that high levels of social security and strong economic performance correlate closely (Chassard 1992, cited in Reissert and Schmid 1994: 116; Wilensky 1975). This demonstrates that a well-developed social security system not only protects workers against the risks of structural economic change, but also may facilitate long-term adjustments which translate into higher rates of economic growth. Furthermore, the supposed negative relation between the level of employment and relative labour costs is subject to the usual Keynesian objection that a decrease in labour costs would increase the demand for goods and services only in the special case of a perfectly functioning neo-classical labour market (Maier and Rapp 1995: 54).

Different methods of financing social security expenditures also have direct implications for equal opportunities in employment. For example, employer and employee contributions to the social security system may be organised in a progressive or a regressive manner, according to the rate of contributory payments for different levels of earnings. Given the tendency for women to be concentrated among the low paid in each member state,

175

regressive systems will worsen the relative position of women in employment compared to men.

We can identify five general principles present in the contributory payment systems of different member states, each of which has a different
impact upon the patterns of employment demand and women's relative
degree of protection. The first and second principles are regressive. According to the first, contributions are paid at a flat rate for all earnings,
irrespective of the individual employment contract, offering social security
protection to all employees. The effect is to impose disproportionate costs
on the employment of low-paid or part-time employees thus acting as a
disincentive to job growth in these forms of employment. The second
principle applies earnings-related contributions up to a maximum earnings,
or hourly, threshold level for the employer or the employee, again imposing
the burden of costs on low-paid employees. The third principle is neither
progressive nor regressive. Contributions are proportional to earnings or
weekly hours for all earnings and thus have a neutral effect on labour
demand. The fourth and fifth principles are progressive features. The fourth
exempts either the employer or the employee from the obligation to pay
social security contributions for low earnings, which may make the creation
or acceptance of low-wage or part-time employment attractive in terms of
net costs, yet unattractive to the employee if it offers a low level of social
protection. The fifth principle involves the payment of higher contributory
rates as earnings increase.

Although it is possible to identify regressive and progressive features in
member states' systems of contributory payments, the impact of these
features on employment depends largely upon the relative size of non-
wage labour costs compared to other countries. For example, although
the old system of flat-rate contributions made by employees in Denmark
prior to the reforms in 1994 was extremely regressive in principle, because
the rate of payment as a proportion of earnings was extremely low
(DK3,552 per year, which was approximately 2 per cent of average earnings
in manufacturing), the impact of this form of payment was minimal. Low
contributory payments were made possible by an almost complete reliance
on general taxation as a means of financing social security expenditures
rather than employment contributions (Boje 1995: 60–66). In contrast, the
regressive structure found in Greece does impose high social security costs
on the employer and the employee, and therefore will have a greater
influence on employment patterns, particularly between informal and
formal sectors. Payments in Greece are earnings related up to a maximum
earnings threshold, which was approximately four times the minimum
wage and two and a half times greater than the average wage in 1994,
and costs are among the highest in the European Union – 27 per cent
for the employer and 16 per cent for the employee (Cavouriaris et al.
1995: 47).

In addition to whether social security contributions are high or low, some member states may place more weight on contributions from the employer rather than the employee, which adds a further dimension to the potential impact on the dynamics of the employment structure. For example, in Belgium, Italy, Spain and Portugal, employers contribute between two and four times the rate paid by the employee, whereas in Germany and the UK contributory rates are approximately equal, and employees in the Netherlands pay a substantially higher rate than employers. The following comparison of contributory payment systems in member states will outline where payments are regressive or progressive in principle and, accounting for the relative size of payments compared to other member states, will identify those features which are relatively advantageous for women's employment.

Categorisation of member states according to whether the system of payments is progressive or regressive is difficult both because of recent experience of substantial reorganisation in some member states and because each social security system invariably contains some combination of the five principles described above. Since the early 1980s, many member states have made substantial changes in the levels of social security contributions collected from the employer and the employee. In Germany, Greece, Spain and Denmark, contributory rates have been increased in response to the demands of high unemployment expenditures, whereas in Belgium and Luxembourg additional financing has been secured from alternative sources. Also, in France permanent measures have been introduced to reduce employers' non-wage labour costs for low-paid workers (see Box 5.1 for details). Consequently, the grouping of countries presented in Table 5.7 represents a general characterisation – so that regressive systems in Luxembourg, Spain and Germany also include the progressive principle of exempting employers and employees from payments for earnings below a minimum earnings threshold. In general, systems of payments found in most member states are regressive – primarily as a result of exemptions at the top end of the earnings distribution (Luxembourg, Spain, Greece, Ireland, Germany and the Netherlands). In the UK, exemptions exist for employees earnings high wages, but it is the only member state where contributions paid by employers are progressive across the whole earnings distribution and is therefore categorised as 'partially progressive'. Finally, five countries (Belgium, Denmark, France, Italy and Portugal) have neutral systems of social security contributions with respect to the creation or acceptance of particular forms of employment contract; contributory rates are earnings related and payable on all earnings. The social security system in France is slightly complicated as employer contributions to family benefit increase as earnings increase (from 0 per cent to 5.4 per cent, see Box 5.1). Compared to the UK, however, total employer contributions in France do not vary substantially with earnings and it is unlikely that they will have a non-neutral impact on patterns of employment creation.

Box 5.1   Changes in the financing of social security protection

Where change has occurred in the financing of the social security system in member states, this has largely been driven by the need to fund increasing unemployment benefit expenditures due to persistent high rates of unemployment and the increasing duration of periods in unemployment.

In **Germany**, total social security contributions rose from 32.4 per cent of gross earnings in 1980 to 39.1 per cent in 1994 and total contributions to unemployment insurance rose from 3 per cent to 6.5 per cent during the same period. These increases primarily reflect the crisis in the East German labour market (Maier and Rapp 1995: 55-56).

Reforms in **Greece** (legislation in 1990, 1991 and 1992) have increased the rates of contributions to 27.45 per cent for employers and 15.8 per cent for employees, compared to 20.9 per cent for employers in 1974. Proposals in 1994 to increase unemployment insurance contributions by 0.5 and 0.2 percentage points to the employer and employee respectively have not yet been implemented due to the employers' reactions. Given the limited success of including the informal sectors of employment in the social security structure of payments, it is expected that further increases in social labour costs will deepen the segregation between formal and informal sectors (Cavouriaris *et al.*, 1995: 48).

In **Spain**, the minimum level of contributions increased by 6.6 per cent and the maximum by 8.4 per cent between 1983 and 1994 (taking weighted measures for the different occupational levels). The lower rises occurred among the lowest paid occupational groups, serving, it is claimed, to increase the creation of low-paid jobs (Moltó, 1995: 125-126). However, the maximum threshold levels are still relatively low in comparison to other member states, so that the system still concentrates social security costs disproportionably among low-paid workers.

Changes in the method of financing active labour market policies in **Denmark** have also increased employer and employee contributions. Prior to 1994, Denmark was the only member state where employee contributions to social security were voluntarily paid at a flat rate through membership of trade union unemployment insurance funds (although according to OECD (1995a), voluntary systems also exist in Finland and Sweden). These contributions were used to finance unemployment insurance expenditures, and general tax revenue was used to finance active labour market policies, vocational training and sickness benefits. Legislative changes in 1994 secured increased financing from earnings contributions by introducing earnings-related payments of 5 percent for employees from January 1994, to increase to 8 per cent in 1998, and payments of 0.3 per cent of gross earnings for employers from 1997, to increase to 0.6 per cent by 1988 (Boje 1995: 60-66).

Other countries have lowered contributory payments in line with mainstream economic arguments. In **Belgium**, adjustments in the means of financing have secured additional funds for the system of social security from the energy tax in order to avoid increasing employer costs (Meulders 1995: 63).

In **Luxembourg**, since 1995 family allowances have been financed by the public authorities, reducing the employer's contribution from 14.2 per cent to 12.5 per cent (Plasman 1995: 32).

Permanent measures were introduced in **France** in July 1993 (and extended in December 1993) to reduce employer contributions to family benefits. Prior to the reforms, employers paid 0 per cent on earnings up to 1.2 x minimum wage, 2.7 per cent on earnings between 1.2 and 1.3 x minimum wage, and 5.4 per cent on all earnings above this level. By 1998, when the reforms are fully implemented, employers will pay 0 per cent on earnings up to 1.5 x the minimum wage and 2.7 per cent on earnings between 1.5 and 1.6 x the minimum wage. The aim of the policy is to create a positive incentive to the creation of low paying jobs. Estimates predict the creation of 100,000 jobs after five years (Silvera *et al.* 1995).

The systems of contributory payments in Luxembourg, Spain, Germany, the UK and Ireland include non-regressive features for low earnings. In the former four countries, employers and employees are completely exempt from contributory payments where earnings are below a minimum level: the minimum wage in Luxembourg; an occupational-specific minimum level in Spain; the combination of an hours and earnings threshold in Germany; and a fixed income level in the UK. In Ireland, although employees are exempt for earnings below IR£173 per week, the employer pays a reduced contributory rate, thus ensuring coverage for all employees under the social security system. Additional features in Spain include reduced contributions (by a coefficient of 0.3) for employees who fall between the minimum and maximum earnings thresholds and work less than 12 hours per week, and a special fixed rate contribution for employers of full-time domestic staff (Moltó, 1995: 123). In each country the non-regressive element may be expected to act as an incentive to the creation and acceptance of low-paid jobs due to the attractive labour costs and relatively high net earnings. However, these may be outweighed by the increased risks faced by the employee in accepting employment which is excluded from social security protection. Figures for Germany in 1992 show that a total of 3.84 million people, 70 per cent of whom were women, relied on 'marginal' part-time jobs as their primary or secondary source of income, which were completely exempt from social security contributions (Maier and Rapp, 1995: 50). However, the exclusionary impact of the minimum threshold in the UK is potentially higher than in Germany due to the higher relative level of the threshold compared to average earnings. Figures for the UK in 1994 show that the minimum level of UK£57 (the equivalent of approximately 15 to 20 hours per week) was approximately 31 per cent of the average pay of women in full-time, manual manufacturing jobs, compared to an equivalent ratio of 16–18 per cent in Germany.[4] Further details in the UK national report show

Table 5.7 Social security contributions as a percentage of gross salary for the employer and the employee, 1994

	Social security contribution rates, minimum exemption and maximum earnings thresholds			
	Employer contribution rates		Threshold levels	
Employee contribution rates	Threshold levels		*Partially progressive system*	
UK[a]	0.0%	<UK£57	0.0%	<UK£57
	3.6%	UK£57–99.99	2% of £57 +	UK£57-430
	5.6%	UK£100–144.99	10$% of pay, up to UK£430 p.w.	
	7.6%	UK£150–199.99		
	10.2%	>UK£200p.w.		
Neutral system				
Belgium	32.3 %	None	13.1 %	None
Italy	45.96%	None	9.99%	None
Portugal	24%	None	11 %	None
Denmark	0.0%	None	5.0 %	None
France	34.42–39.7%	None, except family benefit contribution (see text)	21.0–21.87%	None, except family benefits contribution (see text)
Regressive system				
Luxembourg	0.0%	Min. wage	0.0 %	Min. wage
	14.2%	Up to 5 x min. wage	12.5 %	Up to 5 x min. wage
Spain	0.0%	Min. income level	0.0 %	Min. income level
	24.4%	Up to max.level (varies for prof. category)	4.9 %	Up to max. level (varies for prof. category)
Greece	27.45%	Up to Dr 417.505	15.80%	Up to Dr417.500
Ireland	9.0%	IR£0–173 p.w.	0.0 %	<IR£60 p.w.
	12.2%	IR£173 p.w.–IR£25,800 p.a.	5.5 %	IR£60–173 p.w.
			7.75%	IR£173 p.w.–IR£20,900 p.a.
			2.25%	>IR20,900
Germany[b]	0.0%	<15 hrs p.w. and < DM560 p.m.	0.0%	<15 hrs p.w. and < DM 560 p.m.
	19.55%			
	16.3%	Up to DM 5,700 p.m. DM 5,700–7,600 p.m.	19.55% 16.3%	Up to DM 5,700 p.m. DM 5,700–7,600 p.m.
Netherlands[c]	2.95%	Up to daily threshold of HFL286	31.25%	Paid on annual earnings HFL 5,925–43,267
	+5.15%	Up to daily threshold of HFL190	+13.9%	Up to daily threshold of HFL286
			+1.2%	Up to daily threshold of HFL190

Sources: National reports

Notes: a For the UK (1995 data), the percentage figures for employer and employee represent the contributions paid by those contracted in to the occupational pension scheme (SERPS), which effectively represents the minimum contribution to social security.

b For Germany, the minimum hours threshold refers to health and pension insurance contributions; 18 weekly hours is the minimum threshold for unemployment insurance contributions.

c In the Netherlands, different contributory rates reflect payments to the different pension, health and unemployment funds.

that if we assume a full-time post requires 36 hours, then the British contribution system will always favour splitting the work between at least two people, with regard to minimising the size of employment costs. Hence, the social security system substantially reduces the relative costs of female part-time to male full-time labour (Rubery and Smith 1995: 177–179).

Among these five countries the non-regressive principles (exemptions or reduced rates for low earnings) are typically outweighed by regressive principles for high earnings. In each country contributory rates for employers or employees do not apply to earnings above a specified maximum earnings threshold.[5] In Luxembourg, Spain and Germany, this is true for employers and employees; for the UK the threshold level applies only to employees; and for Ireland the threshold exists only for employer contributions. The regressive effect of the maximum earnings threshold clearly depends on the proportion of employees that lies above the threshold in each country. For example, in West Germany the threshold is relatively high. In 1990 only 1.4 per cent of full-time men and 0.01 per cent of women in manual employment earned above the higher threshold, and 33 per cent and 3.7 per cent of male and female non-manual workers respectively (Maier and Rapp 1995: 48–49). Hence, the structure is almost neutral for manual employees and female non-manual employees, yet strongly regressive with regard to male non-manual workers. This suggests that the structure of payments in West Germany has a neutral impact on the employment patterns of women, whether part-time or full-time, for jobs of more than 15 hours per week. In contrast, the relatively lower earnings thresholds in the UK and Spain do impose disproportionate costs on the employment of low-paid or part-time employees. In the UK, around one in ten male full-time manual workers in manufacturing earn above the maximum weekly threshold of UK£430 for employee contributions (New Earnings Survey 1994),[6] and in Spain the maximum daily earnings threshold for manual workers in 1994 was approximately equal to the average pay of male manual employees in manufacturing (Moltó 1995: 122; own calculations).

The system of earnings-related social security payments on all earnings which is practised in Belgium, Denmark, France, Italy and Portugal is neutral with regard to the relative costs of various employment contracts, and between high- and low-paid employees. However, in Belgium and Italy, actual contributory payments differ from statutory rates for a number of reasons. In Belgium, reduced contributions exist for public sector employment. As an employer, the Belgian state pays only 3.8 per cent for health and pension insurance and the employee pays 10.5 per cent (the state also makes reduced contributions in Ireland, see p. 328). In Italy, rates are less for small firms and vary by industry. Also, rebates of 25 per cent are available for firms in Southern Italy if they hire long-term unemployed or disabled workers, or provide apprenticeship positions (Bettio and Mazzotta 1995: 46).

The UK is the only country in the European Union where a progressive structure of employer contributions applies to all earnings. For earnings greater than UK£57 per week, the employer pays increased rates as earnings increase through a series of thresholds and each time the threshold is passed the new rate is paid on all gross earnings. This contrasts with the Irish system of employee payments where each higher rate applies only to the additional earnings above each threshold level. In the UK, therefore, there are a number of points in the pay scale where substantial jumps in costs may act as major disincentives to increasing earnings to the higher band. For the employee, earnings above the weekly 'lower earnings limit' are subject to a rate of 2 per cent on the first UK£57 and 10 per cent on all additional earnings up to a ceiling of UK£430 per week (Rubery and Smith 1995: 176).

From the above comparison of different contributory payment systems, it is possible to identify those characteristics which are beneficial to women's equal treatment. Given men's overrepresentation among the high paid and women's overrepresentation among the low paid, it is likely that women benefit most from systems where contributions are earnings related, or increase progressively with income, and are not subject to a ceiling. Where ceilings apply, or contributions are at a flat rate for all earnings, low paid and part-time workers are penalised with disproportionate costs. Of course the size of these penalties is determined by the overall level of contributions, ranging from 46 per cent for the employer in Italy to 0 per cent in Denmark. In member states which do not limit earnings-related payments by the employee to a ceiling (Belgium, Denmark, France, Italy and Portugal), the low paid are clearly not burdened with high contributory payments. Inclusion of other progressive principles, such as exemption of low-paid employees from contributory payments, which in principle would favour women, may have negative consequences as a result of reductions in benefits or perhaps tightening of eligibility rules which could result in reduced access to benefits for those people who benefited from lower contributions in these countries (Maier 1995: 85–86). Hence, the equal treatment of low-paid and part-time employees also depends crucially on allowances within the structure of social security protection which ensures complete coverage to all those in employment. The relation between contributions and protection must therefore combine principles of both individual insurance protection and universal distributive justice based on a taxation principle of benefits. Women will benefit by social security systems which twin progressive contributory payments with a universal entitlement to a minimum level of standard protection funded through a distributive system of financing. This may be combined with the application of insurance principles which equate higher contributions with greater levels of protection to ensure, for example, favourable replacement rates. However, where this imposes excessive pressure on the demands for funding, it may be necessary to introduce or reduce maximum thresholds for receipt of benefits so that maximum compensation is only guaranteed up to a maximum earnings limit.

5.3   Active labour market policies

Active labour market policies are concerned with promoting employment or improving employability, as opposed to passive labour market policies which concentrate on income replacement. Some policies, such as early retirement or leave schemes, may fall in between these definitions, as by providing extra sources of income replacement they may free up job vacancies for the non-employed, and in some cases access to leave or retirement may be directly tied to replacements from the unemployed or non-employed.

In most countries there appears to be relatively little interest or awareness of gender issues in active labour market policies, such that the main targets of such policies are the long-term unemployed, youth unemployed or other groups such as the disabled, and few include women as a main target group. An exception to this is the Netherlands, where women have constituted a main target group of job placement policies, alongside young people and ethnic minorities, and interestingly women constitute the only target group where the share of job placements has actually exceeded their representation within the pool of unemployed (Plantenga and Sloep 1995: 53). However, there have been plans developed in the Netherlands to move away from target demographic groups to a classification of the unemployed according to their 'distance' from the labour market. It is not clear how women will fare within this classification, but more significant is the fact that there has been no discussion of the effect of this change, and the effective abandonment of women as a specific target group on women's labour market prospects. Thus the commitment to deal with gender inequality within the Netherlands active labour market policy does not seem to go very deep. There are other countries where there has also been a move away from policies which allow for some form of positive action for women. In Italy subsidies for young people's employment have been retained while those for women's employment have been removed, on the grounds that in practice this provided a hidden subsidy for the textiles industry. The requirement for firms in Italy to hire from the unemployment register, which tended to favour women, has also been abandoned, in this case on the grounds that it was in any case ineffective. In the UK the change in training schemes has increased incentives to trainers to concentrate resources on those with the highest chance of employment, thus leading to a reduction in training schemes for women to move into non-traditional jobs (Rubery and Smith 1995: 180). And in France a special training programme for single women has been amalgamated with the general jobseekers' training programme (Silvera et al. 1995: 111).

The more general direction of change has been to expand the number of programmes targeted at women, but for these programmes to be very small-scale in relation both to the labour market and to the range of active labour market policies. Only where active labour market policies are relatively restricted – as for example in Greece – do programmes targeted at women and funded by the European Social Fund take on a greater relative importance (Cavouriaris *et al.* 1995: 9). The range of specific active labour market policies for women include subsidies for the creation of permanent jobs (in Spain), women's training schools and women's advice centres (the Netherlands), positive action training programmes (Portugal, Ireland) and special courses for women returners (Ireland) and the development of courses, often in service sectors, under the NOW (New Opportunities for Women) initiative (Greece). In Belgium labour market returners, sometimes including particular reference to women, are among the groups specified to be assisted by employment funds set up either through state legislation or through collective agreements based on a levy of the wage bill.

Where evaluations of these policies have been made the results are not very impressive. In Spain only very few permanent jobs for women have been created under the subsidies scheme because the cash incentive is insufficient to offset the advantages of fixed term contracts (Moltó 1995: 128). In Portugal there has been a low take-up of training opportunities for women in non-traditional jobs, although there is some evidence of women entering training programmes in the areas of building and public works and quality control (Lopes and Perista 1995: 64). However, a new regulation in 1995 will exempt employers from training costs when women are taken on as trainees and priority is being given to the vocational training of women.

Women tend to be overrepresented in unemployment in most countries but still tend to be underrepresented in active labour market policy programmes, even relative to their share of employment. One problem is that women are often less likely to be eligible for unemployment benefit and it is eligibility for benefits rather than being unemployed according to ILO definitions that often determines access to schemes. Eligibility issues are not important in countries such as Denmark, where women are as likely as men to receive benefits, but take on greater importance in the countries where women are 'returners' or are concentrated among first-time jobseekers. There has been some progress in improving access to schemes for women who are non-employed but not registered as unemployed, but there is still progress to be made. Thus the Netherlands has recently decided to allow women returners access to 40,000 new low-wage jobs which are to be created (Plantenga and Sloep 1995: 58). Priority will still go to the unemployed, with women having to make their case at the local level. In Germany, women's access to training has been improved since the 1970s as now the period over which applicants must have significant work experience has been extended from three years by an extra five years for every child for whom the person has had responsibility (Maier and Rapp 1995: 70). Job creation schemes, however, are still targeted on the long-term unemployed. In Ireland most of the schemes are still targeted on recipients of unemployment benefits or unemployment assistance and only in a few instances are even the dependants of benefit recipients eligible. Moreover, those in receipt of benefits for deserted wives are not eligible for any schemes. Irish estimates put the share of unemployed men who are registered at 85 per cent and the share of unemployed women at only 50 per cent. However, a new course for women returners is starting in 1994 which should have some effect on redressing the discrimination present in active labour market policy provision in Ireland (Barry 1995: 37–46).

There have been two other trends in eligibility conditions which have increased access for women; the extension of eligibility to lone parents (Ireland and the UK) and the expansion of childcare facilities or subsidies for those undertaking training (the UK, Ireland, Germany and Portugal). In part, however, these policies could also be considered a restriction on women's rights to claim state support for their role as lone parents. In the Netherlands, for example, there is now a discretionary and not an automatic exemption to the requirement to look for work for welfare recipients with responsibilities for children over 5 years old, and automatic exemption applies to single parents or to one adult from a married couple only if they have a child under 5 (Plantenga and Sloep 1995: 47). Women are also less likely to be eligible for early retirement schemes, if only because they constitute an even smaller share of the older than the total labour force. Thus in Belgium and in Germany, the share of women in early retirement schemes has been low (Meulders 1995: 11), except in East Germany (Maier and Rapp 1995: 63–64). In Denmark, however, a higher share of employed older women have moved into early retirement schemes than is the case for men (Boje 1995: 17).

While it is by no means the case that women are always underrepresented in active labour market policies, there does seem to be some consensus that where schemes are effective at integration, underrepresentation is more likely. Countries where women are not underrepresented include Denmark, France, Portugal and the Netherlands, with females accounting for more than 50 per cent of participants in most schemes in the first two countries and for 47 per cent of those successfully placed in jobs in the Netherlands compared to a 43 per cent female share of the unemployed (Plantenga and Sloep 1995: 53). In Denmark, women are overrepresented not only in the new leave schemes but also in the job creation and educational and training programmes (Boje 1995: 72). Some of these women may face low realistic chances of re-employment but need to remain on schemes in order to be able to claim full-time unemployment benefit; the option of withdrawing and relying on spouse's income has become increasingly unrealistic and uncommon in Denmark (Boje 1995: 72). In France, women's overrepresentation increases in schemes which involve atypical employment or training schemes that are not integrated into employment (Silvera *et al.* 1995: 109). In Portugal, women until recently accounted for over four-fifths of those engaged on occupational programmes for the unemployed, but this ratio has fallen to just over two-thirds by 1994, in part because of the phasing out of a scheme for the long-term unemployed among whom women are overrepresented (Lopes and Perista 1995: 58–59).

There is also a variety of rates of involvement of women in active labour market policies in the other countries where women are on average probably underrepresented. In Ireland, women are underrepresented in most schemes for the reasons already outlined, but their share of a subsidised employment scheme was only 19 per cent compared to a 42 per cent female share of trainees (Barry 1995: 44). Germany also shows wide diversity of experience both between men and women and between East and West Germany. West German women tend to be underrepresented in short-time working schemes, which are targeted at industry and construction, and in early retirement schemes, but their shares of vocational training schemes and job creation schemes have been rising, from 24 per cent to 43 per cent between 1970 and 1992 for vocational training schemes and from 29 per cent to 41 per cent of job creation schemes between 1983 and 1989 (Maier and Rapp 1995: 63, 68, 70). The reasons for these changes in female shares are diverse. For the training schemes, the share of men has declined because of the restrictions on training introduced for those already in work, as previously many men in work used to use these schemes to upgrade their skills, while the share of women increased in part because of the change in eligibility rules allowing access to women returners. However, women are still underrepresented in advanced training and on-the-job training, indicating that the closer the schemes are integrated into employment the lower the female representation. The share of women in job creation schemes has increased in part because of a shift in policy from job creation in construction to social and community services. However, the manufacturing bias is still evident in schemes to support the unemployed moving into self-employment and this could be one factor responsible for the low 22 per cent share of women on this scheme.

The experience of East German women is similar to that of West German women, with the main difference that women account for a higher share of all schemes in the East, but still below their share of unemployment. For East German women there is not the same problem of an interrupted employment record as in the West and thus the underrepresentation results from the targeting of policies in male job areas or the discriminatory selection of men for schemes, and not from differences in eligibility requirements. Thus, women in the East account for 57 per cent for all trainees but again are underrepresented in further training and on-the-job training and overrepresented on short refresher courses. Women account for a rising share of job creation schemes (from 36 per cent in 1991 to 47 per cent in 1993) but a decreasing share of short-time working as these schemes in the East have moved from general to specific policies favouring mainly industrial jobs as in the West. Both older men and women in the East took early retirement in large numbers rather than face the high unemployment levels experienced by prime-age and younger workers.

So far we have been mainly discussing countries which have widespread and established active labour market schemes. This is not necessarily the case in all EU countries. The UK has a relatively limited programme of active labour market policies; there are few job creation schemes and women are underrepresented in the Training for Work scheme where priority is given to the long-term unemployed over women returners. Women are also underrepresented in Youth Training, in part because women's jobs have tended historically to involve training outside the labour market, while young men had a tradition of entering apprenticeships, which Youth Training can be said to have replaced, albeit at a lower level of training (Rubery and Smith 1995: 179–181). Spain does have a series of job creation programmes and incentives to employ or train hard to place groups, but all of these measures are relatively insignificant compared to the policy of job creation through flexible and temporary contracts (Moltó 1995: 129). Greece has a relatively limited set of active labour market policies focused mainly on training; women tend to be underrepresented in apprenticeship schemes, and where they are apprentices over two-thirds are training to be hairdressers – but their share of accelerated vocational training programmes exceeds that of men at 53 per cent (Cavouriaris *et al.* 1995: 10–11). Italy has been mainly concerned to promote employment for young people, in small firms and self-employment, through variations in social security levies. Women are underrepresented in the last but overrepresented in the former two. Also, state labour market policy is primarily focused on a very small share of the unemployed, namely those workers, mainly men, made redundant from large industrial firms (see section 5.1). Services where women are mainly employed are largely excluded from these schemes, and some of the most generous schemes to deal with cyclical unemployment are found in the male-dominated construction sector. Not only do those on redundancy schemes receive the most subsidies, but also they are often given priority for inclusion in other active labour market policy schemes. Direct job creation schemes are limited in Italy, but one recent project to support new enterprises in the South did achieve a female participation rate of 33 per cent, somewhat above the female labour force share in the South (Bettio and Mazzotta 1995: 83).

From this overview of women's position within active labour market policies some general issues can be identified that need to be considered when active labour market policies are developed and implemented. The issues to be considered include:

- eligibility requirements, including extending access to women who want to work but who do not fulfil requirements for unemployment benefit
- the design of policies to ensure that women are not concentrated in programmes remote from employment, while men are overrepresented in on-the-job, employer-led programmes;
- the coverage of programmes to ensure that male-dominated jobs or sectors are not given priority over female-dominated jobs and sectors
- the provision of access to childcare especially in countries where childcare is limited;
- closer integration of positive action and women only training courses with actual job opportunities and targeted in areas of expanding employment;
- policies to ensure that the encouragement of participation by welfare recipients does not involve unreasonable pressure on single parents to work without adequate childcare facilities.

5.4   State policies towards atypical and flexible employment

Where labour market policy over recent years has sought to promote flexible and atypical employment as a means of increasing competitiveness and/or adding to the employment rate, these policies may have had an indirect impact in increasing the share of women in employment. However, not all countries have pursued such policies, and not all policies towards flexible employment promote women's employment.

The form of atypical or flexible employment most likely to involve women is part-time employment. Many countries have promoted this form of employment, either directly through incentives and subsidies, or indirectly through changing the law in relation to employment rights. This promotion of part-time work has often gone hand in hand with an extension of rights for part-timers but this extension has often stopped short of full equalisation. The countries which have tended to subsidise part-time work include the UK, with a high hours and earnings threshold before social security is paid, and Germany with a high hours but lower earnings threshold relative to average earnings (see section 5.2). In both countries part-time work including that outside social security payments has increased over recent years; in Germany the number of marginal part-time jobs (that is outside of social security) has increased by 15 per cent since 1987 (Maier and Rapp 1995: 50).

Belgium, Spain, France and again Germany form another group where there have been state policies aimed at promoting part-time work for work sharing. In Belgium, the unemployed have been encouraged to move into part-time work, and subsidies have been provided by the Flemish government to those moving to part-time from full-time work (Meulders 1995: 68), while in Spain subsidies have been introduced for those aged 62 to 65 moving into part-time work prior to retirement (Moltó 1995: 130). In France, in 1993 a new working-time law provides subsidies to firms which reduce working-time, create part-time jobs and develop annualised part-time contracts, provided these lead to job creation or the avoidance of redundancy (Rubery et al. 1995). In Germany those entering part-time work from unemployment will be able to claim full-time benefits if they become unemployed for three and a half years after entering part-time work (Maier and Rapp 1995: 77). The final form of subsidy can be found in countries such as the UK which have increased the number of people receiving in-work benefits, that is top-up income for those on low-paid jobs and have facilitated the unemployed moving not only into low-paid but also into part-time jobs, by reducing the hours of work before Family Credit is payable from 30 to 24 and now to 16 (Rubery and Smith 1995: 223).

In Spain, Ireland, the Netherlands, the UK and Luxembourg, there has been progress in the 1990s in extending part-timers' rights, but from very different starting points and motivations. In Spain and Ireland, there has been a voluntary falling in with current EC policy for pro rata benefits for part-timers (Barry 1995: 47; Moltó 1995: 130), which, particularly in Spain, has regularised part-time work and led to a fairly rapid expansion of part-time work (Moltó 1995: 171). In Luxembourg, the legislation was implemented with the explicit aim of ensuring equal treatment and with no strong commitment to the promotion of flexibility. Here the rights for part-timers were taken a stage further than in any other country, with part-timers given rights to overtime pay when hours exceed contractual hours (Plasman 1995: 34). In the UK, the extension of rights was forced upon the government by rulings against UK legislation as contrary to EC law (Rubery and Smith 1995: 184). In the Netherlands, the country with the highest rate of part-time working, there has been a continuous debate on part-timers' rights (Plantenga and Sloep 1995: 66–68). The minimum wage has recently been extended to cover all part-timers and there has been agreement that part-timers should have full rights to reimbursement of expenses, full access to supra-legal benefits as well as standard pro rata rights according to good employer practice. This will require employers to justify not paying unsocial hours premiums, for example, but the government has stopped short of recommending automatic rights to such payments or indeed a legal right to work part-time as proposed by the Green Party. Some countries, such as Greece and Portugal, have tried to improve the conditions for homeworkers while at the same time regularising their employment by bringing them within the coverage of social security, but in neither case is it felt that these policies have had much practical effect (Cavouriaris et al. 1995: 7; Lopes and Perista 1995: 65). This provides a good example of the limits of state policies in influencing employment organisation.

Other forms of atypical employment to be promoted include temporary work, self-employment and training contracts. In Spain, state policy has mainly been concerned to promote temporary contracts on the grounds that hiring had been restricted by employment protection laws. This has been done by easing the terms under which temporary contracts can be issued (Moltó 1995: 127). Belgium has also followed this route (Meulders 1995: 68), but Portugal and Luxembourg have introduced more restrictions (see Lopes and Perista 1995: 65 for discussion of regulation of agency work; Plasman 1995: 34). Labour market subsidies – in the form of social security rebates – have been targeted mainly at training contracts in Spain and Italy, and Italy also encourages self-employment and jobs in small firms by applying lower social security rates for these forms of employment.

Another means of promoting employment but maintaining employment security is to permit flexible and variable working hours but within a maximum limit for working time. In Denmark (Boje 1995: 81), weekend and unsocial hours working occurs often within stable employment contracts and involves employees receiving time off in lieu for extra hours, thus maintaining a work-sharing element to flexibility policies. In return, employees have received greater job security. This policy arises out of agreement between the social partners and is not as such a state-driven labour market policy.

Thus, flexible and atypical employment has been promoted by state policies in most EU countries, but the form of the promotion and the type of arrangements favoured tend to vary between member states. Nevertheless, part-time employment has become more general, with increases noted over recent years in Spain and Portugal, and active policies adopted in France to promote part-time work as a form of work sharing. In other countries, such as the Netherlands, the promotion of part-time is as much to do with the emphasis in the Netherlands on the importance of caring work as with a specific work-sharing agenda, although the benefits of part-time work for employment are also taken into account (Plantenga and Sloep 1995: 66). Denmark is the first country to move against the trend, with a rapid fall in part-time work from a high level as more younger women seek full-time work. Where part-time is promoted as part of an early retirement programme or as an alternative to unemployment, it may lead to new divisions between part-timers, with those entering part-time work from full-time work or unemployment enjoying better rights to benefits than those entering it direct from inactivity.

5.5 Wage policy

Wage flexibility has been on the policy agenda of many EU member states. But wage flexibility can have different impacts on men and women, not least because women tend to be overrepresented at the bottom of the labour market, on or close to minimum wage rates. Policy to encourage wage flexibility is often in fact a policy to reduce wages at the bottom and allow those at the top to rise, an agenda which would, under most conditions, increase the size of the gender pay gap, although with perhaps some women benefiting as well as some men losing. The Delors White Paper considered that labour costs at the bottom of the labour market have tended to be too high, although it stopped short of recommending reductions in actual wage levels.

One particular shortcoming of the Delors White Paper analysis was the failure to consider whether it is possible to talk not only of occupational segregation by gender but also of wage segmentation by gender. Are there, thus, a set of pay rates which primarily apply to adult women and only rarely apply to adult men except those in training positions, retired or recently unemployed? We do not yet have data on wage dispersion in the EU and are thus are not in a position to answer such questions; however such an analysis is necessary before it can be decided that there is a general need for reductions in minimum wages in all EU member states, for if wage segmentation exists, there may in fact be a strong case for raising rather than lowering minimum wages, both to ease flexibility and to implement the principle of equal pay.

Research in the UK has found that only those living in households with at least one wage earner can afford to take the jobs that are currently available for the unemployed. This kind of wage segmentation can lead to greater inflexibility in the labour market, reducing the possibilities of persons and households moving out of benefits and creating a divide between work rich and work poor households (Gregg and Wadsworth 1995; Rubery and Smith 1995: 172).

The UK stands out as the only country to have abolished all minimum wage protection (except for agricultural workers). No other countries have moved to abolish minimum wages where these are in existence, and in the Netherlands there has been an extension of coverage of the minimum wage system to cover marginal part-time workers (Plantenga and Sloep 1995: 62). However, Spain has witnessed a further decrease in the minimum wage in real terms from an already low level, and there is a high share of underpayment even of this low wage level, with 27 per cent of wage earners paid below this level (Moltó 1995: 133). In the Netherlands there is considerable discussion of policies which would either provide a temporary reduction in the minimum wage – say to 70 per cent for two years for new jobs for the hard to place – or the abolition of legally enforceable minimum rates in collective agreements above the national minimum rate, thus encouraging job creation in the range between the national minimum rate and the collective agreement minimum (Plantenga and Sloep 1995: 64). Such a scheme has been introduced into the agreements covering cleaners, such that new recruits from the unemployed can be paid at the national minimum rate for one year before moving onto a higher level of pay. What is perhaps again significant about the Netherlands' debate is that, despite the high share of women on the minimum wage rate, the issue of gender pay equity has not been discussed in the context of minimum wage policy. In another incidence where policy changes may have had a significant but largely unanalysed impact on women's wages, Italy has moved away from its system of wage indexation, leaving a certain degree of uncertainty over how wage increases in minimum rates are to be negotiated. The result has been a widening of the wage distribution and a decrease in the average real wage, with probably negative consequences for lower-paid and less-qualified women.

Wage policies do not solely refer to minimum wages. In at least two countries policies of restrictions on wage increases in the public sector have tended to have a damaging impact on women. In Greece, public sector wages have gone up by less than the rate of inflation while private sector wages have maintained their real value (Cavouriaris *et al.* 1995: 15). In Denmark, there is a widening gender pay gap arising out of a widening dispersion of earnings in the private sector facilitated by a more decentralised pay determination policy and a reduction in wages in the public sector where most women are employed relative to the private sector (Boje 1995: 82–85).

There has been relatively little progress within member states in direct improvements to equal pay policy. In Ireland (Barry 1995: 50–51), the legislation is being reviewed to allow comparisons with a 'hypothetical' male, thus broadening the scope for equal value legislation. In Spain, some progress has been made in modernising collective agreements, although in some cases the removal of gender-related job classifications has only resulted in the creation of new low-paid job categories, for example for temporary workers, where women are still overrepresented. Some agreements have been concluded, however, which include clauses calling for the progressive equalisation of pay for men and women (Moltó 1995: 133).

5.6   Mainstreaming gender issues in labour market policy debates

This overview of the main elements of passive and active labour market policies has revealed both the centrality of gender to the operation and functioning of labour market policies, and the widespread implicit and explicit discrimination by gender in the application of labour market policies. Thus the standard male employment model is embedded in the systems of unemployment benefit entitlements and active labour market policies, while the flexible, dependent female model of employment is embedded in policies to promote atypical employment or flexibilise wages. However, gender issues remain implicit and not explicit in most labour market policy analyses, conducted either by policymakers or academics.

Recent major contributions to comparative employment analysis by organisations such as the OECD fail to identify even the most basic gender differences in the labour market – such as differences in earnings levels – when calculating comparative unemployment replacement rates for men and women. Part-time work and flexible minimum wage levels are discussed as if they were neutral policies, designed to promote work sharing or the employment of low-skilled workers, while all research reveals the concentration of women in both part-time work and in minimum-wage jobs. Active labour market policies concentrate on the registered unemployed despite the evidence of large reserves of hidden female unemployed in almost all member states.

While the gender aspects remain implicit instead of explicit, many of the policies pursued will have inconsistent and unintended effects. Promotion of atypical employment as a 'normal' form of employment is not consistent with the restriction of social protection to standard, full-time continuing employment careers. Policies to combat social exclusion are not compatible with household-based systems of benefit entitlement, which require all members of the household to withdraw from employment. And policies to encourage the unemployed to move out of benefits and into employment will not be aided by policies which allow wage levels to fall below adult minimum subsistence levels. Consistency and coherence in labour market policies will be achieved only if policy makers recognise both the gender dimensions to the operation of the labour market, and the role of the household or family system in labour market participation patterns. This dimension to the labour market is implicit in all discussions of, for example, part-time work, or unemployment benefit systems but it is rarely explicitly discussed. Instead most analyses are based on either the implicit assumption of a universal male breadwinner system of household organisation, or the alternative implicit assumption that all participants in the labour market may be treated as unattached individuals with independent preferences and choices. It is thus to the household dimension of the economy and its role in shaping gender relations in the labour market that we now turn.

6

HOUSEHOLD ORGANISATION, STATE POLICY AND WOMEN'S EMPLOYMENT RATES

Domestic life and employment are organised around an implicit 'social contract' with two components: a gender contract and an employment contract (OECD 1994c: 19). This contract is manifested in institutional arrangements and dominant social norms concerning gender relations, thus encouraging certain behavioural patterns rather than others in both the labour market and the household. The particular form that the contract takes is historically rooted, and evolves into a new form in response to both economic and political pressures and conflicts of interest (Hirdmann 1988, 1990; Pfau-Effinger 1993, 1996). The resulting social contract is a compromise arrived at through relations between social actors with different bargaining power. Although the contract is rarely articulated explicitly, it may be partly spelt out in state policies, particularly those to do with family policy or welfare provisions, for example in the Beveridge plan laying the foundation for the development of the British welfare state in the post-war period (Wilson 1977).

In most countries the current gender contract still ascribes the primary responsibility for the financial well-being of families to men, while family care and domestic work are mainly undertaken by women. In the employment contract the male norm is to follow a 'breadwinner' pattern of continuous full-time lifelong employment, while women are defined as 'second earners' who commit fewer hours to employment. We can refer to this particular social contract as the 'breadwinner family model'. This gendered division of roles and responsibilities persists despite significant generational change in labour market behaviour. In particular, the gender gap in labour market involvement continues to shrink as younger generations of women adopt more continuous participation patterns, although women's status as second earner is likely to persist in most households for some time due to the lower wages which they receive for their labour market effort.

The particular form which the social contract takes is influenced by labour market conditions and institutional arrangements. In Chapters 2 to 5 we saw how country-specific labour market conditions have a strong impact on employment rates, and a further dimension is the different working-time schedules for both sexes (Rubery *et al.* 1995). Thus the full-time and part-time employment rates vary cross-nationally for women; this coexists with male breadwinners who work much longer and more unsocial hours in some countries than in others. These basic contours are one aspect of how the employment contract varies nationally for both sexes, while other important factors include regulations of wages and other employment conditions (Rubery and Fagan 1994).

In this chapter we turn to how the gender contract and system of household production are organised in the different member states. State policies directed at the household influence the particular form of the gender contract, and in conjunction with policies directed at the labour market, these institutional differences provide an important part of the explanation of national variations in activity and employment patterns for women in particular. Section 6.1 examines women's waged and non-waged contribution to household resources, and their involvement in the informal sector. Section 6.2 follows with a brief discussion of how state policies may reinforce or modify the gender contract, drawing on Lewis's (1992) conceptual distinction between strong and weak breadwinner welfare state regimes. Sections 6.3 to 6.5 then examine three major areas of state policy which impact on women's labour supply and the income protection they receive from the state when non-employed: taxation, state support for childcare, and women's access to social security. General conclusions are drawn together in section 6.6.

6.1 Women's waged and unpaid contribution to household well-being

A variety of theoretical accounts exist for the sexual division of household labour connected with the breadwinner family model of the gender contract. One of the earliest developments was resource theory, which argued that the person in the household with the fewest labour market resources – usually the woman – would do most of the domestic work (Blood 1963; Blood and Hamblin 1958; Blood and Wolfe 1960). The associated prediction was that the distribution of domestic work in couples would become more equal in circumstances where women's employment increased, raising their financial contribution to household resources. An adjustment in the division of domestic labour in couples according to labour market roles is also predicted by the 'New Home Economics' (Becker 1981), although the basis for the adjustment is expressed in terms of specialisation and efficiency rather than resource-based bargaining. Feminist analyses also emphasise resource inequalities between women and men – resulting from capitalism, patriarchy or both – as the basis for the unequal division of domestic labour, and most agree that employment increases women's independence and hence their bargaining position within the household, or at least their ability to escape violent or chauvinistic relationships (J. Pahl 1989). However, feminist theory is generally less optimistic that a smooth adaptation will occur whereby men will take on more domestic labour in response to women's increased involvement in employment. In particular, part-time employment for women may present an insufficient challenge to the male breadwinner model of family life (Hakim 1991; Morris 1984; Vogler 1994). At the same time, the transformative potential of part-time employment depends on labour market conditions and regulations, and whether or not part-time work is used to facilitate women's employment continuity or to construct women as a low-paid labour supply (Fagan and Rubery 1996a; O'Reilly and Fagan 1997).

In this section we look at women's growing financial contribution to household resources and assess whether women's increased labour market involvement is accompanied by an adjustment to the organisation of household domestic labour. This is followed by a discussion of women's involvement in the informal sector, and national differences in the extent of market and public sector substitutes for unpaid domestic labour and care work.

The contribution of women's earnings to household income

Women's earnings constitute a smaller proportion of total household income than men's earnings for two reasons. First, women have lower employment rates, and when employed they work shorter hours. Indeed, the average employed woman in the EU spends eight hours fewer per week at paid work compared to her male counterpart, although the size of this gender difference varies between member states. Second, women are paid less for the hours which they work: not only is their basic hourly wage generally lower, but also they are less likely to receive working-time premiums when they work overtime or 'unsocial' hours (Rubery *et al.* 1995). Finally, even when women are employed full-time on a continuous basis they may be rewarded less favourably than men, due to more limited promotion opportunities and fewer pay increments for seniority.

The contribution which women's earnings make to household income varies across the member states. The highest contribution occurs when women have a high and full-time involvement in employment across the lifecycle. For example, female earnings in East Germany accounted for 40 per cent of total household income in 1988, compared to the lower average contribution (18 per cent) made by women in West Germany, where interrupted and part-time employment is more common for mothers. The difference in the contribution made by East and West German women is smaller when the comparison is restricted to dual earner households, but a gap still remains (see Box 6.1).

Box 6.1   Contribution of women's earnings to household income

Among dual earner households, women contribute nearly half (44 per cent) of joint net income in the former **East Germany**, compared to 38 per cent in former **West Germany**. The difference is even larger when households with non-employed women are included: in the average East German household, 40 per cent of the net household income came from women's earnings in 1988, compared to only 18 per cent in the West. Even in households with a child under 4 years old, East German women contributed 27 per cent of net household income in 1992, compared to 9 per cent by their West German counterparts (Maier and Rapp 1995: 87 and Table 3.1.4).

Among married couples aged 24–55 years in the **UK**, the female earnings contribution to total household income rose from 16 per cent in 1979 to nearly 20 per cent in 1990. This increase, combined with the growing role of unearned income and transfer payments, meant that the male 'breadwinner' earnings contribution has fallen from 74 per cent to 63 per cent of total household income over this period (Machin and Waldfogel 1994). Women now contribute a quarter of all earnings in these households.

In both **Belgium** and **Luxembourg** women's earned income accounted for 20 per cent of the average total household income in 1992. This is less than half the contribution made by male earnings, but the gender difference has declined slightly over a four-year period (1988–92). Excluding social benefits, women contribute one-third of total household earnings (Meulders 1995: 75; Plasman 1995: 42–44).

According to tax records for waged and salaried workers in **Greece**, wives contribute about 16 per cent of household earned income. Assessment of their contribution among farmers and the self-employed appears to be higher, but this is likely to be biased by the widespread underreporting of non-employee income for tax evasion reasons (Cavouriaris *et al.* 1995: 55). In **Spain** women's earnings account for about 25 per cent of total household earnings. This average hides a wide variation according to household type. Among couple households where at least one spouse is employed, the contribution made by female earnings is greatest in households based on self-employment (excluding agriculture) (Moltó 1995: Table 3.1.10).

Time series data available for Belgium, Luxembourg and the UK show that women's average wage contribution to the household has increased in these countries to around 20 per cent by the early 1990s, similar to the proportion contributed by women in West German households. Women's earnings make a slightly higher contribution in Spain (25 per cent), while the available data suggest that a lower wage contribution is made by women in Greek households (see Box 6.1). In these countries – as well as those for which we do not have data – women's wage contribution to the household is likely to continue to increase over time because younger generations of women are following a pattern of higher and more continuous involvement in the labour market. The small decline in the average gender wage gap in some countries over the 1980s will have also contributed to this trend (Rubery and Fagan 1994). Another important, but negative, equalising effect is high and persistent unemployment levels for men, particularly those with few skills, for industrial restructuring is reducing the capacity of these men to be primary breadwinners.

Even when women's earnings are much lower than that of their partners, the degree of independence that independent income offers may be crucial. Qualitative research has revealed that women value the autonomy associated with having their own source of earnings, rather than relying on their partner for money. Indeed, financial dependency on the breadwinning partner is frequently a source of tension, and can be associated with extreme deprivation when relationships are breaking up (J. Pahl 1989).

Furthermore, women are generally responsible for budgeting and 'making ends meet', particularly in low-income households (Brannen and Wilson 1987; J. Pahl 1989; Vogler 1994). In these circumstances women's wages, even if small, often make a critical difference to the budgeting process and to protecting the household from poverty. Thus, although female earnings are concentrated at the bottom of the wage structure in Portugal, many employed women 'have taken on a decisive role in terms of the balancing of household budgets... the likelihood of a household being poor is much greater whenever the woman is non-employed' (Lopes and Perista 1995: 86). Similarly, the relatively small contribution made to total household income by female homeworkers in Spain (less than 10 per cent) may be vital to meet household needs (Moltó 1995: 126 and Table 3.1.10). Another example is France, where employment for the wives of manual workers raises the aggregate taxable household income by 44 per cent, compared to only 4 per cent in households where the man is employed in the high level *cadres* and professional occupations (Silvera *et al.* 1995: 30).

It is clear that state policies which stimulate higher female employment rates over the lifecycle and which close the wage gap between men and women will increase women's financial independence and their contribution to aggregate household income, thus weakening the breadwinner model of family life. Higher earnings for women will also have wider social effects: it will raise the average standard of living for dual earner households, and may provide the necessary financial springboard for lone mothers or wives of unemployed men to escape from reliance on income-related state benefits.

Contribution of women's unpaid domestic work to household well-being

Most unpaid domestic work in the household is done by women. Once time spent on domestic work is added to hours of paid work, the length of the total week for women increases substantially. Thus, regardless of employment status, married couples aged 20–50 in Flanders both devote 69 hours per week to work (Meulders 1995: 76). The average length of the total working week for all men and women in Germany was also similar for both sexes (Maier and Rapp 1995: 82) and in the Netherlands men perform 70 per cent of all paid work, while women carry out 70 per cent of unpaid work (Plantenga and Sloep 1995: 15). These broad data disguise differences between household types. Time budget studies show that it is in households supported by a male breadwinner that women and men have the same total work time (domestic labour + paid work time). However, when both members of a couple are employed, women spend longer working than men – a pattern which holds cross-nationally (Gershuny *et al.* 1994). Thus the increased involvement of women in employment has resulted in an overall increase in their workload because they come home to the 'second shift' of domestic labour (Hochschild 1990).

That women's employment has increased without a notable increase in the amount of domestic labour done by men lends support to the 'dependent labour' thesis, namely that women take responsibility for domestic labour almost irrespective of their wage work commitments. There is no evidence of a smooth 'adaptive partnership', whereby men do more domestic labour when women allocate more time to employment. However, Gershuny *et al.* (1994) have posited a third, mid-way hypothesis of 'lagged adaptation', where the adjustment in the division of labour occurs more slowly and across generations as a result of women's changing employment patterns, coexisting with changes in gender ideology, role models and socialisation.

There are some small signs of change in the division of domestic labour and total work time between women and men, and two key variables have been found to be associated with men's greater involvement in domestic labour (Seymour 1988; Warde and Hetherington 1993). First, men do slightly more domestic work when their partner is employed, particularly if the partner works full-time. Second, gender role ideology is also important, for more egalitarian attitudes are associated with men being more involved in housework.

In Germany, in non-retired households the amount of unpaid work done by men is the same regardless of the employment status of their partners, but fatherhood is associated with men doing more unpaid work in the home. Most of the adjustment to accommodate a dual earner living arrangement in Germany is made by women slightly reducing the amount of time they spend on domestic work, but overall taking on a longer working day. Thus, among employees women work for more hours per week than men once unpaid work is taken into account (Maier and Rapp 1995: Graph 3.1.2 and Table 3.1.2a). The same broad pattern of adjustment is found in Denmark and France (Boje 1994: Table 21; Silvera *et al.* 1995:

134–137). In the UK, it is only when women are employed full-time that men do more of the unpaid household work, and even then this amounts to only around 27 per cent of the household's unpaid work, compared to 18 per cent in households where the women are non-employed or employed part-time (Gershuny *et al.* 1994). This increased contribution from men in the UK is mainly through doing more of the shopping and food preparation, but is a result of a reallocation of their domestic time from other tasks, such as repair work, rather than an increase in men's total domestic input (Horrell 1994). Similarly, in Greece the increase in female participation rates coexists with minimal male involvement in domestic work. The only concession is that men are more involved in shopping for food, but this simply reflects an extension of what was always a primarily male task in Greece, corresponding to the image of men as 'providers' (Cavouriaris *et al.* 1995: 56). Even at weekends men in Spain spend less time than women caring for their children (Moltó 1995: Table 3.1.15).

Unpaid domestic work makes a substantial contribution to economic production. For example, in Germany the value of unpaid domestic and voluntary work is estimated to be in the order of 38 per cent of the Gross National Product (GNP) (Maier and Rapp 1995: 86). In the Netherlands, the annual volume of labour input to unpaid domestic work exceeds that in the formal sector (Plantenga and Sloep 1995: 71). There is also some evidence from Denmark that the fall in the length of the average employment week over the period 1964 to 1987 has been more than compensated for by an increase in the amount of time spent on unpaid work, so that the length of the working week has actually grown. The increase in unpaid work was greater for men than for women (Boje 1995: Table 22), although they still do substantially less unpaid work than women (Boje 1994: Table 21; Kiernan 1992: 497).

The evidence from time budget studies suggests that there is only a limited scope for reductions in domestic labour when both partners are employed. The total amount of time allocated to housework falls, mainly because less time is spent on cleaning and tidying and in the preparation of meals. This is likely to be associated with fewer meals being eaten at home (Horrell 1994), as well as a drop in self-imposed standards (Oakley 1974). Men do more of the shopping, cooking and routine housework, but compensate by spending less time on traditional male tasks (gardening, car and household maintenance), so that the amount of time men spend on domestic labour remains broadly the same. Overall, the main difference in the allocation of time according to women's employment status is that employed women have less time for leisure, sleep and to spend with their children (Horrell 1994: 212).

From a long-term perspective, international data do show that the male share of domestic labour and contribution to total household work time has increased since the 1960s (Gershuny *et al.* 1994). But the historical changes are very small when considered as a proportion of the total work time for women and men. Thus, while the lagged adaptation thesis (Gershuny *et al.* 1994) directs attention to the underlying processes of change in the domestic division of labour, the rate of change is much slower than the change in women's employment roles, and the adaptation made by men may remain partial and incomplete.

Women's involvement in the non-waged and informal sector

As well as the extensive amount of unpaid self-provisioning in the domestic sphere, a wide range of other activities fall outside the formal economy. These include non-wage activities and services in the community; waged work done at or from home; moonlighting; irregular or casual employment; and explicitly illegal activities (Rubery and Smith 1995: 195). The boundary between the formal and informal sector is likely to vary between countries. Indeed, Plantenga and Sloep (1995: 18) argue the 'specific organization of the formal economy always implies a specific organization of the informal or grey economy'. In the UK, for example, the exemption of the low-paid labour force from both tax and social security charges may mean that more of the economy is found within the visible formal sector than may be the case in other societies, for there is no financial incentive to disguise it (Rubery and Smith 1995: 198). One of the main reasons behind the extensive involvement of men, women and children in the informal sector in Portugal – either as a main or second activity – is the low wages obtained in the formal sector (Lopes and Perista 1995: 86).

Just as official labour market statistics do not capture women's hidden unemployment and underemployment, they may also be an unreliable measure of women's activity in many countries where women can be expected to have a major role in the informal sector on account of their high rates of open and hidden unemployment and underemployment, combined with their greater involvement in homeworking and domestic work (Silvera *et al.* 1995: 77). A Dutch study also found marked gender differences in the way that people engage in informal work. Men were found to be mainly involved in informal work for companies, often substituting directly for more regulated, alternative sources of labour, while women were overrepresented in informal work carried out for households. Finally, women contributed more hours to informal work, and at a lower hourly rate. The average wage gap (32 per cent) in the informal sector 'bears a striking resemblance to wage differences between men and women in the formal economy' (Plantenga and Sloep 1995: 12–14).

Women's involvement in homeworking and other forms of paid work within the informal sector is particularly extensive in some countries where employment in the formal sector is highly regulated, such as in many of the

Southern countries. Homeworkers and informal workers in some sectors like clothing and footwear are frequently undeclared in Spain and in Portugal, and so are not captured by measured employment rates. Such employment is characterised by low pay and long hours, with no entitlement to social security benefits. In Spain, a 1985 survey found that 18 per cent of all employment was informal or irregular. Women accounted for 48 per cent of these workers, which is greater than their share of formal employment. Once age is controlled for their involvement in irregular work exceeds that for men. The most common reason for women being categorised as irregular workers was that they were not covered by the social security system (82 per cent). This reason applied to half the irregular male workers (Moltó 1995: 59–60). Informal employment is likely to be highest in the Southern regions of Italy, where overall around 15 per cent of all employment is irregular. This estimate has remained stable over the past decade, so there is little indication that irregular employment has increased with rising unemployment (Bettio and Mazzotta 1995: 95).

Although the informal sector may be larger in the Southern countries, irregular paid work is also found in certain sectors in Northern countries. For example, in Belgium several sectors have been targeted for workplace checks – including hotels, cleaning and private services and construction – in order to increase the numbers of workers registered with the National Social Security Offices and to reduce the numbers receiving unemployment benefits (Meulders 1995: 52). In the Netherlands the volume of informal employment is estimated to be equivalent to between 2 and 4 per cent of the volume of formal employment (Plantenga and Sloep 1995: 12).

Large shares of the population with recorded employment in the formal economy are also involved in the informal sector. Unpaid voluntary work makes an important contribution to the well-being of societies, yet in Denmark and the Netherlands it is mainly done in addition to formal employment, rather than as a replacement. In both countries most voluntary work is done by the employed population in their middle age and there is little gender difference in involvement. In the Netherlands the amount of voluntary work people do is positively associated with education, income, church attendance and living in rural communities (Boje 1995: 45; Plantenga and Sloep 1995: 14).

Moonlighting is another way in which the employed population participates in the informal economy. In Denmark multiple job-holding increased over the 1980s. By the end of the decade more than one-fifth of employed Danes had at least two jobs, an incidence which is two-thirds higher than that recorded in official labour market statistics (Boje 1995: Table 23). This is primarily a male pattern of work, concentrated among skilled workers. In contrast to the pattern in the late 1960s, multiple job-holders in Denmark in the late 1990s are mostly those workers with their main job in the primary sector, indicating the growing differentiation of the Danish labour force into insiders – mainly men – who work long hours and under-employed outsiders – which is where women are overrepresented (Boje 1995: 45).

The involvement of the employed in voluntary work and moonlighting suggests a polarisation between overworked and underworked households, creating an additional dimension to the social exclusion of the long-term unemployed. The processes by which this concentration of work arises has been indicated by case study research in Britain, which revealed that individuals who are integrated into the labour market also do more domestic self-provisioning and informal work because they have the necessary resources and social contacts (R. Pahl 1984).

The potential of market services to substitute for non-wage work

As well as national differences in the boundary between the formal and informal economy, the distribution of work between the family and the public sphere varies between countries (Esping-Andersen 1990, 1995). Broadly, countries fall into three groupings. In the US and the UK, many services such as food preparation, laundry and cleaning and some care services are marketised and retail opening hours are relatively long. These services are provided by women in low-wage, private sector employment. In contast in the Nordic countries – and to a lesser extent France – many care activities have been collectivised and are carried out by women employed in the public sector. These public sector jobs are generally better rewarded than the private sector equivalents found in the low-wage service sector economies of the UK and the US. In the rest of continental Western Europe, most welfare resources are distributed via transfer payments to those with a breadwinner employment history, combined with relatively generous derived rights for 'dependent' spouses. In these countries a large share of services such as food preparation, laundry and care of children and elderly people or incapacitated adults is still provided by women in the home. This is illustrated by the relatively underdeveloped service sector in Germany. If Germany had the same sectoral distribution as the EU average, the relative expansion of the service sector would mean that female participation rates would increase by more than 4 percentage points on the basis of current female employment shares in each sector (CERC (Centre d'etudes de revenue et de coûts) 1994: 95).

The increasing involvement of women in employment may itself generate job creation if the household makes more use of formal and informal market services to replace unpaid domestic work (e.g. childcare, cleaning) and the higher income levels associated with a second wage may stimulate increased demand for labour saving purchases (e.g. ready-prepared food, electrical goods) and items associated with a higher standard of living and previously considered luxuries (Silvera *et al.* 1995: 142). The extent to which this market substitution occurs will be influenced by relative income and price levels, as well as social conventions concerning appropriate consumption patterns.

Once total household income is controlled for, the expenditure patterns of dual earner and sole earner households are broadly similar in the UK, suggesting that there is no simple process of market substitution for self-provisioning (Horrell 1991). Dual earner households do purchase more prepared food (Horrell 1991), and they are also more likely to purchase certain services, notably childcare and to a lesser extent cleaning and some household maintenance work (Gregson and Lowe 1994; Warde 1990). Similarly, in Germany there is a slight increase in the amount of household services purchased in two earner or high-income one earner households, accompanied by a rapid increase in the number of marginal part-timers employed in such services, particularly in private households. In Germany this consumption is likely to be in addition to self-servicing, rather than as a substitute, for the volume of unpaid work in households has remained stable (Maier and Rapp 1995: 89). However, even if there is no direct difference in consumption patterns between dual earner and other households, it is still likely that over time women's participation has affected consumption patterns generally, so that changing societal norms, rather than simply whether the wife is employed or not, influence household expenditure patterns on household appliances, convenience foods, etc. (Rubery and Smith 1995: 205).

These actual and potential developments in household behaviour and consumption patterns have stimulated policy debates about the need to assess the job-creation possibilities of an expanded informal sector or deregulation of labour costs in low-skilled services in the formal economy (CEC 1993a). A 1990 Dutch study which attempted to make such an assessment explored the unfulfilled service needs of dual earner households compared to sole earners, on the basis that the first category has more income but less time (Plantenga and Sloep 1995: 72–73). The main concern of dual earner households was for more convenient store opening hours, although only a few were prepared to pay more for extended services. The other demand was for domestic help, but they were generally unwilling to pay more than the usual informal rate. A quarter of those with children had unsatisfied childcare demands, mainly because of the long waiting lists at crèches and kindergartens. Even on cautious estimates, this would generate additional employment in principle, yet the problem is a lack of coincidence between the prices households are willing to pay and the rates at which people are willing to work for in the formal economy. The authors suggest a combination of initiatives to raise the quality of formal services so that consumers would be willing to pay more, or reducing prices through various subsidies or reductions in labour-related costs. One suggestion was that a portion of social security benefits could be retained as an in-work benefit to subsidise certain activities – such as childcare and household work – which are not in direct competition with existing formal services.

This study of informal work in the Netherlands suggests that the inability, or unwillingness, of many households to pay the formal market rates for some services is a constraint on the development of these activities in the formal sector. Trading of these activities may increase in some countries either in the informal sector or in the formal economy in countries like the UK and the US where private sector service jobs are low paid and poorly regulated. In contrast, public sector service provision is likely to remain relatively high by international standards in countries such as Denmark, even in the face of public expenditure constraints. Clearly the type of state intervention both as employer and as labour market regulator has a major influence on the amount and quality of formal sector job creation in household-related services. The organisation of certain aspects of socially necessary work is likely to change in the future, for there are already indications that some areas of informal and voluntary care work currently carried out by women may decline due to their changing employment patterns as well as wider contemporary processes of urbanisation, individualisation and the fragmentation of family life. It may therefore be increasingly necessary for policy initiatives to stimulate state or market substitutes for some of this socially necessary work (Lopes and Perista 1995: 87; Plantenga and Sloep 1995: 15), and the way that this is done will have a major effect on the conditions of women's paid and unpaid work.

6.2 The influence of welfare state regimes on women's household and labour market roles

The tax and social security system and state childcare and family policies either reinforce or modify the gender contract in two related ways. First, these policies shape female employment patterns through creating a range of labour supply incentives and disincentives. Second, women's employment patterns may be penalised in systems where benefit entitlements rest upon a record of full-time continuous involvement in the formal labour market. These penalties may be incurred in the formal economy through employment interruptions or periods of part-time work (see section 5.1), while employment in the informal sector – which applies to significant pools of women in the Southern member states – may fall outside the insurance system. This lower benefit entitlement both increases female dependency on a male breadwinner for financial transfers and increases their risk of hardship and poverty when they do not have access to intra-household transfers.

Economic theory emphasises that the financial returns from employment have to be sufficient to reward the individual for giving up time which would otherwise be spent in household work and leisure. Of course factors other than the immediate financial returns are important. For example, some individuals may have a strong non-financial commitment to a particular type of job or to employment in itself. Others may be willing to work for a small immediate financial gain if they have calculated that this will enhance their future employment and earnings prospects. Nevertheless, short-term financial rewards will have some influence on most people's labour supply decisions.

Incentives to participate may be created when eligibility for income transfers or welfare services rests upon an individual record of insurance contributions. Thus, the prospect of building up an individual entitlement to a pension and other income transfers over the earlier years of the lifecycle may encourage women to move from non-employment or informal employment into the formal economy; but conversely, they will be penalised if they fail to accumulate the requisite contributory record. Fewer incentives are created when there is a system of derived benefit rights based on their spouse's insurance record, or where universal citizenship rights exist, but the obvious advantage is that protection is extended to those outside as well as inside the formal sector. One such example is health care, for the development of national health systems in the Southern countries since the mid-1980s means that all member states now provide universal access to free, or highly subsidised, health care, either on the basis of citizenship or through a comprehensive system of derived benefits in insurance-based systems (CEC 1993b).

The other way that state policies affect labour supply incentives is through altering individuals' earnings prospects. Active labour market policies and wage policies influence the gross wage (see Chapter 5). Other policies affect the net wage, including deductions due to income tax and social insurance contributions, the withdrawal of certain welfare benefits as earned income rises, and employment-related subsidies, such as for childcare costs. The net wage at which an individual will consider employment to be worthwhile (the reservation wage) will also be influenced by other sources of income which they may have access to, such as spouse's earnings or property income.

Since women's employment is disproportionately concentrated in the lower-paying sectors and lower occupational levels (e.g. Rubery and Fagan 1993, 1994) the man will be the higher earner in most married and cohabiting couples (see section 6.1). This provides a financial incentive for men to specialise in the breadwinning role while women take responsibility for most of the domestic work and childcare. Of course married or cohabiting couples rarely pool all their earnings, and individuals value the autonomy derived from having some control over the disposal of their own earnings, rather than being dependent on an income transfer from their partner (Brannen and Wilson 1987; J. Pahl 1983). However, the concern here is the way in which the state reinforces or modifies the breadwinner model of household organisation through fiscal policy, transfer payments and childcare policies.

A useful starting-point for cross-national comparisons is the classification of countries into strong, modified and weak breadwinner states based on the strength of the state's adherence to the presumption that households are, or should be, organised around a male breadwinner (Lewis 1992). This is reflected in the way in which women are treated primarily as mothers, wives or workers in the tax and social security system and the level and form of childcare support. A strong breadwinner state draws a sharp line between public and private responsibility and defines wives as dependent upon their spouse. This type of state either discourages, or provides little incentive for, women's employment when they are married or have children. In this system the state distributes additional financial resources to married men on the presumption that they are supporting a dependent spouse (e.g. tax relief) and provides women with some derived benefits on the basis of their marital status (e.g. health care, widow's pensions). A modified breadwinner state provides some public support to working mothers via its family policy with some benefits derived from household status and some from labour market status. In contrast, a weak breadwinner state is organised on the presumption that all fit adults of working age are employed or looking for work, and parental employment is facilitated through a combination of childcare subsidies and leave for care responsibilities. A full classification of countries according to whether they are strong, modified or weak breadwinner states has not yet been developed, and there is some disagreement in the literature about the categorisation of certain countries. However, there is a consensus that Ireland and Unified Germany are examples of strong breadwinner states, that France is a modified state, and that the weakest breadwinner states are found in the Nordic countries (S. Duncan 1995; Sainsbury 1994).

Some elements of the breadwinner state have been dismantled over time in every EU state in response to a variety of pressures. Certain reforms have been explicitly introduced to reduce unequal treatment of the sexes, notably in response to the EU Directives on equal treatment in social security. Some countries have also developed policies to provide fiscal support to the growing number of female lone parents, thus acknowledging that not all families are organised around a male breadwinner. At the same time, other policy reforms have been driven by expenditure considerations which have made it more difficult for women to obtain independent benefit entitlements. In particular, eligibility for unemployment benefit has been tightened in some countries (see section 5.1) with the effect that it has become even more difficult for those without a previous record of full-time, continuous employment to gain benefits.

Partly as a result of piecemeal reform there are contradictions in the welfare state regime in many countries. For example, the organisation of the social security system may have a strong breadwinner logic while the taxation system has a weak breadwinner logic. Nevertheless, the interaction of these different institutions establishes a variety of incentives and disincentives which influence the extent and form of women's involvement in employment and the culmination is to establish different 'models of motherhood' (Siim 1993).

Policy reform to weaken the presumption in welfare state policies that women should be dependent on a male breadwinner have to be accompanied by labour market policies which give women access to decent wage and employment opportunities; otherwise the result is simply to push women into low-paid work where the autonomy and independence gained through employment is minimal. Indeed, state policies which encourage women to be independent labour market participants in an unequal labour market may simply replace financial dependence upon individual men with financial dependence upon the state – in other words 'private patriarchy' is replaced by 'public patriarchy' (Walby 1990). In such a situation men continue to derive benefits from women's unpaid household work while women rely upon state public expenditure decisions rather than marital obligations to provide them with financial compensation for their unpaid care work. Therefore, as long as women bear the cost of parenthood in terms of forgone earnings and earnings-related benefits such as pensions, it may be necessary to preserve existing benefits for women which are derived from their marital status rather than moving too quickly to dismantle men's household obligations (H. Davies and Joshi 1995). One solution may be to direct such benefits on the basis of past and current care responsibilities, rather than simply on the basis of marital status.

State policies are generally more 'female friendly' in weak breadwinner states than elsewhere precisely because there is little, if any, policy presumption that men are breadwinners with little obligation to spend time caring for their children while women are second earners who can rely upon financial support from an employed spouse. Instead 'female friendly' policies create incentives and distribute resources which enable women to act as independent labour market participants and independent householders, thereby increasing their autonomy and reducing the dominance of the traditional gender contract (see Box 6.2).

The remainder of this chapter examines three areas of state policy in the member states which are likely to influence women's employment decisions and financial autonomy. Section 6.3 focuses on the potential effect of systems of income tax on women's employment decisions, as well as highlighting the way in which women's labour supply may be affected by the withdrawal of benefits as aggregate household earnings increase. Section 6.4 compares the different systems of state support for child-rearing. Section 6.5 assesses the impact of employment interruptions or periods of part-time work on women's entitlements to two major state transfers: unemployment benefits and retirement pensions.

Box 6.2   Criteria for assessing 'female-friendly' state systems of tax, social security and child support

- Assist women to be independent labour market participants:
  - individualised rather than household assessment for tax and social security benefits so that marginal tax rates on individual earnings are not affected by marital status or cohabitation
  - subsidised childcare via public provision or tax relief to reduce the work-related costs for employed mothers and to increase non-employed mothers' ability to enter the labour market
  - child-raising credits for employment interruptions in contributory based systems of benefit entitlements (e.g. unemployment, invalidity, retirement).

- Additional provisions to assist women to be independent householders:
  - extra tax relief and/or transfer payments for lone parents in recognition of their child-rearing responsibilities
  - provisions which protect women against the risk of income loss arising from divorce or widowhood, particularly for older generations who have had longer interruptions in their labour market participation
  - provisions which protect women against the risk of poverty in old age, which is greater than that for men because of lower female wages and lifetime earnings.

6.3   Taxation on earned income and women's employment

Economic theory suggests that taxation has two contradictory effects on individual labour supply. A tax increase will produce an *income effect*, encouraging the individual to work longer hours to maintain the same total disposable income. The fall in net hourly earnings also creates a disincentive or *substitution effect* because the returns from employment have fallen relative to the value of time for household and leisure activities (and vice versa if tax rates are cut). The influence of fiscal policy on married or cohabiting couples may be more complex if there is some interdependency in their labour supply decisions. In the typical case where the man has the higher earnings, then the trade-off of reduced labour supply in exchange for increased domestic activities (substitution effect) is likely to be stronger for the woman, because this minimises the reduction in aggregate household income.

The strength of the substitution effect on the individual's labour supply decisions is likely to increase at higher income levels, on one hand because in most tax systems the marginal tax rate increases for earnings above certain thresholds, and on the other because trading reduced earnings for increased leisure is not an option for the low paid (Killingsworth 1983; Meulders 1986). However, a trade-off may be made when low pay interacts with the withdrawal of income-tested welfare benefits plus the entry into the income tax system to produce very high effective marginal tax rates which create an 'unemployment trap'.

The calculation of income tax is determined by three factors: the selection of the tax unit (the individual or the household) the definition of taxable income (earnings minus tax allowances and reductions),[1] and the structure of tax rates (Meulders 1986). It is particularly when the household is selected as the tax unit, as well as when tax allowances and reductions are designed on the basis of marital status, that the main differences in tax treatment between the sexes results. This becomes clear when we compare the way in which household and individual based systems of taxation work when the system of tax rates is progressive (i.e. income up to a certain threshold is taxed at one rate, the excess at a higher rate until the next threshold is crossed, and so forth). Progressive tax rate structures are found in most countries, although these have generally been simplified since the mid-1970s (OECD 1994d).

Household taxation

The basic system of household taxation is the aggregation of the earnings of married couples in order to calculate the total household tax bill: the second income (generally the wife's) is added to the first, and the joint income is set against the marginal tax structure. This means that taxation of the second income starts at the highest marginal tax rate faced by the first income, i.e. at a higher rate than if it were taxed on an individual basis.

A variant of this is income splitting, where the aggregated income is divided equally in two; tax is calculated on one half and then doubled to arrive at the total tax bill. This is extended in the family quotient system, where the aggregation includes children's income and the total is no longer divided by two, but by a larger factor which takes into account the number of children. Unless both spouses have the same earnings, income splitting increases the tax on the lower income and reduces the tax on the higher income compared to that paid if taxed on an individual basis.

Therefore, when the tax unit is the married couple rather than the individual, a breadwinner model of household organisation is sanctioned in two ways. First, the net hourly earnings at a given wage are lower for married women compared to other workers, so there is a stronger substitution effect for married women to reduce their labour supply in favour of more time for domestic work. Second, income splitting systems reduce the tax bill for married men, particularly when their spouses are not employed, thus reinforcing their role as breadwinner. Both of these outcomes can be modified through providing additional tax relief to married couples. Extra allowances for married persons reduce the amount of taxable household income, thus lowering the marginal tax rates faced by married workers compared to their single counterparts. An alternative is when the breadwinner logic is explicitly reduced through directing extra tax relief at dual earner couples. However, tax relief is unlikely to be sufficient to counteract the negative effect of income splitting on the marginal tax rates faced by married women.

Individual taxation

In this system the tax unit is the individual, and each faces the same structure of tax rates. The simplest system gives each individual the same amount of personal tax allowances or reductions. Modified systems provide additional tax relief to individuals with household dependents, such as permitting the transferability of any unused personal allowance from one spouse to set against the earnings of the other, or through providing allowances for dependent children or elderly parents. Nevertheless, individuals' tax bills will mainly vary according to their earnings levels rather than marital status.

Under a system of individual taxation the influence of tax on married women's decisions whether to increase or reduce their employment will depend on the marginal tax rate. This will depend on their own wage rate and not on that of their spouse. Thus, the potential labour supply disincentives created by the tax system are no greater for married women than those faced by other workers with comparable wage rates. This does not mean that the labour supply decisions of couples are fully individualised and unaffected by what their spouse is doing, but it does mean that the state is no longer encouraging a breadwinner family model through tax subsidies.

What constitutes a female-friendly taxation system?

Two basic tax principles are necessary to escape from the presumption that women are financially dependent upon their spouses, and to prevent them being taxed at a higher marginal tax rate simply because they are married:

- the individual is the tax unit;
- if extra tax relief is given for other household members this should be directed at the costs of raising children rather than marital 'dependency' (although some transitional protection may be necessary for the lower labour market involvement of older generations of women).

Table 6.1 shows how the member states compare on these criteria. The attention is directed mainly to the elements of the tax system rather than their value relative to earnings, and specific arrangements for the self-employed are excluded.[2] Individual taxation is the rule in five member states (Denmark, Greece, Italy, the Netherlands and the UK), is optional in another five, but is not available in France and Luxembourg. The income splitting is slightly weaker for one earner couples in Belgium than in other countries with this system, because only 30 per cent instead of 50 per cent of the earnings of the breadwinner can be assigned to the non-employed spouse. Opting for individual taxation increases the joint tax bill for the married couple compared to a household-based assessment unless the spouses have similar earnings. This applies particularly in countries where there are numerous increases in the marginal tax over a wide range of earnings (e.g. Germany) compared to those where there are few marginal rate increases (e.g. Ireland). In seven countries, therefore, most married women will probably be making labour supply decisions in response to higher marginal tax rates than their single counterparts.

Household-based systems are organised to provide significant aggregate tax relief for a non-employed spouse. More limited tax relief for a non-employed or low-earning spouse is also given in individual taxation systems through the ability to transfer unused allowances from one spouse to the other, with the exception of Greece. The UK is the only country where individuals are taxed separately but receive an extra allowance simply because they are married. However, the real value of this 'married couple's allowance' has deliberately been allowed to fall over time (Rubery and Smith 1995: 206). Transferable allowances provide some reinforcement of the breadwinner role, and may discourage labour market re-entry for some women because of a tax increase or 'breadwinner levy' on the husband's income (Plantenga and Sloep 1995: 40). However, this disincentive will be less than that faced in a household-based tax system.

Tax relief for dependent children can not be properly interpreted unless state support for children via cash payments is also taken into account, for the form and level of support varies markedly between countries. Tax relief is available in nine countries, but not in Denmark, the Netherlands or the UK, while a system of universal payments for children exists in every country except Spain and Italy; the picture is more complicated when

Table 6.1 Elements of national systems of earned income tax in the EU.

Tax unit	Individual taxation			Income splitting, but can opt for individual taxation				Aggregation, but can opt for individual taxation			Family quotient, individual taxation is not an option	
	Denmark	Netherlands	UK	Greece	Italy	Belgium	Germany	Spain	Ireland	Portugal	France	Luxembourg
Allowances/deductions												
Personal tax relief is the same for married + single people	✓ but transferable to spouse	✓ extra allowance equivalent to marriage allowance	X extra marriage allowance per couple (can share)	✓	X extra deduction for dependent spouse	X lower if married	✓ but spouses benefit from income splitting	X extra deduction for dependent spouse	X	X one tax deduction per married couple, slightly higher than for single people	X extra relief via quotient system	X
For children	X	X	X	✓ usually set against husband's income	✓	✓ usually set against husband's income	✓	✓	✓	✓	✓ via quotient	✓
For other dependents	X	X	X	✓	✓	X	X	✓	X	✓	X	X
Allowances/deductions for costs of childcare, domestic help, etc	X	✓	X	✓	X if both employed Usually set against husband's income	X	✓ for second child or if one parent is disabled/ill	✓ if both employed and income below a threshold	X	✓	✓ if both employed	✓ if both are employees
Additional tax relief for lone parents	X additional help with childcare costs	✓		X extra tax reductions	✓	✓ Additional personal allowance	✓ Additional personal allowance and childcare costs from 1st child	X	✓ child allowance via quotient	X	✓ additional allowance	✓

Sources: National reports, plus supplementary information provided by the experts country systems of income-related family benefits are taken into account (Bradshaw *et al.* 1993). Tax relief for children is particularly high in Luxembourg, Germany, Belgium and France, and these countries also spend relatively large amounts on family benefits (Table 6.2). In contrast, Denmark delivers a high level of child support solely through benefit payments, with the result that the amount of support for families with average earnings and one or two children is similar to that found in Germany. High levels of tax relief or universal child benefits may reduce the financial pressure on women to seek employment, but they may also help to cover employment-related childcare costs in countries where the state provides few direct subsidies for childcare costs.

Table 6.2 Comparison of the level of financial support for children, 1993

Countries ranked by level of family allowance for 2 children	Level of tax concessions[a]	Spending on family benefits[b]	Family allowances (tax relief plus transfer payments) as % of net average earnings		
			1 child	2 children	3 children
Luxembourg	Extremely high	Very high	22	28	40
France	High	High	1	22	50
Belgium	Very high	Very high	7	20	38
Germany	Extremely high	Very high	6	12	21
Denmark	None	Extremely high	6	11	15
Netherlands	None	Average	4	10	16
UK	None	High	5	9	13
Portugal	High average	Low average	4	9	14
Greece	Very low	Extremely low	4	8	12
Italy	Low	Low average	3	6	11
Ireland	Low average	Average	2	4	6
Spain	High average	Extremely low	2	3	5

Sources: Bradshaw *et al.* (1993: Table 2.17) for tax classification and spending on family benefits; CEC (1993b: Table 16) for family allowances
Notes: a Value of tax relief for dependent children as % of average gross earnings; ranking: extremely high, very high, high, high average, average, low average, low, extremely low, none (for details, see original source)
   b Universal child benefits plus income-related family assistance as a % of GDP standardised by % of population who are children

Tax relief targeted at childcare costs can be expected to increase the labour supply of mothers, but the effectiveness depends on the availability of childcare services. Such services are both costly and in short supply in Portugal, for example, so women often resort to the informal economy of private childminders and cannot provide the receipts required to take advantage of tax relief (Lopes and Perista 1995: 89). In contrast the tax relief for childcare costs in France coexists with a much higher proportion of children in formal childcare services, including publicly funded services. There is no tax relief for childcare costs in five countries, but in three (Denmark, Belgium and Italy) this is because state financial support is directed through subsidising services instead. The other two countries are the UK and Ireland, where the lack of tax relief for childcare costs coexists with few state subsidies for childcare services (see section 6.4).

Most countries which provide child support through the tax system enhance these allowances for lone parents. This additional tax relief has been gained only recently in Luxembourg, but the relief will provide a significant degree of support to employed lone parents (Plasman 1995). While the UK gives no specific tax relief for children, lone parents receive an extra allowance equivalent to the married couple's allowance.

Finally, since policies influence social norms as well as providing financial incentives for certain behavioural patterns, they give some indication of they way in which intergenerational family obligations and household organisation vary between countries. The organisation of state policies suggests that a child is considered to be financially dependent on parents until a much later age in some countries than others. For example, tax relief may be claimed for unmarried children with low income until they are in their late 20s in Spain and Italy and also in Germany providing they are students, disabled or doing military service. In contrast, state support to parents through the child benefit system stops once children reach 18 in the Netherlands and 16 in the UK unless they are students. In turn, there may be a stronger obligation to provide financial support to elderly parents in the Southern countries, where additional tax relief is provided for this purpose, and this pattern of tax relief corresponds with extended family households being more common in the Southern countries than in the North (Bettio and Villa 1993; CEC 1992a: 42–43). Germany again stands out as one Northern country where inter-generational obligations may be stronger, because the social assistance system places some responsibility on children to provide financial support to elderly parents in need, even if they live in separate households.

High effective taxes and the 'unemployment trap'

The withdrawal of social security benefits as earned income rises, combined with the entry into the tax system, can produce high effective marginal tax rates which creates a potential 'unemployment trap'. Individuals in this situation make few financial gains from entering employment, or if employed, from increasing their hours of work. Women are particularly vulnerable because their lower average wages plus childcare costs make them less able to escape from this trap, and because when the assessment is household based then their increased labour supply may lead to the loss of benefits claimed by their partner.

There is some degree of joint assessment for spouses in the unemployment insurance (UI) systems in Ireland, the UK, Luxembourg, Greece, Spain and Belgium (see Box 6.3). In the other six countries the rate of UI benefit received by claimants is unaffected by their spouse's labour supply and is simply determined by their individual earnings and employment record, with some additions for dependent children or elderly parents.[3] However, when the unemployed apply for means-tested assistance because their eligibility for insurance benefits are exhausted or inadequate, a household income test is applied in every country where means-tested support is available. This aggregated assessment for social assistance is made on the basis that economies of scale arise when individuals live together, and is normally extended to treat cohabiting couples as spouses, in sharp contrast to the way in which the tax system restricts additional tax relief to married couples.

Box 6.3   The assessment of spouse earnings for claimants of unemployment insurance benefits

In **Belgium** a claimant who is married or cohabiting with a partner who has no income receives a benefit which is calculated at 60 per cent of previous earnings, similar to that paid to a single person. However, if his or her partner enters employment; the benefit is reduced to 55 per cent of previous earnings. Similarly, in **Greece** the earnings replacement rate is 10 percentage points higher for married claimants if their spouse is dependent; a higher threshold is also applied in **Spain**. In **Luxembourg** there is no benefit addition, but the claimant's benefit is withdrawn at a rate of 50 per cent if another household member has income which is more than 2.5 times greater than the statutory minimum wage. The flat-rate individual benefit in **Ireland** is supplemented by a flat-rate addition for a spouse whose earnings remain below a certain threshold after which it is withdrawn rapidly; a similar system exists in the **UK**.

This household assessment has two implications. First, not only are women less likely to be eligible for contributory-based unemployment benefits (see Chapter 5), but also they are unable to claim independent social assistance because the state presumes that they will be supported by their spouse or cohabiting partner. One exception is that cohabiting couples are not jointly assessed in the guaranteed minimum income system (CRMG) in Luxembourg, and the higher support given to single people provides an incentive for couples to cohabit instead of marrying (Plasman 1995: 63).

The second implication is that the withdrawal of household benefits as earnings increase may place a high effective tax on the labour supply decisions of women living with unemployed men. Indeed, the likelihood of an individual being unemployed is increased if his or her spouse is also unemployed (Table 6.3). This concentration of unemployment upon certain households is likely to be partly correlated with the characteristics of household members, such as educational level, as well as local labour market conditions. However, the household pull into unemployment is much greater for women, while male unemployment rates are less affected by the employment status of their wives, suggesting that the benefit system may encourage women to withdraw from employment, or discourage them from entering employment, when their spouse is unemployed. Such a pressure is likely to be heightened by household means testing, which has become more extensive in most countries, particularly the UK, as part of an attempt to reduce public expenditure (CEC 1993b). In particular, the

Table 6.3 Unemployment rates for women and men by unemployment of spouse, 1993

		Unemployment rate for	
		Persons with unemployed spouse	All persons with spouse[a]
Belgium	Female	36.5	12.2
	Male	6.2	3.4
Denmark	Female	(20.5)[b]	7.5
	Male	11.4	10.8
Germany	Female	35.3	7.5
	Male	12.5	4.1
Greece	Female	(27.8)[b]	7.7
	Male	(5.5)[b]	2.1
Spain	Female	34.3	18.8
	Male	14.4	7.7
France	Female	31.3	11.3
	Male	11.7	5.4
Ireland	Female	38.6	17.4
	Male	27.5	14.2
Italy	Female	45.5	11.3
	Male	10.4	2.8
Luxembourg	Female	c	c
	Male	d	d
Netherlands	Female	34.0	10.1
	Male	9.6	5.8
Portugal	Female	(21.2)[b]	5.8
	Male	(6.2)[b]	1.8
UK	Female	28.2	6.0
	Male	14.1	6.4
E12	Female	33.2	9.8
	Male	11.9	5.0

Source: Eurostat (1993a: Table 3.6)
Notes: a Relates to male 'heads of household' and female spouses
b Unreliable data due to small sample size
c Zero or not available
d Not zero, but extremely unreliable

progressive reduction in the value of UI benefits in the UK over the 1980s means that more of the unemployed are forced onto means tested benefits (Rubery and Smith 1995: 220). Means testing has also increased in the Netherlands where claimants of UI are eligible for a supplement to raise their income to the guaranteed social minimum, but since 1983 partner's income has been counted in the assessment and means testing of a spouse's income has subsequently been extended into other parts of the social security system (Plantenga and Sloep 1995: 48–50). The constraint which household-based assessments place on women's labour supply decisions is indicated by the lower activity rates for women when their partner is claiming income-tested benefits in both countries (R. Davies *et al.* 1994; Plantenga and Sloep 1995: 52). Since a growing proportion of the unemployed live in households containing no employed member, social exclusion and economic hardship is becoming increasingly concentrated on jobless households across Europe (OECD 1995a: 34–38). Reforming the benefit system to reduce the household pull into unemployment might help to reduce this social polarisation.

The influence of a household-based assessment for means-tested benefits on individual labour supply decisions is mitigated when the system allows some income to be earned before benefits are reduced. However, the impact of the earnings disregard depends upon whether the disregard is per individual or per couple, the amount of the disregard and the rate of benefit withdrawal once earnings exceed the threshold. This can be illustrated by a comparison of the disregards in the Irish, British and Dutch systems. In Ireland, a woman with a partner in receipt of unemployment insurance or assistance benefits can earn some income before it affects his social benefit. In 1995 she could earn up to IR£30 per week before the household lost benefits if her partner is claiming unemployment assistance. Each pound (punt) of earnings above this is matched by a pound reduction in benefit, and once earnings exceed IR£45, her partner's core benefit is reduced by 50 per cent for earnings above the threshold on the assumption that he receives half of this earned income. A third threshold occurs at IR£60, when the entire 'dependent spouse addition' plus 50 per cent of the 'dependent child additions' are immediately withdrawn. This last threshold is the only one which operates in the unemployment insurance system, so that all spouses' earnings below IR£60 per week are disregarded. These disregards create a strong discouragement for the woman to increase her labour supply unless she can obtain a job with earnings significantly above the upper threshold (Barry 1995: 31–32, 56).

A lower disregard for spouse earnings operated in the UK unemployment insurance system until it was abolished as part of a wider reform implemented in 1996 (UK£28.05 per week in 1995).[4] In itself, this is a positive change, for it removes the punitive tax rate faced by women whose earnings exceed the threshold. However, in practice this will be countered by the interaction with other changes to the system which increase the aggregation of household income for means-tested assessment (Rubery and Smith 1995: 169–174). Thus, the low level of UI benefit means that most unemployed men will still be eligible to claim a means-tested spouse addition through unemployment assistance to supplement their insurance benefit ('Jobseeker's Allowance') if their partner has little or no earnings. Under this means-tested household assessment the weekly earnings disregard for couples increased from the old rate of UK£5 to UK£10. However, this is still a negligible disregard, above which benefits will be reduced pound for pound (with 50 per cent of the excess 'saved' by the state and repaid in a lump sum if the household moves out of social assistance).

The British system, therefore, provides less scope for women with unemployed partners to make independent labour supply decisions compared to the higher and individual earnings disregard in Ireland, although in Ireland women with low earnings potential are still constrained to work part-time below the threshold. In the Netherlands, the system is slightly different, for there is no threshold below which earnings are disregarded. Instead, 25 per cent of all earnings are discounted from the benefit assessment up to a maximum 15 per cent of the net benefit entitlement for up to two years in order to enhance work incentives. This means that households can increase their total income through employment, but this is subject to high marginal tax rates. This entitlement is likely to be abolished and replaced by a discretionary entitlement determined at municipal level in a Bill which is currently being debated (Plantenga and Sloep 1995: 48). In these countries, and other member states with a household-based assessment for social assistance, the introduction of higher and individual earnings disregards would provide some degree of individualisation in the system, and at least enable women to retain some foothold in employment when their spouse cannot.

Lone parents are particularly vulnerable to being caught in the 'unemployment trap' in Denmark and the UK, where a large proportion receive welfare benefits (Boje 1995: 69–71; Rubery and Smith 1995: 221). This is a significant problem, for lone parents now account for about 15 per cent of all families with children in both countries (Boje 1995: 70; EC Childcare Network 1993). Although lone parenthood is less prevalent in many of the other countries, a similar trap frequently exists because lone parents account for a disproportionately large share of households claiming social assistance, for example in Germany and the Netherlands (Maier and Rapp 1995: 100; Plantenga and Sloep 1995: 46). In Denmark, it is in households with a child under 6 years that the 'unemployment trap' seems to bite most, for in these households lone mothers have significantly lower participation rates, and when employed are more likely to work full-time than other mothers. The effect is much weaker when children are older, and overall Danish lone mothers have high employment rates similar to those for comparable mothers living in couple households. In contrast, lone mothers have much lower activity and employment rates than mothers in couple households in the UK, mainly due to the lower levels of part-time employment found among lone mothers. Ireland and the Netherlands are the only other member states with such a low level of labour market integration for lone mothers (CEC 1993b: Graph 37). In order to reduce the effective tax rates lone parents face when entering employment in the UK the government has reinstated the right – abolished in the early 1980s – for lone parents to charge childcare costs against earnings up to a threshold; the amount which they can earn before benefits are withdrawn has also been increased to UK£25 compared to the UK£5 permitted for a single person and UK£10 for a couple in 1995.

Finally in 1988 the UK introduced a system of in-work benefits ('Family Credit'), designed to reduce the effective tax rate faced by household heads. This has increased the opportunity for lone parents to work, especially when their children are at school and do not require full-time care, but the system imposes high effective tax rates (70–96 per cent) on second income earners. Not only does this create an unemployment trap for the second earner, but also the introduction of in-work benefits in the absence of minimum wage provisions appears to be altering the wage structure of jobs. Very low-paid jobs are being created for the unemployed, with the difference made up by benefits paid for through the tax system. In effect, some employers are paying 'below subsistence' wages, which are subsidised by the taxes paid on wages received from higher-paying firms (McLaughlin 1995).

Actual effect of taxes on married women's labour supply

Would tax reform increase women's labour supply? How important is this compared to other possible policy reforms? Two cross-national studies reveal that national differences in married women's participation patterns are only loosely correlated with the effective tax rates faced by second earners (CERC 1994; Vermeulen et al. 1994). For example, one study predicted what the employment rates for married women would be in six countries if their labour supply was driven solely by net financial returns and compared these estimates with observed employment rates. This exercise showed that married mothers had higher full-time employment rates and lower part-time employment rates than predicted in Belgium, France and Spain, while the situation was reversed in the Netherlands, Germany and the UK (CERC 1994). The authors of both reports conclude that the influence of taxes can not be considered in isolation from other societal features which have a strong influence on female labour supply, particularly childcare provision, gender role attitudes and the organisation of employment.

In a similar vein, other researchers emphasise that a higher female labour supply is more dependent upon action to improve women's wage and job prospects than upon tax reform (Meulders 1995; Moltó 1995). Nevertheless, individualisation would have an important effect even if there is no short-run change in labour supply because it would raise the net wage rate for the second earner. This would increase their financial contribution to the household finances, thus weakening the breadwinner model of family life and increasing women's independence and intra-household bargaining position (Maier and Rapp 1995: 104).

The relevance of the emphasis which neo-classical theory places on the marginal financial gains from an extra hour of employment for understanding labour supply decisions is also questioned by Schettkat's (1989) analysis of the impact of individualisation of taxation in Sweden. He found that the reduction in marginal tax rates had little measurable effect on the activity rate of younger generations of women, for this had already began to increase rapidly prior to the reform, although it did stimulate an increased labour supply for the older female cohort (aged 45–55). On this basis he concludes that other societal features may be more important, and emphasises changes in consumption preferences and societal norms concerning what is a suitable standard of living or 'target household income'.

While policies which affect wages, job prospects and childcare may have an even greater impact on women's employment patterns than the tax system, econometric studies which have used data on net wages, means-tested benefits and household circumstances do reveal that tax reform could contribute to increasing the labour supply of some groups of women. Estimating the magnitude of individual responses to tax changes is fraught with complex methodological problems (see Gustafsson 1996), so the results are highly dependent upon the methodology and the type of data used. Indeed an OECD report notes that the actual size of the labour response to marginal tax rates 'is still the subject of debate among empirical economists after more than 20 years of analysis' (OECD 1994d: 58).

However, the general finding is that individual labour supply is most responsive to marginal tax rates at the point of entry to the labour market and for those with short part-time jobs, particularly married women. Among women and men working longer (full-time) hours the marginal tax rate has less of an effect on the number of hours worked (OECD 1994d). Since the marginal tax rates for those on low incomes have increased in most countries since the late 1970s, the financial incentives for married women to re-enter employment or move into full-time employment may have decreased. Therefore, the OECD (1994d) concludes that a tax cut targeted at married women's earnings could be expected to increase their labour supply.

For lone parents and women living with unemployed or low-paid men it may be as important to reform the effective tax rates created by means-tested assessments for benefits as to tackle the income tax system. For example, econometric studies for Denmark show that benefit reform to reduce the high effective marginal tax rate imposed on lone parents would increase their participation in both full-time and part-time work (Boje 1995: 71), while a higher earnings disregard for benefits in the UK would encourage more women to enter employment (A. Duncan *et al.* 1994).

Therefore, the OECD (1994d) concludes that two reforms to the taxation system might have beneficial effects on women's labour supply decisions, to which we add one reform which specifically addresses the issue of aggregated assessment in the benefit system:

- targeted cuts in marginal tax rates for married women and lone parents through the individualisation of taxation and tax deductions for childcare expenses;
- reduction in average income tax rates for those with low wage prospects in order to reduce the 'unemployment trap';
- reduction in the aggregation of spouse's earnings for the assessment of benefit entitlement so that there is at least a partial individualisation of the system, for example through higher, individual earnings disregards for those living in couples. This would mirror the principle of personal tax exemptions in the income tax system.

We now turn to examine another area of state policy which probably has the most significant influence on the level and form of women's labour supply over the lifecycle; namely support for child-raising through the provision of subsidised childcare facilities and entitlements to parental leave.

6.4 Recent developments in state support for childcare

Most of the work involved in raising children is done by women, and this domestic responsibility constrains their labour supply in three ways. There are financial considerations, for childcare costs create an additional effective tax on earnings. When substitute unpaid family carers are available, such as the father or grandmother, this reduces the need to pay for childcare. The third influence is the normative environment concerning whether mothers of young children should or should not be in employment. The extent and form of the resulting care constraint varies for different groups of mothers. Within countries, those mothers with high wage and employment prospects, low childcare costs and a strong non-financial attachment to employment will have the highest employment rates. The strength of the care constraint also varies across countries, evidenced by sharp differences in maternal employment rates, due to different state child support policies combined with prevailing labour market conditions (e.g. EC Childcare Network 1993; Rubery *et al.* 1995). State support to facilitate the combination of employment with meeting care responsibilities fall into two categories: leave which enables parents to redistribute some of their time from the workplace to the home while retaining an employment contract; and state financing and regulation of non-parental childcare to redistribute some care tasks from the home to the public sphere.

Statutory leave arrangements

Maternity leave is essential to preserve women's right to return to employment. Research in the UK at the end of the 1980s, when many women did not have an entitlement to maternity leave, showed that this right had an independent and positive effect on the share who returned to employment after giving birth (McRae 1991). The adoption of the EU Maternity Leave Directive in 1992 gave all women a statutory entitlement to fourteen weeks of paid maternity leave and can be expected to contribute to an increased rate of return among mothers in the UK. Maternity legislation is also being revised in Portugal to increase the statutory leave entitlement (currently it is just over twelve weeks long) and significant changes will have to be implemented in Spain to provide the required protection from dismissal (Lopes and Perista 1995: 90; Moltó 1995: 137). The Directive will have a more limited impact in the other member states, for most employed women already had a virtually automatic entitlement to between fourteen and eighteen weeks – slightly longer in France and Italy – combined with a high, earnings-related benefit, or a high flat-rate payment in the case of Denmark (EC Childcare Network 1994; Rubery *et al.* 1995). However, those women with very marginal employment records who previously did not fulfil the minimal employment or contributory records will benefit from receiving an automatic entitlement to maternity leave.

Parental leave is a more recent development than maternity leave. A Directive to establish a statutory entitlement to Parental Leave and Leave for Family Reasons was proposed in 1983; following continual blocking by the UK, an agreement has now been reached for up to three months' parental leave for each parent under the Maastricht social protocol for fourteen countries (the question of payment is to be determined at member state level). The funding, flexibility and availability of parental leave is quite diverse in the member states (see Appendix Table 6.1). Statutory parental leave payments are made in only five countries. Denmark provides the highest earnings replacement rate, paid to all members of the workforce. More limited financial support is offered in Belgium and Italy, for employees only. In both Germany and France the parental leave payment may be claimed not only by employed parents but also by the unemployed or inactive. The benefit is income-tested in Germany and restricted to the second and third child in France. These, then, are more equivalent to a system of unpaid parental leave combined with targeted family benefits where at least one parent stays at home, than a system of financial redistribution targeted at reconciling caring and employment *per se*. In both countries the scheme has been extended. In Germany, a third year of unpaid leave was introduced in 1993, and in France the benefit became payable for the second as well as the third child in 1995.

In Belgium, the career break scheme offers the potential for the longest period of leave – up to five years subject to various conditions (see Appendix Table 6.1). Statutory entitlements range from three years per family in France, Germany and Spain to a mere four weeks' extension to maternity leave for the mother in Ireland. Parental leave usually starts immediately after maternity leave and runs continuously, although in four countries there is the option to take the leave in one or more 'fractions' over an extended period (Belgium, Denmark, Germany and Greece). Employees who take leave have the right to return to work in all countries, and normally remain on the payroll so that welfare entitlements are maintained. This job guarantee applied only to the first year of leave in Spain until March 1995, but since then both employment protection and seniority have been extended to cover the full three-year period (OECD 1995a: 179). Leave may still not count for seniority in some countries, which may have an important effect on wage increases and promotion prospects, for example in Portugal and Greece (EC Childcare Network 1994: 22–23).

Reduced hours, rather than full-time leave, may have the advantage of enabling parents to retain contact with employment and maintain their skill levels, but the ability to work short full-time or part-time hours will depend upon the availability of childcare. There is a legal entitlement to take leave on a part-time basis in France, and this is the only option in the Netherlands, while part-time leave can also be taken in Belgium and Germany subject to the employer's agreement. Other entitlements permit mothers to reduce their working day by up to two hours in the child's first year in Portugal, Italy and Greece, while in Spain hours can be reduced by up to 50 per cent until the child is 6 years old (Rubery *et al.* 1995: Table 1.13). Finally, the most generous statutory paid leave arrangements to care for sick children in the twelve member states are found in Germany (EC Childcare Network 1994). Here, the entitlement is ten days' paid leave per child per year, funded from statutory health insurance.

Parental leave entitlements are often enhanced in the public sector. For example, public sector workers receive their full pay in Denmark, 75 per cent of their pay in the Netherlands and in Italy the full wage is paid for the first month of leave, and 80 per cent for the next two, while it is only public sector workers who are entitled to parental leave in Luxembourg. To a lesser extent, collective bargaining has enhanced parental leave provisions in some parts of the private sectors (EC Childcare Network 1994; OECD 1995a: Annex 5.A; Plantenga and Sloep 1995: 81; Rubery *et al.* 1995: appendix Table 1.8). New provisions for paid leave for sick children have also been negotiated in Denmark in exchange for increased working-time flexibility (Boje 1995: 82) and in Luxembourg for civil servants (Plasman 1995: 63).

Extended maternity leave and parental leave are important, for they provide some public recognition of the parental responsibilities of many workers, and enable leave takers to preserve their wage and occupational position while putting time into family care work. The effects on women's labour supply are complex. Long leave entitlements may encourage some women to reduce their labour supply when their children are young. But the right to withdraw from employment or to move to part-time hours without quitting the labour market or switching jobs is likely to produce a net increase in female labour supply in two ways. First, the entitlement may encourage women to enter employment and or work full-time up to the birth of their first child in order to build up an entitlement (OECD 1995a: 189). Second, rewards from employment are largely protected from deterioration, in contrast to the reduced prospects and downward mobility experienced by women who are forced to quit when they want time-off for care work and then re-enter the labour market.

At the same time, while parental leave strengthens women's labour market attachment, it may also reinforce their second earner status in the breadwinner family model, depending on the details of the scheme and how these interact with the societal and economic context. Furthermore, the experience of taking a long period of leave may reduce women's labour market attachment and be associated with an actual, or perceived, erosion of skills. Partly in recognition of this, France and Spain have introduced legislation granting the right to reinsertion training at the end of leave (OECD 1995a: 189).

The presumption behind parental leave arrangements which are unpaid (e.g. Portugal, Greece) or supported by a low rate of benefit (e.g. Belgium, Germany) is that the leave taker has an employed spouse or other means of financial support. Where parental leave involves a sharp drop in income, then low-income dual earner families or lone parents will not be able to afford to take leave, while in other two income households this form of leave does little to transform gender relations. The lower average earnings of women creates a financial incentive for the leave to be taken by the mother, which reinforces, or introduces, the presumption that women are second earners who interrupt their labour market activity. This second earner bias in leave taking is likely to be exacerbated when unpaid leave is explicitly restricted to women as an extension of maternity leave (UK, Ireland), or where parental leave is

225

allocated per family. In contrast, a non-transferable individual entitlement provides some incentive for men to take leave as well (e.g. Belgium, Denmark, the Netherlands).

Moreover, when there is a shortage of suitable childcare services, parental leave may enable some women to resume their jobs who would have otherwise quit, but the result for many others may simply be to postpone labour market quits. For example, the German statutory parental leave was extended from one to three years in 1993 in the context of the post-unification rise in unemployment, a dismantling of childcare services in the new Länder, and a general emphasis upon the harmonisation of social policies. This reform gives women an extended right to retain their employment contract for a longer period, but their ability to return remains heavily constrained by the lack of childcare services. Women in the old Länder typically follow a 'women returner' pattern, with more than half quitting their jobs at the end of the leave period and delaying their return to employment (Maier *et al.* 1994: 9). Although women in the new Länder maintain a high and continuous labour market involvement (Maier *et al.* 1994), their ability to do so is increasingly constrained by the lack of childcare combined with high unemployment. In both West and East, therefore, the extension of parental leave as a substitute for childcare services, instead of a complement, has the effect of institutionalising an interrupted employment pattern for women. Similarly, introducing or extending parental leave in societies with a relatively well-established system of childcare subsidies may divert resources and shift, rather than expand, the options for reconciling earning and caring work, which may reinforce gender division in household and labour market roles if the leave is taken only by women. For example, few Danish women interrupt their employment when they have young children, and even the tendency to switch to part-time work seems to be falling (Boje 1994). This pattern of labour market activity is facilitated by a relatively high level of publicly funded childcare services (see the following sub-section). The January 1994 reform to the Danish leave scheme permits the municipal authorities to supplement the national rate of payment for parental leave, which is due to fall in the coming years. One incentive for this local addition might be to reduce the demand for childcare services which are subsidised by municipal authorities (Boje 1994: 80). This may assist parents in areas where there is a shortage of childcare places, but the long-term outcome may be a gradual dismantling of service provision in favour of leave arrangements. Increased leave entitlements, potentially accommodated by a decline in childcare places, may therefore enforce the notion of women as second earners unless extended parental leave also becomes a feature of male employment patterns.

Parental leave in Belgium and Denmark has developed as part of broader schemes to encourage work sharing through 'job rotation'. There has been

---

Box 6.4   Recent reform to the Danish leave scheme, January 1995

In **Denmark** The basic parental leave entitlement is 10 weeks per family, paid at the same flat rate as maternity pay. A supplementary period was introduced under a programme of temporary leave for parental and non-parental reasons implemented in 1992. This additional period of 13 to 52 weeks per parent was conditional on the employer's agreement and acceptance of a previously unemployed person as a replacement. In January 1994 the temporary leave programme was significantly expanded. This gave parents an unconditional entitlement to leave. Legislation in December 1994 made the parental and training leave schemes permanent, while the pilot sabbatical scheme has been extended until 31 March 1999. Overall 80 per cent of the labour force can now apply for parental, educational or sabbatical leave.

	Eligibility conditions	Length of leave	Acceptance of leave	Economic support	Employment of substitute
Educational leave	Membership of unemployment insurance; 3 years' employment in past 5 years.	1 year for employed; 2 years for unemployed	Acceptance by employer	100 % of max. UI[a] benefit	Not required
Parental leave	All parents eligible for sickness benefits; child aged 0–8 years	13 to 52 weeks	13–26 weeks: right for all; 26–52 weeks: acceptance by employer	70% of max. UI benefit[bc]	Not required
Sabbatical leave	Membership of unemployment insurance; 3 years' employment in past 5 years; currently employed; 25 years of age or older	1 year	Acceptance by employer	70% of max. UI benefit[b]	Substitute required (same amount of weekly hours)

a Unemployment Insurance (UI) benefit approximately equals 65% of the average industrial wage
b Reduced from 80 per cent which was established at the beginning of 1994, to 60 per cent by April 1997
c In many local communities the local authorities have decided to pay an additional subsidy for parental leave; this means that the income reduction for most parents on leave has been minimal

The option of local supplements in addition to the common national payment was introduced in 1994, so that local authorities can supplement the basic benefit (80 per cent of unemployment benefit) if they wish; one incentive to do this would be to reduce the demand for childcare services which they also subsidise (Boje 1994: 80; EC Childcare Network 1994).

---

an entitlement of ten weeks' parental leave per family since 1984 in Denmark, paid, like maternity leave, at the same rate as unemployment benefit (about 65 per cent of the average industrial wage). An additional, individual entitlement has been progressively developed since 1992, along-side the introduction of educational and sabbatical leave. This started with a conditional right to between 13 and 52 weeks per parent, subject to the employer agreeing and recruiting a previously unemployed person as a replacement. Legislation gave parents an unconditional leave entitlement from January 1994 and extended this entitlement to the unemployed (see Boje 1995). It also abolished the obligation for employers to recruit a replacement unemployed person for parental or educational leave as it was judged to reduce employers' interest in the schemes (OECD 1995a: 180). Figures from the Danish Ministry of Labour indicate the popularity of the expanded scheme, with more than 140,000 persons, or 5 per cent of the labour force, participating in one of the three schemes in 1994. Parental leave accounted for 58 per cent of this total, educational leave for 33 per cent and sabbatical leave for 9 per cent (Boje 1995: Table 38). Paradox-ically, the popularity of the scheme has led to criticism: parental leave for creating supply bottlenecks among some skilled workers such as nurses, and sabbatical leave for subsidising holidays. Further legislation at the end of 1994 made the leave programme a permanent part of labour market policy, but a reduction in the benefit payments for parental and sabbatical leave is being phased in, so that by 1997 the benefit will be equivalent to 60 per cent of unemployment benefit. However, this will still provide a replacement rate equivalent to about 40 per cent of the average industrial wage (see Box 6.4), which is still favourable by comparison with other member states.

In Belgium, subject to certain conditions, a worker may take 'career breaks' for up to a maximum of 60 months over the period of their working life, with a replacement recruited who is registered unemployed and receiv-ing UI benefits (see Meulders 1994; Rubery et al. 1995: Box 1.6). Legislation in Spain has granted reductions in social security contributions to employ-ers who recruit the long-term unemployed as replacements for workers going on parental leave (OECD 1995a: 196).

Take-up of parental leave

Current survey sources and administrative records are not designed to provide adequate information on the take-up and form of parental leave (see OECD 1995a: 183). The limited available data indicate that the incid-ence of parental leave is rather low, although increasing, and the majority of leave takers are women.

The distinction between maternity and parental leave is made in the labour force surveys in only three OECD countries (the Netherlands, Sweden and the US). However, some indication of the share of women on leave is provided by Table 6.4 which records the number of employed women who were absent from work due to maternity leave and other leave taken for 'family or personal reasons' in the survey reference week in nine member states. This may underestimate the numbers on parental leave in some countries. First, it may exclude some people on long-term leave if they do not report having a job at the start of the questionnaire. Second, the unemployed are also not covered by this question, yet by January 1995 more than half of the people on parental leave in Denmark had previously been registered as unemployed (OECD 1995a: 180). Finally, a measurement based on absence does not provide information on those who were eligible but did not take leave (OECD 1995a: 184). In general, these absences account for a very small percentage of women's employment overall, although the incidence is obviously higher among women with a child under 5 years old. Over time there has been an increase in these family-related leave of absence. This increase may reflect the extension of parental leave entitlements (OECD 1995a: 184), but it may also indicate a greater take-up associated with more women remaining in employment when they have young children instead of quitting the labour market (Rubery et al. 1995).

Table 6.4 Absence from work for reasons of maternity leave and for other reasons, including personal/family reasons, for women aged 15–49, 1983–92

		Maternity leave (A) (000)	Other reasons, including family/ personal (B) (000)	A + B as a % of female employment	A + B as a % of employed women with children under 5 years
Belgium	1983	10.8	7.8	2.3	7.1
	1992	13.9	14.9	2.6	9.7
Denmark	1983	13.9	12.2	3.1	13.2
	1992	24.5	11.0	4.1	18.4
France	1983	122.7	34.1	2.6	9.6
	1992	157.1	22.5	2.5	9.7
Germany	1983	35.7	27.3	1.0	a
	1992	206.8	163.1	3.7	19.9
Italy	1983	a	a	a	a
	1992	82.9	41.3	3.1	11.5
Netherlands	1983	b	b	b	b
	1992	17.1	5.7	1.2	6.6
Portugal	1983	b	b	b	b
	1992	14.4	a	1.7	6.1
Spain	1983	b	b	b	b
	1992	16.1	15.6	1.7	6.2
UK	1983	36.0	52.9	1.7	11.0
	1992	123.9	83.7	2.9	13.7
E12[c]	1983	228.5	144.9	1.5	8.5
	1992	667.1	365.0	2.9	12.6

Source: OECD (1995a: table 5.3), based on European Labour Force Survey data
Notes: a Data unreliable
 b Data not available
 c E12 data include Greece, Ireland, Italy (for 1983) and Luxembourg

Table 6.5 presents the available data on the take-up of parental leave from different national sources. In most countries less than 5 per cent of eligible fathers take parental leave, although a notably higher rate (11 per cent) is recorded in the recently introduced scheme of part-time leave in the Netherlands. The individual entitlement to work part-time in the Dutch scheme may be important for stimulating male take-up. Short periods of leave, often combined with part-time work is the typical way in which fathers take leave in Sweden, the only country where a significant minority of men take leave (see Chapter 7). The male share of other types of leave is generally higher than that for parental leave, suggesting that these forms of leave are perceived of as more legitimate for men, whether for educational and sabbatical reasons in Denmark or partial retirement under the Belgian career break scheme (Boje 1995: 76; Meulders *et al.* 1994: Tables 1.2.1 to 1.2.3).

Table 6.5 Take-up of parental leave[a]

	Number of claimants	% of claimants who are women	Claimants as % of employed women	Claimants as % of eligible leave takers
Belgium	51,000 (1991)	86	3.2	b
Denmark	80,788[c]	90[c]	b	82% of eligible mothers[d] < 5% fathers[e]
Germany (W)	790,000 paid leave 405,605 unpaid leave (1992)	99	6.8 (paid)	95% of all registered births claim parental leave, < 5% are fathers[e]
France	175,000 paid (1991) 95,000 on unpaid leave	97	1.7 (paid)	< 2% in 1992[f]
Netherlands	b	b	b	27% of women[e] 11% of men
Spain	< 20,000 (1991)	100	b	b
Portugal	Rarely used[d]	b	b	b
Greece	Rarely used[d]	b	b	b

Source: CERC (1994: 52), unless otherwise stated
Notes: a No information for Italy; no statutory parental leave for either sex in Luxembourg, UK and Ireland
   b Information not available
   c Boje (1995: 77)
   d EC Childcare Network (1994)
   e OECD (1995a)
   f Gauvin *et al.* (1994: 74).

The majority of people on parental leave are women in every EU country. Take-up by eligible mothers is high in Denmark (82 per cent) and in the former West Germany (96 per cent in 1992). In the Netherlands the recently introduced scheme is used by only 27 per cent of eligible women, but a full assessment must wait until the scheme has become more established. In contrast, less than 2 per cent of entitled parents took either paid or unpaid leave in France in 1992, and a disproportionate share were women with three or more children who thus received some financial support (Gauvin *et al.* 1994: 74). The unpaid leave provisions are also estimated to be rarely used in Greece, Portugal and Spain (EC Childcare Network 1994). Finally, the use of the part-time leave option varies between countries: less than 1 per cent of mothers on leave work part-time in Germany, while in France part-time leave accounted for 5 per cent of leave taken in the public sector and 13 per cent in the private sector use it. In contrast, in Belgium just over half (55 per cent) of women taking career breaks opt for reduced hours rather than a full interruption (Meulders *et al.* 1994: 21). Furthermore, in the Netherlands more than half the mothers remained in part-time work at the end of their leave period, and interestingly 14 per cent of fathers also reduced their hours at the end of the leave period (Plantenga and Sloep 1995: 81).

The amount of benefit paid, the flexibility of the provisions and the professional status of the eligible individual affect take-up (EC Childcare Network 1994; OECD 1995a). National rates of female take-up are greatest when the leave payment is high (Denmark), or where there are few alternatives to mothers of young children due to the limited childcare services (Germany). In some countries low take-up results from mothers making alternative arrangements to combine employment with family duties. For example, in France parental leave competes directly with the alternative of part-time work, particularly in the public sector where the opportunity to work between 50 per cent and 90 per cent of normal working time constitutes a significant amount of flexibility for mothers (Gauvin *et al.* 1994: 16), and where working-time decisions are made within a context of a relatively high availability of childcare services (see the following sub-section). In others, the reluctance to take leave may stem directly from limits in the design and application of the scheme.

Women with high qualifications and high earnings take fewer, or shorter, periods of leave (EC Childcare Network 1994; Sundstrom and Stafford 1994). Part of the explanation is likely to be their higher 'human capital' investment and greater loss of earnings (e.g. Becker 1981), but high earnings also make it more feasible to pay for childcare. Women at this occupational level are also likely to have stronger non-financial career orientations (Dex 1988; Hakim 1991). Indeed, research in the Nordic countries indicates that the rate of return to employment at the end of leave is highest among mothers with good jobs and among those who report that working is important (OECD 1995a: 188). In Germany data also indicate that employers may be more reluctant to grant leave to workers in high-level occupations because the recruitment of replacements is difficult (OECD 1995a: 188). Longer leave also tends to be taken by women in the public than in the private sector, partly because enhanced financial support is frequently available. It may also reflect a more supportive workplace culture (Bettio and Villa 1994: 44; Plantenga and Sloep 1995: 80).

Slightly different factors influence men's propensity to take parental leave (EC Childcare Network 1994; OECD 1995a). Unlike women, they are more likely to take leave if they are well educated, well paid and with permanent jobs. Take-up of parental leave is also higher for men if their partners have a strong attachment to the labour market, indicating some collective adjustment in child-raising. Finally, similar to the finding for women, the workplace culture and enhanced financial support is important, for men are more likely to take parental leave if they are employed in the public sector and in female-dominated jobs.

Low male take-up undermines the equality objectives, since it means that it is still only women who take time off to fulfil parental responsibilities. This may increase employment segregation, for the costs of parental leave may make employers reluctant to hire women in certain jobs. Within internal labour markets, interruptions for leave make women vulnerable to segregation into the 'mummy track' of reduced promotion prospects while the persistent presumption is that men do, or should, follow full-time employment trajectories, which in the UK in particular involves a commitment of very long hours (C. Marsh 1991; Rubery *et al.* 1995). Low male take-up also undermines the effective contribution that leave arrangements can make to work sharing objectives, because the redistribution via leave may become concentrated in the female-dominated sectors, with very little impact on work sharing between men or between the sexes.

The EC Childcare Network (1994) concluded that the main features which deter parents from taking parental leave in some countries are: the loss of income; the inflexibility of schemes which do not allow several short leave periods or the option for part-time leave; inadequate guarantees of employment conditions on the return to work; employer reluctance to grant leave, particularly among those with small businesses; and a general lack of information on both sides. Workplace culture is also important, particularly for men, and a lack of workplace support for those on leave is most evident in workplaces characterised by direct competition and a lack of solidarity. Where part-time leave is possible but rarely used, the particular deterrents are that the problem of finding childcare persists, particularly since the two parents cannot take leave at the same time in most countries; more restrictive conditions than for full-time leave; and maternal preferences for full-time leave (OECD 1995a: 187).

The impact of parental leave on labour demand and worksharing

If parental leave raises employer costs then employment may fall where labour demand is elastic. Of course, as for any policy intervention, the net actual effects are likely to be 'dynamic, long-term and very difficult to isolate' (OECD 1995a: 177).

The costs which an employer will face include those connected with the benefit and welfare entitlements of the leave taker, plus the costs of providing cover, such as through overtime or the recruitment of a temporary replacement. The requirement for advance notice, combined with the low average incidence among the workforce reduces the disruption costs, although a higher incidence of leave will occur in those sectors which rely upon a young female workforce. Some, if not all, of the employers' costs may be shifted to the worker in the long run, in the form of lower wages or higher general taxes, depending on how the scheme is financed and the degree of wage flexibility. Furthermore, large employers may reduce their costs through the reorganisation of working time and other aspects of personnel planning to better accommodate leave entitlements (OECD 1995a). Costs will also be offset by productivity gains, associated with the retention of skilled workers, high staff morale, etc. (Holtermann 1995).

At the aggregate level, public expenditure savings may lower the net costs. For example, in Belgium the scheme appears to produce a net saving because the benefit paid to those taking a career break is less than the unemployment benefit and is paid only when an unemployed replacement is recruited (OECD 1995a: 193). Efficiency gains for the economy may also result to the extent that parental leave makes a long-term contribution to raising the female employment rate and reducing the inflexibility and other costs associated with a segregated labour market and breadwinner family norm (Fagan and Rubery 1996b). However, as long as leave is predominantly taken by women, the costs will be primarily borne by employers with a female workforce, and this may increase sex discrimination, particularly for recruitment to high-level positions.

There is little empirical evidence of the impact of parental leave on labour demand, but some information is available on how employers accommodate parental leave. Parental leave does not create serious personnel problems for large employers, who are able to plan on the basis of experience, the stable patterns of leave claims and advance notice. However, some problems emerge concerning qualified labour in short supply. And little is known about how small firms react and adjust to parental leave (OECD 1995a: 176).

Replacement from the external labour market is obviously subject to existing regulations on fixed term contracts (OECD 1995a: 190) or the scheme's requirement to recruit unemployed replacements. Low-skilled workers are more likely to be replaced, since replacement and training costs tend to be lower, although in France the picture is reversed for the public sector. Full-timers are also more likely to be replaced. In Denmark the strategies of firms appear to vary according to the gender of the leave taker: two-thirds of women are covered by a substitute, while the most common option for men (54 per cent) is worksharing (EC Childcare Network 1994). However, this is partly correlated with the high share of female employment concentrated in the public sector, where replacement rates are much higher. Nevertheless, replacement rates are steadily growing, particularly with the increasing requests for educational leave (Boje 1995: Table

40). In the Netherlands just over half the part-time vacancies were filled with temporary cover, and in the public sector, in education, a replacement is always recruited while this is much rarer in the police and ministries, on the grounds that no suitable candidates were available (Plantenga and Sloep 1995: 80). These different national data suggest that the impact of extended leave on worksharing is likely to vary across the employment structure. At the same time, a large segment of the long-term unemployed are likely to remain untouched by the job openings to provide temporary cover (Boje 1995: 79).

State funding of childcare

State financing of childcare helps to raise women's labour supply through reducing the financial costs incurred when employed. A less direct effect may result from state regulations which establish minimum quality standards for collective services if this increases parental preferences for this form of childcare. The positive impact of state investment in childcare on women's labour supply has been demonstrated in a comparison of the effects of children on female labour supply in France and the UK while controlling for other important influences, such as wages and education (Dex *et al.* 1993). The authors concluded that the constraint of dependent children was much less in France due to the system of subsidised childcare and long school days. The different state policies in both countries are also likely to have influenced the normative environment, for maternal employment is viewed more positively in countries where public childcare services are widespread (Alwin *et al.* 1992). However, while a preference for staying at home when children are young exerts a significant effect on women's labour supply decisions in the UK, a much stronger effect is the difficulty of arranging childcare (Dex 1988; McRae 1991).

A comprehensive review by the EC Childcare Network (1996: 2) concluded that developments in services for children across the European Union since the late 1980s means that

> Most countries have achieved or are moving towards comprehensive publicly-funded services for children aged 3–6 years either in pre-primary schooling or *kindergarten*; the main exceptions are Ireland, the Netherlands and the UK. Levels of provision in services for children under 3 years and in services providing care and recreation for school-age children... are generally far lower... the gap between supply and demand is greatest for these services.

Appendix Table 6.2 shows that there is very little publicly funded childcare for children under the age of 3 in most countries, regardless of the length or availability of parental leave. By far the highest provision is found in Denmark (48 per cent), former East Germany (50 per cent), Belgium (30 per cent) and France (23 per cent).

In most EU countries compulsory schooling begins at 6 years of age, and there is generally some form of pre-primary education, or scope for children to enter primary school prior to the compulsory starting age (Appendix Table 6.2). The combination of opening hours for pre-primary education and childcare, followed by primary school hours, provides some indication of the way in which mothers have to organise their daily schedules. Either they fit their hours of work within school opening hours, or they arrange other childcare – with family and friends or by purchasing services in the informal or formal market.

A comprehensive system of pre-school education exists in France and Belgium which children begin to enter at the age of 2. In both countries around one-third of 2 year olds have a place, rising to nearly complete coverage by the age of 3 (OECD 1995b: 130–131). Most children aged 3–6 years are also in funded places in former East Germany, Denmark, Italy and Spain (82+ per cent). With the exception of Spain, in these countries pre-school weekday provision is long, at seven to eight hours per day. In Spain there is a three-hour lunch break, although this is supervised in a growing number of urban schools (EC Childcare Network 1996). In France and Belgium schools are closed on Wednesday afternoon and out-of-school care on this day is not available for all children. As a result, many mothers in France arrange their working hours to be off on this day (Dex *et al.* 1993; Hantrais 1994). In Denmark and Italy daily attendance hours are shorter once the child enters primary school, partly compensated in Denmark by a comparatively high coverage of out-of-school hours. In Italy the system of six mornings per week largely coincides with public sector working hours, providing some incentive for women to enter this area of employment (Bettio and Villa 1994).

Pre-school provision is lower in the other member states shown. Coverage generally increases with the age of the child, but the opening hours of pre-school and primary institutions vary markedly in these countries and publicly funded out-of-school care is generally very limited. By the age of 4 nearly all children in Luxembourg and the Netherlands are in primary school. Children aged 4 years upwards attend for seven hours per day in the Netherlands, but mothers have to arrange non-school care on Wednesday afternoons. In Luxembourg, mothers have to accommodate the schools closing for two afternoons per week and sometimes a two-hour lunch break on the other three days, but their children attend school on Saturday mornings. In the UK, 90 per cent of 4 year olds are in primary school but they attend for only half a day, progressing to a longer six-and-a-half hour day for 5 year olds. West German kindergartens and primary schools operate on a part-time basis, and once children enter primary school in Greece, Portugal and Ireland they too attend on a part-time basis.

In sum, the national system of funded childcare places in pre-school and primary care creates an important structural influence on whether mothers are available for paid work, and on whether they can manage to work part-time or full-time without having to organise out-of-school care. The length of school holidays is another dimension, not considered here, and a final part of the jigsaw is the organisation of working-time itself. Not only are holiday entitlements longer in some countries than others (Industrial Relations Services (IRS) 1991), but also daily and weekly working hours vary. Trends towards more flexible and non-standard working-time arrangements may make it easier for some parents to negotiate arrangements which are compatible with their childcare needs, but for others the organisational complexity of daily life will increase. Finally, national data hide marked regional variations in provision of pre-school care, with services tending to be concentrated in major urban areas (EC Childcare Network 1990).

Even in countries with comparatively high levels of childcare, there are gaps in provision. For example, in France, there appears to be an un-satisfied demand for day nurseries, since 19 per cent of the population consider this to be the most satisfactory form of childcare when the mother is at work, yet only 11 per cent of employed mothers have actually used nurseries (Silvera et al. 1995: 146). In Belgium, recent initiatives have focused upon developing facilities for sick children, out-of-school care and care for children whose parents have to work outside the normal opening hours of creches and nurseries. There is also an initiative to stimulate new, lower cost communal childcare services (MCAEs) (Meulders 1995: 81–82).

Several countries with lower levels of childcare have attempted to stimul-ate an expansion in national services, but the initiatives have either been curtailed, had limited results, or where childcare places have expanded rapidly the number still remains insufficient (see Box 6.5). Funding from the NOW initiative has also helped to stimulate local childcare projects. For example, pilot projects have been set up in three Athenian municipalities to train unemployed women as childminders, and so far eighty women aged between 25 and 45 years have participated. Childcare facilities have also been provided within many NOW- funded projects in Ireland (Barry 1995: 64).

In the Netherlands the emphasis of policy has shifted over time to funding employer-run facilities. This policy has been criticised on the grounds that it does little to establish a permanent national system of provision because firms are sensitive to cyclical economic pressures, as well as being likely to limit this 'fringe benefit' to higher-level staff (Plan-tenga and Sloep 1995: 78). This prediction was largely borne out in the UK when various initiatives in the banking sector were stalled or dismantled once labour shortages gave way to rationalisation and rising un-employment.

Box 6.5   Examples of national initiatives to stimulate childcare services

In 1989 in the **Netherlands**, the government adopted a four-year action programme designed to stimulate the provision of collective childcare facilities from 21,000 to almost 70,000 over a four-year period through subsidising day care centres, with more limited funding also being directed to employer day care centres (1990–3 Stimulatory Measure for Childcare). By 1992 a total of 47,829 places was in existence. However, many of these places are part-time, and the coverage for children under 4 is still just 5 per cent. The programme was extended until 1996, after which responsibility for childcare was devolved to the municipalities (Plantenga and Sloep 1995: 78).

In **Germany** a Federal Länder commitment to provide nursery places for all children aged 3 to 6 by 1996 was almost immediately followed by a discussion about postponement of this objective on the grounds of budget constraints (Maier and Rapp 1995: 107) so that this legal entitlement will not be implemented until 1999 (EC Childcare Network 1996).

In **Greece** a law passed in 1992 reorganised all childcare under the responsibility of the Ministry of Health, Welfare and Social Services (except pre-school kindergarten, which remain at the Ministry of Education), and set out several new initiatives to expand childcare services. Unfortunately, the initiatives were not implemented. The limited public childcare facilities in Greece, particularly for children under 4 years, are further hampered by staff and funding shortages which mean that some places remain vacant. At the end of 1994 the government announced its intention to fill 25 per cent of the total 4,178 vacant places. Since 1988 all public sector departments which employ more than 300 people have been required to provide a day care centre when erecting a new building. The public sector now accounts for 39 of the 75 employer-run nurseries. This decree was extended to large private sector firms in 1992, but is unlikely to have a major impact because most firms are not covered due to their small size (Cavouriaris *et al.* 1995: 63–65).

The **Luxembourg** government has also been increasing its investment in childcare services. For example, childcare places for those under 2 years increased at a rate of 49 per cent between 1992 and 1993. As from 1994, subsidies have been increased for firms which provide workplace childcare facilities (Plasman 1995: 64).

Ireland and the **UK** are the only member countries where state-funded nursery provision is designed primarily for children 'at risk' because of extreme emotional or material deprivation at home. Lobbying for more subsidised childcare in **Ireland** has had two definite outcomes. Legislation has been passed which requires private sector childcare services to be registered and more childcare facilities have been made available in local labour market initiatives, as well as the introduction of childcare allowances for lone parents who take part in the Community Employment Scheme (Barry 1995: 58–64). In July 1995, the **UK** government announced a new scheme to distribute childcare vouchers to contribute to parents' childcare costs. To date, the reaction of local authorities has been muted, and some have suggested that this will redirect rather than increase total public funding (*Guardian*, 21 July 1995).

An alternative to publicly-funded childcare places is to give tax concessions to parents who purchase childcare (discussed in section 6.3). In some countries, this might target the available childcare places to employed mothers. For example, in the Netherlands around 30 per cent of childcare places are occupied by the children of non-employed mothers, while 40 per cent of employed mothers rely upon other forms of childcare (Plantenga and Sloep 1995: 78). Tax relief may also stimulate additional market provision in some countries, but the effectiveness may be limited in other national contexts, and in particular the market may fail to deliver quality care at a suitable price for those on low income. Furthermore, some low-income groups may not earn sufficient income to take full advantage of the tax relief.

Indeed, the cost of childcare relative to women's wages remains a persistent obstacle to their ability to use formal, non-subsidised provision. For example, an evaluation of initiatives to increase out-of-school childcare in the UK concluded that it is difficult to sustain such provision without public resources, particularly in low-income neighbourhoods (Sanderson *et al.* 1995). In countries where the state provides few childcare subsidies, women often rely upon informal care (see Box 6.6). Increased charges for subsidised services may also lead some women to switch to informal provisions. The cost of formally purchased childcare services has risen markedly since 1994 in the Netherlands as a result of the government setting higher standard changes for subsidised places combined with a reduction in the amount of tax relief to set against childcare costs. The fiscal saving will be diverted into maintaining the existing level of childcare services. Feminists are concerned that the increased cost of institutionalised

---

Box 6.6   Reliance upon informal childcare by employed mothers

In **Portugal** employed women frequently rely upon private childminders in the informal sector, which means they are unable to claim tax relief (Lopes and Perista 1995: 74). The shortage of publicly funded services in the **Netherlands** means that 40 per cent of employed mothers rely upon other forms of care (Plantenga and Sloep 1995:78). In the **UK** most employed mothers also rely on informal care, but around 20 per cent pay for care, spending an average of 25 per cent of their net earnings (A. Marsh and McKay 1993). In **Greece** private nursery provision is negligible. A 1993–5 study in Greater Athens found that 45 per cent of employed mothers with a child under 6 years old relied upon another family member to provide childcare, usually a grandmother. Another 32 per cent relied upon a friend. Family and informal arrangements were even more common outside Athens. It is also common for Greek mothers to employ clandestine migrant workers from Poland, Sri Lanka or the Philippines to provide childcare in their home (Cavouriaris *et al.* 1995: 24–26).

---

childcare will encourage some women to rely on informal arrangements, especially those in the high income brackets who have faced the largest increase in childcare costs (Plantenga and Sloep 1995: 78–79).

Raising children involves an enormous amount of socially necessary work. Most of this is done in the household or through the informal sector. The demand for childcare services is likely to grow in many countries as more women aspire to combine motherhood with paid employment, but the price of non-subsidised childcare is likely to remain prohibitive for many women. Thus, as noted in the European Commission's White Paper on Employment (CEC 1993a), the expansion of childcare services is potentially an important area of job creation, but the market is unlikely to deliver this expansion without some public funding.

Assessment: state support for childcare

The particular combination of policies which exists in any country affects the way in which the early years of child-raising impact on the employment patterns of mothers, and to a lesser extent, that of fathers.

Leave arrangements are only one aspect of more general working-time policies which affect the ability of parents to combine employment with family responsibilities. The opportunity to switch to part-time work has expanded in the public sector in several Northern countries over the 1980s as a result of policies to promote equal opportunities or working-time flexibility, and in some, such as France and Belgium, this coexists with a right to return to full-time work (Hewitt 1993: Table 2.1). This is part of a wider trend towards working-time adjustments and flexibility driven mainly by employers' needs, while employee needs and preferences have been largely subordinated (Bosch et al. 1994; Rubery et al. 1995). The Directive on Working Time places a responsibility on employers and unions to consider the impact of reforms upon family and social life (Bercusson 1994), which may provide some redress in countries with strong industrial relations systems. The Netherlands is possibly one such example, where the draft working-time Act adopts an explicit recognition of the need to promote the combination of work and care tasks, but the wording has still to be finalised (Plantenga and Sloep 1995: 86). But in general, increasing employer demands for variable and non-standard hours are likely to make the organisation of family life and employment more complex, and may place increased costs on households in terms of individual fatigue, reduced time together for family and social activities, etc. (Fagan 1996).

Childcare services, extended leave and flexible working-time arrangements all offer workers a range of options with which to fulfil the dual demands of employment and family life. The needs of parents vary according to their employment and household situation and the stage in the child's life. Similarly, some arrangements will be suitable for certain employers, depending on the sector, occupation or size of workforce. Yet according to the OECD:

> with public spending considerations becoming more binding in most countries, cost considerations loom large in the debate and the different choices are increasingly seen as alternatives rather than complements.
>
> (OECD 1995a: 195)

Simple cost calculations may indicate that it is cheaper for the state to rely upon extended leave and increased working-time flexibility rather than funding childcare services. Such an assessment may be misguided, particularly when wider social costs and benefits and long-term economic gains are considered. One major cost is that gender differences may deepen or emerge around the use of extended leave or the involvement in non-standard working-time patterns, unless men's lifetime employment and care patterns change, thus reinforcing the breadwinner family model and segregated employment patterns.

6.5. Women's employment patterns and their access to social security

Female activity rates are rising rapidly, particularly for younger generations, but women remain less integrated into the employment system than men. Unlike men, they interrupt their employment or work fewer hours in order to put time into raising their children. In most countries women's employment is also more likely to be punctuated by periods of unemployment or temporary or precarious employment, and of course to be rewarded by lower wages. Therefore, women are less likely to follow a pattern of full-time continuous employment over their working lives than men, even though rising unemployment is also undermining men's ability to follow this pattern of employment. Even when they do follow a 'male' employment pattern, the state may still treat them as dependent upon a male breadwinner with the result that their benefit entitlements are reduced due to their household position. When women's household circumstances and labour market opportunities mean that their working life includes periods of interrupted or part-time employment, this impacts on the individual retirement pension that they receive.

The impact of women's household position on their unemployment benefits

The eligibility conditions for unemployment insurance benefits and the share of the registered unemployed in receipt of unemployment compensation were analysed in Chapter 5. This showed that a smaller share of unemployed women have an entitlement to an independent unemployment benefit through the insurance system than unemployed men in eight out of twelve member states, while female entitlement is approximately similar or higher in Denmark, Belgium, Germany and Luxembourg (see Table 5.1). In this section we draw out the way that certain elements of different national unemployment insurance systems create penalties – leading to either a reduced ability to claim benefit or a lower level of benefit – which impact disproportionately upon women because of their household circumstances.

To start with, when entitlement to claim unemployment benefit rests upon recent employment or contributory records, this makes it difficult for women to make a claim if they have recently interrupted their labour market activity to care full-time for their children and are now unemployed. Few countries make explicit allowance in the UI system for such interruptions. One exception is Germany, where the introduction of statutory parental leave in 1986 also introduced credits for periods of statutory parental leave in the qualifying period for unemployment insurance. This is likely to have increased the share of women who are entitled to unemployment benefits. However, longer absences for child-raising are not counted, even though many women have an interruption which exceeds the length of the statutory leave period (on average mothers interrupt their activity for six years) (Maier and Rapp 1995: 60). Some compensation for periods of child-raising is also given in the unemployment insurance system in the Netherlands and in the system of unemployment assistance in France (see section 5.1 for details).

Second, women may still receive a lower benefit than men (or single women) with a comparable record of employment and contributions because they are treated as household dependants or as mothers. The main cause of this discriminatory outcome is either that the availability for work test is stricter for women who have children or live with a male partner, or that a lower benefit is paid on the basis of household status.

In countries where the work availability test is stricter for women with dependent children than for fathers and childless claimants, this can create a major hurdle which prevents women from succeeding in their claim for unemployment benefit. This is particularly difficult in countries with only limited public support for childcare (see section 6.4). In the UK, mothers have to show that childcare arrangements are already in place in order to be accepted as available for work, even though women are unlikely to want to purchase childcare before they have some earnings guarantee to meet this cost. In Germany a similar requirement applied to mothers until recently, but recognition of the discriminatory nature of this regulation means that it is no longer applied. The number of hours which the claimant must be available for work are also important. For example, a stricter test was introduced in the UK in 1996 whereby claimants now have to be available to work a minimum of 40 hours per week. This is longer than the norm for most women in employment, and there are only vague, discretionary provisions for those with caring responsibilities to be available for fewer hours. In contrast, the requirements are clearer in Germany, where claimants who are caring for children or incapacitated adults are permitted to restrict their availability to part-time work providing they can work at least 18 hours a week. However, other claimants have to be available for full-time work even if they previously worked part-time. This means that some part-timers pay contributions into a system which they are then ineligible to draw upon (Maier and Rapp 1995: 57).

Even when unemployed women pass the availability for work test, the amount of UI benefit which they receive may be reduced because of their status as dependent on their partner. This discriminatory outcome occurs in Belgium, Ireland and Germany, driven by different features of these national systems. In Belgium, the sex-biased outcome arises from the different UI benefit rates paid to claimants according to whether their partner is either employed or receiving benefits: an unemployed household head is treated in the same way as a single person, while a lower payment is paid to a claimant who is classified as an unemployed partner on the basis that his/her partner is either employed or receiving benefits (see Box 6.7). Most of those claiming the unemployed household head benefit are men, while women account for two-thirds of those in receipt of benefit as the unemployed partner. Therefore, women generally receive a lower benefit relative to their contributions and their earnings compared with men and single women.

Box 6.7   Differential treatment in the Belgian unemployment insurance system according to household status

In **Belgium** the amount of unemployment benefit received by married or cohabiting claimants is affected by the income of their partner (and similar principles inform the payment of sickness and invalidity benefits). The benefit is paid at a rate of 60 per cent of previous earnings for those workers with a spouse who has neither earned nor replacement income. A lower earnings-related benefit (55 per cent) is paid to claimants defined as unemployed partners on the basis that their partners are either employed or receiving benefits. As the duration of unemployment increases the rate of benefit for unemployed partners is reduced further, and may even be stopped. Furthermore, a means-test is applied to unemployed partners but not to the 'household head' (Meulders 1995).

Aggregation is also present in the Irish system, so that an unemployed couple receive the same total benefit regardless of whether one or both partners are eligible for an insurance benefit. Both partners can make an independent claim, but the benefit is calculated as one personal rate plus a lower dependant's addition, the sum of which is split between the two claimants. This means the couple receive a lower rate of benefit for their contributions than two single claimants and that women are treated as dependent even if they have fulfilled the work history and contributory requirements. A side-effect is that there is little incentive for the wives of unemployed men to register as unemployed since this does not raise their benefit entitlement, which contributes to the under-recording of women's unemployment (Barry 1995: 31).

In Germany, the tax system is the source of a negative effect on the rate of unemployment insurance benefit received by married women. Income splitting for the tax assessment of married couples means that women frequently pay more tax on their earnings solely because they are married (see section 6.3), and in turn this lower net earnings is used to calculate their benefit entitlement (Maier and Rapp 1995). As a result, married women receive a lower benefit than other claimants with comparable earnings and contribution records.

It is clear that while the Equal Treatment Directive has removed many explicit forms of sex discrimination, sex-biased outcomes still result in systems which discriminate indirectly by treating most women as dependent adults or carers with different rights from those held by household heads. This implicit emphasis upon women's roles as wives or mothers rather than as unemployed workers makes it more difficult for women than for men to secure an independent benefit related to their previous employment and earnings. Thus, women's care responsibilities make it more difficult for them to achieve the requisite continuity in employment and contributory payments to gain insurance benefits, and when they do achieve the necessary employment pattern their access to insurance benefits is further squeezed in some countries through rules related to their maternal or marital status. This coexists with a labour market in which recorded female unemployment rates exceed those for men in most countries, a gap which would be even greater in some countries if the significant shares of women's hidden unemployment were recorded. A large share of unemployed women in many countries are, therefore, forced to rely upon private family income transfers, supplemented by household-based means-tested assessments.

This squeeze which state policies exert on women's access to unemployment insurance payments in many countries also exists in the aggregation of household income for means-tested social assistance schemes.[5] This means that when a woman becomes unemployed and has exhausted any entitlement to an insurance benefit, her access to an independent state transfer is low or non-existent if she lives with a partner who is employed or in receipt of benefits. For example, in Germany fewer women who are registered as unemployed receive unemployment assistance compared to men (Maier and Rapp 1995: 59). Thus, a woman is treated as dependent on her employed spouse in a household-based means tests for social assistance even if her previous earnings made a substantial contribution to the household's financial well-being.

In some countries, the principle of treating women as essentially dependent upon a male breadwinner is extended such that women in couple households are exempt from the obligation to seek work when the couple claims social assistance. In contrast, this obligation applies to all other fit adults of working age. This occurs in systems, for example in the UK, where an unemployed claimant receives a means-tested benefit addition for a dependent spouse based on the claimant's availability for work and regardless of the availability of his or her partner. In the current system in the Netherlands, there is a separate category for people whose limited labour market ties makes them exempt from the requirement to be available for work (ABW-sec benefits). This applies mainly to women in their caring role as lone parents and to some single people. A proposed reform, which was expected to become law in January 1996, will merge this element of the system with the general one for unemployed employees (RWW), thus extending the work availability obligation to many women. Those caring for a child under 5 years will remain exempt, and the municipalities may extend this exemption to those caring for older children. This shift in emphasis towards treating women as workers is accompanied by new rights to help them achieve this obligation, including increased access to employment services combined with reimbursements for childcare and training costs (Plantenga and Sloep 1995: 47). A similar shift in emphasis has occurred in the UK in relation to lone mothers, through increasing the financial incentives to work (increased disregards for childcare costs, more generous in-work benefits, etc.), but without the introduction of an explicit work availability requirement (Rubery and Smith 1995).

Finally, it is important not to neglect the way that the introduction or enhancement of means-tested benefits for lone parents provides an important means of state support to assist such women when they lack employment, and a recognition that not all households are organised around a male breadwinner or a female carer. For example, an enhanced benefit rate was introduced for lone parents in Germany in 1992, providing some protection from the general cuts to social assistance spending (Maier and Rapp 1995: 100). Lone parents in the UK have become the focus of attention for the 'New Right', who argue that support for lone parents should be cut in order to discourage this form of living arrangement. However, the actual policy of the Conservative government was mainly to try to cut expenditure through initiatives to move lone parents off benefits. Reforms to benefits have been designed to reduce the unemployment trap for lone mothers rather than actually to cut the rate of support. Another policy direction is the establishment of the Child Support Agency to trace the absent fathers of children when lone parents make a claim for state support, thus shifting part of the claim for support from the state directly to the child's father. This latter development has been particularly controversial and its effectiveness – both in reducing public expenditure and in raising the financial situation of lone parents – is still being hotly debated.

Women's lifetime employment patterns and individual pension entitlements

Pension provision is a subject of policy debate and reform in most countries, due to the ageing of the population, escalating pension costs and a general concern to constrain public expenditure costs. Reforms have also been introduced to promote formal equality between women and men, stimulated by the Equal Treatment Directive on this issue. The most visible reform is the equalisation of pension ages, usually by raising the retirement age for women, as occurred, for example, in the recent Italian reform. Less attention, however, has been given to the issue of how women's ability to obtain an independent pension depends on both their lifetime employment patterns and the extent to which the pension system discriminates against those without full-time, continuous employment records (Ginn and Arber 1994).

A typology of state contributory pension systems has been developed by Ginn and Arber (1994) to classify European welfare states (see Table 6.6). This identifies three pension systems: 'basic security' (Denmark and the Netherlands), 'residual' (the UK and Ireland) and an 'income security' model which underpins the system in the other eight member states. This distinction is closely linked to different national principles of redistributive justice and reliance on employment-related insurance, and hence also reflects the different approaches to organising support for unemployment (see Chapter 5). The extent to which additional pension support is provided through voluntary private company pension schemes must also be taken into account. Ginn and Arber argue that this is inversely related to the type of state provision, for countries with very different ratios of public to private provision devote similar total shares of GNP to pension transfers (Tamburi and Mouton 1986, cited in Ginn and Arber 1994). Thus, relatively generous state provision is associated with lower non-state provision than in residual welfare states. Indeed, the size of the private sector for pension provision in much higher in the UK than in other European states. However, private pension provision does not provide a complete substitute for state provision. This is because personal private pensions yield a low replacement rate for women compared to men, and workplace pension scheme coverage is unevenly distributed across the workforce (B. Davies and Ward 1992).

Table 6.6 Typology of pension systems

Political philosophy	Liberal	Conservative/corporatist	Social Democratic/ socialist
Welfare policy orientation	Residual welfare	Industrial achievement performance	Institutional redistributive
	State plays a minimal role, family and market roles emphasised	Social needs are met mainly according to work-merit	State support based on citizenship, as a universal right
Type of pension system	Residual	Income security	Basic security
	State provides a minimal safety net for those lacking an occupational pension	State ensures a high income replacement rate for those with an adequate employment record	State provides a universal benefit
	UK Ireland	Germany Belgium France Greece Italy Spain Portugal Luxembourg	Denmark Netherlands

Source: Adapted from Ginn and Arber (1994: Table 3.1)

How do these different pension systems impact on women's income in retirement? One indication is the poverty rates for elderly households, which Ginn and Arber (1994) compare for exemplar countries (the UK, Germany and Denmark) of the three model pension systems they identify. This analysis reveals that elderly women are particularly vulnerable to poverty in the UK, in contrast to the absence of a gender bias in Denmark, while in Germany there is a moderate concentration of poverty in old age on women. This indicates, not surprisingly, that the Danish 'basic security' model of a citizenship entitlement to a relatively generous pension provides the best protection against poverty in old age for women and other vulnerable groups.

Another indication is the estimated net replacement rate of a full insurance-based pension compared to that provided through means-tested social assistance. This has been calculated using average net manual earnings in *Social Protection in Europe* (CEC 1993b). This shows that the replacement rate for an individual contributory pension ranges from less than 45 per cent in the UK and Ireland, to 70 per cent or more in the eight 'income security' countries, with the basic security countries, Denmark and the Netherlands, in between. For those individuals forced to rely upon social assistance, the minimum is only slightly less than the contributory insurance pensions in both the residual insurance pension systems of Ireland and the UK, and the basic security systems in Denmark and the Netherlands, but significantly less than the earnings-related contributory pension in the remaining member states (see Table 6.8).

However, to gain a better understanding it is necessary to examine the different elements of the pension systems and how these interact with women's employment patterns. Employment interruptions affect the acquisition of non-means-tested pensions in three ways. First, the number of contributions and total lifetime earnings are lower. At least one of these two factors is used to calculate state pension entitlement in most countries, although in the basic security countries (Denmark and the Netherlands) a large part of the pension entitlement rests simply upon citizenship (see Appendix Table 6.3). The number of qualifying years for a full pension varies across countries, but are slightly lower in the Southern countries. In Greece, women in the public sector used to have the right to retire with a reduced pension after fifteen years' service, and other public sector workers could do the same after twenty-five years' service. This privilege was abolished in 1990, and may encourage women to remain in employment in their later years in order to secure their pension (Cavouriaris *et al.* 1995). Another important aspect of pension acquisition in the Southern countries is that it is related to employment history in the formal economy, yet the proportion of the labour force with access to this stable, formal employment and associated pension is relatively small, particularly for women. Few, if any, pension rights are built up through work in the informal economy in these countries.

Contributory systems usually provide credits for periods of involuntary unemployment or incapacity, but in some countries, such as the UK and Ireland, women may be less likely to register as unemployed as they are more likely to be ineligible for unemployment benefit. In both countries this is exacerbated by the lack of requirement for them to register as available for work when they live with an unemployed spouse who is claiming a dependent spouse addition. Gaps for child-raising are only partially compensated in most of the state 'income security' systems since contributions are credited only for specific periods of maternity and parental leave (Belgium, Germany, Greece, Spain and Portugal) or statutory leave plus a bonus of roughly six months' child-raising per child in Italy. Longer credits are available in the two 'residual' countries (Ireland and the UK) and in Luxembourg for non-employed periods for children under 6 years old (Appendix Table 6.3). Credits give important recognition to women's unpaid work, but they are double-edged. They may reinforce the presumption that mothers should interrupt employment, and the German and UK system of care credits for part-time maternal employment below a certain threshold endorses this form of employment, while providing no pension incentive for these women to increase their labour supply.

The second effect of employment interruptions on pensions is that non-employment generally reduces earnings in subsequent periods of employment. Labour market re-entry for women who quit employment to raise young children is associated with downward occupational mobility and reduced earnings (and hence pension contributions), in countries such as the UK and Germany where this employment pattern is still common for many women. Conversely, earnings increase with employment continuity, particularly in non-manual occupations, so that contributions to earnings-related pension schemes tend to be highest in the final years prior to retirement. This emphasis upon earnings in the last few years has a particularly strong impact in 'final salary' pension schemes, but of course also influences the pension received when a 'lifetime earnings' formula is used.

Private company pension schemes generally place a further penalty on employment interruptions because, unlike state schemes, they generally require a minimum period of service to gain entry, and early leavers often lose at least part of the value of their pension on leaving their employer (Ginn and Arber 1994). Another problem is that non-standard workers, as well as women full-timers, may be concentrated in occupations or industries in the private sector which are not covered by company schemes. At the same time, the concentration of women in the public sector in many countries may reduce this gender bias if public sector workers have access to more generous pension entitlements.

Periods of part-time employment also affect pension acquisition, not simply because of the effect of this form of employment on earnings, but because this employment form may be excluded from pension coverage in both state and company systems. For example, periods of short part-time work do not count towards the statutory contributory record in Germany and the UK, although this effect is moderated for those in short part-time jobs who receive credits for childcare responsibilities (discussed in section 6.4). Research has also shown that company-based pension schemes often exclude part-timers in general, or those working less than 50 per cent of standard hours or below a certain income (Maier 1994: 166). A number of European Court judgments, including the influential 1986 Bilka–Kaufhaus and 1990 Barber rulings, have outlawed the exclusion of part-timers from company pension schemes since this disproportionately discriminates against women. This has directly improved pension entitlements of part-timers in the Netherlands, for example, where they were excluded from the Dutch supplementary pension scheme until 1990 (Plantenga and Sloep 1995: 68). Although governments have generally been reluctant to intervene directly in the rules for company pension schemes to speed the process of reform, the European legal rulings can be expected to exert pressure on collective bargaining and to increase the inclusion of part-timers in such schemes over time (Maier 1994: 166). However, the coverage of part-timers may still remain lower than that for full-timers if they are concentrated in workplaces without company schemes, such as in Britain (see Table 6.7).

Table 6.7 Membership of employers' pension schemes in the UK by gender and working-time

	Men (%)			Women (%)		
	Working full-time	Working part-time	Total	Working full-time	Working part-time	Total
Present employer has a pension scheme						
Member	62	12	58	54	19	38
Not a member	15	34	17	22	34	28
Present employer does not have a pension scheme	21	39	22	21	39	29
Does not know if present employer has a pension scheme – not a member	2	14	3	2	7	4

Source: Rubery and Smith (1995: Table 3.17), taken from *General Household Survey* (1992: Table 6.2).

Ginn and Arber (1994) identify three important elements which affect how non-standard employment patterns are either accommodated or discriminated against in state pension systems, plus the potential for unequal access to private occupational or company schemes:

State pension schemes

- treatment of gaps in employment and job changes;
- coverage of part-time, temporary or low-paid workers;
- pension formulae (e.g. based on average lifetime earnings, 'best' years of earnings or final salary).

Private occupational and company schemes

- the entry and exit rules in these forms of pension provision may discriminate against workers with non-standard employment records, an issue of particular importance in national systems which rely heavily upon this form of pension provision;
- such schemes may be more common in some sectors and for some occupational categories, making women vulnerable to exclusion through employment segregation.

Given the impact of these different elements of the system on women's ability to obtain their own pension entitlement, how do the three European models of pension provision compare? In the Danish example of a 'basic security' pension system, the pension is only weakly dependent upon the employment history. A flat-rate state pension is universally paid to all retired citizens with 40 years' residence; it has a replacement rate equivalent to 40 per cent of the average production wage (Palme 1990, cited in Ginn and Arber 1994). On top of this, there is a compulsory employment-related scheme (ATP) which pays a small pension linked to the number of years of contributions (but not earnings or hours) and a third tier of private, earnings-related occupational schemes. Currently less than half of employees are covered by private occupational schemes; over the age of 35 coverage is lower for women than for men, although the gender gap is modest compared to that found for occupational pension coverage in the UK (Ginn and Arber 1994).

In contrast, in the UK the state pension is lower, and is tied more closely to previous employment. The basic flat-rate state pension is set below the level of means-tested benefits, with a low earnings-related addition (SERPS). Those without a complete contributory record or an occupational pension therefore rely upon means-tested benefits to bring their pension up to a low guaranteed minimum. Women are particularly vulnerable. Fewer employed women belong to an occupational pension scheme compared to men (see Table 6.7) and women are around twice as likely as men to rely upon means-tested additions in old age (Ginn and Arber 1994).

Germany, as an example of a corporatist 'income security' pension model, falls between the two extremes illustrated by the UK and Denmark. Here, the state pension scheme provides a relatively generous earnings-related pension for those with the requisite employment record. However, the net earnings replaced by the pension is heavily influenced by the insured lifetime. For example, a ten-year gap in employment produces a gross replacement rate of 39 per cent compared to 50 per cent for someone with a full employment record (Maier and Rapp 1995: 110). Furthermore, it does not count periods of short part-time hours so that such workers, together with others with low lifetime earnings, are unable to acquire an independent pension above the level of means-tested benefits. The private occupational system is less widespread than that found in the UK, but like the UK it is also more generally available to men than women.

This corporatist model of income security generally provides women with stronger derived rights than those available in a residual state, which provide some help to women to build up their own pension. First, the couple's contribution records from the state scheme are split equally upon divorce, and funds from occupational schemes may also be split. Pension contributions are also apportioned in the Spanish system, according to the

250

duration of marriage (Moltó 1995). In contrast, divorced women in the UK currently lose any right to their husbands' pensions upon divorce, although reforms are currently being debated. Second, the widow's pension available from 'income security' schemes is generally higher than that provided in 'residual' regimes.

The implications of an incomplete contributory record on pension entitlements in the different member states have been estimated by the European Commission by modelling the proportion of state benefit received for specified lifetime profiles (Table 6.8). This shows that the pension entitlement is largely protected in most countries except Portugal for a worker with average industrial earnings but a five-year employment gap in the middle of his or her working life due to unemployment or illness. A similar five-year break to care for a disabled parent is generally protected to the same extent, except in Denmark, the Netherlands, Belgium and Germany, where the pension replacement rate is roughly 10 to 20 percentage points lower. Someone who takes a ten-year complete break from full-time employment to care for children also has his or her pension largely protected, although the protection offered falls below 80 per cent in Denmark and the Netherlands.

Divorce or lone parenthood reduce pension entitlements for women. In eight countries, the scenario for a divorced women with a significant gap in her employment history followed by a return to full-time employment at the end of her marriage is a loss of between 25 and 50 per cent of the pension, with an even more negative effect in Portugal and Italy, while the best protection is offered in Denmark, Belgium and Ireland. A four-year break from employment for lone parents in low-paid jobs produces a similar or slightly lower penalty to that of divorce in most countries.

There are some limitations with the specification of these scenarios because they are not concerned with examining gender differences directly. For example, the models are based on average industrial earnings, neglecting women's lower average earnings and their concentration in the service sector. The scenario used for assessing the impact of a period of part-time employment is particularly problematic and dramatically underestimates the likely effect of this employment form on pension rights for many women. This is because it assumes half-time hours are worked at average industrial wages in the middle of the working life, followed by a return to full-time employment. Yet in many countries women work shorter part-time hours and wages are lower, which may pull them below the contributory threshold, as seen, for example, in the UK. A more important distortion of the analysis is the failure to explore the impact on pensions for part-timers who do not move back into full-time employment, which is common in the UK, for example, or for those who work part-time prior to retirement. When a more realistic scenario is modelled for someone in Germany in a middle income group who interrupts employment and subsequently works part-time

Table 6.8 Average replacement rate for a full contributory state pension and the impact of an incomplete contributory record on pension entitlement

	Individual retirement benefit: % average net earnings manual worker in manufacturing		Case 1: five-year break due to unemployment (or sickness) (%)[a]	Case 2: five-year break due to caring for disabled parent (%)[b]	Case 3: ten-year break due to caring for child (%)[c]	Case 4: divorce (%)[d]	Case 5: lone parent (%)[e]	Case 6: part-time work (%)[f]	Case 7: negligible contributions (%)[g]
	Contributory pension	*Social assistance*							
Basic security model									
Denmark	60	52	99 (100)	78	79	98	100	98	93
Netherlands	49	49	89 (100)	88	76	73	57	82	57
Income security model									
Belgium	73	47	100 (100)	91	90	92	80	89	53
Germany	77	39	100 (100)	90	>100	68	82	86	63
Greece	107	8	94–100 (94–100)	86–100	93–100	68	70–74	93–100	11
Spain	97	32	94–100 (94–100)	100	100	75	80	100	33
France	88	46	100 (100)	100	96	46–62	80	97	58
Italy	89	19	(91–100) (91–100)	88–100	80	46	74	83	23
Luxembourg	78	46	90 (100)	>100	94	62	82	88	54
Portugal	94	30	70–100 (70–100)	100	100	36	51	100	28
Residual model									
Ireland	42	35	100 (100)	98–100	98–100	100	99–100	100	86
UK	44	31	100 (100)	100	100	53–77	85	96	67

Source: CEC (1993b: Table 8 and Graphs 42–49)

Notes: a Single full-time industrial worker on average earnings; regular employment for full period required except a five-year spell of unemployment in middle of career (similar interruption, but for illness instead of unemployment)
b Full-time manual industrial worker on average earnings; regular employment from age 16 to retirement, except period 41– 5 years old caring for disabled parent
c Full-time manual industrial worker on average earnings; regular employment from age 16 to retirement, except period 26–35 years old caring for child; married to an average industrial wage earner in regular employment; regular employment from age 16 to retirement
d Aged 20–45 years: at home and married to manual industrial worker on average earnings; divorced at 45 years, from 45 years to retirement in regular full-time employment in industrial sector on average earnings
e No dependants; full-time manual industrial work at 75% average earnings from 18 years to retirement, except 29–33 years old caring for child
f Full-time manual industrial worker on average earnings in full-time regular work; regular full-time employment from age 16 to retirement, except period 29–43 years part-time work
g Never-married person aged 70; no dependants; no significant contributions record; negligible independent means of support

until retirement, the replacement rate falls to a mere 45 per cent (Maier and Rapp 1995: 111). This illustrates the importance of integrating gender inequalities directly into labour market policy evaluations.

Finally, an elderly, never-married person with a negligible contributory record and no other independent means of support would receive a sub-stantially reduced level of income support in every country except Den-mark. In Denmark and the Netherlands, support for such a person is guaranteed through the system of non-means-tested, residency based pen-sions, but in the other countries the pension received in this scenario depends largely upon the receipt of minimum non-contributory entitlements or means-tested social assistance. This safety net is particularly important for women, given their lifetime employment patterns plus a greater life expectancy than men. Another important form of pension protection for married women with an incomplete contributory record is the provision of widow/er's pensions, which exists in all member states.

Box 6.8   Pension reform in Italy and France produces both gains and losses for women relative to men

The basis for calculating pensions has been reformed in **France** to contain expenditure. Pensions are now indexed to prices, the minimum contributory record has been raised from 37.5 years to 40 years, and the pension is calculated on the basis of earnings in the best 25 years instead of the best 10. Among those with full-time, continuous employment careers this reform has reduced the earnings replacement rate for men and raised it slightly for women, because women's wages are more stable over the lifetime. However, women with interrupted or part-time employment history will suffer from this tightening of pension entitlement (Silvera *et al.* 1995).

A comprehensive reform to the pension system is underway in **Italy** to contain expenditure by levelling down the pension entitlements of more affluent workers. Within this context there will be some relative gains and losses for women. On the plus side, the shift away from a 'final salary' calculation to a 'lifetime earnings' calculation will place a higher penalty on men than women because of the steeper growth of male earnings over the lifetime. However, several other reforms have a direct negative impact on women. Firstly, the pension age for women has been raised to equal that for men, and early retirement will be penalised. Second, survivors' pensions are to be income-tested. Finally, the provisions for atypical workers have not been finalised, and seem likely to produce penalties for part-time and temporary work, while the treatment of the self-employed has been improved.

In Greece, there have been several important reforms which have extended the safety net for retired women without an independent pension through the introduction of a means-tested non-contributory retirement pension and the granting of a basic independent pension for farmers' wives in 1982, subsequently extended to all unpaid family workers in 1988. All three categories receive a pension equal to that paid to farmers, but the level of the pension is far below that available from the contributory system and is too low to live on (see Table 6.8), equivalent to about 10 per cent of the minimum wage (Cavouriaris *et al.* 1995: 30). Furthermore, in 1992 widow/ers who are low-paid or disabled became entitled to claim a portion of their deceased spouse's pension (their own contributory pension entitlement can not be claimed as well).

Reforms have also been made to the pension system in France and Italy, mainly driven by the objective of curtailing public expenditure (Box 6.8). In both reforms, the change has produced relative gains and losses for women. On one hand, the calculation of earnings replacement rates has penalised men more than women. On the other hand, the penalty for an interrupted or atypical employment career has increased, which will probably hit women hardest.

Ginn and Arber (1994) conclude that women are more likely to acquire an adequate independent pension in a basic security model (such as in Denmark) than in the income security or residual models. Furthermore, where occupational pensions are a major component of the pension system, the effect is to widen the gender gap in access to an adequate pension. Their comparison of the three countries reveals that there is an internal logic to the Danish and German pensions systems which is lacking in the UK. Thus, the Nordic model combines universal entitlements with childcare policies which enable women to follow continuous employment patterns (and thus contribute to the financing of universal pensions). In contrast, the German model does not facilitate employment continuity for women, but provides some protection to women in old age through relatively generous derived rights. In the UK, the state provides little support to help women combine employment with care responsibilities, yet it does little to ensure that women without full-time lifetime employment receive anything other than a residual level of income support in old age.

Rising public expenditure costs are encouraging governments to move away from universal provision above a residual minimum and to encourage market provision of pensions. There is also a tendency to reduce women's derived rights to widows' pensions in some countries, driven partly by costs and partly by the changing employment patterns of women. Both types of reforms will have a negative impact on women's pension entitlements in old age. Reforms which move away from universal or derived pension provision must, therefore, be accompanied by measures which protect workers with interrupted and non-standard employment patterns, and are co-ordinated with wider child support policies to enable women to follow standard employment patterns.

6.6 Summary

In this chapter we have argued that the social contract of the breadwinner family model is under strain due to the rapidly changing labour market behaviour of women in particular.

Women's contribution to household income is growing, mainly due to their greater involvement in the labour market but also as more men experience low wages and unemployment as economies restructure. But while women are taking on more paid work, men are making only a slight increase in their contribution to unpaid domestic work, so that in dual earner households women have a longer total working week than men. A substantial amount of work is done away from the formal economy in household self-servicing and production, in voluntary work and in waged work in the informal sector. The changing employment patterns of women mean they have less time for non-market work combined with higher income, fuelling speculation that this might drive job creation as market goods and services are substituted for household and informal activity. In particular, the scope for job creation in care work and related activities are potentially great, but the main obstacle is the lack of effective demand at market prices.

The welfare state regime has a major effect on women's labour market and household roles. It underpins the social contract between the sexes through institutional definitions of family responsibilities and social protection entitlements. It also has a major effect on women's employment conditions, either as the public employer or labour market regulator. The traditional strong breadwinner regimes do most to obstruct women's emancipation compared to the more moderate and weak breadwinner states in countries such as France and Denmark. In Denmark, for example, state policies facilitate a high female employment rate over the lifecycle, combined with a pension system which provides a reasonable level of income in old age regardless of the previous employment history. The stronger breadwinner logic in other countries encourages women to interrupt or reduce their employment, partly compensated for by derived rights on the basis of their marital status. These rights are an important means of providing women with income security in old age, but this protection is extended to divorced women in only some countries.

There have been some policy reforms in recognition of changing household living arrangements and women's labour market patterns. Thus, family taxation has been reformed in the direction of individualisation in many countries, and explicit sex discrimination has largely been removed from the eligibility conditions for social security benefits. However, where systems are still designed around the breadwinner family model, certain rules impact disproportionately upon women because of their household role as primary carer for dependent children. Individual social security entitlements still largely rest upon a full-time, lifetime, labour market involvement, and severe penalties are often incurred for labour market interruptions and periods of part-time employment. This frequently coexists with other state policies which provide strong incentives for women to withdraw from the labour market and depend upon their male partners for support; namely, limited subsidies for childcare services and elements of aggregation which are still found in parts of the tax and social security system.

The breadwinner model of family life is under increasing strain across Europe. Higher levels of female employment alongside higher male unemployment rates is challenging the division between second earner and breadwinner. Other social and demographic trends – later and fewer marriages, divorce, cohabitation, lower fertility rates, increased life expectancy, etc. – are leading to a more diverse range of households. All these developments challenge the relevance of organising state policies upon the presumption that men and women of working age live together in family breadwinner arrangements. At the same time, social security systems still need to accommodate gender differences whereby women still do more unpaid care work than men, and are paid less. In this context it may be important to preserve certain derived rights unless substitute forms of social protection are developed. But policy should not remain simply directed at women; complementary initiatives are needed to encourage men to do more household and care work. Thus initiatives are required to increase male take-up of parental leave, and more generally to make men's working-time and employment patterns more compatible with family life.

7

THE NEW MEMBER STATES[1]

With the entry of Sweden, Finland and Austria to the European Union in 1995 the balance of the European Community changed: from having only one country, Denmark, which belonged to the high female employment Nordic countries, the EU now had three such member states. Not only do they have high employment rates, but also they have had a tradition of state policies designed around a weak male breadwinner model, providing support to women to enter employment through provision of paid parental leave, childcare and plentiful employment opportunities in the public sector. Despite these similarities within the Nordic bloc, there are still major differences between Scandinavian countries: Finland has high female employment rates based on full-time work, while Sweden has one of the highest part-time rates in the EU. The entry of Sweden and Finland into the EU also has the simultaneous effect of raising the average employment rate and increasing the trends towards employment loss as both countries have suffered from very severe economic crises in the 1990s.

The entry of Austria increases the number of countries within the EU which could be said to follow a German-type employment system. The similarities between Germany and Austria extend beyond those of language to include, for example, the dual training system for young people, and a tendency to favour a strong male breadwinner form of household organisation. Austria, like Germany, has been affected by the changes in Eastern Europe, in part because of its geographical location. However, Austria has its own distinct range of policies which do not by any means all follow those adopted by Germany; for example it makes less use of part-time work and has long adopted a system of individualised taxation.

7.1 The female contribution to the evolution of the European employment rate

Trends in employment rates in the new member states

The employment rate patterns of the three new member states are both distinctive and diverse.[2] As discussed above, the two new Nordic countries share certain similarities with Denmark, while Austria has a social and economic system which shares certain similarities with Germany. Sweden has the highest employment rate in all EU member states, and this first rank is maintained despite falls in employment which began in 1991 (Table 7.1). Finland's employment rate, however, is located in the middle of the distribution of EU states, at rank seventh or eighth (dependent upon the data used – see Table 7.2) out of fourteen member states, excluding Luxembourg.[3] This relatively poor employment performance is based on extremely low employment rates for men, placing Finland at the bottom of the EU ranking, having fallen from ninth place in 1985 (or eighth using national data). In contrast, female employment rates have remained high, with Finland still ranked third after Sweden and Denmark,[4] compared to second place in 1985 (joint with Denmark in the *Employment in Europe* data). This high employment rate for women in Finland is that much more significant when we take account of the high share of full-time work among women, in contrast to the other high female employment countries where part-time rates are much more significant, including especially Sweden. Austria's employment rate, by contrast, fits more into the average EU pattern, its overall employment rate fifth highest out of fourteen, with its male employment rate also ranked fifth and its female employment rate ranked sixth.

Austria also fits the more standard EU pattern in having experienced an overall upward trend in its employment rate during the period 1985 to 1992 (the period for which we have comparable data), based on a downward trend in the male employment rate but compensated by an upward trend in the female employment rate. These trends appear to have been fairly consistent over the period, although the employment rate fell slightly overall and for women after 1992. The upward trend in the employment rate also reflects an increased absorption of immigrant labour after the opening up of Eastern European borders. The immigrants are concentrated in low-skilled jobs which Austrians tend to shun but still suffer from significantly higher unemployment rates than the Austrians.

In the two Nordic countries, in contrast, the employment rate fell over the same period; the fall in Finland was much more dramatic than in Sweden, at 8.6 percentage points compared to just under 3 percentage points in Sweden. However, this comparison is somewhat misleading because of the artificial fixing of the beginning and end dates. Employment rates actually rose in both countries after 1985, so that the fall to 1992 was in fact more dramatic than a comparison of end dates implies and both countries experienced a dramatic fall in employment rates between 1992 and 1993.[5] The Finnish employment rate reached 70.1 per cent in 1990 before falling to 61.2 per cent by 1992 and indeed 57.2 per cent by 1993.[6] In Sweden the employment rate rose from 80.1 per cent in 1985 to 82.7 per cent in 1990, before falling to 77.2 per cent in 1992, followed by a dramatic

Table 7.1 Employment rates in the EU (E14), 1985–92[a]

	All (%)				Women (%)				Men (%)		
	1985	1990	1992		1985	1990	1992		1985	1990	1992
Sweden	80.1	82.7	77.2	Sweden	76.7	80.6	76.1	Portugal	80.9	82.8	80.5
Denmark	74.5	74.0	72.1	Denmark	67.5	68.9	67.8	Sweden	83.4	84.7	78.3
Portugal	65.0	69.3	69.5	Finland	67.5	67.5	60.4	Germany	75.6	76.1	76.5[b]
UK	66.0	71.3	67.5	UK	55.1	62.0	60.4	Denmark	81.3	79.1	76.3
Austria	63.4	65.5	66.3	Portugal	49.9	56.6	59.0	Austria	78.3	75.3	75.6
Germany[c]	62.0	64.9	65.6[b]	Austria	49.1	55.7	56.8	Netherlands	67.2	74.1	75.6
Netherlands	51.6	60.5	63.4	Germany	48.3	53.2	54.4[b]	UK	76.9	80.5	74.5
Finland	69.8	70.1	61.2	France	49.3	51.0	51.3	Italy	74.1	72.2	71.1
France	59.4	60.1	59.3	Netherlands	35.7	46.5	50.8	Greece	73.6	71.3	69.5
Belgium	53.6	56.4	56.2	Belgium	37.7	42.5	44.5	Belgium	69.3	70.1	67.6
Italy	54.3	54.7	54.4	Italy	34.9	37.5	37.8	France	69.4	69.3	67.3
Greece	55.2	54.7	53.1	Greece	37.0	38.3	36.8	Spain	63.5	68.8	66.2
Ireland	50.8	52.5	51.3	Ireland	31.6	35.0	36.5	Ireland	69.6	69.8	66.0
Spain	44.7	50.3	49.2	Spain	26.1	32.0	32.3	Finland	72.1	72.6	62.1

Source: CEC (1995a: Annex, 187–202)
Notes: a Employment rate = all in employment divided by the working age population
b Data refer to 1991
c Data exclude the new Länder

Table 7.2 Employment rates for new member states[a]

	All (%)				Women (%)				Men (%)			
	Austria	*Sweden*	*Finland*	*Finland[b]*	*Austria*	*Sweden*	*Finland*	*Finland[b]*	*Austria*	*Sweden*	*Finland*	*Finland[b]*
1985	63.4	80.1	69.8	72.4[c]	49.1	76.7	67.5	69.8[c]	78.3	83.4	72.1	72.4[c]
1990	65.5	82.7	70.1		55.7	80.6	67.5		75.3	84.7	72.6	
1991	65.9	81.1	66.1		56.3	79.3	64.6		75.4	82.9	67.7	
1992	66.3	77.2	61.2	64.3	56.8	76.1	60.4	63.3	75.6	78.3	62.1	65.2
1993	65.5	72.7	57.2		56.4	72.2	56.0		74.4	73.1	58.3	
1994	65.3	71.7	56.5		56.3	71.2	55.6		74.0	72.1	57.5	

Source: CEC (1995a: Annex, 187–202)
Notes: a Employment rate = all in employment divided by the working age population
    b Source: Ilmakunnas (1995)
    c Data refer to 1987

fall to 72.7 per cent by 1993. In both Sweden and Finland male and female employment rates rose or remained stable between 1985 and 1990, with all the fall in employment rates concentrated over the later part of the period. The falls in employment in Finland are associated with the economic crisis, triggered by the collapse of its export markets in the USSR. Sweden also moved into economic crisis in the 1990s as its trading position declined and its public sector deficits rose.

The female employment has played a critical but somewhat different role in the evolution of employment rates in the three new member states: high female employment in comparative terms has prevented Finland falling yet further down the ranking of countries by employment rates; Sweden has achieved its high employment rate position through high employment levels of both men and women, but with women's employment rate boosted, as we shall see, by opportunities for flexible working among those in employment; in Austria there has been a relatively late but steady rise in female employment leading to a steady upward movement of Austria in the league of European employment rates.

Employment rates by age and education

Finland and Sweden both have the inverted U pattern of female participation typical of Scandinavian countries, and showing a similar pattern to the participation rates of men by age (see Figure 7.1). Changes over the period have reaffirmed the absence of interrupted or curtailed careers for women, associated with the M-shape or the left-hand peak participation curves; indeed there has been a trend towards a right-hand peak as participation rates fall at younger ages and rise at older ages. In Austria there has been a move away from a left-hand peak distribution to a much flatter participation pattern over the core working-age ranges, although there is still a sharp fall in participation rates for the over 50s, suggesting the continuation of a generation effect depressing employment rates among older women. However, the flatter participation rate curve of women aged 20 to 50 still lies significantly below the higher participation rate lines of Finland and Sweden.

Finnish data on employment rates by age confirm the pattern found for activity rates. Most of the decrease in employment is concentrated on younger age groups, with even steeper falls for men. Male employment has fallen more than female employment in all age groups. High female employment rates are found in all age ranges in Finland up until age 55, where the rates fall from the 70–80 plateau to closer to 50 per cent. In Austria female activity rates fall from 75 per cent in the 20–24 age range to 66 per cent for age 40–49, before plummeting to 42 per cent for 50–59 year olds. Austria also has wide variations in participation rates by education, with 77 per cent of university graduates active in the labour market in 1992

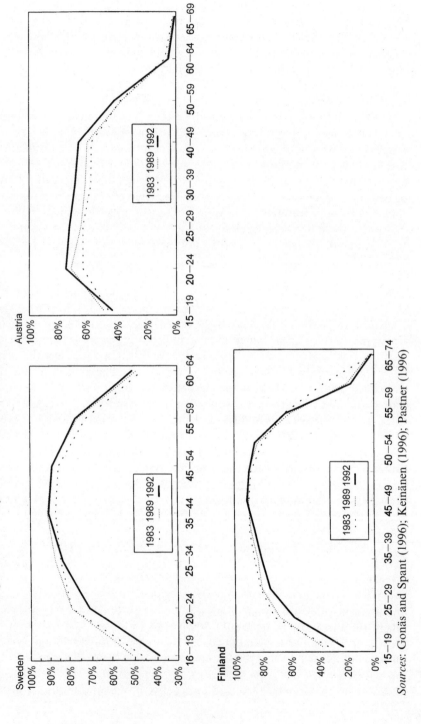

Figure 7.1 Female age-related activity rates in Sweden, Finland and Austria, 1983–92

Sources: Gonäs and Spant (1996); Keinänen (1996); Pastner (1996) compared to only 32 per cent of women with just compulsory school education and 51 per cent of those with secondary school education. The very high participation rates for women of all ages in Sweden and Finland means that differences in educational attainment have a much less important impact on participation in these two countries.

In all three countries mothers have relatively high employment rates (Figure 7.2 and EC Network 1996). Sweden has the highest rate of employment for mothers in all EU countries, Finland the fourth-highest and Austria the fifth (or fifth and sixth respectively if East Germany is considered separately from the rest of Germany). Note here that the motherhood employment rate in Sweden is likely in fact to be underestimated as the data refer to mothers with a child of 7 or under. These data may in contrast exaggerate Austrian mothers' relative employment rate as for the E12 countries plus Finland the data refer to mothers with a child under 11 while for Austria the data refer to mothers with a child up to 15. Finnish mothers have, however, the second highest full-time employment rate after Portugal. Sweden has the highest part-time employment rate for mothers but the motherhood full-time employment rate is only just above that found in low participation countries such as Luxembourg and Spain, although still well above that found in Germany, the UK and the Netherlands.

Employment rates and part-time employment

Finland and Austria have below average shares of part-time employment in total employment, while Sweden has the second-highest share in the Union after the Netherlands (*Employment in Europe* (CEC 1995a) and Table 7.3). Austria's share of part-time work is likely to be underestimated as currently data on part-time employment exclude those working less than 12 hours a week. New estimates (Pastner 1995), more comparable with the ELFS, put the share of women working part-time at 27.8 per cent and men at 6.2 per cent compared to 17.3 per cent and 1.6 per cent in *Employment in Europe* data. However, in none of the three countries has there been any significant growth in part-time jobs over the period 1983 to 1994, and indeed in both the Scandinavian countries, despite one having a high and the other a low part-time rate, the share of employed women in part-time work actually fell. In Austria the share rose slightly between 1985 and 1990 but has remained relatively stable since. The share of men in part-time work grew in all three countries but from a very low level in Austria. In Finland the share of men in part-time work rose to just above the EU average and Sweden ended with the third-highest male part-time employment rate in the EU after the Netherlands and Denmark. Taking into account part-time work, through the calculation of full-time equivalent employment rates, has only a limited impact on estimates of changes in male and female employment rates in the three new member states (see Figure 7.3).

Figure 7.2 Full-time and part-time employment rates of mothers with a child aged under 11 years, 1993

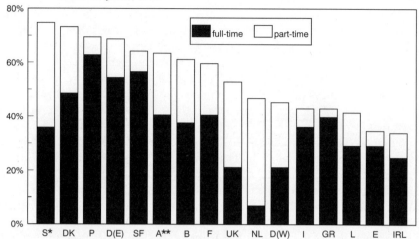

Source: EC Childcare Network (1996)
Notes: * Child aged under 7
       ** Child aged under 15

Table 7.3 Part-time rates by gender in the EU (E15), 1985–92

	All (%)			Women (%)			Men (%)		
	1985	1990	1992	1985	1990	1992	1985	1990	1992
Belgium	8.6	10.9	12.4	21.1	25.8	28.1	1.8	2.0	2.1
Denmark	24.3	23.3	22.5	43.9	38.4	36.7	8.4	10.4	10.1
Germany[a]	12.8	15.2	15.5[b]	29.6	33.8	34.3[b]	2.0	2.6	2.7[b]
Greece	5.3	4.1	4.8	10.0	7.6	8.4	2.8	2.2	2.8
Spain	5.8	4.9	5.8	13.9	12.1	13.7	2.4	1.6	2.0
France	10.9	11.9	12.7	21.8	23.6	24.5	3.2	3.3	3.6
Ireland	6.4	8.1	9.1	15.5	17.7	18.6	2.4	3.4	3.9
Italy	5.3	4.9	5.9	10.0	9.5	11.5	3.0	2.4	2.9
Luxembourg	7.2	6.9	6.9	16.3	16.5	16.5	2.6	1.9	1.3
Netherlands	22.4	31.7	34.5	51.0	59.2	63.8	7.6	15.0	15.4
Austria	7.0	8.4	8.2	15.7	17.2	17.3	1.4	1.8	1.6
Portugal	6.0	6.0	7.3	10.0	9.4	11.5	3.4	3.5	4.1
Finland	8.2	6.7	7.4	12.2	9.6	9.8	4.5	4.1	5.1
Sweden	25.4	23.5	24.3	45.5	40.9	41.2	6.8	7.4	8.3
UK	20.9	21.3	23.2	44.3	42.6	44.5	4.3	5.2	6.2
E15	12.5	13.5	14.2	27.2	28.0	28.7	3.3	3.8	4.2

Source: CEC (1995a: Annex, 187–202)
Notes: a Data exclude the new Länder
       b Data refer to 1991

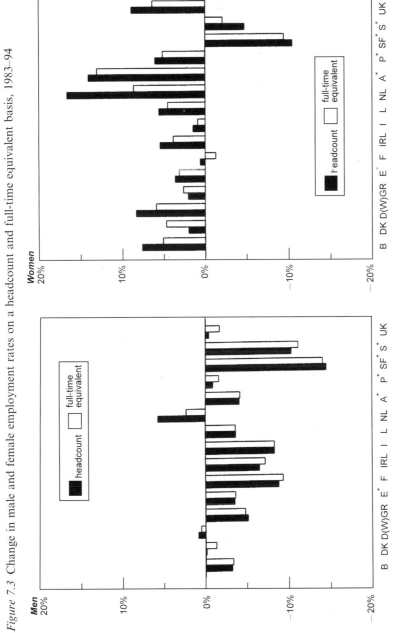

Figure 7.3 Change in male and female employment rates on a headcount and full-time equivalent basis, 1983–94

Sources: European Labour Force Surveys (1983–94); OECD (1995)
Notes: * 1987–94 D(W) 1983–92

Non-employment by age group and gender

Unemployment in Finland in 1992 was the third highest in the EU after Ireland and Spain and by 1993 had overtaken Ireland as well (CEC 1995a – see Appendix Table 7.1). Sweden's unemployment rate in 1992 was in fact relatively low, well below the EU average and below the rates for all states apart from Luxembourg, the Netherlands, Austria and Portugal. However, by 1994 just before Sweden joined the EU, the Swedish unemployment rate had risen by 4 percentage points, and exceeded the rate in the UK, Germany and Greece in addition to the above countries. Nevertheless its unemployment rate remained over 8 percentage points below that for Finland. In contrast Austria has a very low unemployment with only Luxembourg recording lower rates. Austria has retained a low unemployment rate since 1985 while rates in Sweden and Finland have moved sharply upwards. Sweden's and Finland's welfare state systems have been designed around a high level of employment, and the rise in unemployment levels has been a major shock to its public expenditure and welfare state system.

Sweden and Finland join the UK in having higher unemployment rates for men than for women, while in Austria unemployment rates are roughly equal. In both Sweden and Finland the unemployment rates for men and women were very similar in 1985 and it is primarily over the 1990s that the gender gap has emerged.

So far we have been considering unemployment rates by the conventional measure of shares of the labour force. If instead we consider unemployment as a share of the working-age population we can arrive at a consistent way of comparing employment, unemployment and inactivity rates across the EU, including the new member states (CEC 1995a). Figure 7.4 shows the shares of the female working-age population in non-employment divided into unemployment and inactivity. Finland has a relatively high share of its female population in unemployment at 7.4 per cent, the fourth-highest in the EU, but a low share in inactivity, at 32.2 per cent, the third-lowest in the EU. Austria has an opposite pattern with a very low share in unemployment (the lowest of the fourteen states, excluding Luxembourg, for which we have data), but falls in the middle of the ranking of countries by inactivity rates. Sweden in contrast has both a low share of female working-age population in unemployment (twelfth out of fourteen) and the lowest share of women in inactivity. As we shall discuss later, there are problems with the data for all three new member states about exactly how inactivity, unemployment and employment are defined, but the relative positioning of the countries would not necessarily change significantly if all the problems of comparability could be resolved.

The fall in employment rates in Sweden and Finland from 1990 to 1993 has been absorbed primarily by rises in unemployment, although the share

Figure 7.4 Female working-age non-employment in the EU, 1992

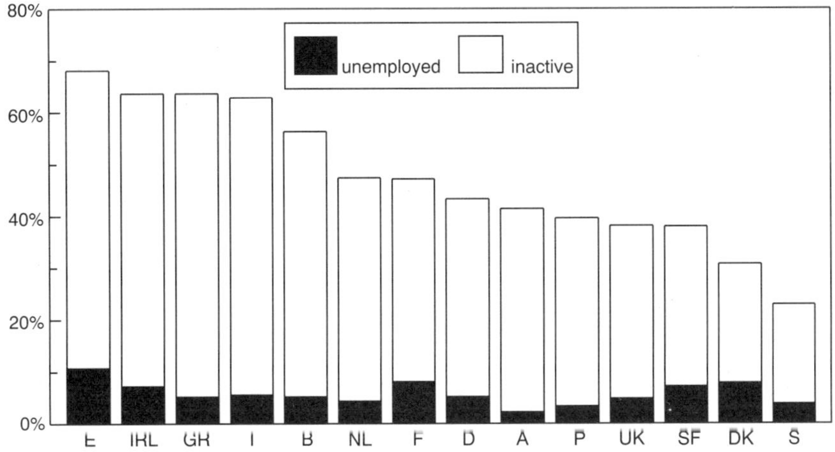

Source: CEC (1995a: Annex, 187–202)
Notes: Data for Germany include the new German Länder
Unemployed and inactive as share of working-age population

in inactivity for both men and women has risen in both countries. The rise in inactivity in Finland has been lower in percentage point terms, despite more rapid falls in employment rates. However, inactivity levels in Sweden were still lower than in Finland in 1993. The share of the non-employed who are involved in domestic work has fallen in Sweden as the share of the unemployed has risen. Thus while 31 per cent of non-employed women were classed as housewives in 1987 by 1994 that figure had fallen to 15 per cent (Löfström 1995). In Austria there has been a gradual fall in the share of the female population classed as housewives, from 21.9 per cent in 1985, to 18.1 per cent in 1992 (Pastner 1995).

Data from Finland (Ilmakunnas 1995) disaggregates the change in employment and non-employment by age group into the various categories of non-employment including unemployment, studying, housework and retirement (Table 7.4). Taking the population aged 15–64 as a whole, it is clear that unemployment has absorbed most of the fall in the employment rate from 1987 to 1992, accounting in the case of men for 7.3 percentage points out of a total fall in the employment rate of 9.5 percentage points and for 4.2 out of the 6.5 percentage point fall for women. After unemployment, increased participation in education is the next most important factor, with increases of 1.6 and 1.9 percentage points for the male and female 15–64 population respectively. Housework absorbed only an additional 0.2 of a percentage point for men and 0.4 for women, while the share of women in retirement fell by 0.2 of a percentage point and that for men rose by 0.6.

Table 7.4 Percentage point changes in unemployment and forms of inactivity resulting from decreases in the Finnish employment rate, 1987–92

Age		Unemployment	Studying	Housework	Retirement	Other	Change in employment rate
15–19	Total	3.1	9.6	0.3	0.0	−0.3	−12.6
	Male	3.1	11.2	0.1	0.1	−0.5	−14.0
	Female	3.1	8.0	0.6	−0.2	0.0	−11.5
20–24	Total	9.9	4.7	1.2	−0.1	0.2	−15.9
	Male	12.3	4.9	0.0	0.0	0.6	−17.8
	Female	7.4	4.7	2.5	−0.1	−0.2	−14.3
25–29	Total	7.9	2.3	2.5	0.1	−0.1	−12.7
	Male	10.2	2.4	0.2	0.3	−0.2	−12.9
	Female	5.6	2.3	5.0	−0.2	0.2	−12.9
30–34	Total	6.7	2.2	1.3	−0.2	0.1	−10.2
	Male	8.5	1.5	0.4	−0.2	0.0	−10.2
	Female	4.8	2.9	2.1	−0.2	0.1	−9.7
35–39	Total	5.8	1.8	1.0	0.0	−0.1	−8.5
	Male	7.9	0.8	0.2	0.3	0.0	−9.2
	Female	3.8	2.9	2.0	−0.4	0.0	−8.3
40–44	Total	6.0	1.5	0.0	0.0	0.0	−7.5
	Male	7.4	0.8	0.1	0.2	−0.1	−8.4
	Female	4.6	2.1	−0.1	0.0	0.2	−6.8
45–49	Total	5.1	1.1	−0.8	−0.1	0.1	−5.4
	Male	6.0	0.6	0.0	0.9	0.1	−7.6
	Female	4.2	1.5	−1.5	−1.1	0.2	−3.3
50–54	Total	4.2	0.3	−1.3	−0.8	0.3	−2.5
	Male	5.7	0.1	0.1	−0.4	0.3	−5.8
	Female	2.5	0.4	−2.7	−0.8	0.1	0.5
55–59	Total	6.5	0.1	−1.3	−3.0	0.1	−2.3
	Male	7.8	0.0	0.1	−1.8	−0.1	−6.0
	Female	5.4	0.1	−2.6	−3.9	0.1	0.9
60–64	Total	1.5	0.0	−2.2	5.5	0.1	−4.9
	Male	2.1	0.0	−0.1	3.5	0.4	−5.9
	Female	1.0	0.0	−3.6	7.2	−0.1	−4.5
15–64	Total	5.8	1.8	0.2	0.2	−0.2	−8.0
	Male	7.3	1.6	0.2	0.6	−0.1	−9.5
	Female	4.2	1.9	0.4	−0.2	0.0	−6.5

Source: Ilmakunnas (1995)

A more complex picture emerges when we look at the data by age group.
Unemployment accounts for a very low share of the fall in employment
rates for the population aged 15–19, with the falls in employment of 14
percentage points for men and 11.5 for women mainly accounted for by the
rise in participation in education. By age 20–24 most of the employment fall
is absorbed into unemployment, particularly for men, although both men
and women register a 5 percentage point rise in the share in education. The
lower increase in the unemployment rate for women is partly explained by a
lower employment rate fall but also by a 2.5 percentage point rise in the
share categorised as undertaking domestic work. The female share in these
activities rises even more steeply for the 25–29 population – a rise of 5
percentage points – and 2 percentage point rises are recorded for the age
30–34 and 34–39 year old populations, although for older women the shares
classified in domestic work fell. These increases are associated with the

increasing take-up of the child homecare allowance, which effectively allows women to take paid leave from employment or to receive benefits if out of employment when they have children. High marginal tax rates, plus limited employment opportunities may have swelled the number remaining on these benefits for longer. Among the older age ranges, increased unemployment accounts for the vast majority of the fall in the employment rate, although the increased participation in education is evident to some extent all the way up the age hierarchy. Retirement accounts for a significant part of the fall in employment rates only for the over 60s. This increase is due to new early retirement schemes.

Reconsidering current definitions of economic activity

Problems of defining economic activity status apply to the new member states as much, if not more, than those encountered for the twelve older members. In Austria one of the main problems has been a national definition of employment that excludes those working less than 12 hours a week. The number included in this category are estimated at around a quarter of a million, one-third men and two-thirds women. However, the men in this category are almost exclusively pensioners and students, that is they are involved in marginal work only at particular points in their working lives. Among women there are more prime-age workers, particularly unpaid family workers in Austria's relatively large agricultural sector. This issue of whether to include marginal workers is one of considerable concern in other parts of the EU; national data sources in the Netherlands now exclude such workers, although Eurostat still includes short part-time hours workers.

Another major problem concerns how to classify women who are on paid parental leave – as employed or as inactive? In Austria there has been an expansion of parental leave from one year to two years which has attracted a high take-up rate among women and has boosted estimated female employment rates. Moreover there is considerable discussion in Sweden about whether the particular form of the welfare state which grants mothers and fathers considerable flexibility in their working-time arrangements, while retaining their employment position, leads to an overestimate of female but also to some extent of male participation rates in comparison to other countries (Jonung and Persson 1993). In the Finnish data the women who have taken up the child homecare allowance are treated as inactive, although only after they have exhausted parental leave entitlements.

Austria has only recently started to collect data based on the ILO unemployment rate definition. Most data are based on the old system of counting only registered unemployed and calculating the unemployment rate by dividing the registered unemployed by the active population, defined as dependent employees working more than twelve hours plus the registered unemployed. This contrasts with the ILO definition which counts all those available and looking for work as unemployed and also includes in the denominator all those who worked for at least one hour. Moves towards the new definitions reduce the measured unemployment rate as it brings in the self-employed and the marginally employed including unpaid family workers, and excludes those unemployed who are not looking for work because of the highly cyclical nature of Austria's labour market. Many men in the construction industry, for example, do not look for work in the closed season, and many women who work in the tourist industry do not seek work in-between, confident that they can return to their old job when the season starts again. The new definitions are excluding many of the traditional unemployed while discovering some hidden unemployed, many of whom are women.

In Sweden hidden unemployment – that is those who are outside the measured workforce but who would like to work and are available immediately for work – used to be more common among women than men, but relatively infrequent for both. In 1983 it accounted for around 5 per cent of the population but the share rose to around 18 per cent for men and 13 to 14 per cent for women by 1994. There has also been a major rise in the share who are underemployed – that is wanting to work more. In 1983 around 100,000 women wanted to work more but by 1994 this number had risen to a quarter of a million. For men the rise was also significant albeit to a lower level – from 30,000 to 110,000. The high share of women wanting to work more reflects the tendency for women to become trapped into shorter part-time hours when perhaps the family need for shorter hours has disappeared.

7.2 Women's employment rates and structural and regional change

Regional patterns of change in economic activity by gender

In Sweden there has been a long-standing policy to reduce regional differentials through providing incentives for employers to move to more distant regions and by using the public sector to even out employment levels. This policy has been largely successful with relatively even employment rates across all regions. In the recent recession male participation rates have fallen fairly evenly across all regions while female participation rates have fallen more in regions such as Stockholm where participation rates have been above average, thus leading to a further convergence of rates. Unemployment rates in Stockholm and other densely populated areas are still below those in the more rural areas. The cutback in public sector employment can be expected to have a particularly severe impact on those regions where women are especially concentrated in public employment and participation rates may begin to diverge.

Austria, although a small country, has very divergent female employment rates by region and quite different patterns of women's employment. Employment rates are highest in the urban areas such as Vienna at 68 per cent but fall to around 56 per cent in the more rural areas of the Tyrol, Carinthia, Vorarlberg and Styria. However, there are also significant seasonal variations in employment rates by region. The manufacturing sector in some regions, such as Vorarlberg, has suffered particular employment losses from the transfer of clothing sectors to the newly opened up Eastern European countries on the borders with Austria. The whole clothing industry in the Waldviertel, a northern part of Lower Austria was transferred to the Czech Republic. In these border areas the displaced women have little to look forward to other than long-term unemployment. In many regions women move between employment and unemployment or inactivity because of their involvement in the highly seasonal tourist industry. Some women also move between tourism and agriculture, in the same way as men move between agriculture and construction. Thus employment rates in some regions of Austria are far from stable over the year.

In Finland the rate of growth of female employment was greater than male employment taking the country as a whole for both the period 1983–7 and the period 1987–92. However, during the first period there was some divergence between regions in the relative performance of male and female employment, with stronger growth rates for men in four out of the twelve regions. In the recessionary period, however, female employment fell less then male employment in all twelve regions. Unemployment rates by region in Finland have been divergent for a long time, with a difference of no less than 8 percentage points in 1987. Northern and Eastern Finland have had the highest unemployment rates. Despite the regional divergence, the pattern of male unemployment rates exceeding female rates is found in almost all regions. During the recession all regions suffered dramatic rises in unemployment but the wide regional disparities were largely maintained.

Impact of segregation by industry, occupation and employment contract

In Finland the employment losses faced by women in the 1990s have been concentrated in the private sector, and have been brought about primarily by change in the scale of employment and not by restructuring between sectors or changes in female shares within sectors. Public sector employment has increased from 38.5 per cent of female employment in 1990 to 41.5 per cent in 1994 as private sector employment has declined. The importance of the changing scale of employment over the composition of jobs or the female share of jobs is highlighted by a shift-share analysis of changes by occupation using 42 occupational categories. More than 100 per cent of the decrease in employment between 1988 and 1994 was due to the change in scale of employment (minus 195,000 jobs), while changes in the composition of jobs added only 19,000 jobs, and changes in the female share within occupations actually further decreased jobs by 11,000, giving a total fall of 184,000 jobs (including the interaction term).

While Finland's public sector employment share for women has been rising it has still not reached the level of importance of the public sector for Swedish women. Nearly three-fifths of Swedish women work for the state or the municipalities sector. Most women in Sweden work in caring occupations such as the health sector, social work, education followed by public administration and are thus particularly vulnerable to planned cutbacks in the welfare state.

In Austria, as in all EU countries, the growth of female employment has been primarily associated with a growth of services and of clerical and office work. However, although this growth has been significant for Austrian women, the actual size of the service sector remains low by international comparison. This places Austria in stark contrast with service-oriented Sweden. The Austrian share of female employment in agriculture and manufacturing remains markedly above that for both Sweden and the UK for example. Moreover the relative share of the public sector is low and is set to decline under current budget cuts proposals.

Small and medium-sized enterprises are regarded as being of key importance for Finland in moving out of the recession. Women tend to be overrepresented in this sector although they lost employment disproportionately in small firms in the beginning years of the recession, thereby demonstrating the fragility of employment in this sector. In Sweden there has been rapid growth of self-employment over the 1980s and early 1990s, associated with the development of small businesses. The growth has been considerably stronger for men than for women, and although there have been some steps taken to encourage female entrepreneurship, with extra resources available to women since the middle of the 1980s, so far the results of this policy appear to have been modest. In Austria there has been a massive decrease in self-employment and family workers over recent decades, with the share of women working as family workers dropping from one-third in 1951 to only just over 5 per cent in 1992. Although most of the decline had occurred before the 1980s, female family workers declined from 115,000 to 85,000 between 1982 and 1992. Small businesses remain important in Austria and women are overrepresented in these firms not only because they are found more often in the female-dominated sectors, but also because even within sectors women tend to be overrepresented in small firms.

7.3   Unemployment, gender and labour market organisation

Youth unemployment rates are high in Finland and Sweden and have indeed grown dramatically in the 1990s recession; in Sweden from 7.8 per cent in 1991 to 22.6 per cent in 1993 and in Finland from 14.5 per cent in 1991 to over 33 per cent in 1993 (Appendix Table 7.2). In contrast, Austria's youth unemployment rates are very low, almost identical to average rates. The absence of a specific problem of youth unemployment in Austria may be associated with the dual training systems which exists in Austria as well as Germany and may provide a better transition from school to work as the training posts are integrated in organisations.[7] The problem of youth unemployment is even more severe for young men than for young women in the two Scandinavian countries and is also somewhat higher among Austrian young men than young women.

Female unemployment rates are lower than male unemployment rates in both Finland and Sweden and women also fare better in terms of duration of unemployment in these two countries. In contrast, in Austria, where women's unemployment rate is similar to men's, women's duration of unemployment is also longer and has risen faster than men's.

Only a very small percentage of Sweden's unemployed are first time job seekers: only 6 per cent of male unemployed and 7 per cent of female unemployed in 1994. More women than men who are unemployed are re-entrants to the labour market (14 per cent compared to 12 per cent for men) but the vast majority of the unemployed of both sexes entered unemployment directly as a result of job loss. In Finland in 1993 only a very small percentage of women entered unemployment from domestic responsibilities (under 6 per cent), and over 81 per cent entered unemployment direct from employment, including 39 per cent who entered unemployment due to the termination of a fixed term contract, a somewhat higher share than for men. In Austria women's unemployment rates tend to be highest for those age groups where women may be returning to work after childbirth, age 25–29 and 30–39. Around a quarter of women who are on maternity benefit do not in fact have a job to return to and they may face particular problems of unemployment.

Education and unemployment

In Sweden there has been an increase in the share of the unemployed with upper secondary level as opposed to basic education, for both men and women. This reflects the increasing trend towards a more highly educated workforce, as well as perhaps a reduction in the effectiveness of education as a protection against unemployment. In Finland unemployment rates are higher among the less well educated, but with the exception of the highly educated all educational groups fared equally badly in the recession. Young women in Finland are particularly well educated and this, together with their extensive work experience, may have provided women with some relative protection against unemployment. In Austria women have been catching up with men in their involvement in higher education so that the female share of entrants to universities is now 51 per cent. This change is all the more remarkable given Austria's large gender deficit in educational attainment according to OECD (1995b) statistics. Unemployment rates in Austria are strongly inversely related to educational levels so that women's enhanced education should protect young women in the labour market, although female unemployment rates still tend to be higher at a given level of education. Young women have traditionally been underrepresented in apprenticeship training, still accounting for only one-third of all apprentices in 1992.

7.4   State policies and women's employment and unemployment rates

Women and the unemployment benefit system

Table 7.5 provides a classification of unemployment benefit systems and women's access to these schemes across all fifteen member states. We have divided the member states according to whether the continuity requirements for unemployment benefits are high, medium or low, whether the duration of non-means-tested benefits is short, medium or long and whether access of part-timers to unemployment benefits are low, medium or high. The unemployment benefit systems of the three new member states can thus be put in comparative perspective. Sweden and Finland have low continuity requirements for benefits and Austria medium requirements. More specifically, in Finland recipients need to have worked for at least six months in the past two years, while in Sweden they need to have been in membership of an unemployment insurance system for a least a year before becoming unemployed and to have worked for at least 80 days out of 5 months during a reference period of one year (Gonäs and Spant 1996). In Austria they must have been employed for one year within the preceding two, except for young people under 25 where six months within the last year is sufficient. Non-means-tested benefits normally last for 300 days in Sweden and between 5 and 7.5 months in Austria, putting both into the short duration category for non-means-tested unemployment benefits. Finland is in the medium duration category as earnings-related benefit is available for 500 days followed by labour market support which is non-means-tested for 180 days.[8] After 180 days means testing is applied for labour market support.

In all three countries unemployment benefits are earnings-related. In Austria the replacement rate is 60 per cent of net earnings up to a maximum

Table 7.5 Unemployment benefit system in member states

	% of unemployed receiving benefits		Continuity requirements for unemployment benefits[a]	Access of part-timers to unemployment benefits[b]	Duration of non-means-tested benefits[c]
	Men	Women			
Belgium	85.2	84.0	Medium	Low	Long
Denmark	84.4	84.3	Low	Medium	Long
Germany	75.7	73.7	Low	Low	Medium
Greece	11.3	5.8	Low	—	Short
Spain	38.7	21.9	Low	High	Medium
France	51.7	42.5	Medium	High	Medium
Ireland	83.1	43.8	High	Low	Short
Italy	6.0	5.2	Medium[d]	—	Short
Luxembourg	26.6	30.7	Medium	Medium	Medium
Netherlands	58.8	25.9	Medium	High	Long
Austria			Medium	High[e]	Short
Portugal	18.2	16.2	High	—	Medium
Finland	90.4	91.6	Low	Low	Medium
Sweden	78.7	76.8[f]	Low	Low	Short
UK	70.0	32.0	Medium	Low	Short

Sources: National reports
Notes: a Continuity requirements
Low = less than 6 months in past year or equivalent
Medium = approximately equal to 6 months in past year or equivalent
High = greater than 6 months in past year
b Access of part-timers to unemployment benefits
Low = minimum hours threshold of 7 hours or more, or minimum earnings requirement or requirement to be available for full-time work
Medium = minimum hours threshold more than 12 but less than 7; no requirement to be available for full-time work
High = minimum hours threshold of 12 hours or less; no requirement to be available for full-time work
c Duration of non-means-tested benefits
Short = 15 months maximum or less
Medium = more than 15 months maximum but less than 3 years maximum
Long = more than 3 years maximum
d Refers to 'ordinary unemployment benefits'
e Benefits are earnings related and no minimum level for part-timers
f 1990 data

level of earnings, and there is no basic minimum payment so that part-timers would receive only a low benefit level. In Sweden the unemployment compensation rate in 1996 was high at 75 per cent, having been progressively lowered from 90 per cent as part of the cutback in the welfare state (Gonäs and Spant 1996). In Finland the formula for the earnings adjusted daily allowance is the sum of a flat-rate component (basic daily allowance) and the earnings-adjusted component. The latter is 42 per cent of the difference between the previous daily wage and the basic daily allowance (20 per cent for higher wages). This gives replacement rates varying from around 77 per cent at a wage of 4,000 Finnish marks per month down to 38 per cent at 20,000. Thus only the Finnish system is likely to pay a significantly higher replacement rate to women who tend to be lower paid,[9] although the actual payment received is on average still only 81.5 per cent of the male benefit. However, a very high share of Finnish women receive benefit when they are unemployed – 91.6 per cent, just slightly higher than the share of men.

The low share of part-time employment among women means that female claimants are not strongly penalised by the relatively stringent eligibility conditions in the Finnish system which excludes those working under 18 hours. Part-time work is further discouraged by the requirement for all unemployed claimants to be able and willing to accept full-time employment. The required working-time conditions for entitlement to unemployment benefits in Sweden are 17 hours per week, similar to Finland. Eligibility conditions in Austria are far less stringent with a minimum threshold of 12 hours per week. Austria also has allowances for dependent spouses as well as children, while the Scandinavian systems are based more on the principle of individual rights.

Active labour market policies and women's employment

Active labour market policies, including employment training and the provision of wage subsidies to assist the placement of the unemployed in temporary jobs, have taken on great importance in Finland with the rapid rise in unemployment. So far women's participation in the schemes has been somewhat less than men's, but roughly proportional to women's share among the unemployed.

Sweden's labour market model was designed around the concept of an active labour market approach; high benefits were provided but with strong incentives and policies to ensure most people were in employment or moved quickly back into employment. The rise in unemployment and in unemployment duration in the early 1990s has thus caused problems for the model because of the high costs of benefits. Although originally conceived as a policy aimed at full employment for men, it adjusted to take on board the objective of increasing employment for women. Particularly important in this regard was the spread of public sector services to all regions. Specific polices were also adopted to help women, including wage subsidies and projects to assist women in non-traditional jobs. Since 1994 two people have been given responsibilities in each of the twenty-four regional employment services areas for looking after the interests of women who are trying to enter employment (Gonäs and Spant 1996).

Austria in contrast spends a relatively low share of GDP on active labour market policies. Although some schemes exist such as training programmes, there is little attempt at job creation. Women are underrepresented among the recipients of benefits for this training programme, and the scheme itself tends to reinforce gender stereotypes in relation to appropriate training courses. There has been a specific training programme for women since 1985 but its effects have been limited. During the late 1980s there was a movement within the Employment Services to establish a network of women to promote women's interests which has recently called for a whole range of measures to promote the interests of women seeking work. There have been a number of projects aimed, for example, at providing assistance with childcare, and subsidies have been made available to firms who re-employ women after maternity leave. Prospects for further improvement are not good as budgets have been cut back and there is an increased emphasis on placement measures. The separation of Employment Services from the federal government has resulted in a greater role for the social partners in running the service, and so far they appear disinclined to promote women's initiatives. The importance of female-targeted initiatives must, however, be put in perspective. Women, for example, tend not to be covered by schemes designed to postpone or reduce redundancies in large industrial companies as these companies employ mainly men.

Promotion of flexible employment

The growth of flexible employment forms, evident within the Austrian labour market, has come from employer initiatives and not from specific state policies aimed at promoting such forms of work. The social security system excludes jobs which generate income below a certain level and this provides an incentive for some groups such as pensioners or students on grants to take on these jobs as they retain entitlements to benefits. The state regulates the use of fixed term contracts, not permitting multiple fixed term contracts, and has recently ruled that maternity leave should postpone the end date of a fixed term contract.

In Sweden extensive rights for mothers to work reduced hours (see section 7.5) means that much part-time work may be regarded as voluntary, and indeed promoted by the state. However, there are increasing numbers of employers who offer part-time jobs and will not offer full-time work to those who desire it. Thus involuntary part-time work, developed at the initiative of employers, is also important in Sweden. In Finland the tradition among women has been to work full-time. The parental leave arrangements in Finland tend to favour either full-time work or non-participation, because of high marginal tax rates, and so part-time has not been promoted by state policies. Among those in the labour market there is an increasing share of those who work part-time who would like full-time work (40 per cent in 1993 compared to 24 per cent in 1989) but also an increasing share of those who work full-time who would like part-time work. Temporary contracts have increased especially among new recruits, with around 60 per cent of all new recruits now on fixed term contracts. Government labour market policies include subsidies to employers offering temporary contracts to the unemployed. A higher share of female new recruits are on temporary contracts than male recruits (64 per cent compared to 57 per cent in 1993).

Wage policy

None of the three new member states has a minimum wage, and wage levels are set by collective agreement. All the countries also have highly segregated labour markets, but while in Austria the high level of segregation permits the payment of widely divergent wages to men and women, in Sweden the high gender segregation coexists with a relatively narrow spread of earnings. The narrow wage dispersion in Sweden was achieved as a result of the solidaristic wage policy. The move towards more decentralised pay determination in the 1990s thus threatens the continuation of the narrow wage dispersion. Finland also has narrow wage dispersion and has maintained its centralised system of wage determination. In the 1990s there has been active exploration of the use of job evaluation to implement the principle of equal pay for work of equal value (Keinänen 1996).

7.5 Household organisation, state policies and women's employment rates

Sweden and Finland can be regarded as examples of the weak male breadwinner welfare state, while Austria falls into the opposite end of the spectrum of strong male breadwinner states. This characterisation is reflected in state welfare and taxation policies and in women's role in the household. However, some elements of state policies, for example individualised taxation in Austria, do not fit the characterisation.

Female contributions to the household: income and domestic labour

In Finland women contribute on average 40 per cent of household income; where women work full-time the share rises to 43.5 per cent. Despite the large contribution to household income, time use studies suggest that women still do more of the housework: 236 minutes per day on average compared to 140 for men. The largest differences between men and women are in time spent on meal preparation and cleaning and laundry. If paid and domestic work are taken together the time spent working by men and women is found to be roughly similar as men spend longer on paid work. In Finland there is only a very limited private service sector to substitute for domestic labour and in the current recession there are proposals to try to widen pay differentials to provide an incentive for this form of employment. But such a policy, it is argued, might require unemployment benefits to be adjusted downwards if there were to be an incentive to work.

In Sweden the reform of the tax system towards individual assessment coupled with high marginal tax rates has provided an incentive for families to be organised around two equal earners, and this incentive system may to some extent explain the high female participation in Sweden. However, women still contribute less to household income than in Finland as they more often work part-time and still earn less than men, even after accounting for working time.

The gender gap in time spent on household activities appears to be higher in Austria than in Finland, which, given the high full-time employment rates of Finnish women, is not surprising. In Austria women spend over twice as long on domestic work as men, but also on average spend only half the time on wage work as men. However, the gender gap remains even if only working men and working women are compared, for the latter spend on average 4 hours 13 minutes per day on household tasks, children and care compared to 1 hour 41 minutes by working men. Women who are not in wage work in Austria actually spend as long on domestic activities as working women do on wage and domestic work combined. A comparison of time budget studies in 1981 and 1992 reveals that there has been some change in men's activities: they now spend more time on housework and childcare, but change is in fact more evident among older than younger men.

Taxation on earned income and women's employment

All three new member states base their taxation system on the individual as the tax unit. However, while the Swedish and Finnish systems do not provide for dependent spouses, the Austrian system includes a dependent spouse allowance. This has been increased twice, in the 1988 and the 1994 tax reforms, although it still remains at a low level. The result is that in Austria married women may face a slightly higher marginal tax rate when entering the labour market than their single counterparts. Moreover, although the switch from household to individual taxation was agreed as

279

long ago as 1974, the argument for household taxation has recently resurfaced, associated with an ideological trend to stress the value of the traditional family.

The high marginal tax rates in Sweden reinforced the individualisation of the tax system as it was beneficial to have two fairly equal income earners in each household. Now that marginal tax rates have been reduced in Sweden, it may be that there will be less incentive for a dual earner household, but that will not necessarily mean that women will be happy to reduce their participation in wage work.

Although in Finland there is an individualised taxation system, women still encounter some problems of high marginal taxation due to the interplay between the taxation system and means-tested benefits. The most important means-tested benefits are housing benefit, child homecare allowance and the living allowance which is paid when incomes are too low. In all these cases the level of benefits is dependent upon aggregate household income, and the impact of the withdrawal of benefits can be exacerbated by the kicking in of requirements to pay fees for day care in nurseries which again are means tested. Another problem is that sometimes the child homecare allowance provides a higher subsidy than unemployment benefit, thus providing an incentive for women not to participate in the labour market. In Sweden parental leave payments are linked to continuing employment status and are not means tested. Benefit systems as well as taxation systems are individualised in Sweden while in Austria the period of non-means-tested unemployment benefit is short. In Austria women tend not to be eligible for the means-tested benefits as these are based on household income, and these benefits may restrict spouses' participation in the labour market.

State support for childcare

Parental leave is generous in comparative terms in all three new member states. However, major differences are found between the three countries in the form of the leave arrangements and the level of compensation. Moreover in each of the three countries there has been a marked reform of the system over recent years.

In Sweden parental leave is relatively long-term, flexible and well remunerated. Paid leave is available for up to 15 months, and although the level of compensation has recently been cut from 90 per cent to around 80 per cent for most of the time it is still remunerated at a more generous level than elsewhere in the EU. This leave can be taken full-time or part-time or in any combination up until the child is 8 years old. In addition each parent can take up to 18 months' unpaid leave, and has the right to work only 75 per cent of normal hours up until the child is 8 if the parent so chooses. Although fathers have the same rights as mothers to take parental leave, in practice in 1992 they accounted for only about 9 per cent of leave actually taken, although 40 per cent or so of fathers took some leave.[10]

In Finland the child homecare allowance was introduced in 1990 to give all parents the right to child homecare benefits and not solely those on parental leave from work. Those on parental leave receive an income-related benefit, but there has been an increase in the share of women receiving just the flat-rate allowance with the rising number of mothers without labour market attachment. Parental income-related allowances have also been cut, with the maximum rate now 66 per cent compared to 80 per cent in 1992 (Keinänen 1996). Even at its peak the compensation was lower than in Sweden. Although reduced hours are possible in Finland most parental leave is taken on a full-time basis. In Finland men can take the parental leave instead of women after the first 105 days, but men have only a few days of leave reserved exclusively for them (Keinänen 1996).

In 1990 the Austrian government introduced a new package of measures, called the Family Package. This involved parental leave for fathers, the extension of parental leave and benefits from one year to two years, the possibility of part-time parental leave and some help for mothers who are not eligible for parental leave because they did not have the required continuity of employment. There was a very high take-up of the extended normal parental leave, as would be expected given the low provision of childcare, but few fathers have taken up parental leave opportunities so that there are only eight fathers for every thousand mothers on parental leave. Parental leave payments are low, not related to earnings and have not been uprated in recent years. Moreover there is considerable opposition to the extension of paid leave to two years and the higher entitlements for single mothers,[11] both of which are seen by some to be a rather generous form of social expenditure.

There are also marked differences in childcare provision. According to the European Commission Network on Childcare only 3 per cent of Austrian children aged up to 3 were in publicly funded day care compared to 21 per cent of Finnish children and 33 per cent of Swedish (EC Network 1996; see also Table 7.6). From 1990 in Finland all children under 3 have been entitled to municipal day care. In Sweden municipalities also have to provide childcare for children under 12, but places are sometimes limited and an increasing share of the costs are borne by parents. In Finland childcare fees are earnings related. Attempts in Austria to expand public provision of childcare have been blocked until recently and current facilities are open only in the morning and close for two months in the summer, neither of which arrangements helps working mothers.

Table 7.6 Parental leave and childcare in member states

	Length of maternity and parental leave in months after birth of each child	Payment for parental leave[a]	Publicly funded childcare 0–3 years[f] per cent of age group covered	School hours
Belgium	27	FR	30	Long day
Denmark	30	FR	48	Medium day
Germany	36	FR[b]	2 (W), 50 (E)	Half day
Greece	9	U	3	Half day
Spain	36	U	2	Long day[g]
France	36	FR[c]	23	Long day
Ireland	3	—	2	Medium day
Italy	9	ER[d]	6	Half day
Luxembourg	2	—	n.a.	Half day
Netherlands	15[e]	U	8	Long day[g]
Austria	24	FR	3	—
Portugal	27	U	12	Half day[h]
Finland	36[i]	ER + FR	21	—
Sweden	36	ER	33	—
UK	7	—	2	Medium day

Sources: EC Childcare Network (1994, 1996)
Notes: a FR = flat rate, ER = earnings related, U = unpaid
      b Means tested
      c Only paid for families with 2 or more children
      d Low earnings-related benefit
      e Includes 6 months per parent part-time leave only
      f Greece 0–2 1/2, Netherlands 0–4, UK 0–5
      g Long day but with a long lunch break which may or may not be supervised
      h Half day as shortage of places has meant children attending in shifts
      i Including childcare leave in addition to maternal and parental leave

Social protection and pensions

In Austria access to social protection is based on employment records or derived employment rights through one's spouse. In contrast in Finland and Sweden there are universal benefits paid to citizens (Gonäs and Spant 1996; Keinänen 1996). The latter principle is more consistent with individualised rights and with a weak male breadwinner model. However, individualisation has its costs. Pensions in Sweden are based upon the individual's employment history and as women work less and for lower pay they are disadvantaged. No credits are granted within the supplementary pension system for years spent out of the labour market raising children. Similarly in Finland more women receive only the basic pension which is not adequate for subsistence, although the share receiving supplementary earnings related pensions is rising as women with long work histories move into retirement (Keinänen 1996).

In Austria no less than 38 per cent of pension expenses for women are widow's pensions. Men now have the right to a widower's pension but this token equality gesture has tended to reinforce the position of women by apparently making the policy sex-neutral. Since 1993 women can claim credit for bringing up children towards their pension, but they theoretically would need to look after children for 60 years to reach the minimum poverty income level pension. However, this reform is still an important step in improving the situation of mothers. Women's pension age is also to be equalised upwards in line with recent judgments over the application of European equality law.

7.6 Summary

This analysis of women's position within the three new member states of the European Union has provided further confirmation and examples of some of the key findings with respect to women's employment within the other twelve member states. In particular these three new member states help to illustrate and confirm the following points.

- There are wide differences between member states in the extent to which the male breadwinner model of household and family organisation has been modified.
- Despite these differences women in all countries, including those with a strong male breadwinner state such as Austria, are demanding and achieving greater access to employment.
- Women's employment position within EU labour markets has remained relatively robust compared to that of men's, boosted in part by the increased participation in education by women.
- Women tend to bear more of the burden of flexible employment than men, but differences in the form and extent of flexible employment are so great between member states that it is not possible to argue that flexible or atypical employment is a requirement for the integration of women into the labour market.
- Where states such as Finland and Sweden have taken the road towards a weak breadwinner model and dual earner households, the road back to the single breadwinner model is effectively closed despite the fall in employment opportunities and pressure on the welfare state.
- Nevertheless, the rights won by women for greater state and social support for childrearing and domestic work are vulnerable under current recessionary conditions and cutbacks in the welfare state are likely to have negative effects both on women's employment prospects and on support for caring work.
- Although welfare state systems based on derived rights reinforce women's subordinate position in the economy, a premature move towards individualisation, without first securing greater equality in the labour market, might have damaging effects on women's position in countries such as Austria. Even in Sweden and Finland where women's labour market position is more robust, women do face unequal access to social protection as this is based on women's own but unequal employment histories and earnings.

8

CONCLUSIONS

This book has been concerned with the gendering of employment systems and the consequent need to identify the gender dimension to labour market institutions and policies. At the same time it has highlighted the differences between countries and the ways in which gender relations or the gender order are shaped by the path-dependent evolution of country-specific employment systems. These concerns can be regarded as both complementary and potentially contradictory: complementary in the sense that both emphasise the significance of institutions for gender, but potentially contradictory in the sense that there is no simple or universal gender dimension to employment. The gendering of institutions takes different forms and thus what constitutes a female-friendly policy or institution within one society does not necessarily play the same role in another.

In dealing with women's employment position in all fifteen member states we inevitably come up against the complex problem of how and to what extent we can maintain the general need for a gender perspective while doing justice to the complex reality of gender relations in modernday Europe. This problem is possibly exacerbated, or possibly modified, by the further finding, that has been evident throughout the above discussion, of increasing disparities among women, located not only in different EU states but also within single EU states. Moreover, these differences in part reflect a breakdown of the traditional gender order even in countries maintaining, for example, a strong male breadwinner welfare state. Thus, while some countries are even reinforcing their traditional policy stance towards the family in their welfare and labour market policies, it is by no means the case that state policies can be considered sufficient to hold back a tide of social change.

To conclude this book we need to address three main issues:

- First, to what extent have we found a variety of both employment systems and gender orders within Europe; and to the extent that diversity currently prevails, how likely is it that there will be an increasing tendency of convergence, reducing over time the significance of member states in shaping women's role in European employment?

284

- Second, to what extent is the pattern of development of women's employment over recent years a consequence of the continued segregation of the labour market or can it be considered a move towards a more integrated and more equal labour market system?

- Third, and contingent on our assessment of the first two issues, is there a case for developing a gender perspective to European employment analysis and policy, and in what particular ways should we seek to 'mainstream' gender into current debates and practices?

8.1 Convergence or divergence in the gender order in Europe?

At a statistical level, there is some strong evidence of a process of convergence in women's position in the labour market across EU states. The most compelling argument in this direction comes from changes in employment rates themselves: the increases in employment rates have tended to be higher in those countries with the lowest employment rates and there is a general move toward a closing of the gender gap in employment, fuelled in part by another general trend, that towards lower employment rates for men in most EU countries. The significance of this finding is that over time there should be a reduction in the dispersion of employment rates across European member states as those with low employment rates 'catch up' with those with higher employment rates, and possibly as those at the top end of the spectrum converge also somewhat towards the mean, as has in fact happened in the high employment rate Scandinavian countries. These trends in the high employment countries demonstrate (as we discuss further in section 8.2) that any trend towards convergence across countries is not necessarily indicative of the desegregation of the labour market or the achievement of gender equality. The growing problem of employment shortage for men may restrict further equalisation of employment rates by gender at the top end of the spectrum, and the impetus towards greater female employment rates may still be found primarily in the gender-segregated pattern of labour demand. Nevertheless, the trend towards convergence will reduce gender differences in countries with low employment rates.

There is already evidence of convergence in the participation patterns of highly educated women across Europe (see Rubery *et al.* 1995) and as there is marked growth in the share of highly educated women across Europe, this development in itself will ensure some convergence. These predictions relate to projected supply side changes, based on past trends, and do not directly address issues of demand. However, it is also probable that the progressive integration of women into the economy will in the future, as it has in the past, be associated with a growth in the service sector economy, particularly as those countries with low female employment rates tend to have relatively underdeveloped welfare services or low shares of private service work (Esping-Andersen 1990, 1995). Constraints on the transition to a high female employment, high service economy may arise through, for example, restrictions on the development of the welfare state because of its fiscal implications. Nevertheless, some long-term convergence in female employment rates can be expected, leading to a reduction in dispersion of overall employment rates within the EU.

Beyond this statistical convergence in employment rates there is much less strong evidence to support the notion of a convergence in either employment systems or the gender order across Europe. Perhaps the strongest evidence for convergence, other than the change in employment rates, comes from the changing behaviour and attitudes of women themselves; in all member states, regardless of whether state policy supports the strong or the weak version of the male breadwinner model, women are refusing to accept their traditional roles and are participating in the labour market on a more continuous basis. However, the aspirations of women are still being constrained by both divergent employment and divergent social and welfare systems. The importance of divergence in country-specific employment systems has been shown in particular in three areas: first, in patterns of employment and unemployment at the regional and sectoral level within countries; second, in labour market systems and the pattern of unemployment; third, in the welfare and household regimes which underpin labour market systems.

When we looked at regional patterns of employment and unemployment we in fact found strong evidence in support of the significance of the nation-state. The wide variations in female employment and unemployment rates at the nation-state level were largely replicated at the regional level. Thus where female unemployment exceeded male unemployment at the national level, this pattern was also found at the regional level, and vice versa. Trends in male and female employment and unemployment at the national level were also largely mirrored at the regional level. Exceptions are found to this pattern – in particular North/South Italy and East/West Germany do not fit into a universal national model – but by and large societal-specific characteristics are reproduced at the regional level.

The importance of societal differences also emerges in any investigation of the pattern of part-time work; divergences at the national level are reproduced at both the regional and at the sectoral level (Rubery *et al.* 1995), so that for example a low share of part-time work cannot be explained by a low share of service work. There is also little evidence that women's employment rates have been suppressed by restrictions on the development of part-time work; high employment rate countries include those with and those without high shares of women working part-time. Moreover, the share of unemployed women seeking part-time work very much follows the share working part-time in the country concerned. If one reason for female unemployment were a mismatch between demand and supply of part-time work, one might expect to find a high share of women seeking part-time work in countries with a low share of part-time jobs.

The detailed investigation of labour market systems and unemployment patterns revealed even stronger country-specific characteristics. Countries were found to vary not only according to the level of unemployment and the relative risk of unemployment by gender, but also according to the patterns of flows in and out of employment, unemployment and inactivity. Gender differences in these flows in part explain the higher female unemployment rates in many countries, for as women move more rapidly between economic activity statuses they often have a higher risk of being trapped by unemployment, particularly as unemployed women face greater competition from inactive women when trying to re-enter employment than is the equivalent situation for men. Yet there are also major differences in the pattern of flows and in the gender dimension to the labour market system which impact on both the level of unemployment and on the relative incidence. Countries which share a similar high female unemployment rate may in fact face very different labour market systems and unemployment problems. For example, in some cases much of the female unemployment is concentrated among the young, and sometimes among women returners or job losers; in some cases education provides a relatively strong defence against unemployment, while in others it may seem to exacerbate problems in the search for a first job or fail to protect against unemployment for those returning to the labour market. Superficial similarities, such as a higher female unemployment rate or a higher share of women among the long-term unemployed, may disguise very strong differences in the under-lying problem of unemployment for women, and indeed for men.

Perhaps the greatest differences, however, are found in the welfare and social regimes within Europe. Of most significance for women are the marked disparities in systems of support for childcare and parenting. Only a few countries have up until now provided paid parental leave, although the new agreement on parental leave at the EU level may trigger some further developments in this area. Remarkably wide differences persist in the availability of publicly supported childcare. These differences in child-care provision provide at most only part of the explanation of different rates of female employment; for example the UK has virtually no childcare for children under 3 supported by the state but a relatively high female employment rate. These differences in provision are perhaps more import-ant in influencing the quality of female employment opportunities, with women in countries without state support seeking part-time employment, often in different jobs than those for which they have been trained and forced to accept occupational and earnings downgrading, while women in countries where there is more state support may be able to retain their jobs on a full-time or a part-time basis. However, while some state policies for parental leave clearly promote the integration of women into good-quality employment, some leave schemes encourage women to take leave on an unpaid or low-paid basis but fail to provide the necessary childcare support to allow eventual reintegration into employment. Thus the adoption and development of policies such as parental leave systems are not in themselves sufficient to ensure that state policy is promoting female employment.

The majority of EU welfare regimes are still based on some element of household-based taxation and on a system of derived rights for access to benefits. It is arguable that the taxation system in particular does not have a major direct impact on participation of women: for example, one of the countries with a taxation system most likely to disadvantage second income earners – France – has a high female participation rate apparently relatively unaffected by the taxation regime. Household-based systems do have more general indirect effects, for example by making transfers which support the male breadwinner family and thus reduce the impetus towards dual earner households. Specific groups of women are directly affected, particularly those in households dependent upon benefits and where the general trend towards more means-tested benefits restricts the opportunities for household members to integrate into wage work.

Systems of benefits based on derived rights and with limited entitlements for those without full-time continuous careers may encourage women to participate in the informal economy or in jobs outside the system of social protection as there are few penalties from not participating in the social security system for women whose main hope of access to reasonable benefit levels comes through their husbands' labour market opportunities. On the other hand, a move towards individualised benefits can really be contemplated only as part of a general policy move towards a new gender contract based on much greater equality in the labour market. Even in Scandinavian countries where there has been most progress towards equal pay, the shorter hours worked by women together with their still lower hourly pay rates mean that women do receive lower benefits than men when these are provided on an individualised basis.

Thus one of the factors constraining convergence in welfare systems is the need for a co-ordinated package of measures, including both labour market and welfare reforms, if a society is to move, for example, from a strong to a weak male breadwinner system. Although individual women and, in particular, groups of highly educated women, may be abandoning their traditional roles within strong male breadwinner states, this piecemeal fragmentation of the system is not likely to lead to a smooth adjustment to a new coherent match between the employment and welfare system and the changing needs of the population in both the labour market and in the household spheres. The absence of a strong movement towards convergence can in fact be detected in the parallel absence of any evidence of a co-ordinated and systematic approach to reforming labour market and welfare policy to meet the needs of gender equality.

8.2 Gender segregation and women's employment: a form of protection for female employment growth?

While employment rates have converged, there is ample evidence to suggest that a large part of this process of convergence comes not through the integration of men and women on an equal basis in the labour market but through the growth of female-dominated employment sectors. The overall increase in the female employment rate was in fact attributed about equally to the growth of female dominated sectors and to increasing female shares within sectors. While the latter process involved some desegregation of traditional male growth areas, the increasing female shares were also found in already female-dominated sectors and occupations, suggesting an intensification of the process of segregation. The growth of part-time jobs has also served to reinforce the feminisation of the labour force, for while most new jobs are part-time, most part-timers continue to be female.

Thus, segregation has continued to foster female employment growth, while at the same time acting as a basis for female inequality, facilitating the development of atypical employment forms geared to women workers and enabling the payment of wages which contravene the principle of equal pay for work of equal value. However, while there is strong evidence of continued and in some sense intensified segregation, there are other trends within the labour market which do suggest some convergence between women and men, and thus a decrease in the extent to which men and women correspond to polarised stereotypes of gender employment patterns. The areas in which we have found convergence include: an increasing share of men found in part-time jobs; an increasing share of prime-age men who are inactive, both measured by flows from employment or unemployment into inactivity and by the stock of men categorised as inactive; an opposite tendency for inactivity levels to reduce among women, for flows into employment to increase and for women to be less likely to move into inactivity to have children; a narrowing of the gender gap in unemployment rates in countries where women's unemployment exceeds men's, and the emergence of more countries where men's unemployment exceeds women's.

Much of the apparent convergence in patterns of behaviour from the male side comes from two factors: first, a deterioration in male employment prospects leading to more part-time work, more inactivity and more unemployment; second, a greater convergence in male and female lifestyles at the beginning and end of employment careers. Thus the periods when men's labour market behaviour most resembles that of women are when young men and women are trying to make entry into employment or are preparing for employment through education. This initial transition period leads to both sexes accepting, for example, part-time or temporary jobs as adjuncts to study or as possible bridges into full-time work. Even at this stage there is far from gender equality, but it may be the case that the labour market is less clearly differentiated along gender lines than is the case in prime-age years. Similarly among older workers there is a convergence in employment rates brought about by more women seeking and remaining in work and more men accepting early retirement and/or participating in atypical work after retirement. There is much less evidence of convergence among prime-age workers of both sexes and it is women alone who face entrapment in part-time and temporary work even during prime working years. Obviously more prime-age men are finding it difficult to gain access to employment but this results in higher unemployment rates and to a more limited extent in higher inactivity rates. There is, therefore, a danger of overestimating convergence trends among women and men if one fails to account for patterns by age. The male unemployed or otherwise disadvantaged may also be under pressure to accept low-paid or part-time employment, but this is still a much more common form of economic activity for prime-age women than for prime-age men.

Thus despite the wide variations between countries already discussed, and indeed despite the trends towards some convergence in participation and employment patterns between men and women, the labour market remains gendered, in both a supply side and a demand side sense. On the supply side there are still differences in participation patterns over the lifecycle which interrelate with tendencies for women to be more involved in atypical employment and non-employment during prime working-age years. On the demand side gender segregation is still pervasive and although women have made entry into non-traditional jobs, this has been offset, and sometimes more than offset, by increasing female concentration in traditional job areas and by the growth of part-time employment, primarily in female-dominated sectors. Overall, we must conclude that labour markets remain gendered and that there is, therefore, a strong prima facie case for developing a gender perspective to employment analysis and policy.

8.3   Mainstreaming gender into labour market and welfare policy

Mainstreaming gender into European labour market and welfare policy analysis should not be regarded as an optional development, to satisfy a pressure group, but an essential measure to improve the accuracy of the diagnosis and the appropriateness of selected remedies. From this investigation of the effects of placing gender at the centre of an analysis of the European employment rate we can identify three main areas for further investigation and policy development.

Mainstreaming gender into labour market trends analysis and active labour market policies

The first area where there is a need for further analysis from a gender perspective relates to the general field of labour market analysis and policy development. We have demonstrated that men and women face different employment trajectories, with different implications for policy at the European and national level. Segregation of the labour market has resulted in a gender-specific pattern of demand, and recent trends suggest an increase in gender segregation, with women increasing their share of female-dominated areas such as services, reinforced in part by the significant growth in part-time jobs in many member states. Therefore discussions of labour demand and future employment prospects which do not take on board the continued specificity of demand for labour by gender fail to diagnose the issues correctly.

For example, more information is still required in order to determine the extent to which the demand for low-skilled labour, as identified in the Delors White Paper on *Growth, Competitiveness, Employment* (CEC 1993a), has declined, absolutely, or whether the problem is a specific decline in demand for male low-skilled labour through changes in both industrial structure and a further feminisation of service sectors. What is certain, however, is that it is inappropriate to discuss changes in demand for the less-skilled or low-paid labour as if they were all pointing in one direction. Indeed, from a gender perspective, the problem may not be a decrease in low-skilled jobs relative to low-skilled labour, but a persistent tendency towards the underutilisation of women's skills which tends to increase competition at the bottom of the labour market (Maier 1995). The policy solutions from this perspective would involve finding mechanisms to move people up the labour market into jobs which were more likely to utilise their skills fully, and not to fall into the trap of calling for ever-increasing numbers of low-productivity jobs. Thus if the segmentation of the labour market by gender is taken into account, the results may not be a marginal change to policy analysis and development, but a fundamental reanalysis of the main challenges for employment policy in the future.

An important side-effect of developing a gender dimension to European employment policy is, however, the simultaneous recognition of the important role of country-specific labour market and social institutions in shaping current employment and non-employment patterns. We have seen that differences between countries in gender relations in employment can to a large extent be traced to differences in social and institutional practices within European member states, which then call into question the possibility of developing universal policy programmes at the European level. For example, even under conventional definitions of activity status, women still experience higher rates of unemployment than men, and this higher risk of

291

unemployment needs to be understood in a context of gender differences both in participation patterns and in employment opportunities. Yet these two factors interact in different ways in member states, according to differences in women's tendency to be continuous or discontinuous participants in the labour market, as well as according to differences in labour market organisation and forms of discrimination in access to employment. In some countries policies to help unemployed women may need to focus on training and re-employment opportunities for women returners. In others the main objective may need to be to increase young women's initial access to employment, through changes both in employer practices and in family attitudes, in circumstances where young men are given greater assistance than young women in finding employment (Pugliese 1995). Thus, adopting a gender perspective highlights the impact of labour market institutions and social and family organisation on patterns of unemployment and employment but does not provide a simple universal set of conclusions on appropriate policy tools.

Mainstreaming gender into statistical analysis of economic activity

The second area that is a priority for further research and policy action is that of statistical categorisation of economic activity status. Men and women differ both in their experience of employment and of non-employment. Current definitions of economic activity status have been found to be particularly inappropriate for describing women's economic activity status. For women there is both a blurring of the distinctions between employment and non-employment as a consequence of the growth of marginal part-time employment, and a blurring of the distinctions between unemployment and inactivity as a consequence of women's greater involvement in domestic work. This, on the one hand, provides women with an alternative social identity when without work, but on the other hand inhibits their opportunities to comply with the job search requirements of current definitions of unemployment. The higher rates at which women make transitions between different activity statuses reinforces the blurring of these activity definitions which at least in the past have been relatively clear-cut for the male population.

These problems of definitions, as we have seen, are now also increasingly applying to men's economic activity status, suggesting that there is some weakening of the tendency for men to participate on a permanent and continuing full-time basis in the labour market. Men are now more likely to work part-time and to move into inactivity even during prime working years, while women are increasing their permanency of attachment to the labour force.

On balance, the complexity of categorising economic activity status is likely to increase further. The simple three-way divide between employment and unemployment and inactivity is challenged by a number of labour market developments. These include, among others, the search for alternative and imaginative ways of work sharing such as special leave arrangements; active labour market policies which involve training or employment contracts that fall between conventional employment and inactivity statuses; the tendency for periods spent in education to lengthen but to be combined with employment; the continued growth of flexible short hours and precarious employment which increase flows between employment and non-employment; and new working-time arrangements such as annualised hours which increase the ambiguity of economic activity status over the annual cycle. Many of these developments are not specifically related to gender, yet further analysis suggests that gender will continue to play an important role in shaping access to and involvement in economic activity. Thus women tend, for example, to be overrepresented in leave arrangements, even when these are not specifically related to childcare, and to be overrepresented in active labour market policy programmes which are not closely integrated into the labour market. They are also overrepresented in short hours and temporary work, but perhaps are not as likely as men to be offered new employment contracts which combine flexibility over the year with continuous employment contracts, such as under annualised hours systems, and instead to move more often between activity statuses.

Most importantly, whenever new and alternative definitions of economic activity are calculated, significant gender differences are found (see Chapters 2 and 5) in the effects on economic status. It is well known that the registered unemployed and the survey-based definitions of unemployment include quite different populations, particularly of women, but the implications of these differences are not fully explored, particularly when official and survey-based definitions conveniently often give rise to fairly similar unemployment percentages.

Further research into the effects of definitions on how we understand the development of both employment and non-employment is unlikely to give rise to simple alternative definitions of economic activity status to substitute for current categories. Instead the need is for more complex and alternative sets of definitions according to the purpose of the categorisation, which allow individuals to be placed in more than one category, and for categories to be subdivided into forms of employment and non-employment status. A move to a more complex set of definitions would in fact increase the accuracy of information for employment policy, and would also highlight the fact that individuals cannot be simply divided into those with non-economic and those with economic identities and statuses. Such changes to statistical categorisations would do much to make more visible women's hidden unemployment and underemployment at the same time as allowing a more explicit recognition of the dual roles that women still hold in society.

Mainstreaming gender into social protection policies

The third area for research and policy is in the analysis of the gender impact of current state welfare, social protection and active labour market policies and the extent to which these policies reinforce or modify a male breadwinner model of household organisation. The identification of the implicit gender dimension to social and labour market policies is essential in a context where most analyses either take these policies to be gender-neutral or assume that a male breadwinner model of social organisation is normal, universal and uncontroversial. Conventional labour market theory and analysis tends to be based on the assumption that all workers are unattached individuals, while in social policy and social protection debate, the male breadwinner model is taken as the assumed norm. These two different starting-points lead to the failure to identify contradictions between policies pursued on the labour market and the social policy front.

These contradictions or lack of coherence between social and labour market policy may be regarded as simply an example of gender-blindness; more seriously such gender-blindness may represent a convenient excuse for evading consideration of the consequences of proposed policies for equality of access to employment and income. Thus proposals to promote part-time and flexible work are made simultaneously with proposals to reduce entitlements to unemployment benefit for those without full-time continuous insurance or who are not available for full-time work. Increased means testing of benefits is presented as a better method of targeting state support, without an analysis of its effects on either women's rights to independent benefits or the impact on participation patterns within households. Social exclusion will undoubtedly be greater if no members of a household participate in work, yet social protection systems based on male breadwinner models still impose punitive effective marginal tax rates on spouses of unemployed benefit recipients. Similarly, wage flexibility policies are presented as policies to reduce unemployment, without taking into account the likely consequences of such policies on the value of women's work in the labour market. Many of these policies have implications for inequalities between social groups as well as between men and women, and the argument may be made that it is more important to target protection at poor households than at women directly. However, many of the problems faced by poor households can be related to the problems faced by women in the labour market and in the social benefit system; low-paid and part-time jobs and punitive effective rates of tax on benefits are the factors which maintain and reinforce social exclusion. Families are more likely to escape from poverty if both the man and the woman are in work, and targeted policies which constrain participation of partners are likely to reinforce both social as well as gender inequalities.

This study has also highlighted the need for co-ordinated policies at the labour market and social policy level. Social and taxation policy has tended to lag behind changes in social organisation and in women's aspirations for independence. In many countries policies remain predicated on the male breadwinner, thus reinforcing a model which may be considered increasingly outmoded and inappropriate. Much more clearly needs to be done to ensure that women have independent and equal access to social protection. However, in assessing the merits of individualisation of benefits and entitlements within social protection policies, it is important to bear in mind the continued discrimination faced by women in the labour market, and the consequent need for co-ordinated policies covering the labour market, social welfare and the household, if individualisation is not potentially to result in women facing reduced access to total resources. For example, a full-scale switch from derived rights to independent rights may have the consequence of confining women to the low levels of rights and benefits that can be established by those working intermittently or in low-paid jobs and may deprive women of their shares in the much higher benefit entitlements accumulated by their male partner. Such moves could reinforce men's monopoly control of earned income resources, while removing the rights that women currently have to at least partial compensation for the domestic support they have provided for their male partners. In particular it must be recognised that calls for independent rights can be used by governments as much to cut benefits based on derived rights, such as widow's benefits, thereby increasing the potential risk of women entering into poverty, as to extend benefit entitlements to women.

These reservations relate to the method and the speed by which a move away from a breadwinner model is accomplished. Many women have entered, whether voluntarily or otherwise, into a gender contract whereby they expect their partner to provide support through market work and through his social protection entitlements. Moves away from such a situation need to ensure that in the process the value of domestic work is not downgraded and that the interests of those women who are not able to provide for their own entitlements are protected. In practice, while discrimination prevails in the labour market all women face some degree of difficulty in providing for their individual social security protection.

Independent rights remain an essential element of a reformed gender contract, involving greater equality in the labour market, the home and the social system. Changes in social protection policy are, however, unlikely by themselves to bring about such a transformation of major institutions and relationships. A similar argument applies to the principle of independent taxation which needs to be fought for in its own right, but which is likely to have less impact on women's employment decisions than changes in the employment opportunities for women, measured by both job opportunities and women's wage earning opportunities. Greater equality in the labour market thus becomes a first priority in a co-ordinated programme of change. Nevertheless, for certain groups of women the individualisation of rights is an important priority, for example for unemployed women who are finding their rights to benefits for which they have contributed eroded by greater means testing or by requirements to make provision for childcare or to work full-time. Another important group for whom individualisation is critical in some countries is that of the wives of unemployed men, as here greater opportunities to earn their own independent income could reduce social exclusion for individuals and indeed for whole families as it would allow members of the household to retain independent access to the labour market.

Towards 'mainstreaming gender' at the national and European level

This book has emphasised the importance and the urgent necessity for systematic inclusion of a gender perspective into all social and labour market analysis and policy development. Such a development is long over-due. Debates over how to move towards greater gender equality in employment have progressed beyond the concern with specific measures to more general concerns with the thrust of economic and social policy and institutions. The legitimacy of this approach has been recognised in principle by European member states. The governments of the member states of the United Nations European region, including all EU member states, agreed to incorporate in the regional platform of action in preparation for the 1995 Beijing UN World Conference on Women, Equality and Peace a statement that

> Rethinking employment policies is necessary to integrate the gender perspective and to draw attention to a wider range of opportunities as well as to address any negative gender implications of current patterns of work and employment. Major shifts in employment policies need . . . to ensure *all macro and micro economic policies are subjected to a gender impact analysis and that results of the analysis are recognised and acted upon.*
> (UN E/ECE/RW/HLM/L.3/Rev. 2. para. 81, emphasis added)

This policy approach was reaffirmed in Beijing. It is now time for this policy to be adopted and implemented systematically at both the European level and the national policy level within the European Union.

APPENDICES

Appendix Table 2.1 Percentage point contribution by gender to changing employment rates within EU member states between 1983 and 1992 (15–64 population): decomposition by population structure and age-specific employment rates

1983–7	Men				Women				Rate change
	Population effect	Changing age-specific employment rates	Interaction term	Male contribution	Population effect	Changing age-specific employment rates	Interaction term	Female contribution[a]	
Belgium	0.15	-1.51	-0.00	-1.36	0.09	0.43	0.03	0.55	-0.82
Denmark	0.12	2.31	-0.00	2.43	0.51	2.99	-0.17	3.33	5.76
Germany[b]	0.31	-0.65	-0.05	-0.40	0.18	0.96	0.00	1.15	0.75
Greece	-0.16	-1.09	-0.07	-1.32	-0.10	1.07	-0.00	0.97	-0.35
Spain	0.00	0.00	0.00	0.00	0.00	0.00	0.00	0.00	0.00
France	-0.16	-2.05	-0.01	-2.22	-0.01	-0.32	-0.01	-0.33	-2.55
Ireland	0.07	-2.78	0.01	-2.70	-0.14	-0.02	0.04	-0.12	-2.82
Italy	-0.05	-1.42	0.01	-1.46	0.02	0.38	-0.01	0.39	-1.07
Luxembourg	0.26	-0.51	0.10	-0.15	-0.02	1.49	0.14	1.62	1.47
Netherlands	0.34	2.38	-0.08	2.64	0.12	3.79	-0.01	3.90	6.54
Portugal	0.00	0.00	0.00	0.00	0.00	0.00	0.00	0.00	0.00
UK	0.37	0.43	-0.03	0.77	0.31	2.18	0.00	2.49	3.26

Appendix Table 2.1 (Contd . . .)

1987–92	Men				Women				Rate change
	Population effect	Changing age-specific employment rates	Interaction term	Male contribution	Population effect	Changing age-specific employment rates	Interaction term	Female contribution[a]	
Belgium	0.76	-0.21	0.07	0.62	0.45	3.01	0.13	3.58	4.21
Denmark	0.42	-1.72	0.02	-1.28	0.15	-0.51	0.07	-0.29	-1.58
Germany[b]	0.35	0.53	0.11	1.00	0.25	3.04	0.23	3.53	4.52
Greece	-0.40	-0.59	-0.01	-1.00	-0.20	0.21	-0.06	-0.05	-1.05
Spain	0.39	0.16	0.01	0.55	0.18	2.09	0.09	2.36	2.92
France	0.34	-1.36	0.03	-1.00	0.37	0.27	0.10	0.74	-0.26
Ireland	0.26	-1.04	0.02	-0.76	-0.08	1.76	0.10	1.78	1.02
Italy	0.08	-1.46	-0.02	-1.39	0.12	0.88	-0.00	1.00	-0.40
Luxembourg	0.24	-1.31	0.05	-1.02	0.15	1.88	0.14	2.17	1.15
Netherlands	0.77	0.49	-0.04	1.21	0.21	3.99	0.04	4.23	5.44
Portugal	0.40	-0.49	0.09	0.01	0.43	2.65	0.13	3.22	3.23
UK	0.54	-1.00	0.06	-0.40	0.28	1.85	0.13	2.26	1.86

1983–92	Men				Women				Rate change
	Population effect	Changing age-specific employment rates	Interaction term	Male contribution	Population effect	Changing age-specific employment rates	Interaction term	Female contribution[a]	
Belgium	0.87	-1.78	0.17	-0.74	0.44	3.41	0.29	4.14	3.40
Denmark	0.69	0.67	-0.20	1.16	0.67	2.49	-0.13	3.03	4.20
Germany[b]	0.75	-0.22	0.05	0.58	0.46	4.04	0.24	4.74	5.32
Greece	-0.47	-1.66	-0.19	-2.31	-0.27	1.34	-0.14	0.92	-1.39
Spain	0.00	0.00	0.00	0.00	0.00	0.00	0.00	0.00	0.00
France	0.15	-3.39	0.02	-3.22	0.29	-0.05	0.16	0.40	-2.82
Ireland	0.32	-3.85	0.07	-3.46	-0.23	1.64	0.24	1.65	-1.81
Italy	0.06	-2.86	-0.04	-2.85	0.17	1.29	-0.07	1.40	-1.45
Luxembourg	0.42	-1.87	0.29	-1.17	-0.01	3.31	0.48	3.78	2.62
Netherlands	1.32	2.87	-0.34	3.85	0.36	7.77	0.01	8.14	11.99
Portugal	0.00	0.00	0.00	0.00	0.00	0.00	0.00	0.00	0.00
UK	1.04	-0.57	-0.10	0.37	0.62	3.96	0.17	4.75	5.12

Source: Special tabulation provided by Eurostat
Notes: a Male/female contribution = population effect + changing age-specific employment rates + interaction term
     b Data for Germany exclude the new Länder

Appendix Table 2.2 Decomposition of the change in male and female part-time employment, 1983–92[a]

Men 1983–7 (%)

	Population effect	Changing age-specific part-time rates	Interaction effect	Scale effect	Composition effect	Residual effect	Total	Net change in part-time employment (000)
Belgium	-2926.6	4268.0	-1441.4	-1371.1	-1589.2	33.7	-100.0	-0.06
Denmark[b]	38.6	46.5	14.9	-11.3	53.0	-3.1	100.0	40.87
Germany[b]	8.5	85.9	5.5	-15.8	26.1	-1.8	100.0	80.10
Greece	-4.0	-97.1	1.0	59.5	-55.5	-7.9	-100.0	-16.55
France	-11.4	121.2	-9.8	-26.4	17.2	-2.2	100.0	128.26
Ireland	-177.3	313.5	-36.3	-225.1	55.2	-7.4	100.0	1.11
Italy	-2.5	103.7	-1.2	37.8	-34.2	-6.1	100.0	122.45
Luxembourg	-20.1	174.9	-54.8	52.8	-57.1	-15.7	100.0	0.54
Netherlands	16.2	66.3	17.5	-9.2	28.8	-3.4	100.0	277.02
UK[b]	7.1	87.1	5.9	-13.5	23.4	-2.8	100.0	277.61
E10[b]	0.9	98.5	0.6	-6.5	7.7	-0.3	100.0	911.48

Men 1987–92 (%)

	Population effect	Changing age-specific part-time rates	Interaction effect	Scale effect	Composition effect	Residual effect	Total	Net change in part-time employment (000)
Belgium	-56.9	186.2	-29.2	75.9	-121.8	-11.0	100.0	4.87
Denmark[b]	-219.2	394.3	-75.1	-212.0	-8.1	0.9	100.0	6.04
Germany[b]	16.4	83.9	-0.2	22.8	-5.5	-0.9	100.0	191.05
Greece	19.1	99.5	-18.6	134.0	-102.0	-12.9	100.0	4.95
Spain	50.6	-151.6	1.0	77.2	-24.9	-1.7	100.0	-15.09
France	-235.2	339.3	-4.1	-575.0	453.6	-113.8	100.0	17.35
Ireland	-13.6	116.4	-2.8	-28.1	15.9	-1.4	100.0	6.16
Italy	-17.3	-85.8	3.1	-136.9	135.3	-15.7	100.0	-32.31
Luxembourg	-70.8	-74.9	45.7	-8.4	-64.0	1.6	100.0	-0.47
Netherlands	17.8	89.6	-7.4	-108.0	159.5	-33.7	100.0	95.84
Portugal	-32.9	153.8	-20.9	14.0	-46.1	-0.9	100.0	8.43
UK[b]	-56.7	184.3	-27.6	6.8	-62.6	-0.8	100.0	110.58
E10[b]	-23.8	137.9	-14.1	-16.2	-7.9	0.2	100.0	403.64
E12[b]	-21.3	133.0	-11.8	-7.3	-14.1	0.2	100.0	396.50

Appendix Table 2.2 (Contd . . .)

Men 1983–92 (%)

	Population effect	Changing age-specific part-time rates	Interaction effect	Scale effect	Composition effect	Residual effect	Total	Net change in part-time employment (000)
Belgium	-55.6	291.8	-136.2	57.4	-105.9	-7.1	100.0	4.81
Denmark	12.2	79.7	8.0	-26.8	46.4	-7.4	100.0	46.91
Germany[b]	9.5	83.9	6.6	5.7	3.5	0.3	100.0	271.15
Greece	6.7	-85.5	-21.2	170.8	-127.5	-36.6	-100.0	-11.60
France	-22.0	148.1	-26.1	-63.8	63.8	-22.0	100.0	145.61
Ireland	-36.4	156.9	-20.6	-54.0	22.2	-4.7	100.0	7.27
Italy	-10.0	110.4	-0.4	12.0	-21.1	-0.9	100.0	90.14
Luxembourg	-306.4	444.8	-38.4	361.4	-537.2	-130.6	100.0	0.07
Netherlands	14.5	66.1	19.4	-17.5	46.0	-14.0	100.0	372.86
UK	-3.8	111.8	-8.0	-8.8	5.5	-0.6	100.0	388.19
E10[b]	-2.2	110.7	-8.5	-7.4	5.6	-0.4	100.0	1315.11

Women 1983–7 (%)

	Population effect	Changing age-specific part-time rates	Interaction effect	Scale effect	Composition effect	Residual effect	Total	Net change in part-time employment (000)
Belgium	21.8	74.4	3.7	-6.9	29.3	-0.6	100.0	70.31
Denmark	302.4	-200.5	-2.0	-166.7	498.3	-29.2	100.0	16.82
Germany[b]	83.8	29.6	-13.5	-315.1	428.7	-29.8	100.0	64.61
Greece	286.9	-332.3	-54.7	442.5	-136.1	-19.4	-100.0	-3.97
France	19.7	82.3	-2.0	-64.7	96.5	-12.1	100.0	332.75
Ireland	129.0	23.8	-52.8	-243.3	429.9	-57.5	100.0	2.81
Italy	28.6	70.8	0.6	111.2	-70.1	-12.5	100.0	94.99
Luxembourg	210.6	-15.3	-95.3	291.4	-63.3	-17.4	100.0	0.80
Netherlands	63.9	26.4	9.6	-25.6	101.7	-12.1	100.0	381.17
UK	52.3	42.6	5.1	-66.3	135.0	-16.4	100.0	710.59
E10[b]	42.1	55.2	2.7	-26.2	71.2	-2.9	100.0	1696.25

Appendix Table 2.2 (Contd....)

	Women 1987–92 (%)							Net change in part-time employment (000)
	Population effect	Changing age-specific part-time rates	Interaction effect	Scale effect	Composition effect	Residual effect	Total	
Belgium	50.5	40.7	8.8	22.8	25.3	2.3	100.0	118.32
Denmark	33.5	-122.9	-10.6	-92.6	141.2	-15.1	-100.0	-57.18
Germany[b]	64.8	28.9	6.3	42.3	19.3	3.2	100.0	1179.60
Greece	22.4	-117.1	-5.3	70.0	-42.3	-5.3	-100.0	-21.53
Spain	100.8	0.4	-1.1	32.9	63.5	4.4	100.0	94.94
France	39.0	59.0	2.0	-187.4	302.3	-75.9	100.0	273.93
Ireland	63.7	35.5	0.8	-23.1	95.2	-8.3	100.0	20.31
Italy	32.9	60.1	7.0	-55.3	99.7	-11.5	100.0	144.04
Luxembourg	202.7	-123.9	21.2	-34.2	243.0	-6.1	100.0	0.68
Netherlands	71.3	25.7	3.0	-55.8	161.0	-34.0	100.0	453.98
Portugal	60.5	45.2	-5.7	8.3	51.2	1.0	100.0	37.39
UK	130.3	-2.4	-27.9	15.5	113.4	1.4	100.0	378.61
E10[b]	63.6	37.4	-1.0	-14.0	79.8	-2.2	100.0	2480.48
E12[b]	67.2	33.8	-1.0	-5.6	73.6	-0.8	100.0	2611.60

Appendix Table 2.2 (Contd....)

	Women 1983–92 (%)							Net change in part-time employment (000)
	Population effect	Changing age-specific part-time rates	Interaction effect	Scale effect	Composition effect	Residual effect	Total	
Belgium	35.9	51.4	12.7	8.1	26.0	1.8	100.0	188.63
Denmark	181.8	-255.9	-25.9	-188.8	440.9	-70.3	-100.0	-40.36
Germany[b]	64.8	28.5	6.7	20.1	41.2	3.5	100.0	1244.21
Greece	65.7	-143.7	-22.1	138.7	-56.7	-16.3	-100.0	-25.50
France	32.0	70.4	-2.3	-97.4	197.6	-68.2	100.0	606.69
Ireland	81.9	35.4	-17.3	-46.2	162.1	-34.0	100.0	23.11
Italy	29.3	62.3	8.3	10.4	18.2	0.8	100.0	239.03
Luxembourg	254.1	-87.5	-66.7	138.8	92.8	22.6	100.0	1.48
Netherlands	65.6	23.1	11.3	-29.9	137.4	-42.0	100.0	835.15
UK	77.5	26.3	-3.9	-39.3	131.2	-14.4	100.0	1089.20
E10[b]	54.4	43.8	1.9	-17.5	77.1	-5.2	100.0	4176.73

Source: Special tabulations provided by Eurostat

Notes: a Growth effect + age-specific part-time rates + interaction effect = net change in employment (100%) where growth effect = scale effect + composition effect + residual effect

b Data for Germany and E10/12 exclude the new Länder

Appendix Table 2.3 Decomposition of the percentage point change in part-time employment rates for total, male and female employment, 1983–92[a]

All	Population effect	Age-specific part-time rates	Interaction effect	Net change
Belgium	0.01	4.58	−0.19	4.39
Denmark	0.37	−2.37	0.21	−1.79
Germany[b]	0.34	3.26	−0.03	3.58
Greece	−0.04	−1.26	−0.06	−1.36
France	−0.13	3.61	−0.35	3.13
Ireland	−0.00	2.76	−0.25	2.51
Italy	−0.04	1.50	0.03	1.49
Luxembourg	0.08	0.24	−0.15	0.17
Netherlands	0.30	12.68	0.23	13.21
UK	−0.02	4.90	−0.49	4.39
E10[b]	0.01	4.13	−0.32	3.82

Men	Population effect	Age-specific part-time rates	Interaction effect	Net change
Belgium	−0.15	0.63	−0.30	0.17
Denmark	−0.01	2.92	0.07	2.99
Germany[b]	0.04	1.45	−0.03	1.45
Greece	−0.03	−0.44	−0.10	−0.57
France	−0.23	1.72	−0.29	1.20
Ireland	−0.27	1.54	−0.15	1.12
Italy	−0.03	0.73	0.01	0.71
Luxembourg	−0.28	0.32	−0.05	−0.00
Netherlands	0.25	7.51	0.54	8.31
UK	−0.18	3.22	−0.32	2.72
E10[b]	−0.12	2.23	−0.25	1.86

Women	Population effect	Age-specific part-time rates	Interaction effect	Net change
Belgium	0.41	8.34	−0.16	8.59
Denmark	1.09	−9.64	0.21	−8.33
Germany[b]	1.35	3.59	0.04	4.98
Greece	0.03	−3.33	−0.06	−3.36
France	0.23	4.95	−0.60	4.58
Ireland	2.23	2.45	−1.40	3.28
Italy	−0.00	2.29	0.03	2.32
Luxembourg	2.28	−2.74	−1.03	−1.49
Netherlands	2.46	11.84	−0.76	13.54
UK	0.60	3.07	−0.89	2.78
E10[b]	0.60	4.61	−0.55	4.65

Source: Special tabulation provided by Eurostat
Notes: a Population effect + change in age-specific part-time rates + interaction effect = net change in part-time employment rates
b Data for Germany and E10 exclude the new Länder

303

Appendix Table 2.4 Distribution of male and female unemployment and inactivity by age group, 1983–92

Male unemployment (%)	15–24			25–49			50–64		
	1983	1987	1992	1983	1987	1992	1983	1987	1992
Belgium	35.0	26.4	23.8	49.6	60.1	66.9	15.4	13.6	9.3
Denmark	36.3	31.7	25.4	49.6	48.8	57.4	14.1	19.6	17.3
Germany[a]	30.6	20.3	14.3/14.4	53.3	57.1	53.2/55.3	16.1	22.6	32.5/30.2
Greece	34.7	37.1	39.9	51.6	49.7	47.2	13.7	13.1	12.9
Spain	–	42.1	34.1	–	41.8	51.1	–	16.1	14.9
France	39.0	32.9	26.3	44.3	52.3	59.5	16.7	14.8	14.2
Ireland	36.6	32.8	28.9	51.7	54.1	59.6	11.8	13.0	11.5
Italy	63.8	57.2	48.5	29.5	35.7	44.5	6.8	7.0	7.0
Luxembourg	44.2	37.0	32.9	48.7	51.9	58.7	7.5	10.5	7.8
Netherlands	33.6	38.3	30.3	55.9	50.1	60.1	10.4	11.5	9.7
Portugal	–	50.0	42.6	–	37.3	41.3	–	12.7	16.1
UK	38.5	32.5	29.3	44.0	49.0	52.6	17.5	18.6	18.0
E10	40.3	35.2	30.5	45.1	49.1	53.3	14.6	15.7	16.2
E12[a]	–	37.0	31.3/30.4	–	47.3	52.7/53.0	–	15.7	16.0/16.6

Female unemployment (%)	15–24			25–49			50–64		
	1983	1987	1992	1983	1987	1992	1983	1987	1992
Belgium	37.0	31.6	23.0	57.3	63.8	71.8	5.6	4.6	5.2
Denmark	37.2	30.0	23.5	51.9	58.0	60.2	10.8	12.0	16.3
Germany[a]	34.3	22.3	15.2/12.8	54.4	60.2	57.1/62.4	11.3	17.5	27.7/24.9
Greece	49.6	48.7	43.3	45.5	47.1	51.2	4.8	4.2	5.5
Spain	–	55.4	36.7	–	39.7	57.7	–	4.9	5.6
France	44.4	35.8	25.9	44.6	53.9	63.6	11.0	10.3	10.5
Ireland	47.0	41.1	35.5	46.0	51.4	57.5	7.0	7.5	7.0
Italy	60.0	53.7	46.4	36.7	43.3	49.6	3.3	3.1	3.9
Luxembourg	51.2	45.9	22.4	42.9	51.2	71.8	6.0	2.9	5.7
Netherlands	42.1	37.0	25.8	53.0	57.1	67.0	4.9	5.9	7.2
Portugal	–	51.3	40.1	–	43.8	55.4	–	4.9	4.4
UK	44.6	35.5	31.5	45.9	52.8	56.9	9.5	11.8	11.6
E10	45.8	38.1	31.2	46.1	52.6	57.9	8.1	9.3	10.9
E12[a]	–	41.5	32.5/30.2	–	50.1	57.8/58.8	–	8.4	9.6/11.0

Appendix Table 2.4 (contd ...)

Male inactivity (%)

	15–24			25–49			50–64		
	1983	1987	1992	1983	1987	1992	1983	1987	1992
Belgium	54.9	46.1	44.6	9.3	9.9	11.9	35.8	44.1	43.4
Denmark	46.1	38.6	39.5	17.7	22.5	22.7	36.2	38.9	37.8
Germany[a]	54.1	44.7	39.2/36.8	13.4	16.6	18.6/16.5	32.4	38.7	42.2/46.7
Greece	55.6	51.4	49.5	10.5	9.7	10.4	33.9	38.9	40.0
Spain	—	55.4	54.2	—	10.8	13.1	—	33.7	32.7
France	45.9	45.5	48.7	8.0	7.4	9.1	46.1	47.1	42.2
Ireland	63.1	62.8	60.0	12.8	14.4	17.2	24.2	22.8	22.8
Italy	50.9	47.7	47.0	8.1	10.5	14.6	41.0	41.8	38.4
Luxembourg	44.1	43.8	40.1	7.3	7.9	10.1	48.5	48.3	49.8
Netherlands	55.7	45.5	40.0	12.5	14.7	17.3	31.8	39.7	42.7
Portugal	—	44.7	53.1	—	12.6	11.8	—	42.6	35.1
UK	50.4	42.6	39.3	14.3	15.6	19.5	35.4	41.9	41.2
E10	51.3	45.8	44.3	11.0	12.3	14.9	37.7	41.9	40.8
E12[a]	—	47.0	45.8/45.0	—	12.2	14.6/14.3	—	40.9	39.6/40.7

Female inactivity (%)

	15–24			25–49			50–64		
	1983	1987	1992	1983	1987	1992	1983	1987	1992
Belgium	25.4	24.2	25.3	36.8	33.8	33.3	37.8	42.0	41.4
Denmark	31.0	23.7	27.2	25.3	28.5	29.2	43.7	47.8	43.6
Germany[a]	22.1	19.9	19.2/19.7	42.1	40.9	39.3/35.6	35.8	39.2	41.6/44.7
Greece	22.8	24.0	26.1	46.7	41.9	38.1	30.6	34.0	37.9
Spain	—	23.4	32.2	—	41.1	39.3	—	35.5	34.6
France	26.3	28.1	27.6	37.2	34.5	31.9	36.5	37.3	35.9
Ireland	21.7	23.8	23.9	51.0	49.4	45.8	27.3	26.8	26.7
Italy	21.2	21.4	17.7	42.9	40.7	38.6	35.9	37.9	37.5
Luxembourg	16.4	17.0	18.6	47.9	46.0	44.2	35.7	37.0	38.1
Netherlands	21.7	19.9	30.3	47.4	46.3	45.2	30.9	33.8	36.2
Portugal	—	23.8	22.6	—	35.9	32.9	—	40.3	36.8
UK	23.5	22.2	24.0	42.1	41.8	41.8	34.3	36.0	35.6
E10	23.0	22.6		41.8	39.9	38.2	35.2	37.5	37.8
E12[a]	—	22.7	24.5/24.5	—	40.0	38.2/37.5	—	37.3	37.3/38.1

Source: Special tabulation provided by Eurostat
Note: a Data for Germany and E12 exclude/include the new Länder

APPENDICES

Appendix Table 3.1 Intra-country range of regional employment rates: headcount and full-time equivalent (FTE) rates, 1983–92[a]

		Male employment rates (%)			Female employment rates (%)		
		1983	1987	1992	1983	1987	1992
Belgium	maximum	72.6	70.7	71.8	41.2	39.8	46.0
	minimum	66.0	60.9	62.3	34.3	35.9	42.1
	range	6.6	9.8	9.4	6.9	3.9	4.0
	maximum (FTE)	66.6	64.9	71.2	37.1	36.1	39.7
	minimum (FTE)	65.0	60.1	61.1	30.6	30.7	35.6
	range (FTE)	1.6	4.8	10.1	6.5	5.4	4.1
Germany	maximum	—	80.1	82.1	—	59.2	62.6
	minimum	—	70.1	69.7	—	36.7	44.7
	range	—	10.0	12.4	—	22.4	17.9
	maximum (FTE)	—	—	81.0	—	—	54.8
	minimum (FTE)	—	—	69.3	—	—	38.0
	range (FTE)	—	—	11.7	—	—	16.8
Greece	maximum	—	—	78.6	—	—	41.6
	minimum	—	—	67.9	—	—	33.5
	range	—	—	10.6	—	—	8.1
	maximum (FTE)	—	—	77.4	—	—	39.8
	minimum (FTE)	—	—	67.3	—	—	32.4
	range (FTE)	—	—	10.1	—	—	7.5
Spain	maximum	—	67.5	70.1	—	37.0	35.6
	minimum	—	56.7	57.1	—	19.7	25.0
	range	—	10.8	13.1	—	17.3	10.6
	maximum (FTE)	—	66.6	69.6	—	35.5	33.6
	minimum (FTE)	—	56.1	55.9	—	18.2	23.3
	range (FTE)	—	10.5	13.7	—	17.2	10.4
France	maximum	78.3	74.2	72.3	58.7	57.1	58.5
	minimum	71.1	62.5	61.1	40.9	41.4	39.8
	range	7.1	11.7	11.3	17.8	15.7	18.7
	maximum (FTE)	77.0	72.6	71.2	54.7	52.3	54.0
	minimum (FTE)	70.5	61.5	60.0	35.9	36.1	34.5
	range (FTE)	6.4	11.1	11.2	18.8	16.2	19.5
Ireland	maximum	—	—	66.6	—	—	39.8
	minimum	—	—	62.7	—	—	32.1
	range	—	—	3.9	—	—	7.7
	maximum (FTE)	—	—	65.1	—	—	36.1
	minimum (FTE)	—	—	61.4	—	—	29.0
	range (FTE)	—	—	3.7	—	—	7.1
Italy	maximum	78.1	75.8	75.2	44.2	46.6	49.1
	minimum	69.3	65.1	61.9	19.3	20.1	21.7
	range	8.8	10.8	13.3	24.9	26.5	27.4
	maximum (FTE)	77.4	75.2	74.3	42.3	44.3	45.9
	minimum (FTE)	68.2	63.6	60.8	18.1	19.0	20.5
	range (FTE)	9.2	11.7	13.5	24.1	25.3	25.4
Netherlands	maximum	—	75.3	77.5	—	45.2	53.8
	minimum	—	69.9	71.7	—	37.5	47.3
	range	—	5.4	5.8	—	7.7	6.5
	maximum (FTE)	—	70.1	71.5	—	32.5	37.1
	minimum (FTE)	—	65.1	66.0	—	25.7	30.9
	range (FTE)	—	5.0	5.5	—	6.8	6.2

306

Portugal								
	maximum	—	—	79.7	—	—	58.1
	minimum	—	—	76.0	—	—	48.4
	range	—	—	3.7	—	—	9.7
	maximum (FTE)	—	—	78.4	—	—	55.4
	minimum (FTE)	—	—	74.7	—	—	43.7
	range (FTE)	—	—	3.7	—	—	11.7
UK	maximum	79.3	81.4	81.2	54.0	60.3	63.3
	minimum	65.0	65.4	68.0	44.1	47.1	53.7
	range	14.3	16.0	13.2	9.9	13.2	9.6
	maximum (FTE)	78.0	79.7	78.3	42.6	47.5	49.1
	minimum (FTE)	64.0	63.6	64.5	35.5	38.3	42.0
	range (FTE)	14.0	16.2	13.8	7.1	9.2	7.1

Source: Special tabulations provided by Eurostat
Note: a Regional employment rates based on the NUTS I regional classification except for Ireland

Appendix Table 3.2 Regional unemployment rates by gender, 1983, 1987 and 1992[a]

		Male unemployment rates (%)						Female unemployment rates (%)					
		Share of the labour force			Share of the population			Share of the labour force			Share of the population		
		1983	1987	1992	1983	1987	1992	1983	1987	1992	1983	1987	1992
Belgium	Flamande	6.8	5.1	2.6	5.3	3.8	1.9	17.5	16.3	7.0	7.8	7.4	3.5
	Walloon	9.5	10.1	7.6	6.9	7.0	5.2	20.3	20.3	13.5	8.7	9.2	6.6
	Brussels	11.7	12.8	10.3	8.7	9.0	7.2	12.8	16.9	11.4	6.0	8.1	5.8
Denmark		9.4	5.3	8.5	7.9	4.5	7.3	10.6	7.2	10.0	7.6	5.5	7.8
Germany	Schleswig-Holstein	—	9.1	4.8	—	7.4	4.0	—	11.7	6.4	—	6.1	3.9
	Hamburg	—	8.5	5.6	—	6.8	4.5	—	7.7	4.7	—	4.5	2.9
	Lower Saxony	—	8.5	4.4	—	6.8	3.6	—	10.0	5.9	—	5.1	3.4
	Bremen	—	11.7	7.5	—	9.3	5.9	—	12.2	8.2	—	6.1	4.8
	North Rhine Westphalia	—	7.0	4.2	—	5.5	3.4	—	9.8	6.0	—	4.5	3.1
	Hessen	—	4.8	2.7	—	4.0	2.2	—	6.4	3.1	—	3.4	1.8
	Rhineland-Palatinate	—	5.1	4.0	—	4.2	3.2	—	9.0	4.8	—	4.4	2.7
	Baden-Württemburg	—	3.7	2.6	—	3.1	2.1	—	5.5	3.2	—	3.1	2.0
	Bavaria	—	4.9	2.3	—	4.2	2.0	—	6.1	3.4	—	3.7	2.2
	Saarland	—	7.1	7.5	—	5.4	5.7	—	7.3	4.8	—	2.9	2.3
	Berlin[b]	—	7.8	9.2	—	6.0	7.7	—	8.2	10.5	—	5.3	7.3
	Brandeburg	—	—	11.1	—	—	8.9	—	—	19.9	—	—	14.5
	Mecklenburg West Pomerania	—	—	12.1	—	—	9.6	—	—	22.3	—	—	16.1
	Saxony	—	—	9.4	—	—	7.4	—	—	19.7	—	—	14.2
	Saxony Anhalt	—	—	9.7	—	—	7.6	—	—	19.9	—	—	14.3
	Thüringia	—	—	8.8	—	—	6.8	—	—	22.1	—	—	15.9
Greece	Northern Greece	—	—	3.9	—	—	3.0	—	—	11.9	—	—	5.1
	Central Greece	—	—	5.3	—	—	4.2	—	—	14.0	—	—	6.1
	Attica	—	—	6.4	—	—	4.7	—	—	15.4	—	—	6.1
	Islands	—	—	2.8	—	—	2.2	—	—	6.0	—	—	2.7
Spain	North West	—	14.4	13.1	—	11.1	9.8	—	17.6	22.4	—	7.9	10.2
	North East	—	14.2	9.5	—	10.9	7.1	—	28.0	25.4	—	9.8	10.8
	Madrid	—	13.0	9.2	—	10.0	7.1	—	22.7	18.5	—	8.3	7.3
	Centre	—	15.3	13.3	—	12.0	10.1	—	26.6	28.9	—	8.4	11.1
	East	—	15.3	10.8	—	12.2	8.5	—	30.3	21.6	—	12.7	9.8
	South	—	26.5	21.8	—	20.4	16.1	—	37.5	33.8	—	11.8	12.8
	Canarics	—	20.5	21.5	—	15.5	15.6	—	36.0	30.4	—	13.0	13.4

307

Appendix Table 3.2 (Contd ...)

		Male unemployment rates (%)		Female unemployment rates (%)	
		Share of the labour force	Share of the population	Share of the labour force	Share of the population
		1983 1987 1992	1983 1987 1992	1983 1987 1992	1983 1987 1992
France	Île de France	5.2 8.2 7.4	4.3 6.6 5.8	7.0 9.9 8.9	4.4 6.3 5.7
	Paris Basin	6.5 8.6 7.9	5.3 6.8 6.1	11.3 15.0 13.4	6.6 8.7 7.9
	North	7.8 13.9 13.4	6.0 10.1 9.4	11.7 16.3 19.0	5.7 8.1 9.4
	East	5.3 8.0 5.8	4.3 6.3 4.4	11.5 13.9 12.4	5.8 7.4 7.0
	West	6.1 8.7 8.0	4.9 6.8 5.9	10.7 14.6 13.4	6.2 8.7 8.0
	South West	5.6 8.0 7.7	4.5 6.1 5.7	12.4 13.5 14.1	6.9 7.8 8.4
	Centre East	5.0 6.7 6.4	4.0 5.3 4.9	9.3 11.2 11.6	5.3 6.5 7.0
	Mediterranean	8.9 10.3 11.4	7.1 7.8 8.5	15.6 18.3 17.5	7.6 9.7 9.3
Ireland	East	— — 16.1	— — 12.4	— — 15.5	— — 7.3
	South West	— — 13.3	— — 10.0	— — 14.8	— — 5.9
	South East	— — 18.2	— — 14.2	— — 19.1	— — 7.6
	North East	— — 15.4	— — 12.1	— — 18.3	— — 7.2
	Mid-West	— — 12.9	— — 9.7	— — 11.7	— — 5.0
	North West & Donegal	— — 15.8	— — 11.7	— — 14.7	— — 6.5
	Midlands	— — 14.7	— — 11.2	— — 15.8	— — 6.1
	West	— — 14.2	— — 10.6	— — 13.9	— — 6.0
Italy	North West	4.4 5.4 5.4	3.5 4.1 3.9	12.2 13.4 11.9	5.4 6.1 5.7
	Lombardia	3.4 3.6 3.5	2.7 2.9 2.7	9.5 9.5 8.0	4.2 4.4 3.8
	North East	4.3 4.5 3.3	3.5 3.6 2.6	10.6 10.8 9.0	4.4 4.6 4.2
	Emilia-Romagna	4.0 3.7 2.7	3.2 2.9 2.1	10.9 11.6 8.3	5.4 6.1 4.5
	Centre	4.5 4.7 4.1	3.6 3.7 3.0	14.0 13.0 10.6	6.2 6.1 5.1
	Lazio	5.5 7.0 6.4	4.3 5.5 4.8	13.3 14.7 12.5	4.6 5.6 5.3
	Campania	10.1 17.2 14.1	7.9 13.5 10.1	21.1 34.0 25.2	7.6 13.1 8.1
	Abruzzi and Molise	5.4 7.0 5.1	4.3 5.5 3.8	13.3 15.4 11.9	5.5 6.8 4.9
	South	7.8 11.4 11.4	6.0 8.7 8.3	18.6 25.6 21.8	6.4 9.0 7.7
	Sicily	7.4 11.9 14.0	5.9 9.5 10.3	26.8 30.7 29.8	7.1 8.9 9.2
	Sardinia	11.7 12.1 11.9	9.2 9.2 8.6	27.4 28.4 26.8	8.6 9.9 9.6
Luxembourg		2.3 1.8 1.6	1.9 1.4 1.2	5.1 3.8 2.8	2.1 1.6 1.3
Netherlands	North	— 9.0 5.3	— 6.9 4.1	— 17.9 10.8	— 8.2 5.7
	East	— 8.1 4.0	— 6.4 3.2	— 15.1 8.0	— 7.2 4.2
	West	— 7.2 3.8	— 5.9 3.1	— 12.9 6.7	— 6.7 3.9
	South	— 7.0 4.2	— 5.5 3.3	— 14.1 8.8	— 6.6 4.7
Portugal	North	— — 2.8	— — 2.3	— — 3.6	— — 2.2
	South	— — 4.4	— — 3.5	— — 6.5	— — 3.7
	Islands	— — 2.5	— — 2.0	— — 5.0	— — 2.5
UK	Scotland	14.1 16.1 11.3	11.9 13.5 9.6	11.6 13.8 7.6	6.6 8.3 5.0
	Northern Ireland	18.8 18.5 15.4	15.0 14.9 12.3	11.7 11.1 7.9	5.8 5.9 4.6
	North	17.0 15.2 14.2	14.1 12.7 11.7	11.7 11.8 7.9	6.4 7.3 5.0
	Yorks & Humberside	14.1 12.9 12.2	11.9 10.9 10.3	8.8 11.0 7.5	6.1 6.7 4.9
	East Midlands	9.4 10.9 10.7	8.1 9.4 9.3	8.8 11.0 6.6	5.1 6.9 4.4
	East Anglia	9.7 8.0 8.3	8.5 7.1 7.3	9.4 10.4 6.0	5.5 6.6 4.0
	South East	8.7 8.0 11.1	7.6 7.1 9.7	8.0 8.1 7.5	4.7 5.3 5.1
	South West	9.0 8.3 10.6	7.7 7.2 9.3	8.4 9.9 7.8	4.8 6.5 5.2
	West Midlands	15.1 14.1 12.7	12.8 12.2 10.8	12.0 11.5 8.2	6.7 7.1 5.3
	North West	15.2 13.7 12.8	12.7 11.6 10.6	11.3 12.6 6.8	6.5 8.0 4.4
	Wales	16.1 14.2 11.9	12.8 11.3 9.6	11.5 12.7 5.5	5.8 7.2 3.4

Source: Special tabulations provided by Eurostat
Notes: a Data are based upon NUTS I regional classification except for Ireland
    b Data refer to West Berlin only in 1987

Appendix Table 3.3 Decomposition of the change in female employment, 1983–92[a]

1983–7	Industry effect (%)	Share effect (%)	Interaction effect (%)	Scale effect (%)	Weight effect (%)	Residual effect (%)	Total (%)	Net change in employment (000)
Belgium	73.41	24.47	2.12	31.53	41.06	0.81	100.00	73.05
Denmark	105.75	−7.68	1.93	93.55	11.13	1.07	100.00	110.28
Germany[b]	95.49	−0.12	4.62	68.70	26.10	0.69	100.00	380.85
Greece	57.41	40.16	2.43	36.39	20.38	0.63	100.00	93.71
Spain	—	—	—	—	—	—	—	—
France	87.94	10.88	1.18	8.64	79.06	0.24	100.00	304.09
Ireland	54.52	43.29	2.19	−76.36	134.13	−3.25	100.00	10.61
Luxembourg	67.79	28.70	3.50	52.15	14.64	1.01	100.00	6.22
Netherlands	69.04	25.96	5.00	63.51	4.69	0.84	100.00	458.73
Portugal	—	—	—	—	—	—	—	—
UK	87.78	11.37	0.84	61.77	24.34	1.68	100.00	1043.98
E9[bc]	86.91	11.97	1.11	56.42	29.26	1.23	100.00	2481.52
E11[bc]	—	—	—	—	—	—	—	—

1987–92	Industry effect (%)	Share effect (%)	Interaction effect (%)	Scale effect (%)	Weight effect (%)	Residual effect (%)	Total (%)	Net change in employment (000)
Belgium	43.92	51.84	4.24	43.39	0.48	0.04	100.00	241.55
Denmark	50.64	40.89	8.47	7.23	43.34	0.07	100.00	24.73
Germany[b]	71.88	24.09	4.03	68.41	3.11	0.37	100.00	1788.97
Greece	43.98	37.52	18.51	61.35	−16.92	−0.45	100.00	52.16
Spain	53.94	40.52	5.54	46.72	6.55	0.67	100.00	724.23
France	69.80	29.63	0.57	49.33	19.86	0.62	100.00	561.37
Ireland	57.36	37.73	4.91	38.50	17.77	1.09	100.00	54.93
Luxembourg	60.70	39.69	−0.40	50.68	9.40	0.63	100.00	7.04
Netherlands	70.75	24.85	4.40	54.42	14.43	1.90	100.00	505.27
Portugal	28.65	56.99	14.36	36.20	−7.19	−0.36	100.00	232.99
UK	61.41	37.18	1.41	37.09	23.62	0.70	100.00	825.35
E9[bc]	68.84	28.54	2.62	57.02	11.11	0.72	100.00	4061.37
E11[bc]	67.20	29.61	3.19	55.37	11.07	0.76	100.00	5018.59

1983–92	Industry effect (%)	Share effect (%)	Interaction effect (%)	Scale effect (%)	Weight effect (%)	Residual effect (%)	Total (%)	Net change in employment (000)
Belgium	49.79	44.44	5.77	39.29	9.49	1.01	100.00	314.60
Denmark	96.55	3.79	−0.34	77.73	17.14	1.68	100.00	135.01
Germany[b]	75.00	18.63	6.37	67.80	6.26	0.93	100.00	2169.82
Greece	51.66	35.21	13.13	44.22	7.03	0.41	100.00	145.87
Spain	—	—	—	—	—	—	—	—
France	75.30	22.82	1.88	34.03	39.90	1.36	100.00	865.46
Ireland	55.14	37.03	7.83	18.15	35.72	1.27	100.00	65.54
Luxembourg	62.93	32.90	4.17	49.87	11.46	1.61	100.00	13.26
Netherlands	68.09	23.27	8.64	56.46	8.72	2.91	100.00	964.00
Portugal	—	—	—	—	—	—	—	—
UK	75.83	22.04	2.13	50.24	23.25	2.33	100.00	1869.33
E9[bc]	74.94	21.15	3.90	55.72	17.33	1.90	100.00	6542.89
E11[bc]	—	—	—	—	—	—	—	—

Source: Special tabulations provided by Eurostat

Notes: a Industry effect + share effect + interaction effect = net change in employment where industry effect = scale effect + weight effect + residual effect

b Data for Germany and E9/11 exclude the new Länder

c E9/11 exclude Italyz

Appendix Table 3.4 Decomposition of the change in the female share of employment, 1983–92[a]

	1983–7 (percentage points)			
	Industry effect	*Share effect*	*Interaction effect*	*Net change*
Belgium	0.88	0.53	0.03	1.45
Denmark	0.52	−0.36	0.11	0.28
Germany[b]	0.39	−0.00	0.07	0.45
Greece	0.57	1.12	0.03	1.72
Spain				
France	1.14	0.16	0.02	1.31
Ireland	1.32	0.43	0.03	1.78
Luxembourg	0.64	1.25	0.06	1.94
Netherlands	0.44	2.42	0.03	2.89
Portugal				
UK	1.11	0.52	0.00	1.63
E9[bc]	0.86	0.35	0.02	1.22

	1987–92 (percentage points)			
	Industry effect	*Share effect*	*Interaction effect*	*Net change*
Belgium	0.03	3.62	−0.01	3.65
Denmark	0.42	0.39	0.08	0.89
Germany[b]	0.21	1.64	0.07	1.92
Greece	−0.25	0.56	0.26	0.57
Spain	0.42	2.63	0.08	3.13
France	0.53	0.78	−0.01	1.30
Ireland	0.93	1.98	0.13	3.03
Luxembourg	0.43	1.82	−0.13	2.12
Netherlands	1.26	2.17	0.09	3.51
Portugal	−0.40	3.21	0.62	3.42
UK	0.80	1.26	0.01	2.06
E9[bc]	0.51	1.31	0.03	1.85
E11[bc]	0.54	1.43	0.05	2.02

	1983–92 (percentage points)			
	Industry effect	*Share effect*	*Interaction effect*	*Net change*
Belgium	0.88	4.12	0.09	5.09
Denmark	0.98	0.22	−0.04	1.16
Germany[b]	0.53	1.58	0.27	2.38
Greece	0.30	1.53	0.45	2.28
Spain				
France	1.63	0.93	0.04	2.61
Ireland	2.18	2.26	0.38	4.82
Luxembourg	1.06	3.04	−0.04	4.07
Netherlands	1.71	4.57	0.13	6.40
Portugal				
UK	1.90	1.80	−0.01	3.70
E9[bc]	1.34	1.63	0.11	3.08

Source: Special tabulations provided by Eurostat

Notes: a Industry effect + share effect + interaction effect = net change in employment rate
     b Data for Germany and E9/11 exclude the new Länder
     c E9/11 exclude data for Italy

Appendix Table 3.5 Full-time and part-time contribution to changes in employment by sector, 1983–92[a]

1983–92	Full-time contribution (%)			Part-time contribution (%)			Total (%)	Absolute change (000)
	Full-time industry effect	Changing share of full-time work	Full-time interaction effect	Part-time industry effect	Changing share of part-time work	Part-time interaction effect		
Belgium	68.62	−20.48	−1.85	9.06	40.96	3.69	100.00	360.19
Denmark	80.53	12.13	3.78	35.38	−24.25	−7.56	100.00	230.26
Germany[b]	74.66	−12.15	−2.26	10.93	24.31	4.52	100.00	3811.81
Greece	107.12	10.26	1.40	4.54	−20.52	−2.80	100.00	197.48
Spain	—	—	—	—	—	—	—	—
France	41.36	−40.84	−4.58	13.22	81.69	9.17	100.00	722.95
Ireland	58.05	−31.20	−6.25	4.50	62.39	12.50	100.00	38.26
Luxembourg	91.93	−0.25	0.78	8.61	0.49	−1.57	100.00	20.07
Netherlands	54.12	−21.93	−5.81	18.14	43.87	11.62	100.00	1640.54
Portugal	—	—	—	—	—	—	—	—
UK	56.22	−18.17	−2.22	23.39	36.33	4.43	100.00	2295.09
E9[b,c]	64.84	−17.60	−2.46	15.11	35.19	4.92	100.00	9316.65
E11	—	—	—	—	—	—	—	—

1987–92	Full-time contribution (%)			Part-time contribution (%)			Total (%)	Absolute change (000)
	Full-time industry effect	Changing share of full-time work	Full-time interaction effect	Part-time industry effect	Changing share of part-time work	Part-time interaction effect		
Belgium	74.94	−16.22	−0.76	8.08	32.44	1.52	100.00	293.12
Denmark	559.94	843.86	18.67	402.59	−1687.72	−37.34	100.00	3.87
Germany[b]	72.98	−14.97	−1.74	10.31	29.95	3.48	100.00	3133.86
Greece	107.54	9.39	0.93	2.78	−18.77	−1.86	100.00	93.04
Spain	93.26	−0.10	−0.17	6.46	0.21	0.34	100.00	1139.25
France	71.40	−15.23	−0.35	13.01	30.47	0.71	100.00	658.46
Ireland	76.48	−16.42	−1.16	5.94	32.84	2.31	100.00	64.36
Luxembourg	95.29	2.37	1.07	8.15	−4.74	−2.14	100.00	10.15
Netherlands	48.35	−18.51	−1.93	31.21	37.02	3.87	100.00	762.35
Portugal	88.93	−14.22	3.05	−0.11	28.45	−6.10	100.00	206
UK	49.88	−18.17	0.00	31.95	36.34	−0.01	100.00	719.34
E9[b,c]	67.59	−15.10	−1.01	16.29	30.20	2.03	100.00	5738.55
E11[b,c]	71.32	−11.56	−0.84	16.27	23.12	1.69	100.00	7083.80

Source: Special tabulations provided by Eurostat

Notes: a Industry effect + changing shares of full/part-time work + interaction effect = net change in employment

b Data for Germany and E9/11 exclude the new Länder

c E9/11 exclude data for Italy

Appendix Table 3.6 Change in female employment, 1983–90[a]

1983-7	Occupation effect (%)	Share effect (%)	Interaction effect (%)	Scale effect (%)	Composition effect (%)	Residual effect (%)	Total (%)	Net change (000)
Belgium	50.95	46.06	3.00	28.23	22.34	0.37	100.00	69.30
Denmark	—	—	—	—	—	—	—	—
Germany[b]	—	—	—	—	—	—	—	—
Greece	34.21	63.63	2.16	32.79	1.39	0.03	100.00	87.66
Spain	—	—	—	—	—	—	—	—
France	63.31	33.65	3.05	4.90	58.31	0.10	100.00	290.55
Ireland	19.78	86.25	−6.02	−124.81	149.12	−4.53	100.00	8.34
Luxembourg	77.85	17.77	4.38	51.77	24.56	1.52	100.00	5.67
Netherlands	—	—	—	—	—	—	—	—
Portugal	—	—	—	—	—	—	—	—
UK	68.53	28.92	2.55	56.05	11.70	0.78	100.00	1117.04
E6[c]	65.56	32.20	2.24	42.51	22.33	0.72	100.00	1578.55
E10[d]	—	—	—	—	—	—	—	—

1987-90	Occupation effect (%)	Share effect (%)	Interaction effect (%)	Scale effect (%)	Composition effect (%)	Residual effect (%)	Total (%)	Net change (000)
Belgium	61.07	37.20	1.73	46.70	13.77	0.60	100.00	116.36
Denmark	—	—	—	—	—	—	—	—
Germany[b]	81.90	15.93	2.17	71.50	9.52	0.87	100.00	1333.00
Greece	56.65	37.89	5.46	54.81	1.78	0.06	100.00	76.34
Spain	64.64	30.23	5.13	59.26	4.85	0.52	100.00	615.38
France	99.87	−2.55	2.69	66.22	32.91	0.74	100.00	303.20
Ireland	65.09	34.12	0.78	64.23	0.82	0.04	100.00	25.68
Luxembourg	266.29	−155.17	−11.11	103.25	159.92	3.12	100.00	1.00
Netherlands	72.02	23.54	4.44	53.40	17.47	1.15	100.00	258.74
Portugal	63.02	31.77	5.21	67.97	−4.64	−0.31	100.00	177.17
UK	111.95	−6.76	−5.19	77.37	32.04	2.54	100.00	1079.23
E6[c]	100.86	0.85	−1.70	71.13	28.29	1.44	100.00	1601.81
E10[d]	87.18	11.76	1.07	69.63	16.41	1.14	100.00	3986.11

1983-90	Occupation effect (%)	Share effect (%)	Interaction effect (%)	Scale effect (%)	Composition effect (%)	Residual effect (%)	Total (%)	Net change (000)
Belgium	56.01	39.68	4.31	38.63	16.37	1.00	100.00	185.66
Denmark	—	—	—	—	—	—	—	—
Germany[b]	—	—	—	—	—	—	—	—
Greece	42.23	49.49	8.28	41.82	0.38	0.02	100.00	164.00
Spain	—	—	—	—	—	—	—	—
France	80.54	14.48	4.98	35.18	44.30	1.06	100.00	593.75
Ireland	51.06	45.35	3.58	15.30	35.23	0.54	100.00	34.03
Luxembourg	104.45	−7.61	3.16	58.69	42.26	3.50	100.00	6.67
Netherlands	—	—	—	—	—	—	—	—
Portugal	—	—	—	—	—	—	—	—
UK	89.07	10.86	0.08	64.75	21.12	3.19	100.00	2196.26
E6[c]	82.28	15.68	2.04	55.47	24.72	2.09	100.00	3180.37
E10[d]	—	—	—	—	—	—	—	—

Source: Special tabulations provided by Eurostat
Notes: a Occupation effect + share effect + interaction effect = net change in employment where occupation effect = scale effect + compositional effect + residual effect
b Data for Germany exclude the new Länder
c E6 data exclude Germany, Netherlands, Denmark, Italy, Portugal and Spain
d E10 data exclude Denmark, Italy and the new Länder

Appendix Table 3.7 Decomposition of the percentage point change in the female share of employment by occupation on a headcount and full-time equivalent basis[a]

Headcount basis	1983–7				1987–90				1983–90			
	Occupation effect	Share effect	Interaction effect	Change in share of employment	Occupation effect	Share effect	Interaction effect	Change in share of employmen	Occupation effect	Share effect	Interaction effect	Change in share of employment
Belgium	0.45	0.93	0.04	1.43	0.46	1.25	0.00	1.71	0.89	2.16	0.10	3.14
Denmark	—	—	—	—	—	—	—	—	—	—	—	—
Germany	—	—	—	—	0.48	0.80	0.03	1.31	—	—	—	—
Greece	0.03	1.59	0.01	1.64	0.04	0.80	0.09	0.93	0.02	2.31	0.23	2.57
Spain	0.00	0.00	0.00	0.00	0.26	1.64	0.09	2.00	—	—	—	—
France	0.79	0.46	0.04	1.29	0.47	-0.04	0.04	0.47	1.23	0.40	0.13	1.76
Ireland	1.11	0.64	-0.03	1.73	0.02	0.81	-0.02	0.81	1.07	1.38	0.09	2.54
Luxembourg	0.96	0.70	0.12	1.78	1.04	-1.01	-0.05	-0.02	1.95	-0.35	0.16	1.76
Netherlands	—	—	—	—	0.77	1.04	0.12	1.93	—	—	—	—
Portugal	—	—	—	—	-0.19	1.29	0.12	1.22	—	—	—	—
UK	0.56	1.39	0.03	1.98	1.39	-0.29	-0.19	0.91	1.99	1.02	-0.13	2.85
E6[b]	0.67	0.96	0.03	1.66	0.83	0.02	-0.05	0.81	1.49	0.94	0.04	2.47
E10[c]	—	—	—	—	0.64	0.46	0.01	1.10	—	—	—	—

Appendix Table 3.7 (Contd...)

Full-time equivalent basis	1983–7				1987–90				1983–90			
	Occupation effect	Share effect	Interaction effect	Change in share of employment	Occupation effect	Share effect	Interaction effect	Change in share of employment	Occupation effect	Share effect	Interaction effect	Change in share of employment
Belgium	0.35	0.45	0.03	0.83	0.35	1.09	–0.00	1.44	0.68	1.54	0.06	2.27
Denmark	–	–	–	–	–	–	–	–	–	–	–	–
Germany	-0.01	1.66	0.01	1.66	0.44	0.29	0.02	0.75	0.01	2.64	0.24	2.89
Greece	–	–	–	–	0.08	1.06	0.09	1.23	–	–	–	–
Spain	–	–	–	–	0.29	1.69	0.09	2.07	–	–	–	–
France	0.63	0.33	0.03	0.99	0.40	-0.08	0.03	0.36	1.02	0.24	0.08	1.34
Ireland	0.96	0.80	-0.05	1.71	-0.03	0.66	-0.02	0.61	0.87	1.40	0.04	2.31
Luxembourg	0.82	0.93	0.09	1.84	1.19	-1.12	-0.05	0.01	1.93	-0.23	0.14	1.85
Netherlands	–	–	–	–	0.60	0.92	0.09	1.62	–	–	–	–
Portugal	–	–	–	–	-0.20	1.41	0.12	1.34	–	–	–	–
UK	0.46	1.24	0.03	1.73	1.02	0.24	-0.15	1.11	1.53	1.39	-0.09	2.83
E6[b]	0.51	0.80	0.03	1.34	0.62	0.23	-0.04	0.81	1.14	0.98	0.03	2.15
E10[c]	–	–	–	–	0.51	0.44	0.01	0.97	–	–	–	–

Source: Special tabulations provided by Eurostat

Notes: a Occupation effect + share effect + interaction effect = change in share of employment

b E6 data excludes Germany, Netherlands, Denmark, Italy, Portugal and Spain

c E10 data exclude Denmark and Italy

Appendix Table 5.1 Duration of standard rate of unemployment benefits in member states (E12)

Country	Duration	Conditions
Belgium	Unlimited for claimants with responsibility for dependants 12 months for married/ cohabiting partner, plus reduced rate for six months and a flat rate thereafter	Benefits may be suspended if duration exceeds twice the regional average.
Denmark	Up to 7 years 1 year extensions for parental and educational leave	First 3 years involves participation in subsidised work/ training for 12 months; in next 4 years, eligible for minimum 12 months employment offer
Germany	6 months 12 months Up to 32 months	Requires 1 year of contributory employment Requires 2 years contributions For claimants over 42 years old; maximum duration for age over 54 with at least 5.5 years contributions
Greece	Minimum 5 months Up to 12 months	If younger than 49 years, max duration requires at least 250 working days; if older than 49 years, 210 working days are required
Spain	Minimum 120 days Up to 720 days	Minimum duration requires 360 to 539 contributory days; maximum duration requires at least 2,160 days
France	Minimum 4 months Up to 27 months	Minimum duration requires 6 months contributions in the past 12 months for any age; maximum duration requires 27 months in the past 36, and is restricted to claimants at least 55 years old
Ireland	Up to 6 months Up to 15 months Up to age 66	Claimants under 18 years old Aged 18 to 64 Aged 65 or over with at least 3 years' contributions
Italy	Up to 180 days 270 days minus number of days worked in previous year	Employment in industry and services Employment in agriculture (Also, for occasional and seasonal workers duration equals number of days worked in previous year)
Luxembourg	Minimum 12 months Extension up to additional 12 months	Extension for persons aged at least 50 years Also, up to 182 days extension for hard-to-place unemployed
Netherlands	6 months Extension up to 4.5 years	Basic benefit: 26 weeks contributions in last 52 weeks and loss of at least 5 hours per week Extended benefit: minimum extension of 3 months for 5-10 labour history; maximum duration for 40 or more years employment (see text for reform)
Portugal	Minimum 10 months Up to 30 months	Minimum duration for age less than 25 years and increases in 5 year age bands up to maximum for age over 55 years, also extensions for age over 55 up to early retirement at 60
UK	12 months	Reforms from August 1996 will reduce duration to 6 months

Sources: National reports
Notes: All details refer to the duration of the standard rate only, which refers to 'ordinary unemployment benefits' in Italy. Extended periods for reduced rates not mentioned here are available in France and a 'continuation payment' is available in the Netherlands.

Appendix Table 5.2 Calculation of replacement rates in member states for the initial period based on average gross hourly earnings and average weekly working-time of full-time manual workers in manufacturing

	Average gross hourly earnings (NACE 1–5; October 1993; national currency)		Average hours per week (1992)		Average gross weekly earnings		Formula for replacement rate; threshold levels; adult dependency allowance; year of application	Ratio of unemployment benefit to average gross earnings for a single person	
	M	F	M	F	M	F		M	F
B[a]	407	308	38.9	38.4	15,832	11,827	55% +5% for claimants with dependants; earnings threshold of BF 54,780 p.m.; 1993	44	55
DK[b]	108,64	91,76	38.6	37.4	4,193	3,432	90%; max. earnings threshold of DKR 2,927; 1993	63	77
D	n/a	n/a	n/a	n/a	n/a	n/a	60% of net wage + 7% for claimants with children 1995; earnings threshold = DM7,600 (gross) p.m.; 1994	34	32
GR	n/a	n/a	n/a	n/a	(7,443 per day)	(5,859 per day)	40% of daily wage; max. daily payment of Dr 1894; +10% of benefit for each dependant (spouse or child); 1993	25	32
E[a]	995	767	40.5	40.2	40,298	30,833	70%; payment limited to 100–170% of min. wage, or 100–220% with children; min. wage = 68285p.m.; 1993	66	70
F	52,51	42,44	40.2	39.4	2,111	1,672	The higher of (40.4 per cent + FF1,645 p.m.) or 57.4%; min. payment is FF 3,983, max. payment is 75% of wage; 1995	58	63
IRL	7.12	4.96	41.5	38.7	295.5	192.0	Flat rate of IR£55.60 p.w.; adult dependant allowance IR£35.50; child allowance IR£12.80; average pay related benefit IR£6.80; 1993	21	33
I	—	—	n/a	n/a	—	—	20%; no threshold (ordinary unemployment benefits); or 80% for wage supplementation/ turnover benefits, up to a threshold level; 1994	20	20
L	425	300	40.4	38.4	17170	11520	80 per cent + 5% for dependent children; max. payment = 2.5 x min. wage (=Fl40,300 p.m.); 1993	80	80
NL	22,07	17,18	39.2	38.8	865,14	666,58	70% of daily wage; earnings threshold = HFL 286,84 per day; 1993	70	70
P	499	363	43.3	42.3	21,607	15,355	65%; earnings threshold = 3 x min wage = 181% of average manufacturing pay	65	65
UK	6.67	4.56	44.8	39.9	298.8	181.9	Flat rate of UK£45.45 + adult dependant allowance UK£28.05; 1994	15	25

Sources: Eurostat (1994b); national reports and additional consultation; own calculations

Notes: a Earnings data are for April 1993.
b earnings data are for NACE 1-5 except 16 and 17; Denmark also excludes NACE 50

Appendix Table 5.2

Explanatory notes

The information in Appendix Table 5.2 refers only to those unemployed workers who are fully eligible to the standard rate of unemployment benefits in an initial period, the duration of which varies enormously between countries (see Table 5.4). Calculation of actual replacement rates applies the particular formula to average gross weekly earnings for manufacturing (the product of average gross hourly earnings for 1993 and average weekly hours for 1992). Also, presentation of both benefits and wages are pre- tax and therefore do not reveal the extent of differences between countries regarding the taxation of benefits.

In three countries (Germany, Greece and Italy) it is not possible to utilise Eurostat earnings data either because they are not recorded, or because they do not combine with the specific method of calculation of replacement rates. In Italy, Eurostat earnings data have not been recorded since 1985. However, as the replacement-rate formula of 20% is not subject to a maximum earnings threshold and no allowances are payable for dependants, the actual replacement rates for all workers will also be 20%, regardless of previous earnings (80% is payable to those eligible for the wage supplementation scheme in the initial period). In Germany and Greece, the specific methods of calculating replacement rates have forced us to refer to calculations based on national earnings data provided by the national experts, rather than the available comparative earnings data provided by Eurostat. In Germany, calculation of the replacement rate applies to net earnings. As Eurostat refers to gross earnings and we have not obtained tax details for 1993, the information in the Table represents the ratio of pre-tax unemployment benefits to gross income for manual workers in industry in 1992 (national data). In Greece, as the application of replacement rates and threshold levels refers to daily wages, the information shown refers to the daily average wage of manual workers in manufacturing for the first quarter of 1993, again based on national earnings data (the formula for replacement rates for non-manual workers is 50% in Greece).

Further approximations include the case of France, where calculations apply 1995 rules to 1993 earnings. Consequently, the actual replacement rates shown are slightly overestimated as they are partially derived from use of the fixed sum – FF 1,645 p.m. – which applies to 1995 earnings. Also, calculation of the replacement rates in Ireland include the average level of 'pay-related benefits' received by claimants in 1993, and calculations for the Netherlands assume a weekly earnings threshold that is five times greater than the daily threshold for which we have information.

Appendix Table 6.1 Statutory provisions for parental leave

Type of leave	Restrictions in coverage	Employment conditions	Individual or family right	Duration of leave Maximum duration	Leave period	Flexibility of leave Part-time	Fractioning[a]
Paid							
B	None, but conditional on employer's agreement	12 months' continuous service	Individual	260 weeks[b]	Throughout the whole career	Yes[c]	Yes
DK[d]	None	F leave: No I leave: 120 hours within a minimum employment period of 3 consecutive months with the employer	F family I: individual	F leave: 10 weeks I leave: 26 weeks[e]	F leave: following maternity leave I leave: up to the child's 9th birthday	F leave: no I leave: no	F leave: no I leave: yes
I	Excludes farmers, self-employed, domestic services	No	Family	26 weeks	From the 4th month after the birth to the 10th month inclusive, following maternity leave	No	No
D	None	4 weeks' gainful employment with the same employer	Family	Until the child is aged 3 years[f]	Until the child is aged 3 years	Yes[c]	Yes
F	None	12 months' continuous service	Family	Until the child is aged 3 years[f]	Until the child is aged 3 years	Yes	Yes
Part-time							
NL	None	12 months continuous service	Individual	26 weeks	Until the child's 4th birthday	Leave can be taken only on a part-time basis	No
Unpaid							
E[g]	None	No	Family	Until the child is aged 1 year[h]	Until the child is aged 1 year[h]	No	No

Appendix Table 6.1 (Contd...)

	Restrictions in coverage	Employment conditions	Individual or family right	Duration of leave		Flexibility of leave	
				Maximum duration	Leave period	Part-time	Fractioning[a]
P	None	6 months	Family	26 weeks[i]	Following maternity leave	No	No
GR	Excludes companies with 100 employees or fewer	12 months continuous service[k]	Individual	13 weeks[l]	From the end of the maternity leave until the child is aged $2\frac{1}{2}$ years	No	Yes
Unpaid and limited entitlement							
L	Only public sector	Public sector employee	Individual	52 weeks	Until the child's 4th birthday	Yes[l]	
UK	Only women	2 years with the current employer for women working 16 hours or more per week 5 years with the current employer for women working less than 8 hours per week	Mother	22 weeks	Extension of maternity leave	No	No
IRL	Only women	Conditional on employer's agreement	Mother	4 weeks	Extension of maternity leave	No	No

Appendix Table 6.1 (Contd...)
Parental leave payment

	Restrictions in coverage	Employment conditions	Type of benefit	Level of benefit — Full-time	Partial benefit available	Maximum duration
B	Excludes self-employed, unemployed and those not in the labour force	12 months with the employer	Flat-rate, conditional on replacement	20-25% average manual industrial wage	Yes	260 weeks[b]
DK	Excludes those not in the labour force	Parental (F) benefit: worked 120 hours within 13 weeks preceding leave	Flat-rate	Family: 100% UI Individual: 80% UI, falling to 60% in 1997. (UI = 65% average manual industrial wage)	No	F benefit: 10 weeks I benefit: 26 weeks[c]
I	Excludes self-employed, unemployed and those not in the labour force	None	Earnings-related	30% of earnings	No	26 weeks
D	None	None	Flat-rate, income-tested from 7th month; income-test applied to married and cohabiting couples; since 1994 high income households also excluded from payment in the first 6 months	22% average manual wage for first 6 months	No	104 weeks
F	Not available for first child	2 years of work in the last 5 years preceding leave[m]	Flat-rate	≈ 35-40% average net manual industrial wage	Yes	Until the child is aged 3 years

Sources: OECD (1995a: Tables 5.1 and 5.2); information for Luxembourg and Ireland from Rubery *et al.* (1995: appendix Table 1.8); benefit rates from CERC (1994)

Notes:
a Fractioning = the possibility of taking the leave in more than one portion over an extended period rather than taking it in one continuous period
b The duration of a 'career break' in Belgium is not directly comparable with that of parental leave in other countries as it refers to the whole career period and not to each child
c Only with employer's agreement
d The subscripts F and I stand for the shareable family leave and the individual family leave respectively
e 13 weeks if the child is over 1 year; the leave is expandable to 52 weeks with the agreement of the employer
f Including maternity leave period
g The last four weeks of paid maternity leave can be transferred to the father
h A further period of two years may be taken. From March 1995, job guarantee and security extends over the 3 full years
i Leave duration can be extended up to 2 years under special circumstances
j Employer may refuse leave if it has been claimed by more than 8% of the workforce during the year
k The other parent should also be employed
l The entitlement to work part-time may be extended until the child reaches 15 years
m Two years of work in the last ten years, for the second child onwards

Appendix Table 6.2 Publicly-funded childcare services and school weekly opening hours

	Compulsory primary school age	Pre-school services — Type of service and hours of operation	% Pre-school coverage by age — 0-3	% Pre-school coverage by age — 3-6	Primary school hours	Out-of-school care and recreation services
Denmark	7	Range of types of childcare centres open for up to 10 hours, plus pre-primary[a]	48	82	Weekly hours increase with age from 15-22 at 7 years to 20-27 for 10 year olds; may vary daily and locally, usually set within 0800-1500 range	Two-thirds attend out-of-school and holiday care services
France	6	Pre-primary from 2 years; term and hours same as primary school	23	99	0830-630, closed Wednesday	Some out-of-school, Wednesday and holiday care
Belgium	6	Pre-primary from $2\frac{1}{2}$ years; term and hours same as primary school	30	95+	0830-530, lunch break usually supervised; schools closed Wednesday afternoon	Some out of school, Wednesday and holiday care
Italy	6	Pre-primary from 3 years; open 8-10 hours, e.g. 730-1730 in state-run, others may have shorter hours	6	91	27-30 hours, schedule set by school; 6 days 0830-1300 common in South; For others 5 days with afternoon sessions on 2 days is common	Limited and mainly in urban areas
Spain	6	Pre-primary from 3 years; term and hours same as primary school; some nursery provision	< 5	84	0900-1200 and 1500-1700[b]	Very limited
Germany	6	West: Kindergarten from 3 years in term time; 3-4 hours a.m., closed for lunch, 2 hours p.m. East: full-day attendance[c]	West: 2 East: 50	W: 78 E: 100	0800-1200 or 1300 hours; hours may vary day to day	West: 5% East: 88%
Greece	6	Pre-primary from $3\frac{1}{2}$ years, 4 hours a.m. in term time; some nurseries open 0700-1600	<5	70[d]	Weekly hours increase with age from 20 at 6-8 1/2 years to 24-26 hours. Many attend in a.m. or p.m. 4-hour shifts due to shortage of school buildings	Very limited

Appendix Table 6.2 (Contd . . .)

Portugal	6	Pre-primary; term and hours same as primary school; some nurseries – open 8 hours daily	12	48	0900-1500, 1-hour lunch break usually unsupervised	10%
Luxembourg	6	Compulsory pre-primary from 4 years	6	13% for 0-2 years 49% for 2-4 years[e]	0800-1600, 2-hour lunch break usually unsupervised. schools closed on Tuesday and Thursday afternoons	No information
UK	5	Can enter primary school at 3 years on shift basis ($2\frac{1}{2}$ hours a.m. or p.m.), full-time at 4 years; limited nursery provision	2	60[f]	0900-1530 with a supervised lunch break	< 5%
Netherlands	5	Can enter primary school at 4 years; limited subsidised nursery provision, often part-time	8	71[f]	0900-1600, 2-hour lunch break; lunch break increasingly supervised; schools closed Wednesday afternoons	< 5%
Ireland	6	Can enter primary school from 3 years; limited nursery provision	2	55	4 hours 40 minutes per day until 6 years, then an extra hour per day; the half-hour lunch break is supervised	< 5%

Sources: EC Childcare Network (1990, 1996); OECD (1995b).

Notes: a In Denmark, children also start pre-primary school attendance for 3-4 hours per day at 6 years, with some starting at 5 years; most 5-6 year olds attend other childcare services as well as pre-primary school (70% in 1989)

b In Spain an increasing proportion of lunch breaks are supervised in urban pre-primary and primary schools; pre-primary is attended by nearly all 4-5 year olds, but only half of 3 year olds; places are being expanded for 3 year olds

c In West Germany there is a trend towards longer hours in some kindergartens, and in others to shorter hours of morning or afternoon shifts; unification has meant that the two previous systems are being integrated; in practice this means that the childcare system in the East is adapting pedagogical standards of the West; parental leave has been increased to 3 years, and some centres in the East have been closed; from 1999 all children will have the legal right to a kindergarten place from their 3rd birthday

d In Greece the statistics relate to the age bands 0-2 1/2 and 2.1/2-5.1/2 years; children can enter school from 5.1/2 years, and this is included in the data

e The data for Luxembourg relate to *foyers de jour conventionnés*, which are centres with which the Ministry of the Family have an agreement; statistics for other subsidised services are not available

f In the UK and the Netherlands this includes children aged 5 attending compulsory schooling

Appendix Table 6.3 Impact of employment gaps on retirement pensions in the member states (E12), 1995

Type of pension system[a]	Eligibility related to employment continuity		Relationship to earnings	Derived rights for spouse without own individual pension	
	Qualifying period	Credits for employment gaps due to child-raising[b]		Addition for dependent spouse	Survivor's pension
Basic security					
Denmark	*Folkpension*: citizenship + residency; Additional labour market pension (*ATP*): all employees aged 16+ years and employed >9 hours per week pay flat-rate hourly contribution (lower in public sector)	Largely not applicable – gaps have no direct impact on *folkpension*	*Folkpension: flat-rate*; *ATP*: *Lifetime earnings* reduced by periods of inactivity or short-hours employment, but is a smaller element of the total pension + only a minority of women interrupt (maximum value is approx. 25% of basic *Folkpension* for those employees who retired in 1994 + had contributed to scheme since it started in 1964)	Not applicable – independent pension	Not applicable - independent pension.
Netherlands	State (*AOW*): residency (50 years); Supplementary: years worked for an employer who offered this scheme	Largely not applicable – gaps have no direct impact on AOW – credits in supplementary schemes for maternity leave: parental leave credits may be negotiated in collective agreement	*AOW: flat-rate* (70% of Statutory Minimum Wage (SMW)); Supplementary: *final salary* × years contributed (70% × 2/40); Ceiling for high earners	Married/cohabiting receive a lower individual pension, i.e. 50 per cent of SMW each	Revert to flat-rate individual pension (i.e. 70% SMW)
Income security					
Belgium	Employment years (full = 45 for men, 40 for women)	1 year credit for career break, extended to 2 years when household received family allowances for child <6 years old during career break	*Final salary* × qualifying years (60% × 1/40 (1/45 for men)); Guaranteed minima set for complete contributory record	Increased earnings-related pension formula (75% instead of 60%) + higher guaranteed minima	Yes (80% of deceased's pension)
Germany	Employment years (minimum 5)	Credits for maternity + parental leave	*Lifetime earnings*: calculated as proportion of lifetime earnings (ceiling for high earners); employment history has direct + significant impact on pension	No	Yes

Appendix Table 6.3 (Contd . . .)

Spain	Employment years (10 = 50% of qualifying period, +2% for each additional year ie full record = 35 years)	Credits for maternity + parental leave	*Final salary* (last 8 years of earnings); minimum = 85% of Statutory Minimum Wage	Yes, if his/her own pension is less than the minimum	Yes
Greece	Employment years (full = 35), except for minimal agricultural pension	Credits for maternity + parental leave	Non-agricultural: *final salary* × qualifying years (80% of average gross monthly salary for months employed in last 5 years) Agricultural: *flat-rate*	+ 1.5 × daily wage of unskilled worker for dependent spouse	Yes (70% of deceased's pension)
France	Employment years (40 = full)	Credit of 2 years per child and for maternity leave	*Lifetime earnings:* best 25 years	No	Yes
Italy[c]	Employment years (40 = full) Contribution threshold to retire earlier with full pension (estimated 14-15 years full-time employment on average salary)	Credits for maternity + parental leave. +170 days contributory credits for absences to raise child under 6 years: additional credits of up to 2 years for disabled dependants over 6 years; 4 months reduction in pension age for each of first 3 children	*Lifetime earnings*	No	Yes
Luxembourg	Employment years (40 = full)	Credits for maternity + parental leave; credits for periods of non-employment when child is under 6 years	*Lifetime earnings*, within fixed range of a reference amount (MR)	Yes (minimum 73% of MR)	Yes, but reduced by 30% if earn >150% of MR
Portugal	Employment years (15 = full)	Credits for maternity + parental leave	*Lifetime earnings:* best 10 years in previous 15	Yes, providing spouse's own income does not exceed the joint pension	Yes (60% of the deceased's pension, also paid to cohabiting partners)
Residual Ireland	Employment years (40 = full)	Credits for raising child until 12 years old (pre-1995 was for children under 6 years old)	*Flat-rate* (reduced for those with incomplete contributory record)	Yes, providing spouse's own income does not exceed a threshold	Yes
UK	Employment years (44 for men, 39 for women)	Credits for raising child until 16 years old providing earnings do not exceed a part-time threshold	*Flat-rate basic* (reduced for those with incomplete contributory record) + earnings-related addition based on lifetime earnings	Yes	Yes

Sources: National reports plus personal communication from the authors of the national reports; CEC (1993b)
Notes: a Typology developed by Ginn and Arber (1994)
   b All countries with qualifying periods for a pension provide credits for interruptions due to unemployment, sickness, disability, military service
   c Details refer to the recent pension reforms

Appendix Table 7.1 Unemployment rates by gender, 1985–94

All (%)	1985	1990	1991	1992	1993	1994
Spain	21.7	16.2	16.4	18.5	22.8	24.1
Finland	6.3	3.4	7.6	13.1	17.9	18.4
Ireland	16.9	13.4	14.8	15.4	15.7	15.2
France	10.2	9.0	9.5	10.5	11.8	12.6
Italy	8.1	8.3	8.3	8.8	10.3	11.3
Denmark	7.1	7.7	8.4	9.2	10.5	10.3
Belgium	10.3	6.7	6.6	7.3	8.9	10.1
Sweden	3.0	1.8	3.3	5.8	9.5	9.8
UK	11.5	7.1	8.7	10.0	10.1	9.3
Greece	7.0	6.4	7.0	7.9	8.6	8.9
Germany			5.6	6.6	7.9	8.4
Germany (W)[a]	7.2	4.8	4.2			
Netherlands	8.4	6.2	5.8	5.6	6.6	7.0
Portugal	8.7	4.6	4.0	4.2	5.7	7.0
Austria	4.4	3.6	3.8	3.3	3.9	4.0
Luxembourg	2.9	1.7	1.7	2.1	2.6	3.5
E15[b]	9.8	7.6	8.2	9.2	10.7	11.1

Women (%)	1985	1990	1991	1992	1993	1994
Spain	25.1	24.1	23.9	25.6	29.3	31.4
Finland	6.1	2.8	5.7	10.5	15.7	16.7
Ireland	18.5	14.6	15.9	16.0	16.2	15.8
Italy	13.0	12.8	12.6	13.1	14.8	15.7
France	12.6	11.9	12.2	13.0	13.9	14.7
Greece	10.6	10.8	11.8	13.0	13.6	13.7
Belgium	16.7	10.6	10.0	10.2	11.8	13.0
Denmark	8.6	8.4	9.5	10.1	11.1	11.1
Germany			7.0	8.5	9.7	10.1
Germany (W)[a]	8.7	5.9	4.9			
Sweden	2.9	1.8	2.9	4.7	7.7	8.2
Netherlands	10.8	9.1	8.4	7.6	7.9	8.2
Portugal	11.7	6.3	5.4	5.0	6.8	8.1
UK	11.0	6.6	7.4	7.4	7.6	7.1
Luxembourg	4.4	2.5	2.3	2.8	3.3	4.0
Austria	3.8	3.6	3.7	3.3	3.7	
E15[b]	11.6	9.7	10.0	10.8	12.2	12.8

Men (%)	1985	1990	1991	1992	1993	1994
Finland	6.5	4.0	9.3	15.5	19.9	19.9
Spain	20.2	11.9	12.3	14.5	19.1	19.7
Ireland	16.1	12.8	14.2	15.1	15.4	14.8
Sweden	3.1	1.8	3.6	6.9	11.1	11.2
UK	11.8	7.4	9.8	12.0	12.1	10.9
France	8.3	6.8	7.4	8.4	10.1	10.8
Denmark	5.8	7.0	7.5	8.3	10.0	9.7
Italy	5.5	5.7	5.9	6.4	7.8	8.7
Belgium	6.5	4.1	4.3	5.3	6.9	8.0
Germany	–	–	4.6	5.2	6.6	7.1
Germany (W)[a]	6.2	4.0	3.7	–	–	–
Netherlands	7.0	4.3	4.1	4.3	5.6	6.3
Portugal	6.6	3.3	2.8	3.6	4.8	6.1
Greece	5.0	3.9	4.4	5.0	5.7	6.0
Luxembourg	2.2	1.2	1.3	1.7	2.3	3.2
Austria	4.8	3.6	3.9	3.2	4.1	
E15[b]	8.7	6.1	6.9	8.1	9.7	10.0

Source: CEC (1995a: Annex, 187–202)

Notes
a Data exclude the new Länder
b Data include the new Länder

Appendix Table 7.2 Youth unemployment rates by gender, 1985–94

All (%)	1985	1990	1991	1992	1993	1994
Belgium	23.0	15.3	14.9	16.2	21.8	24.1
Denmark	11.1	11.3	11.6	12.7	14.3	13.4
Germany			5.9	6.4	7.8	7.9
Germany (W)[a]	10.3	4.5	4.0			
Greece	21.9	21.5	22.9	25.2	26.8	27.7
Spain	47.8	32.3	31.1	34.6	43.4	45.0
France	25.5	19.5	21.4	23.5	27.5	29.5
Ireland	24.2	19.4	22.4	24.4	25.4	24.0
Italy	28.6	25.7	25.2	27.3	30.6	32.1
Luxembourg	6.7	3.9	3.2	4.0	5.1	6.5
Netherlands	13.2	8.6	8.3	8.5	11.1	10.7
Austria	5.3	4.4	3.2	3.7	3.5	
Portugal	20.0	10.0	8.8	10.1	12.9	15.2
Finland	9.7	6.7	14.5	25.2	33.3	33.6
Sweden	7.1	4.5	7.8	13.6	22.6	22.6
UK	18.5	10.8	14.0	15.3	15.9	14.7
E15[b]	21.8	15.4	15.9	17.7	20.8	21.2

Women (%)	1985	1990	1991	1992	1993	1994
Belgium	29.4	19.9	18.0	18.2	23.0	25.8
Denmark	12.5	11.5	12.2	13.2	14.7	14.0
Germany			6.3	7.0	8.1	8.2
Germany (W)[a]	11.2	4.7	4.0			
Greece	29.4	29.9	31.3	34.3	36.1	36.9
Spain	51.0	39.7	37.9	40.6	47.6	50.1
France	28.9	23.2	24.9	26.9	29.8	31.9
Ireland	22.7	18.2	20.9	22.8	23.4	22.3
Italy	34.6	30.8	29.4	31.8	35.3	36.3
Luxembourg	7.1	4.6	3.1	3.7	5.7	7.4
Netherlands	13.5	9.6	9.1	8.6	10.2	9.5
Austria	4.8	4.2	3.0	3.0	2.9	
Portugal	24.6	11.9	11.1	11.3	15.3	17.1
Finland	8.9	5.2	11.1	20.9	29.2	29.9
Sweden	6.8	4.5	7.1	11.1	19.0	19.8
UK	17.0	9.6	11.4	11.2	12.0	11.4
E15[b]	23.3	17.3	17.2	18.6	21.3	21.9

Men (%)	1985	1990	1991	1992	1993	1994
Belgium	16.9	11.0	11.9	14.3	20.7	22.6
Denmark	10.0	11.2	11.0	12.2	13.8	12.7
Germany			5.4	5.8	7.5	7.7
Germany (W)[a]	9.5	4.3	3.9			
Greece	15.9	14.4	16.0	17.4	18.9	19.7
Spain	45.6	26.2	25.7	29.9	40.0	40.9
France	22.3	16.0	18.1	20.2	25.3	27.2
Ireland	25.5	20.4	23.7	25.8	27.0	25.4
Italy	23.7	21.5	21.8	23.7	26.8	28.8
Luxembourg	6.4	3.2	3.3	4.2	4.7	5.6
Netherlands	13.0	7.5	7.4	8.5	11.9	11.9
Austria	5.8	4.5	3.3	4.3	3.9	
Portugal	16.3	8.4	6.8	9.1	10.8	13.7
Finland	10.5	8.2	17.7	29.2	36.9	36.9
Sweden	7.4	4.6	8.5	16.0	26.0	25.3
UK	19.7	11.9	16.3	18.7	19.2	17.4
E15[b]	20.5	13.7	14.8	16.9	20.3	20.5

Source: CEC (1995a: Annex, 187–202)
Notes: a Data exclude the new Länder
b Data include the new Länder

NOTES

2 THE FEMALE CONTRIBUTION TO THE EVOLUTION OF THE EUROPEAN EMPLOYMENT RATE

1 With the employment rate measured here as persons in employment divided by the working age-population.
2 Some of this change and the 5 per cent fall in male unemployment must be accounted for by the changes to the labour force survey in the Netherlands.

3 WOMEN'S EMPLOYMENT RATES AND STRUCTURAL AND REGIONAL CHANGE

1 Women's umemployment is higher than the men's in one out of three regions in Belgium, two out of seven regions in Spain, two out of eight regions in France, one out of three regions in Portugal and three out of eleven regions in Italy, all in the South. In France, Portugal and Italy, the specified regions include those with the highest unemployment rates.
2 Closer examination by member state reveals that large structural shifts in women's favour were particularly evident in France, in the first part of the period (1983–7), where the weight effect accounted for 79 per cent of the total female employment change. In Ireland, the weight effect was even more important accounting for no less than 134 per cent of the female employment change but this had less impact on the E9 rate. In both cases it was the change in composition towards other services that increased employment for women at the same time as men faced declines in agriculture in both countries and in metal manufacture in France and construction work in Ireland.
3 The analysis of occupational change also covers a different time period from that of industrial change.

4 UNEMPLOYMENT, GENDER AND LABOUR MARKET ORGANISATION

1. A majority of school leavers in Germany enter an apprenticeship, often known as the dual training system, which involves work experience, training and part-time education. Fewer young people thus fail to obtain any employment experience before falling into employment.
2. In principle further data are collected from the LFS which should enable us to identify the form of inactivity that has increased over recent years; in practice most of the increase in inactivity for both women and men is concentrated in the inactive 'not stated' category or for women also in the inactivity 'other' category. These together with the 'no answer' category account for about 27 per cent of the

327

female unemployed compared to a total of 29 per cent moving into inactivity and for over 16 per cent of the male unemployed compared to a total of 20 per cent moving into inactivity. The shares moving into retirement, full-time education and into disability have also risen but these account for a very small share of all the flows into inactivity for both men and women. However, the important role of disability benefits in the Netherlands for both men and women does show up in the data; 14.6 per cent of male unemployed and 7.8 per cent of female unemployed became disabled between 1991 and 1992.

3. Note that in Italy those with education levels 6/7 still face the highest unemployment rates in the age category 25–29 and national data in fact give high unemployment rates only for university graduates in this age range (Bettio and Mazzotta, 1995: Table A10); and in Spain the unemployment rates for the higher educated in this age range are still significant, but in Portugal the 25 to 29 year olds with higher education have unemployment rates significantly below average.

5 STATE POLICIES AND WOMEN'S EMPLOYMENT AND UNEMPLOYMENT RATES

1 According to the current exchange rate, the Irish currency is approximately equivalent to British sterling, so IR£45 represents a significantly higher figure than UK£10.

2 This problem is also true of 'job-search' models which argue that higher levels of benefits and longer periods of duration combine to raise the reservation wage of unemployed workers, which in turn acts to reduce the incentives for comprehensive job search. This problem has been addressed above in relation to the impact of the social security system on the labour market participation of persons seeking part-time work.

3 A comparison of actual replacement rates for different lengths of periods in unemployment can be found in OECD (1991: Annex 7.B), OECD (1994b: Table 8.1) and Reissert and Schmid (1994: 101–103). As the spell of unemployment increases, differences in replacement rates between married claimants with a working spouse and those with a dependent spouse become more pronounced. This reflects the impact of means-tested unemployment assistance schemes which continue to compensate married persons with a dependent spouse, as well as single persons, albeit at a lower level than during the initial period.

4 Calculations for the UK refer to New Earnings Survey data for 1994. An approximation is made for Germany as the figure of DM560 applies to 1994 and earnings information was obtained only for 1992.

5 Two earnings thresholds exist in Germany: the lower for the payment of health and pension insurance and the higher for the payment of unemployment insurance (Maier and Rapp 1995). In Ireland, the state, as employer, pays 2.01 per cent for each civil servant on gross earnings up to IR£25,800 and 2.35 per cent for public servants on all earnings (Barry 1995).

6 Exact figures are unattainable as UK national earnings data only provides information for certain income thresholds: 14.1 per cent of males working full-time in manufacturing earn at least UK£400 per week and 6.6 per cent earn at least UK£470 per week. It is reasonable to assume, therefore, that approximately 10 per cent earn at least UK£430 per week (New Earnings Survey 1994: Part C).

6 HOUSEHOLD ORGANISATION, STATE POLICY AND WOMEN'S EMPLOYMENT RATES

1 Property and investment income are excluded from the analysis.

2 The tax treatment of spouses in family businesses is particularly important where this form of activity is common, such as in Italy and Greece. Both countries tax employees individually, but the treatment of family businesses differs. In Greece the total revenue is assessed as the man's earnings (Meulders 1986), while in Italy part of the income from the business is treated as belonging to the married women. The portion is 50 per cent when the business is declared as a married partners' enterprise ('*impresa conjugale*') or proportionate to her share of the work as formally specified in the deed of partnership for a family business ('*impresa familiare*') (Bettio and Mazzota 1995).

3 Additions for dependent children are paid in seven countries (Germany, Luxembourg, Greece, Spain, Italy, Ireland and the UK) and for elderly parents in Spain and Italy.

4 The UK and Irish currency exchange rate is virtually pound for punt.

5 While a severely reduced access to means-tested social assistance means that women are dependent upon other family members for support the state does of course provide an important safety net for low income households. The lack of a general system of guaranteed minimum social assistance in the Southern countries means that women are also forced to rely upon family members, but without any state guarantee that the household income will be maintained at a certain level.

7 THE NEW MEMBER STATES

1 Except where otherwise stated, this chapter draws its information from the national reports on the new member states, by Löfström (1995), Pastner (1995) and Ilmakunnas (1995). These reports were commissioned and completed after the work on the synthesis report for the twelve member states had already been carried out. This chapter follows the outline of the main report, but is not able to provide comparable data as the new member states are not included in the European Labour Force Survey for the relevant years.

2 For this discussion on employment rates we rely largely on the data provided by *Employment in Europe 1995* (CEC 1995a) covering all fifteen member states. These data are compiled in a different way from the Labour Force Survey as employment data are taken from national accounts and not the Labour Force Survey. Thus the employment rates referred to for the twelve member states may differ from those referred to in Chapters 1 and 2.

3 Luxembourg is excluded as the data on employment are drawn from national accounts and relate to employment within the country. This includes the work of many transborder commuters who are not resident in Luxembourg, but the employment rate is calculated by dividing employment by the resident working age population; this procedure gives rise to a very high employment rate in Luxembourg. Of course the employment rates of surrounding countries are reduced by the exclusion of transborder workers, and thus for the calculation of the overall E15 employment rate Luxembourg should be included, but the data give a misleading impression of the employment rate level within the Luxembourg population.

4 Or joint third with the UK, dependent upon the data used.

5 This study examined the period 1983 to 1992, with 1992 the latest data available when the study was undertaken in 1995; the section on the new member states was added in 1996 when more up- to-date information was available.

6 These data calculated by *Employment in Europe* give a lower employment rate than national Labour Force Survey data, but the latter gives a consistent picture of decline in employment rates, albeit with the start and end points at a higher level – see Table 6.1.2.

7 Under the dual training system most school leavers enter workplace-based apprenticeships and continue with part-time education.

8 This extra 180 days non-means-tested benefit is available only for those who fulfil certain employment history criteria.

9 In Austria some higher paid workers, most of them men, would also receive a lower replacement rate due to the setting of a maximum earnings level for the replacement formula.

10 From 1995 30 days of leave are reserved solely for men.

11 The leave has in fact since been cut to eighteen months with a further six months available only to fathers.

REFERENCES

Alwin, D.F., Braun, M. and Scott, J. (1992) 'The separation of work and the family: attitudes towards women's labour force participation in Germany, Great Britain, and the United States', *European Sociological Review* 8, 1: 13–37.

Barry, U. (in collaboration with A. O'Connor) (1995) *Women and the Employment Rate in Ireland: The Causes and Effects of Variations in Patterns of Female Participation and Employment*. Report for the European Commission. Working Paper, EC Network on the Situation of Women in the Labour Market: Manchester School of Management, UMIST.

Becker, G. (1981) *A Treatise on the Family*. Cambridge, Mass.: Harvard University Press.

Bercusson, B. (1994) *Working Time in Britain: Towards a European Model. Part 1: The European Union Directive*. London: Institute of Employment Rights.

Bettio, F. and Mazzotta, F. (1995) *Women and the Employment Rate in Italy: The Causes and Effects of Variations in Patterns of Female Participation and Employment*. Report for the European Commission. Working Paper, EC Network on the Situation of Women in the Labour Market: Manchester School of Management, UMIST.

Bettio, F. and Villa, P. (1993) 'Family structures and labour markets in the developed countries: the emergence of a Mediterranean route to the integration of women into the labour market'. Published in Italian: 'Strutture familiari e mercati del lavoro nei paesi sviluppati. L'emergere di un percorso mediterraneo per l'integrazione delle donne nel mercato del lavaro', *Economia e Lavoro* 2: 3–30.

Bettio, F. and Villa, P. (1994) *Changing Patterns of Work and Working-Time for Men and Women*. Report for the European Commission. Working Paper, EC Network of Experts on the Situation of Women in the Labour Market: Manchester School of Management, UMIST.

Beveridge, W. H. (1944) *Report on Full Employment in a Free Society*. White Paper. London: HMSO.

Blood, R. (1963) 'The husband and wife relationship', in F. Nye and L. Hoffman (eds) *The Employed Mother in America*. Chicago: Rand McNally.

Blood, R. and Hamblin, R. (1958) 'The effects of the wife's employment on the family power structure', *Social Forces* 36: 347–352.

Blood, R. and Wolfe, D. (1960) *Husbands and Wives: The Dynamics of Married Living*. New York: Free Press.

Boje, T. (1994) *Changing Patterns of Work and Working-Time for Men and Women in Denmark: Towards the Integration or the Segmentation of the Labour Market*.

Report for the European Commission. Working Paper, EC Network of Experts on the Situation of Women in the Labour Market: Manchester School of Management, UMIST. UK.

Boje, T. (1995) *Women and the Employment Rate in Denmark: The Causes and Effects of Variations in Patterns of Female Participation and Employment.* Report for the European Commission. Working Paper, EC Network on the Situation of Women in the Labour Market: Manchester School of Management, UMIST.

Bosch, G., Dawkins, P. and Michon, F. (1994) *Times are Changing. Working Time in 14 Industrialised Countries.* Geneva: ILO.

Bradshaw, J., Ditch, J., Holmes, H. and Whiteford, P. (1993) *Support for Children: A Comparison of Arrangements in 15 Countries.* London: HMSO.

Braithwaite, M. (1994) *The Economic Role and Situation of Women in Rural Areas.* Luxembourg: Green Europe, Office for Official Publications of the European Communities.

Brannen, J. and Wilson, G. (1987) *Give and Take in Families: Studies in Resource Distribution.* London: Unwin Hyman.

Cavouriaris, M., Karamessini, K. and Symeonidou, H. (1995) *Women and the Employment Rate in Greece: The Causes and Effects of Variations in Patterns of Female Participation and Employment.* Report for the European Commission. Working Paper, EC Network on the Situation of Women in the Labour Market: Manchester School of Management, UMIST.

CEC (Commission of the European Communities) (1992a) *Women in the European Community.* Luxembourg: Office for Official Publications of the European Community.

CEC (Commission of the European Communities) (1992b) *Employment in Europe.* Luxembourg: Office for Official Publications of the European Community

CEC (Commission of the European Communities) (1993a) *Growth, Competitiveness, Employment: The Challenges and Ways Forward into the 21st Century: White Paper.* Luxembourg: Office for Official Publications of the European Community.

CEC (Commission of the European Communities) (1993b) *Social Protection in Europe.* Luxembourg: Office for Official Publications of the European Community.

CEC (Commission of the European Communities) (1994) *Employment in Europe.* Luxembourg: Office for Official Publications of the European Community

CEC (Commission of the European Communities) (1995a) *Employment in Europe.* Luxembourg: Office for Official Publications of the European Community

CEC (Commission of the European Communities) (1995b) *The Demographic Situation in the European Union.* DGV COM/94/595. Luxembourg: Office for Official Publications of the European Community.

CEC (Commission of the European Communities) (1996) *Incorporating Equal Opportunities for Women and Men into all Community Policies and Activities.* Com ((96)67.

CERC (Centre d'etudes de revenue et de coûts) (1994) *Social Welfare and Economic Activity of Women in Europe.* V/2184/94–EN. Brussels: European Commission.

Chassard, Y. (1992) 'The convergence of social protection objectives and policies. A new approach', in CEC (Commission of the European Communities) *The Convergence of Social Protection Objectives and Policies.* Luxembourg: Office for Official Publications of the European Community.

Connell, R. W. (1987) *Gender and Power.* Cambridge: Polity Press.

332

Davies, B. and Ward, S. (1992) *Women and Personal Pensions*. Equal Opportunities Commission Research Series. London: HMSO.

Davies, H. and Joshi, H. (1995) 'Social and family security in the redress of equal opportunities', in J. Humphries and J. Rubery (eds) *The Economics of Equal Opportunities*. Manchester: Equal Opportunities Commission.

Davies, R., Elias, P. and Penn, R. (1994) 'The relationship between a husband's unemployment and his wife's participation in the labour market', in D. Gallie, C. Marsh and C. Vogler (eds) *Social Change and the Experience of Unemployment*. Oxford: Oxford University Press.

Dex, S. (1988) *Women's Attitudes towards Work*. London: Macmillan.

Dex, S., Walters, P. and Alden, D. (1993) *French and British Mothers at Work*. London: Macmillan.

Dreze, J. H. and Malinvaud, E. (1994) 'Growth and employment: the scope for a European initiative', *European Economy* 1: 77– 106.

Duncan, A., Giles, C. and Webb, S. (1994) *Social Security Reform and Women's Independent Incomes*. Research Discussion Series no. 6. Manchester: Equal Opportunities Commission.

Duncan, S. (1995) 'Theorising European gender systems', *Journal of European Social Policy* 5, 4: 263–284.

EC Childcare Network (1990) 'Childcare in the European Communities 1985–90', *Women of Europe Supplement* no. 31, DGX. Brussels: European Commission.

EC Childcare Network (1993) 'Mothers, fathers and employment 1985–1991'. Equal Opportunities Unit, DGV. V/5787/93–EN. Brussels: European Commission.

EC Childcare Network (1994) 'Leave arrangements for workers with children: a review of leave arrangements in the Member States of the European Community and Austria, Finland, Norway and Sweden'. Equal Opportunities Unit, DGV. Brussels: European Commission.

EC Childcare Network (1996) 'A review of services for young children in the European Union 1990–1995'. Equal Opportunities Unit, DGV. Brussels: European Commission.

EOC (Equal Opportunities Commission) (1996) *Briefing on Mainstreaming*. Manchester: Equal Opportunities Commission.

Esping-Andersen, G. (1990) *The Three Worlds of Welfare Capitalism*. London: Polity Press.

Esping-Andersen, G. (1995) 'Europe's welfare states at the end of the century: frozen Fordism or postindustrial adaptation?' Paper presented at the 17th Conference of the International Working Party on Labour Market Segmentation. University of Siena, July.

Eurostat (1988) *Labour Force Survey – Methods and Definitions*. Luxembourg: Office for Official Publications of the European Communities.

Eurostat (1992) *Labour Force Survey – Methods and Definitions*. Luxembourg: Office for Official Publications of the European Communities.

Eurostat (1993a) *Unemployed Women in the EC*. Luxembourg: Office for Official Publications of the European Communities.

Eurostat (1993b) *Old Age Replacement Ratios – Volume 1*. Luxembourg: Office for Official Publications of the European Communities.

Eurostat (1993c) *Labour Force Survey – Results 1991*. Luxembourg: Office for Official Publications of the European Communities.

Eurostat (1994a) *Demographic Statistics*. Luxembourg: Office for Official Publications of the European Communities.

Eurostat (1994b) *Earnings: Industry and Services*. Luxembourg: Office for Official Publications of the European Communities.

Eurostat (1994c) *Labour Force Survey – Results 1992*. Luxembourg: Office for Official Publications of the European Communities.

Eurostat (1995a) *Labour Force Survey – Results 1993*. Luxembourg: Office for Official Publications of the European Communities.

Eurostat (1995b) *Labour Force Survey – Principal Results 1994*. Luxembourg: Office for Official Publications of the European Communities.

Fagan, C. (1996) 'Gendered time schedules: paid work in Great Britain', *Social Politics* 3, 1: 72–106.

Fagan, C. and Rubery, J. (1996a) 'The salience of the part-time divide in the European Union', *European Sociological Review* 12, 3: 227–250.

Fagan, C. and Rubery, J. (1996b) 'Transitions between family formation and paid employment in the European Union', in G. Schmid, J. O'Reilly and K. Schöman (eds) *International Handbook of Labour Market Policy and Policy Evaluation*. Cheltenham, UK: Edward Elgar.

Freeman, R. (1995) 'Are your wages set in Beijing?', *Journal of Economic Perspectives* 9, 3: 15–32.

Freyssinet, J. (1984) *Le Chômage*. Collection 'Repères' no. 22. Paris: La Découverte.

Gauvin, A., Granie, C. and Silvera, R. (1994) *The Evolution of Employment Forms and Working Time among Men and Women in France: Towards the Integration or the Segmentation of the Labour Market*. Report for the European Commission. Working Paper, EC Network of Experts on the Situation of Women in the Labour Market: Manchester School of Management, UMIST.

General Household Survey (1992) London: HMSO.

Gershuny, J., Godwin, M. and Jones, S. (1994) 'The domestic labour revolution: a process of lagged adaptation', in M. Anderson, F. Bechhofer and J. Gershuny (eds) *The Social and Political Economy of the Household*. Social Change and Economic Life Initiative, Oxford: Oxford University Press.

Ginn, J. and Arber, S. (1994) 'Gender and pensions in Europe: current trends in women's pension acquisition', in P. Brown and R. Crompton (eds) *A New Europe? Economic Restructuring and Social Exclusion*. Canterbury: UCL Press.

Gonäs, L. and Spant, A. (1996) *Trends and Prospects for Women's Employment in the 1990s in Sweden*. Report for the European Commission. Working Paper, EC Network on the Situation of Women in the Labour Market: Manchester School of Management, UMIST.

González, P. and Castro, A. (1995) 'The Portuguese labour market: did European integration make a difference?' Paper presented at the 17th Conference of the International Working Party on Labour Market Segmentation. University of Siena, July.

Green, F. (1991) 'Sex discrimination in job-related training', *British Journal of Industrial Relations* 29, 2: 295–304.

Gregg, P. and Wadsworth, J. (1995) 'Gender, households and access to employment', in J. Humphries and J. Rubery (eds) *The Economics of Equal Opportunities*. Manchester: Equal Opportunities Commission.

Gregson, N. and Lowe, M. (1994) *Servicing the Middle Classes: Class, Gender and Waged Domestic Labour in Contemporary Britain*. London: Routledge.

Gustafsson, S. (1996) 'Tax regimes and labour market performance', in G. Schmid, J. O'Reilly and K. Schöman (eds) *International Handbook of Labour Market Policy and Policy Evaluation.* Cheltenham, UK: Edward Elgar.

Hakim, C. (1991) 'Grateful slaves and self-made women: fact and fantasy in women's work orientations', *European Sociological Review* 7, 2: 101–121.

Hantrais, L. (1994) 'Comparing family policy in Britain, France and Germany', *Journal of Social Policy* 23, 2: 135–160.

Hewitt, P. (1993) *About Time: The Revolution in Work and Family Life.* London: Institute for Public Policy Research/Rivers Oram Press.

Hirdmann, Y. (1988) 'Genussystemet – reflexioner kring kvinnors sociala under-ordning', *Kvinnovetenskaplig Tidskrift* 3: 49– 63.

Hirdmann, Y. (1990) 'Genussystemet', in Statens Offentliga Utredningar (SOU), *Demokrati och Makt I Sverige.* Stockholm: SOU.

Hochschild, A. (1990) *The Second Shift.* London: Piatkus.

Holtermann, S. (1995) 'The costs and benefits to British employers of measures to promote equality of opportunity', in J. Humphries and J. Rubery (eds) *The Economics of Equal Opportunities.* Manchester: Equal Opportunities Commission.

Horrell, S. (1991) 'Working-wife households: inside and outside the home'. unpublished Ph.D. dissertation, University of Cambridge.

Horrell, S. (1994) 'Household time allocation and women's labour force participation', in M. Anderson, F. Bechhofer and J. Gershuny (eds) *The Social and Political Economy of the Household.* Oxford: Oxford University Press.

Horrell, S. and Rubery, J. (1991) *Employers' Working-time Policies and Women's Employment.* Equal Opportunities Commission Research Series. London: HMSO.

Humphries, J. and Rubery, J. (1984) 'The reconstitution of the supply side of the labour market: the relative autonomy of social reproduction', *Cambridge Journal of Economics* 8, 4: 331– 346.

Ilmakunnas, S. (1995) *Women and the European Employment Rate: The Causes and Consequences of Variations in Female Activity and Employment Patterns in Finland* Report for the European Commission. Working Paper, EC Network on the Situation of Women in the Labour Market: Manchester School of Management, UMIST.

Industrial Relations Services (IRS) (1991) 'Working-time in Europe', *European Industrial Relations Review*, no. 5. London: IRS.

Jonung, C. and Persson, I. (1993) 'Women and market work: the misleading tale of participation rates in international comparisons', *Work, Employment and Society* 7, 2: 259–274.

Keinänen, P. (1996) *Trends and Prospects for Women's Employment in the 1990s in Finland.* Report for the European Commission. Working Paper, EC Network on the Situation of Women in the Labour Market: Manchester School of Management, UMIST.

Kiernan, K. (1992) 'The role of men and women in tomorrow's Europe', *Employment Gazette* October: 491–500.

Killingsworth, M. (1983) *Labour Supply.* Cambridge: Cambridge University Press.

Lane, C. (1993) 'Gender and the labour market in Europe: Britain, Germany and France compared', *Sociological Review* 41, 2: 274–301.

Lewis, J. (1992) 'Gender and the development of welfare regimes', *Journal of European Social Policy* 2, 3: 159–173.

REFERENCES

Löfström, A. (1995) *Women and the European Employment Rate: The Causes and Consequences of Variations in Female Activity and Employment Patterns in Sweden.* Report for the European Commission. Working Paper, EC Network on the Situation of Women in the Labour Market: Manchester School of Management, UMIST.

Lopes, M. Chagas and Perista, H. (1995) *Women and the Employment Rate in Portugal: The Causes and Effects of Variations in Patterns of Female Participation and Employment.* Report for the European Commission. Working Paper, EC Network on the Situation of Women in the Labour Market: Manchester School of Management, UMIST.

Machin, S. and Waldfogel, J. (1994) 'The decline of the male breadwinner: changing shares of husbands' and wives' earnings in family income', Discussion paper WSP/103, Welfare State Programme. Suntory-Toyota International Centre for Economics and Related Disciplines, London School of Economics.

McLaughlin, E. (1995) 'Towards an egalitarian welfare state', in J. Humphries and J. Rubery (eds) *The Economics of Equal Opportunities.* Manchester: Equal Opportunities Commission.

McRae, S. (1991) *Maternity Rights in Britain: The Experience of Women and Employers.* London: Policy Studies Institute.

Maier, F. (1992) *The Regulation of Part-time Work: A Comparative Study of Six EC Countries.* Report prepared for the Commission of the European Communities (DGV), WZB (Labour Market and Employment) Discussion Paper.

Maier, F. (1994) 'Institutional regimes of part-time working', in G. Schmid (ed.) *Labour Market Institutions in Europe.* New York: M.E. Sharpe.

Maier, F. (1995) 'Wage and non-wage labour costs, social security and public funds to combat unemployment', in *Follow-up to the White Paper on Growth, Competitiveness and Employment: Equal Opportunities for Women and Men.* Report to the European Commission's Employment Task Force (DGV), February 1995, V/5538/95–EN. Brussels: European Commission.

Maier, F. and Rapp Z. (in collaboration with C. Johnson) (1995) *Women and the Employment Rate: The Causes and Consequences of Variations in Patterns of Female Activity and Employment Patterns in Germany.* Report for the European Commission. Working Paper, EC Network on the Situation of Women in the Labour Market: Manchester School of Management, UMIST.

Maier, F., Quack, S. and Rapp, Z. (1994) *Changing Patterns of Work and Working-Time for Men and Women in Germany: Towards the Integration or the Segmentation of the Labour Market.* Report for the European Commission. Working Paper, EC Network of Experts on the Situation of Women in the Labour Market: Manchester School of Management, UMIST.

Marsh, A. and McKay, S. (1993) 'Families, work and the use of childcare', *Employment Gazette* August: 361–370.

Marsh, C. (1991) *Hours of Work of Women and Men in Britain.* EOC Research Series. London: HMSO.

Maruani, M. (1995) 'Inequalities and flexibility', in *Follow-up to the White Paper on Growth, Competitiveness and Employment: Equal Opportunities for Women and Men.* Report to the European Commission's Employment Task Force (DGV), V/5538/95–EN. Brussels: European Commission.

Maurice, M., Sellier, F. and Silvestre, J.J. (1986) *The Social Foundations of Industrial Power.* Cambridge, Mass.: MIT Press.

Meulders, D. (1986) *Income Tax in the European Community*. London: Institute for Fiscal Studies.

Meulders, D. (in collaboration with C. Hecq and R. Ruz Torres) (1994) *Changing Patterns of Work and Working-time for Men and Women in Belgium: Towards the Integration or the Segmentation of the Labour Market*. Report for the European Commission. Working Paper, EC Network on the Situation of Women in the Labour Market: Manchester School of Management, UMIST.

Meulders, D. (in collaboration with C. Hecq and R. Ruz Torres) (1995) *Women and the European Employment Rate in Belgium: The Causes and Effects of Variations in Female Activity and Employment Patterns*. Report for the European Commission. Working Paper, EC Network on the Situation of Women in the Labour Market: Manchester School of Management, UMIST.

Moltó, M.L. (1995) *Women and the Employment Rate in Spain: The Causes and Effects of Variations in Patterns of Female Participation and Employment*. Report for the European Commission. Working Paper, EC Network on the Situation of Women in the Labour Market: Manchester School of Management, UMIST.

Morris, L. (1984) 'Redundancy and patterns of household finance', *Sociological Review* 32, 3: 492–523.

Mósesdóttir, L. (1996) 'Breaking the boundaries: women's encounter with the state in Sweden, Germany and the United States during the post-war period', Paper presented at the 18th Conference of the International Working Party on European Employment Systems and the Welfare State. University of Tampere, Finland, July.

New Earnings Survey (1994) London: HMSO.

Oakley, A. (1974) *Housewife*. Harmondsworth: Penguin.

OECD (1991) *Employment Outlook*. Paris: OECD.

OECD (1992) *Employment Outlook*. Paris: OECD.

OECD (1993a) *Employment Outlook*. Paris: OECD.

OECD (1993b) *Labour Force Statistics*. Paris: OECD.

OECD (1994a) *The OECD Jobs Study: Evidence and Explanations. Part I – Labour Market Trends and Underlying Forces of Change*. Paris: OECD.

OECD (1994b) *The OECD Jobs Study: Evidence and Explanations. Part II – The Adjustment Potential of the Labour Market*. Paris: OECD.

OECD (1994c) *Women and Structural Change: New Perspectives*. Paris: OECD.

OECD (1994d) *The OECD Jobs Study: Taxation, Employment and Unemployment*. Paris: OECD.

OECD (1994e) *Employment Outlook*. Paris: OECD.

OECD (1995a) *Employment Outlook*. Paris: OECD.

OECD. (1995b) *Education at a Glance* Paris: O.E.C.D.

O'Reilly, J. and Fagan, C. (1997) *Part-time Prospects: An International Comparison of Part-time Work*. London: Routledge.

Orloff, A.S. (1993) 'Gender and the social rights of citizenship: the comparative analysis of gender relations and welfare states', *American Sociological Review* 58, 3: 303–308.

Pahl, J. (1983) 'The allocation of money and the structuring of inequality within marriage', *Sociological Review* 31, 2: 237–262.

Pahl, J. (1989) *Money and Marriage*. London: Macmillan.

Pahl, R. (1984) *Divisions of Labour*. Oxford: Blackwell.

Palme, J. (1990) *Pension Rights in Welfare Capitalism: The Development of Old Age Pensions in 18 OECD Countries 1980–85*. Swedish Institute for Social Research 14, Stockholm.

Pastner, U. (1995) *Women and the European Employment Rate: The Causes and Consequences of Variations in Female Activity and Employment Patterns in Austria*. Report for the European Commission. Working Paper, EC Network on the Situation of Women in the Labour Market: Manchester School of Management, UMIST.

Pastner, U. (1996) *Trends and Prospects for Women's Employment in the 1990s in Austria*. Report for the European Commission. Working Paper, EC Network on the Situation of Women in the Labour Market: Manchester School of Management, UMIST.

Pfau-Effinger, B. (1993) 'Modernisation, culture and part-time employment: the example of Finland and West Germany', *Work, Employment and Society* 7, 3: 383–410.

Pfau-Effinger, B. (1996) 'Theorising cross-national differences in the labour force participation of women'. Paper presented to the seminar on Gender Relations, Employment and Occupational Segregation: A Cross-National Study, University of Leicester, February.

Plantenga, J. and Sloep, M. (1995) *Women and the Employment Rate in the Netherlands: The Causes and Effects of Variations in Patterns of Female Participation and Employment*. Report for the European Commission. Working Paper, EC Network on the Situation of Women in the Labour Market: Manchester School of Management, UMIST.

Plasman, R. (1995) *Women and the Employment Rate in Luxembourg: The Causes and Effects of Variations in Patterns of Female Participation and Employment*. Report for the European Commission. Working Paper, EC Network on the Situation of Women in the Labour Market: Manchester School of Management, UMIST.

Pugliese, E. (1995) 'Youth unemployment and the condition of young women in the labour market', in *Follow-up to the White Paper on Growth, Competitiveness and Employment: Equal Opportunities for Women and Men*. Report to the European Commission's Employment Task Force (DGV), V/5538/95–EN. Brussels: European Commission.

Reissert, B. and Schmid, G. (1994) 'Unemployment compensation and active labour market policy: the impact of unemployment benefits on income security, work incentives, and public policy, in G. Schmid (ed.) *Labour Market Institutions in Europe*. New York: M.E. Sharpe.

Rubery, J. (ed.) (1988) *Women and Recession*. London: Routledge and Kegan Paul.

Rubery, J. (1995) 'Synthesis', in *Follow-up to the White Paper on Growth, Competitiveness and Employment: Equal Opportunities for Women and Men*. Report to the European Commission's Employment Task Force (DGV), V/5538/95–EN. Brussels: European Commission.

Rubery, J. and Fagan, C. (1993) *Occupational Segregation of Women and Men in the European Community. Social Europe Supplement 3/93*. Luxembourg: Office for Official Publications of the European Community.

Rubery, J. and Fagan, C. (1994) *Wage Determination and Sex Segregation in the European Community. Social Europe Supplement 4/94*. Luxembourg: Office for Official Publications of the European Community.

Rubery, J. and Fagan, C. (1995) 'Gendered relations in societal context', *Work, Employment and Society* 9, 2: 217–240.

Rubery, J. and Maier, F. (1995) 'Equal opportunity for women and men and the employment policy of the EU – a critical review of the European Union's approach', *Transfer: European Review of Labour and Research* 1, 4: 520–532.

Rubery, J. and Smith, M. (1995) *Women and the European Employment Rate: The Causes and Consequences of Variations in Female Activity and Employment Patterns in the UK*. Report for the European Commission. Working Paper, EC Network on the Situation of Women in the Labour Market: Manchester School of Management, UMIST.

Rubery, J., Fagan, C. and Humphries, J. (1992) *Occupational Segregation of Men and Women in the UK*, Report for the European Commission. Working Paper, EC Network on the Situation of Women in the Labour Market: Manchester School of Management, UMIST.

Rubery, J., Fagan, C. and Smith, M. (1995) *Changing Patterns of Work and Working-Time in the European Union and the Impact on Gender Divisions*. Report to the European Commission, DGV – Equal Opportunities Unit. Brussels: European Commission.

Sainsbury, D. (ed.) (1994) *Gendering Welfare States*. London: Sage.

Sanderson, I. and Percy-Smith, J. with Foreman, A., Wraight, M., Murphy, L. and Petrie, P. (1995) *The Out-of-school Childcare Grant Initiative: An Interim Evaluation*. Research Series Discussion Paper no. 44. London: Employment Department Group.

Schettkat, R. (1989) 'The impact of taxes on female labour supply', *International Review of Applied Economics* 3, 1: 1–24.

Schunter-Kleemann, S. (1996) 'Welfare state cultures and family policies in the European countries – towards a new framework in cross-cultural social policy research'. Paper presented at the 18th Conference of the International Working Party on European Employment Systems and the Welfare State. University of Tampere, Finland, July.

Seymour, J. (1988) 'The division of domestic labour: a review'. Working Papers in Applied Social Research no. 13, University of Manchester: Faculty of Economic and Social Studies.

Siim, B. (1993) 'The gendered Scandinavian welfare states: the interplay between women's roles as mothers, workers and citizens in Denmark', in J. Lewis (ed.) *Women and Social Policies in Europe: Work, Family and the State*. Cheltenham, UK: Edward Elgar.

Silvera, R., Eydoux, A., Gauvin, A. and Granie, C. (1995) *Women and the Employment Rate in France: The Causes and Effects of Variations in Patterns of Female Participation and Employment*. Report for the European Commission. Working Paper, EC Network on the Situation of Women in the Labour Market: Manchester School of Management, UMIST.

Sundstrom, M. and Stafford, F. (1994) 'Time out for childcare and career wages of men and women', *Stockholm Research Reports in Demography no. 85*. University of Stockholm.

Tamburi, G. and Mouton, P. (1986) 'The uncertain frontier between private and public pension schemes', *International Labour Review* 125: 127–40.

UNECE (United Nations Economic Commission for Europe) (1994) *Regional Platform for Action – Women in a Changing World – Call for Action from an ECE*

Perspective. Preambular Declaration. UN E/ECE/RW/HLM/L.3/Rev.2.para.81. United Nations: Economic and Social Council, Economic Commission for Europe.

Varegao, J. and Ruivo, M. (1994) 'Working-time and employment in Portugal'. Paper presented at the 16th Conference of the International Working Party on Labour Market Segmentation. Strasbourg, July.

Vermeulen, H., Dex, S., Callan, T., Dankmeyer, B., Gustafsson, S., Lausten, M., Smith, N., Schmaus, G. and Vlasblom, J.D. (1994) 'Tax systems and married women's labour force participation: a seven country comparison' *ESRC Research Centre on Micro-social Change in Britain Working Paper*, University of Essex.

Vogler, C. (1994) 'Money in the household', in M. Anderson, F. Bechhofer and J. Gershuny (eds) *The Social and Political Economy of the Household*. Oxford: Oxford University Press.

Walby, S. (1990) *Theorising Patriarchy*. Oxford: Basil Blackwell.

Warde, A. (1990) 'Household work strategies and forms of labour: conceptual and empirical issues', *Work, Employment and Society* 4, 4: 495–515.

Warde, A. and Hetherington, K. (1993) 'A changing domestic division of labour? Issues of measurement and interpretation', *Work, Employment and Society* 7, 1: 23–45.

Whitting, R., Moore, J. and Tilson, B. (1995) 'Employment policies and practices towards older worker: an international overview', *Employment Gazette* April: 147–152.

Wilensky, H. (1975) *The Welfare State and Equality*. Berkeley: University of California Press.

Wilson, E. (1977) *Women and the Welfare State*. London: Tavistock.

Wood, A. (1994) *North–South Trade, Employment and Inequality: Changing Fortunes in a Skill-Driven World*. IDS Development Studies Series. Oxford: Clarendon Press.

INDEX

Note: page numbers in italics refer to tables or figures where these are separate from their textual reference.

345

157–9, *160*, 161, 167; unemployment
benefit replacement rates *171*, 174,
316; wage policy 191, 192; work
availability 244; work experience of
jobseekers *123*, 124
New Earnings Survey, (1994)
181
New Home Economics 195
non-employment: gender 266–70,
273–4; domestic responsibilities 267;
education *42*, 43; older age 52–5;
prime age 47–52; regional variations
89–96; youth 39–47
non-wage costs, employer 175–83
non-wage work 201–5
NOW initiative 236
NUTS (Nomenclatures of Territorial
Units) 83, 92, *93*

Oakley, A. 200
occupational data 7
occupational structure 105–8
OECD 193; (1991) 169, 170; (1992) 61,
62; (1994) 1, 13, 162, 169, 194,
210, 221, 222; (1995) 72, 165, 217,
224, 225, 228, 229, 231, 232, 233,
239, 274
O'Reilly, J. 196
Orloff, A. S. 4

Pahl, J. 196, 198, 207
Pahl, R. 203
Palme, J. 250
parental leave 223–4, 228–32, 280, *282*,
287–8, *318–20*
part-time employment: age groups 37;
childcare 239; education 65;
employment rates 29–39, 263–5; full-
time equivalents 32, *33*; gender
differences 37, 188, *299–302*; growth
111; hours worked 65; involuntary 61;
pensions 248–9, 253; restructuring
104–5; societal differences 286–7;
statistics 6–7; unemployment benefits
159–62
Pastner, U. 263, 267
patriarchy, public/private 208
pay inequity, gender 153, 170
pension systems 245–9; basic security
245, 250, *252*, 254, *323*; income
security 245, 250, *252*, *323–4*; residual
245, *252*, *324*

pensions: derived rights 256; divorce
251; employment gaps *323–4*; lone
parents 251; part-time employment
248–9, 253; private 246, 250–5; state
249; women's entitlement 245–55
Perista, H. 59, 70, 129, 149, 156, 184,
186, 190, 198, 201, 205, 214, 223, 238
Persson, I. 269
Pfau-Effinger, B. 3, 194
Plantenga, J. 5, 7, 27, 60, 65, 77, 158,
159, 167, 183, 185, 189, 191, 199, 200,
201, 202, 204, 205, 212, 217, 219, 225,
231, 234, 236, 237, 238, 239, 244,
249
Plasman, R. 63, 179, 189, 190, 197, 215,
216, 225, 237
population growth, male/female 25
Portugal: childcare 238, *322*;
contributory payment systems 177,
180, 181–2; discouraged workers 72,
73, *74–5*, 76; domestic responsibilities
139, 140–1; education 143, *144*, 145–6,
149; employment flexibility 189–91;
employment rates *259*, *297–8*;
employment rates excluding part-time
65, *66*, 67–9; employment rates by
gender/age *20–1*, *24*, *28*, 78–81, *265*,
309, *310*, *312*, 313–14; employment
rates by region 83, *84*, 87–9, *307*, *308*;
employment rates by sector *311*;
inactivity *134*; informal sector 70, 201,
202; labour market flows *115*, 116,
118, *119*, *127*, 128, *135*, *138*; labour
market policies 184–8; non-
employment in older age 53, 54; non-
employment in prime 47, *48*, 50, 52;
non-employment by region 90, *91*, 92,
98, 99; non-employment in youth *40*,
41, *42*, 43–4, *45–6*, *326*; parental leave
224–5, *229*, *230*, *282*; part-time
employment *30*, *31*, 32, *33*, *35*, 37,
111, *264*, *299–302*, *303*; pension
schemes 245, 248, 251, *252*, *324*;
segregation 103, 105, 107; social
security 152–4; statistics 8; taxation
213, 214; unemployment 55–7, 59,
113, *131*, *132*, *304–5*, *325*, *326*;
unemployment benefit 153–6, *164*,
275, *315*; unemployment benefit
eligibility 157, *158*, 163;
unemployment benefit replacement
rates *171*, *316*; women's earnings/

252; segregation 104, 107, 110; social security 152–4; statistics 8; taxation 220, 212, *213*, *214*, 215; unemployment 57, 60, 113, 130, *131*, *132*, *304–5*, *325*, *326*; unemployment benefit 153–6, *164*, *275*, *315*; unemployment benefit eligibility 157, *158*, 159, *160*, 163, 167; unemployment benefit replacement rates *171*, 172, 173, 174, *316*; unemployment insurance 215–16; wage policy 191–2; women's earnings/household income 197, 198; work experience of jobseekers *123*
Spant, A. 274, 276, 277
Stafford, F. 231
state policies: childcare 222–3, 239–40, 280–2; female employment 274–8; unemployed 151
statutory leave: *see* maternity leave; parental leave
subsidies, employment 183–4, 189
Sundstrom, M. 231
Sweden 7, 8; employment rates 17, 257, 258, *259*, *260*, 261; employment rates by age/gender 261–3, *265*; employment by region/structural change 270–3; non-employment by age/gender 266–9, 270, 273–4; parental leave 230, *282*; part-time employment 263–5; state policies 274–83; taxation 221; unemployment benefits *275*

Tamburi, G. 246
tax relief 212, 214, 238
tax unit 211, 212
taxation 279; childcare concessions 238; derived rights 288; employment 269; female employment 279–80; female friendly 209, 211–15; income effect 209–10; household-based 210–11, *213*, 288; lone parents 222; substitution effect 209–10; unemployment trap 215–20
taxes, married women's labour supply 220–2
temporary contracts 109
training 146–7, 225, 274
Training for Work 187

UK: childcare 234, 235, 237, 238, *322*; contributory payment systems 177,

179–80, *180*, 181, 182; discouraged workers 73, *74–5*, 76; domestic responsibilities *139*, 140–1, 200; earnings disregard 218–19; education 142, *144*, 145, 146–7; employment flexibility 188–91; employment rates *259*, *297–8*; employment rates excluding part-time 65, *66*, 67–9; employment rates by gender/age *20–1*, 22, *24*, 25, *26*, *28*, 29, 78–81, *265*, *309*, *310*, *312*, *313–14*; employment rates by region 83, *84*, 85–9, *307*, *308*; employment rates by sector *311*; housewife category 77; inactivity 133, *134*; informal sector 71, 201; in-work benefits 220; labour market flows 114, *115*, 116, *119*, 120, *127*, *135*, *138*; labour market policies 185–8; lone parents 245; non-employment in older age *53*, 54; non-employment in prime *48*, 49, 51, 52; non-employment by region *90*, *91*, 92, 93, 95–6, *97–9*; non-employment in youth *40*, 41, *42*, 43–4, *45–6*, 47, *326*; parental leave 223, *229*, 232, *282*, *319*; part-time employment *30*, *31*, 32, *33*, 34, *35*, *36*, 37, 39, *264*, *299–302*, *303*; pension schemes 245, 246, 247, 248, *249*, 250, 251, *252*, 253, 254; segregation 103, 105; social security 152–4; taxation 221, 222, 212, *213*, *214*, 215; unemployment 112, 113, 114, *131*, *132*, *304–5*, *325*, *326*; unemployment benefit 154–6, *164*, 166, *275*, *315*; unemployment benefit eligibility *158*, 159, 160, 161–2, 168; unemployment benefit replacement rates *171*, 172, 173, 174, *316*; unemployment insurance 215–16; wage policy 191; women's earnings/household income 197–8; women's unpaid domestic work 200; work availability testing 241–2; work experience of jobseekers *123*, 124
UN World Conference on Women, Equality and Peace, Beijing 2, 296
underemployment 71–81
underutilisation 78–81
unemployment 13, 14–15, 44, *45–6*, 58–62; compensation systems 151–3; cyclical 270; disguised 14; distribution 55–7; domestic responsibilities